Communications
in Computer and Information Science 1475

More information about this series at http://www.springer.com/series/7899

Cornel Klein · Markus Helfert · Karsten Berns ·
Oleg Gusikhin (Eds.)

Smart Cities, Green Technologies, and Intelligent Transport Systems

9th International Conference, SMARTGREENS 2020
and 6th International Conference, VEHITS 2020
Prague, Czech Republic, May 2–4, 2020
Revised Selected Papers

 Springer

Editors
Cornel Klein
Siemens
Munich, Germany

Karsten Berns
University of Kaiserslautern
Kaiserslautern, Germany

Markus Helfert
Maynooth University
Maynooth, Kildare, Ireland

Oleg Gusikhin
Ford Research and Advanced Engineering
Dearborn, MI, USA

ISSN 1865-0929   ISSN 1865-0937 (electronic)
Communications in Computer and Information Science
ISBN 978-3-030-89169-5   ISBN 978-3-030-89170-1 (eBook)
https://doi.org/10.1007/978-3-030-89170-1

This Springer imprint is published by the registered company Springer Nature Switzerland AG
The registered company address is: Gewerbestrasse 11, 6330 Cham, Switzerland

Preface

This book includes extended and revised versions of a set of selected papers from SMARTGREENS 2020 (9th International Conference on Smart Cities and Green ICT Systems) and VEHITS 2020 (6th International Conference on Vehicle Technology and Intelligent Transport Systems), held during May 2–4, 2020, as web-based events, due to the COVID-19 pandemic.

SMARTGREENS 2020 received 38 paper submissions from authors in 21 countries, of which 16% were included in this book.

VEHITS 2020 received 94 paper submissions from authors in 30 countries, of which 9% were included in this book.

The papers were selected by the event chairs and their selection is based on a number of criteria that include the classifications and comments provided by the Program Committee members, the session chairs' assessment, and also the program chairs' global view of all papers included in the technical program. The authors of selected papers were then invited to submit revised and extended versions of their papers having at least 30% innovative material.

The purpose of the International Conference on Smart Cities and Green ICT Systems (SMARTGREENS) is to bring together researchers, designers, developers, and practitioners interested in the advances and applications in the field of smart cities, green information and communication technologies, sustainability, and energy aware systems and technologies.

The purpose of the International Conference on Vehicle Technology and Intelligent Transport Systems (VEHITS) is to bring together engineers, researchers, and practitioners interested in the advances and applications in the field of vehicle technology and intelligent transport systems. This conference focuses on innovative applications, tools, and platforms in all technology areas such as signal processing, wireless communications, informatics, and electronics, related to different kinds of vehicles, including cars, off-road vehicles, trains, ships, underwater vehicles, or flying machines, and the intelligent transportation systems that connect and manage large numbers of vehicles, not only in the context of smart cities but in many other application domains.

The papers selected to be included in this book contribute to the understanding of relevant trends of current research on smart cities, green ICT systems, vehicle technology, and intelligent transport systems including the following: connected and autonomous vehicles, advanced driver assistance systems, the Internet of Things, data analytics in application to intelligent road infrastructure and logistics, energy-aware systems and communities, innovative digital services and technologies, security management in smart cities, and, finally, examples of smart infrastructures and sustainable computing.

   We would like to thank all the authors for their contributions and also all the reviewers who have helped to ensure the quality of this publication.

May 2020

Cornel Klein
Markus Helfert
Karsten Berns
Oleg Gusikhin

Organization

SMARTGREENS Conference Chair

Markus Helfert   Maynooth University, Ireland

VEHITS Conference Chair

Oleg Gusikhin   Ford Motor Company, USA

SMARTGREENS Program Chair

Cornel Klein   Siemens AG, Germany

VEHITS Program Co-chairs

Karsten Berns   University of Kaiserslautern, Germany
Markus Helfert   Maynooth University, Ireland

SMARTGREENS Program Committee

Hamdy A. Ziedan	Assiut University, Egypt
Mohamed Abbas	Solar Equipment Development Unit, UDES/CDER, Algeria
Javier M. Aguiar	Universidad de Valladolid, Spain
Carlos Antunes	University of Coimbra/INESC Coimbra, Portugal
Simona Bernardi	Universidad de Zaragoza, Spain
Lasse Berntzen	University of South-Eastern Norway, Norway
Nik Bessis	Edge Hill University, UK
Blanca Caminero	Universidad de Castilla-La Mancha, Spain
Lin Chen	Chinese Academy of Sciences, China
Ken Christensen	University of South Florida, USA
Calin Ciufudean	"Stefan cel Mare" University of Suceava, Romania
Georges Da Costa	IRIT, Paul Sabatier University, France
Wanyang Dai	Nanjing University, China
Cléver Ricardo de Farias	University of São Paulo, Brazil
Venizelos Efthymiou	University of Cyprus, Cyprus
Tullio Facchinetti	University of Pavia, Italy
Adrian Florea	University "Lucian Blaga" of Sibiu, Romania
Christopher Gniady	University of Arizona, USA
Andre Gradvohl	State University of Campinas, Brazil

SMARTGREENS Additional Reviewers

Tasos Bakogiannis   National Technical University of Athens, Greece
Christian Tenllado   Complutense University of Madrid, Spain

VEHITS Program Committee

Kyriakos Agavanakis   University of West Attica, Greece
Felix Albu   Valahia University of Targoviste, Romania
Ramachandran Balakrishna   Caliper Corporation, USA
Paolo Barsocchi   National Research Council, Italy
Sandford Bessler   Austrian Institute of Technology, Austria
Neila Bhouri   IFSTTAR, France
Gergely Biczók   Budapest University of Technology and Economics,
                               Hungary
Nebojša Bojovic   University of Belgrade, Serbia
Jean-Marie Bonnin   IMT Atlantique, France
Christophe Boucher   ULCO, France
Christine Buisson   Université de Lyon, France
Catalin Buiu   Universitatea Politehnica din Bucuresti, Romania
Roberto Caldelli   University of Florence, Italy
Maria Calderon   Universidad Carlos III de Madrid, Spain
Pedro Cardoso   Universidade do Algarve, Portugal
Raffaele Carli   Polytechnic University of Bari, Italy
Rodrigo Carlson   Federal University of Santa Catarina, Brazil
Gino Carrozzo   Nextworks s.r.l., Italy
Graziana Cavone   Polytechnic University of Bari, Italy
Abdelghani Chahmi   Université des Sciences et de la Technologie
                               d'Oran, Algeria
Jun-Dong Chang   Institute for Information Industry, Taiwan, Republic
                               of China
Ioannis Chatzigiannakis   Sapienza University of Rome, Italy
Lin Chen   University of Paris-Saclay, France
Ka Cheok   Oakland University, USA
Gihwan Cho   Chonbuk University, South Korea
Domenico Ciuonzo   University of Naples Federico II, Italy
Michele Colajanni   University of Modena and Reggio Emilia, Italy
Noelia Correia   University of Algarve, Portugal
Bernard Cousin   University of Rennes 1, France
Alfonso Damiano   University of Cagliari, Italy
Fabio D'Andreagiovanni   French National Centre for Scientific Research
                               (CNRS), France
Klaus David   University of Kassel, Germany
Antonio de la Oliva   Universidad Carlos III de Madrid, Spain
Danny De Vleeschauwer   NOKIA, Belgium
Rui Dinis   Universidade Nova de Lisboa, Portugal

Mariagrazia Dotoli	Politecnico di Bari, Italy
Aisling Driscoll	University College Cork, Ireland
Mehmet Efe	Hacettepe University, Turkey
Khaled El-Araby	Schlothauer & Wauer GmbH, Germany, and Ain Shams University, Egypt
Sabeur Elkosantini	University of Carthage, Tunisia
Oscar Esparza	Universitat Politècnica de Catalunya, Spain
Christian Esposito	University of Salerno, Italy
Peppino Fazio	University of Calabria, Italy
Attilio Fiandrotti	Tèlècom ParisTech, France
Dieter Fiems	Ghent University, Belgium
Lino Figueiredo	Instituto Superior de Engenharia do Porto, Portugal
Yi Guo	The University of Texas at Dallas, USA
Kevin Heaslip	Virginia Tech, USA
Sonia Heemstra de Groot	Eindhoven Technical University, The Netherlands
Sin C. Ho	The Chinese University of Hong Kong, Hong Kong
Tamás Holczer	Budapest University of Technology and Economics, Hungary
William Horrey	AAA Foundation for Traffic Safety, USA
Zechun Hu	Tsinghua University, China
Hocine Imine	French Institute of Science and Technology for Transport, Development and Networks (IFSTTAR), France
Govand Kadir	University of Kurdistan-Hewler, Iraq
Thomas Kamalakis	Harokopio University of Athens, Greece
Markus Kampmann	University of Applied Sciences Koblenz, Germany
Athanasios Kanatas	University of Piraeus, Greece
Tetsuya Kawanishi	Waseda University, Japan
Boris Kerner	University of Duisburg-Essen, Germany
Lisimachos Kondi	University of Ioannina, Greece
Anastasios Kouvelas	ETH Zurich, Switzerland
Milan Krbálek	Czech Technical University, Czech Republic
Francine Krief	University of Bordeaux, France
Björn Krüger	University of Bonn, Germany
Yong-Hong Kuo	The University of Hong Kong, Hong Kong
Anis Laouiti	Télécom SudParis, France
Deok Lee	Kunsan National University, USA
Fedor Lehocki	Slovak University of Technology, Slovak Republic
Ruidong Li	National Institute of Information and Communications Technology, Japan
Mingxi Liu	University of Utah, USA
Gabriel Lodewijks	University of New South Wales, Australia
Jonathan Loo	University of West London, UK
Maria del Carmen Lucas-Estañ	Universidad Miguel Hernández de Elche, Spain
Salim M. Zaki	Dijlah University, Iraq
Michael Mackay	Liverpool John Moores University, UK

S. M. Hassan Mahdavi	VEDECOM, France
Zoubir Mammeri	IRIT, Paul Sabatier University, France
Sadko Mandzuka	University of Zagreb, Croatia
Bernd Markscheffel	TU Ilmenau, Germany
Jonas Martesson	KTH Royal Institute of Technology, Sweden
Barbara Masini	Italian National Research Council (CNR), Italy
José Manuel Menéndez	Universidad Politécnica de Madrid, Spain
Lyudmila Mihaylova	University of Sheffield, UK
Aleksandar Milosavljevic	University of Niš, Serbia
Antonella Molinaro	Mediterranean University of Reggio Calabria, Italy
Wrya Monnet	University of Kurdistan-Hewler, Iraq
Jânio Monteiro	Universidade do Algarve, Portugal
Pedro Moura	University of Coimbra, Portugal
Daniela Nechoska	St. Kliment Ohridski University, Bitola, North Macedonia
Marialisa Nigro	Roma Tre University, Italy
Jennie Oxley	Monash University, Australia
Dario Pacciarelli	Roma Tre University, Italy
Brian Park	University of Virginia, USA
Cecilia Pasquale	Università degli Studi di Genova, Italy
Paulo Pereirinha	Polytechnic Institute of Coimbra, Portugal
Fernando Pereñiguez	University Centre of Defence, Spanish Air Force Academy, Spain
Valerio Persico	Network Measurement and Monitoring (NM2) and University of Naples "Federico II", Italy
Hesham Rakha	Virginia Tech, USA
Corina Sandu	Virginia Polytechnic Institute and State University, USA
Jose Santa	Technical University of Cartagena, Spain
Oleg Saprykin	Samara State Aerospace University, Russia
Shih-Lung Shaw	University of Tennessee, USA
Alexander Smirnov	SPIIRAS, Russia
Uwe Stilla	Technische Universitaet Muenchen, Germany
Todor Stoilov	Bulgarian Academy of Sciences, Bulgaria
Wai Yuen Szeto	The University of Hong Kong, Hong Kong
István Varga	Budapest University of Technology and Economics, Hungary
Francesco Viti	University of Luxembourg, Luxembourg
Tara Yahiya	University of Kurdistan-Hewler, Iraq

VEHITS Additional Reviewers

Ioannis Agalliadis	ETH, Switzerland
Emanuele Caimotti	Politecnico di Torino, Italy
Alexander Hanel	Technische Universitaet Muenchen, Germany
Szilvia Lestyan	CrySyS Lab, Hungary
Antonio Meireles	ISEP, Portugal
Shimaossadat Mousavi	ETH, Switzerland
Sleiman Safaoui	The University of Texas at Dallas, USA

Invited Speakers

Reinhold Behringer	Knorr Bremse GmbH, Germany
Tolga Bektas	University of Liverpool, UK
Matthias Jarke	RWTH Aachen, Germany
Lukas Krammer	Siemens, Austria
Meng Lu	Dynniq, The Netherlands

Contents

Smart Cities and Green ICT Systems

Implementation and Operation of Blockchain-Based Energy Communities Under the New Legal Framework

Stephan Cejka[1]([✉])(iD), Franz Zeilinger[1], Mark Stefan[2](iD), Paul Zehetbauer[2],
Argjenta Veseli[3], Katrin Burgstaller[3], and Marie-Theres Holzleitner[3](iD)

[1] Siemens AG Österreich, Vienna, Austria
{stephan.cejka,franz.zeilinger}@siemens.com
[2] AIT Austrian Institute of Technology GmbH, Vienna, Austria
{mark.stefan,paul.zehetbauer}@ait.ac.at
[3] Energieinstitut an der Johannes Kepler Universität Linz, Linz, Austria
{veseli,burgstaller,holzleitner}@energieinstitut-linz.at

Abstract. The current movement within the energy market caused by the need for climate measures along with emerging new technologies leads to an evolution to a more intelligent, decentralized power network. Energy communities are part of this progress by jointly producing, consuming, storing, and sharing energy to increase the self-consumption of locally generated energy. These energy communities are the focus of this article. Besides the legal framework, in particular, the European Union's Clean Energy Package, the implementation of energy communities will depend heavily on suitable information and communications technology (ICT) solutions, e.g., the Blockchain technology which again rises legal implications like privacy issues.

This article provides an interdisciplinary overview about the legal, economic, and technical questions arising due to the deployment of energy communities in their integration into the existing power system. A concrete implementation of a Renewable Energy Community by utilizing Blockchain technology and the implications regarding privacy issues, energy efficiency as well as profitability aspects are discussed and results of a comprehensive stimulative study on energy savings for community customers are presented.

Keywords: Energy community · Energy transition · Clean energy package · Renewable energy · Blockchain · Energy efficiency · Privacy

1 Introduction

To mitigate the climate change the continuing temperature rise needs to be limited according to the globally stipulated values in the 2016 Paris agreement [53]. Countermeasures as well as changes in humans behavior will be necessary to achieve a durable reduction of the greenhouse gas emissions, which are responsible for the continuing increase in temperature [39]. As the energy sector is one

C. Klein et al. (Eds.): SMARTGREENS 2020/VEHITS 2020, CCIS 1475, pp. 3–30, 2021.
https://doi.org/10.1007/978-3-030-89170-1_1

of its biggest sources [39], it is one of the major sectors addressed by proposed countermeasures. The European Union thus issued its 'Clean Energy Package for All Europeans' package in 2018/19 aiming [23]

- to reduce the emissions of greenhouse gases by 40%,
- to reach a share of 32% of renewable energy sources in the energy mix, and
- to improve energy efficiency by 32.5%.

Additionally, the European Union plans to achieve climate neutrality, i.e., net-zero emissions, by 2050 [24] and some member states have even more ambitious goals, such as Austria which plans to achieve climate neutrality already by 2040 [26] as well as a renewable electricity share of 100% by 2030 [49].

Already since the last few decades, the energy market has been in a continuous move, including significant paradigm shifts such as from former monopolies to deregulated markets. New technologies, new local energy producers in the lower voltage grid layers (e.g., windmills, photovoltaic sites), and changed consumer behavior (e.g., electric vehicles, controllable devices) push the ongoing evolution to a more intelligent, decentralized power network (smart grid) [20]. Thus, changes in the energy sector are not limited to producers and energy transmission, but include local energy storage and consumption as well. Traditional final consumers, such as households, increasingly become 'prosumers' as a combination of producers and consumers (i.e., houses with photovoltaic units feeding-in their excess energy) [45].

Energy communities are a third step in an evolution shown in Fig. 1 that started with households optimizing their own energy consumption and continued by applying those procedures to apartment buildings next [31]. In particular, households are not necessarily required to possess and operate their own photovoltaic unit to join a community. In consequence, every individual shall be able to join and thus take over an active part in the energy transition [15]. Those communities generally aim to jointly produce, consume, store, and share energy to increase the self-consumption of locally generated energy, but they could also offer other energy-related services. As a further aspect, energy communities

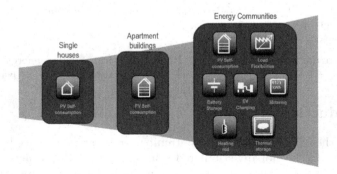

Fig. 1. The transition towards energy communities [12].

allocate the ongoing trend to favor regional products (e.g., in grocery stores), to the energy system [15].

Besides the legal framework, the implementation of energy communities will depend heavily on suitable information and communications technology (ICT) solutions. This article, extending the previous contribution of *Cejka et al.* [12], will thus provide an interdisciplinary view on legal, economic, and technical aspects on those energy communities. The remainder of this paper is structured as follows: We will first introduce the European Union Clean Energy Package in more detail, including an enumeration of the relevant new actors on all three layers (Sect. 2). The actors of the rightmost layer of Fig. 1, the energy communities, are the focus of this article; they are introduced and various aspects are discussed in Sect. 3. In Sect. 4, we describe an implementation of such a community by utilizing Blockchain technology and their implications, especially in energy efficiency and privacy issues. We will then show profitability aspects including simulations on cost savings for the community's participants in Sect. 5. Section 6 concludes this article by providing a summary as well as an outlook to future work.

2 European Union's Clean Energy Package

The Clean Energy Package, adopted by the European Parliament, partly in the end of 2018 and partly in Summer 2019, is the latest development in European Union's energy law. Within its four directive and four regulation acts it includes additional and new measures on the various domains in the energy sector:

- Energy Performance of Buildings Directive (EU) 2018/844,
- **Renewable Energy Directive (EU) 2018/2001 (RED),**
- Energy Efficiency Directive (EU) 2018/2002,
- Governance of the Energy Union and Climate Action Regulation (EU) 2018/1999,
- Electricity Regulation (EU) 2019/943,
- **Electricity Directive (EU) 2019/944 (ED),**
- Regulation on Risk-Preparedness in the Electricity Sector (EU) 2019/941,
- Regulation on the European Union Agency for the Cooperation of Energy Regulators (EU) 2019/942.

The two bold-printed directives are of main interest of this article's scope as they contain several new actors in the energy market. They can be distinguished into three groups based on their level of collaboration and their local area of operation (Fig. 1):

- On layer 1 (Single houses):
  - Renewables self-consumer (included in the RED)
    'a final customer [...] who generates renewable electricity for its own consumption, and who may store or sell self-generated renewable electricity'

- Active customer (included in the ED)
  'a final customer, or a group of jointly acting final customers, who con-
  sumes or stores electricity generated within its premises [...] or who sells
  self-generated electricity or participates in flexibility or energy efficiency
  schemes'
- On layer 2 (Apartment buildings):
  - Jointly acting renewables self-consumers (included in the RED)
    'a group of jointly acting *renewables self-consumers* located in the same
    building or multi-apartment block'
  - Active customer (included in the ED)
    according to their definition above, 'a group of jointly acting final cus-
    tomers' is included
- On layer 3 (Energy Communities):
  - Renewable Energy Community (included in the RED)
    see Sect. 3.1 for its definition
  - Citizen Energy Community (included in the ED)
    see Sect. 3.1 for its definition

Obviously, at each layer there exist definitions for two actors for comparable
concepts in parallel. While their scopes are not completely identical (cf. *Commonalities and Differences* of energy communities in Sect. 3.1), this also stems
from the different application areas of the two directives in question: the ED
being the more general legal act in order to the completion of the internal market and mainly of regulatory nature, the RED to promote deployment and use
of renewable energy sources for energy production including electricity and to
foster their acceptance [43]. Furthermore, the ED aims to provide "level playing
fields", while the RED aims for an "equal footing with other market participants". Therefore, the REC shall become a non-discriminating position among
the other (larger) competing players on the energy market.

Those parties shall be able to 'generate, consume, store, and sell electricity
without facing disproportionate burdens' and '[c]itizens living in apartments [...]
should be able to benefit [...] to the same extent as households in single family
homes'. Thus, they improve the local acceptance of and the local investment in
renewable energy, as well as allow a more comprehensive participation of citizens
in the energy transition. The new actors are expected to be significant members
in the future energy system [50]. It is mentionable, that the term 'prosumer' does
not appear in the legal framework, though those are covered by the concept of
'renewable self-consumers' [21,45].

3   Energy Communities

Among the proposed countermeasures in the Clean Energy Package are the two
types of energy communities to merge the energy production as well as the
consumption of individuals and enterprises. As they are the main field of this
article, various aspects of them will be handled in detail in this section.

3.1 Legal Definitions

The legal definitions of the two types of energy communities can be summarized as [12]:

Renewable Energy Community (REC)

- is a legal entity, autonomous, and based on open and voluntary participation,
- shareholders or members are
  - natural persons, small or medium enterprises, or local authorities,
  - located in the proximity of renewable energy projects owned and developed by that legal entity,
- its primary purpose is to provide environmental, economic or social community benefits rather than financial profits.

Citizen Energy Community (CEC)

- is a legal entity, based on open and voluntary participation,
- is open for participation of all entities,
- is controlled by shareholders or members that are natural persons, small enterprises, or local authorities,
- its primary purpose is to provide environmental, economic or social community benefits rather than financial profits,
- it may engage in generation, including from renewable sources, distribution, supply, consumption, aggregation, energy storage, energy efficiency services or charging services for electric vehicles or provide other energy services.

Commonalities and Differences. Some of the commonalities and differences between the two types are already apparent in their definitions. Though in this publication we will not focus on them (cf. [13,18]), only in summary there are main differences in their

- membership structure:
  Participation is much more regulated in RECs as they are restricted in their types of member. In contrast, participants of CECs are just restricted in terms of the community's effective control[1].
- application area:
  As the CEC is contained in the Electricity Directive it is restricted to electricity, while the REC is restricted to renewable energy in general (e.g., including heating and cooling).
- geographical area:
  The REC contains a proximity aspect further restricting its possible members[2], while the members of a CEC may be widely spread – optionally even over member states' borders.

---

[1] Unclear usage of language (at least) in the german and english versions of the directive have often, including by authorities, led to an understanding of a restriction to certain types of members.

[2] Ambiguous usage of language (at least) in the German and English versions of the directive allows the dissent opinion of *Lowitsch et al.* [43] that just restricts the controlling members to a certain proximity.

– operational area:
  In contrast to RECs, the definition of the CEC explicitly contains an enumeration of services it can provide. RECs' possible operations are more limited, namely to
  - produce, consume, store and sell renewable energy,
  - share produced renewable energy within the community, and
  - access energy markets in a nondiscriminatory manner.

In result, neither one of the community types is a strict subset of the other [12,16]. Note that the term *local energy community* that was contained in the drafts was abandoned in favor of the term CEC and is no longer legally used. This decision makes sense as the CEC does not include any restriction in their geographical area. Generally, in subsequent sections we will mainly focus on RECs, while main aspects are expected to hold also in CECs.

3.2   Structure of a Community

Besides open legal questions for the national implementations, there are other issues concerning the structure and organization of a community (e.g., minimum or maximum size of a community, desired mix of producers and consumers, etc.) [12]. While the concrete structure of communities might be different according to their location in an urban or in a rural area, in general, the following participants (also in combination; cf. prosumers) are assumed to be present in every community (cf. Fig. 2):

– producers (e.g., houses equipped with a photovoltaic unit or small power plants attached to or even owned by the energy community itself),
– consumers (e.g., houses as well as e-car charging points), and
– a (community-owned) battery storage.

Participants can thus be distinguished in community members or shareholders attached to the community and community-owned components, such as a central battery storage. The energy community could temporarily store produced energy that cannot be allocated to a consumer at this time in a battery storage; further excess energy could be sold to another purchaser outside of the community. In contrast, the energy demand of the consumer that cannot be met by the community will still be purchased from a traditional vendor.

In general, the term 'community' indicates at least two members; however, according to *Lowitsch et al.* [43], autonomy permits a share of a third at cap; hence requiring at least three members in an REC. For autonomy from other energy market players further members (e.g., distribution system operators) are precluded from CEC's participation as well as from REC's effective control, namely if they are mainly engaged in commercial activities in the energy sector. This shall restrain utilities or financial investors to setup RECs to benefit from the customer-friendly design of the framework [43].

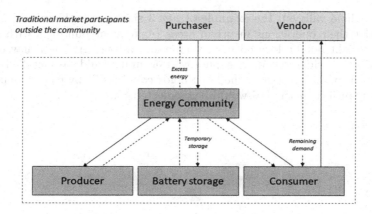

Fig. 2. Energy community structure, including energy flow in dashed lines and cost flow in continuous lines [14].

3.3 National Adaptions

The directives of the Clean Energy Package, including the energy communities, need to be implemented into national law of the Unions member states until End 2020 (ED)/Mid of 2021 (RED); thus, there is a significant movement in this area at the moment. Several open questions for the national implementation have been identified in previous work (e.g., the definition of proximity regarding the RECs operational limits, the choice of a suitable organizational and legal form, or privacy aspects) [15]. Details on the Austrian national adaption can be found in [18,27], summaries of implementations in other member states in [33].

3.4 Local Proximity

RECs will be restricted to a local proximity, to be defined on national level by using either geographical (e.g., maximum distances), administrative (e.g., borders of municipalities or districts) or technical boundaries [14]. For example, in Austria there are seven grid levels (GL) defined; RECs are only allowed to span across these grid levels in a limited way:

1. ultra-high voltage (380 kV and 220 kV),
2. transformation from ultra-high to high voltage,
3. high voltage (110 kV),
4. transformation from high to medium voltage,
5. medium voltage (from more than 1 kV up to and including 36 kV),
6. transformation from medium to low voltage,
7. low voltage (1 kV and below).

While the discussed plans on allowing RECs' operations on the grid levels 6 and 7 seem to be properly suited for rural areas (those would cover small towns and even whole valleys), the example of Fig. 3 shows that this would improperly restrict their operations in urban areas (apartment buildings with several stairwells might not be located in the same low voltage grid and may only be connected over grid level 5). If a photovoltaic unit would be installed on the house's rooftop, only a part of the households could profit by chance depending on which transformer the PV would be connected to.

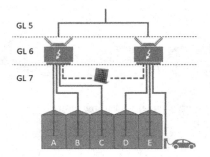

Fig. 3. Example of an apartment building consisting of several stairwells that could not build an energy community in case of a restriction to GL 6 and 7.

The final decision in Austria was to enable two types of RECs: the local REC to span over grid levels 6 and 7; and the regional REC which additionally includes grid level 5 and parts of grid level 4 [14,18,27]. Although relaxed, it is still not guaranteed that direct neighbors may always be able to build up an REC together.

4   Blockchain Technology for Energy Communities

While concrete transpositions of the directives into the member states are still pending, several research projects are already dealing with possible implementations by utilizing Blockchain technology [12,37,41]. This technology is currently not only discussed in the energy system [1–3,10], but also introduced in a variety of different domains [11]. Although new use cases such as energy communities could be an indicator to use emerging technologies, the Blockchain is just one possibility for the technical implementation of energy communities [16]. Nevertheless, the Clean Energy Package contains a definition on 'peer-to-peer trading of renewable energy' as the 'sale of renewable energy between market participants by means of a contract with pre-determined conditions'. It further includes an 'automated execution and settlement of the transaction' in its definition, which indicates to legally consider smart contracts in an environment utilizing Blockchain technology [12,15,43].

As many authors previously engaged with introducing Blockchain technology (e.g., [29,40]), this article will focus only on a few selected aspects of special interest within the use case, especially on questions on Blockchain's energy efficiency and technology-immanent privacy issues. In a nutshell, Blockchain transactions are processed 'peer-to-peer' without requiring intermediaries. Data – in this use case mainly on energy generation and consumption as well as on settlement of the energy exchange – are processed and validated by the attached machines, also known as nodes, and not in a traditional manner by a central server. Several transactions are assembled in a block until its maximum size is reached; in this case a new block is initiated and linked to the previous block using hash functions. These links eventually result in the eponymous chain of blocks; it renders later manipulations of its integrated data difficult, especially if contained in a very antecedent block. In result, a Blockchain approach provides a high level of automation, security, and transparency for the participants [37].

4.1 Energy Efficiency

Among the goals of the Clean Energy Package is an improvement of energy efficiency, though quite on the contrary, Blockchain technology is in fact not known for an energy efficient operation [55,56]. According to estimations, only the (probably best-known) Bitcoin Blockchain reaches an annual electricity consumption of 50–80 TWh, comparable to countries such as Switzerland, Austria, Belgium, Czechia or Finland [54]. An energy-efficient implementation thus needs a special emphasis on this issue, in particular, by avoiding to use the 'proof-of-work' consensus protocol [41,52].

4.2 Privacy Issues

Irrespective of using Blockchain technology, the protection of personal data must be constantly taken into consideration during an implementation. A major advantage of Blockchain technology from a technical point of view is its technology-immanent immutability the persisted data; however, this is the main point of conflict concerning data protection rights [25,28,37]. Thus, in particular when using Blockchain technology for the implementation of energy communities, the focus must not only be laid on the technical feasibility but also on the protection of the processed data. Besides other types of classifications, Blockchains can be divided into two groups based on control and accessibility [35] shown in Table 1 which also influences data protection aspects [37].

Table 1. Public and private blockchains and their implications regarding privacy.

	Public blockchain	Private blockchain
Use	Open to all	Limited to defined actors
Blockchain operator	None defined	Defined
Access to data	Open to the public	Open to the participants
Controller (GDPR)	Unclear	Blockchain operator
User identity exposure	Usually hard when using anonymized or pseudonymized ID	Usually possible due to the limited number of actors – regardless whether they are anonymized or pseudonymized

Scope and Applicability of the GDPR. Since 2018, the data protection regime within the European Union is generally harmonized by the General Data Protection Regulation (GDPR), aiming to ensure a high level of protection for personal data. Precisely, the GDPR is applicable only on 'personal data' of 'natural persons'; thus excluding any data of enterprises, that might also be members of the energy community. The 'processing of personal data', which is the central connecting factor in terms of the GDPR, is defined very wide[3] and since Blockchain technology is designed to distribute its data copies to various servers, it is difficult to identify a locality where data processing takes place. Obviously, Blockchain is a data processing technology that may process a large number of data records, possibly including records of personal data.

The GDPR defines 'personal data' as any information relating to an identified or identifiable natural person ('data subject'). The question of identification needs to consider all means likely to be used to identify a natural person, taking – for example – costs of identification and the time required as well as the state of the technology into account [37]. While pseudonymized data is also counted as identifiable data, the GDPR does not apply to anonymous information, i.e., information that does not relate to an identifiable natural person, or the data subject can no longer be identified. Thus, for GDPR's applicability it is essential whether or not natural persons are identifiable by the processed data. In that context it needs to be mentioned that there are different opinions on whether hashes or encrypted personal data fall under the GDPR as pseudonymized data [5,29]. Obviously, re-identification of pseudonymized users is the easier the fewer users are involved in a system, especially in private Blockchains where by design all users must be known and identifiable for the Blockchain operator. Therefore, it is necessary to classify the involved kind of data that is processed within an energy community to answer the question if personal data is involved.

Energy Data as Personal Data. Within an energy community, data is collected on the energy produced, consumed and stored; as a result, Blockchain will process the electricity consumption and generation data of each member. Generally a high-frequent readout of households' energy consumption data using Smart Meters will be required for a reasonable operation. While it initially appears that those data will be purely of technical nature, the collected data indeed could reveal detailed information of the consumer's behavior and its private life; hence they are considered as personal data [17,34,44,51]. In case of a prosumer, measurement data on the electricity fed into the grid provide information about the available resources of this member. Since personal data is processed, the technical execution of the Blockchain must be adapted to comply with the GDPR.

---

[3] I.e. 'any operation or set of operations which is performed on personal data or on sets of personal data, whether or not by automated means, such as collection, recording, organization, structuring, storage, adaptation or alteration, retrieval, consultation, use, disclosure by transmission, dissemination or otherwise making available, alignment or combination, restriction, erasure or destruction'.

Data Subject Rights. According to the GDPR, the data subject has several rights[4] in the controller's responsibility. Since the Blockchain is designed such that its persisted data cannot be modified, it needs to be shown how this technology can be reconciled with data protection.

The Controller. The primary role of the controller is its responsibility for compliance with the GDPR [4]. However, in Blockchain applications it is not a priori clear, to whom this role is assigned. Various actors who could qualify, e.g., in a public and permissionless Blockchain, among others, the software developer, miners, or even every participating node [22, 25]. Evidently, the assessment of the controller depends on the respective constellation and the concrete design of the Blockchain application [30]. Thus, no generally valid statement can be made and the question therefore needs to be examined on a case-by-case basis. However, with a private Blockchain, it is usually easier to determine a controller due to its structure with a legal entity as operator who is responsible to determine the means of personal data processing and the purposes. For energy communities with a usually delimited group of participants the use of a private Blockchain is feasible, thus the identification of the data controller is rather unproblematic, while in the public Blockchain compliance with data protection obligations is not easily possible.

Right to Erasure. The most problematic rights when using Blockchain technology are the right to rectification and the right to erasure. Later modifications of persisted data on the Blockchain would require all subsequent data blocks to be rewritten, hence this is (depending on the amount of data) infeasible. It is even more difficult with a public Blockchain, since all actors involved would have to make the correction and deletion; coordination would be very complicated because data to be corrected could be distributed over thousands of nodes. Generally, it should be avoided to persist data of identifiable natural persons as plain text on the Blockchain. However, for cases where this is impossible, e.g., for the settlement and the traceability of energy transfers in the community, other solutions need to be found. Anyways, the general principles of data protection law, such as the principles of storage limitation[5] and data minimization[6] need to be followed at all time.

The deletion of data is not only contrary to the Blockchain design, but also among the most essential advantages that result in the high confidence in this technology due to its immutability and transparency. Proposals in the literature for introducing mutability into the Blockchain (e.g., [8, 47]) are thus disapproved by us due to the immutability as one of the main principles of the Blockchain. Potential feasible solutions in related work are, for example, 'zero-knowledge-proofs' [36] or to use a combined system of a Blockchain and a traditional

---

[4] They are the right to information, access to personal data, rectification, erasure, restriction of processing, data portability, objection and not to be subject to a decision based solely on automated processing, including profiling.

[5] I.e., personal data shall only be kept as long as necessary.

[6] I.e., only the minimum required personal data shall be collected.

distributed database [22,57]. In this case only references to mutable records in the database are persisted on the immutable Blockchain accompanied with hashes of the records to proof that no later modifications have been carried out.

There is a distinction between the literal senses of erasure[7] and destruction[8], both mentioned as possible processing operations in the GDPR. Even though the GDPR does not contain definitions of the involved terms, it can be argued merely on the basis of the wording that the requirements on an erasure are lower, i.e., it might not necessarily require a final destruction [37]. It is argued to be sufficient, if the data is no longer usable or accessible for the controller. A practical goal-oriented solution would thus be to correct the data with a supplementary statement [30]. Data removals would be possible likewise by stating information to be no longer usable in such a statement.

Data Protection Impact Assessment. Generally, when processing personal data, the controller must continuously assess the risks posed by the processing operations [6]. Furthermore, the GDPR contains the 'Data Protection Impact Assessment' (DPIA) as an evaluation and decision-making tool to reduce risks of personal injuries resulting from the misuse of personal information as well as for developing more efficient and effective procedures for processing personal data [38]. As the GDPR contains sensitive fines, compliance with obligations of the GDPR including a (correct) implementation of the DPIA is important. Its implementation is mandatory, if a processing operation is 'likely to result in a high risk to the rights and freedoms of natural persons'. The guidelines of the Article 29 Data Protection Working Party [6] can be used to define DPIA, as there is no direct definition in the GDPR. Accordingly, a DPIA 'is a process designed to describe the processing, assess its necessity and proportionality and help manage the risks [...] resulting from the processing of personal data by assessing them and determining the measures to address them'. This process is the key to accountability as it allows the controller to adopt appropriate strategies when developing data processing, but furthermore it is helpful in complying with the GDPR's requirements since the DPIA provides evidence that appropriate measures have been taken to protect personal data. According to the guidelines, a DPIA is particularly necessary if new technological solutions are used, if data processing is carried out on a large scale or if automated processing leads to decisions that have legal effect for natural persons [6]. Especially those listed criteria are of high relevance for Blockchain applications and in result, a DPIA is recommended to be done [12].

4.3 Smart Contracts

Smart Contracts are the automated processing of functions based on pre-determined procedures; their connection to the Blockchain is among Blockchain tech-

---

[7] The Oxford Dictionary defines 'erasure' as 'the act of removing writing, drawing, recorded material or data'.
[8] The Oxford Dictionary defines 'destruction' as 'the act of destroying something; the process of being destroyed'.

nology's other major advantages. In general, they contain a source code defining the rules (i.e., mainly `if-then-else` constructs) under which a contract is concluded. In energy communities they could especially be utilized for allocating energy to the participants [46]. For example, various scenarios depicted in the contract, such as the billing of electricity consumption data and electricity generation data between the participants, could be carried out fully automatically without any influence of third parties [32].

There are several legal issues with smart contracts, e.g., in the area of a possible reverse transaction, but also in terms of privacy as Smart Contracts fall under 'automated-decision making with legal or similar effects' according to the GDPR [7,30]. In summary, legal issues with Smart Contracts are further located in a variety of other legal areas, e.g., civil law, consumer protection law, tax law, e-commerce law, that cannot be dealt with in detail within the scope of this article. For example, as computers are not recognized as a legal entity under current law, the question arises to whom a declaration of intent in a system where a contract is executed only between two machines and the human being is pushed far into the background can be attributed to. In future, the creation of an 'electronic person' may be a possible solution to those legal problems; currently only the human that is eventually behind the autonomous system, such as a user or the programmer, are possible choices.

4.4 Implementation of an Energy Community

A renewable energy community with residential and industrial customers as well as a battery storage system supporting self-consumption optimization and peer-to-peer energy sharing using Blockchain was implemented and validated in a small municipality in Styria, Austria [12]. In regard to the discussed aspects of the previous subsections, the implementation focuses on being privacy-friendly and the use of the energy-efficient and suitable *proof-of-authority* consensus protocol [9]. Different roles and stakeholders are defined to concretize the structure of energy communities as introduced in Subsect. 3.2:

- *Community Representative*: The energy community as legal entity is represented by the *community representative*. This can be a person or a board representing the interests of the community members.
- *Platform Operator*: In this concept, the energy community assigns a service provider to take care of the technical and IT system needed for the community operation. The role is optional; for example, in case the energy community provides this services on its own, this role coincides with the *community representative*.
- *Pro-/Consumer*: This role represents and subsumes a variety of different members of the energy community in Fig. 2, e.g., a household (natural person), a charging station (automation system) or a community storage system.
- *Energy Supplier*: As described before, (traditional) energy suppliers are also needed for the community operation, e.g., for selling excess generated energy or for purchasing remaining demanded energy (cf. Fig. 2). Depending on the

use case at hand, those external market participants may also need a certain yet restricted access to the community's ICT system.
– *External Stakeholders*: Other external stakeholders could be obliged by law (e.g., an observing regulation authority for consumer protection, ministries for tax-related issues etc.), by wish of the energy community or as required by a use case[9] to have some access to the community's ICT system.

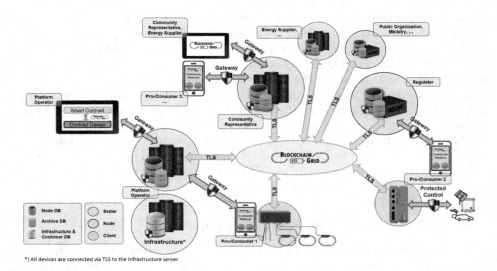

Fig. 4. The architecture used in the *Blockchain Grid* project.

Figure 4 shows the implemented architecture of the *Blockchain Grid* project. Core element of this concept is a permissioned private Blockchain, based on *Parity Ethereum*, smart contracts running on this Blockchain system and an *infrastructure server* to configure and operate the system. Access privileges to the Blockchain and roles within the Blockchain system are managed and assigned over the *infrastructure server*. To ensures that nobody, except authorized participants, can read the data in the system, all data written to the Blockchain (transactions) is stored in encrypted form. The consensus algorithm for new blocks is the *proof-of-authority* procedure, in which a limited number of authorized participants (*validators* or *sealers*) generate blocks in which all transactions of a given time frame are stored into the Blockchain. In the *proof-of-authority* process the sealers generate blocks in a defined sequence in which the data of the participants is stored. Network members put their trust into the authorized sealer nodes and a block is accepted if the majority of sealers signs the block [3]. There are three different types of nodes in this concept (cf. Fig. 4):

---

[9] Note that especially the CEC can offer a high variety of use cases (cf. Subsect. 3.1).

- *Sealer*: These nodes have a complete local image of the Blockchain (*Node DB*) and are responsible to create its blocks. The sealer nodes execute computationally intensive operations like block generation and evaluation of smart contracts and are therefore visualized as machines in data center environments.
- *Nodes* (or "full" nodes): These nodes also hold a full local copy of the Blockchain (*Node DB*), but take no part in the generation of blocks. They can therefore validate all transactions and smart contracts within the Blockchain independently from the sealer nodes, but their operations are not as complex as the sealer nodes'. Therefore, these nodes are visualized as smaller computer systems, e.g., located in an office environment.
- *Clients* (or "light" nodes): These nodes only have a lightweight access to the Blockchain, such that they can send transactions (write data into the Blockchain) or receive transactions (get data for this node out of the Blockchain). For these operations only limited computational efforts and data storage is required; therefore, the client can be executed on an embedded device with very limited capabilities like a smart meter or a measurement system. Furthermore, those nodes do not save a local copy of the whole Blockchain, but only those parts that are currently needed and into which the client is involved.

Sealer nodes in this system are operated by trusted parties, e.g., the *platform operator*, the *community representative* or the use-case associated *energy supplier*. The remaining nodes are operated by other trusted stakeholders like the regulator or other authorities. As all of these nodes have a full local copy of the Blockchain (*Node DB*) they can access all stored data. Over a gateway functionality, provided by sealer and full nodes, stakeholders can access data depending on their roles explained in more detail later in this section. Measuring devices (as shown on the bottom of Fig. 4) and other sensors or actuators like a community storage system are connected as clients. Required control information (e.g., for changing the maximum power of a charging station for electric vehicles) can be retrieved by the clients via protected connections (*protected control*). Within the *Blockchain Grid* project additional measurement and controller hardware was installed at the participants sites. In future, those measurements could be done by a smart meter in addition to its normal metering tasks. The idea is that the connection to the Blockchain could be easily activated over the *infrastructure server* without the need for any hardware handling at the customer site. Likewise, heat pumps or charging stations that have already implemented the Blockchain client software within their control systems can be added to the Blockchain system by the *infrastructure server*.

All necessary information for the system's operation, such as the smart contracts, configurations and roles of the participants as well as the access rights to data are stored on the *infrastructure server*. Customer data (name, address, customer number) are assigned to an ID within the Blockchain. This assignment is managed and can be used depending on the use case, e.g., by the Distribution System Operator (DSO) or an energy supplier to transmit billing-relevant information. In this way, the *platform operator* represents the person responsible in terms of data protection law, which is the only one who can access the server. All data exchange between the infrastructure server and the participants is made via an encrypted connection (TLS).

Blockchain Grid Gateway. To access the data in the Blockchain, each participant receives an access identifier (username and password) which is linked to the customer data by the *infrastructure server*. Each sealer node and full node provides a way to login with the customer access ID to obtain data according to the respective access rights (*gateway* in Fig. 4). In order to strengthen the relationship of trust between the participants and the nodes, the participant can determine which nodes he wants to connect to. As the full nodes validate all transactions and smart contracts within the Blockchain independently the participant could check, if desired, whether every node shows the same data. The credentials are validated via the *infrastructure server*, which notifies the respective node of the Blockchain ID, the role and access rights of the participant asking for data access. For example, a *pro-/consumer* has only access to his own data (like sold energy, measured load data, ...) whereas the *community representative* can access aggregated data of the overall community operation (e.g., sold energy of the community, share of individual participants) to ensure optimal conditions for the community. Furthermore, the gateway provides functionalities to adopt, design and deploy smart contracts to the Blockchain system using the *contract design* function in the gateway.

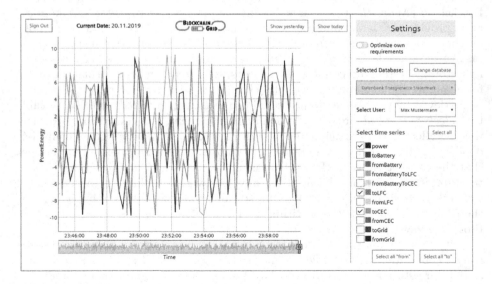

Fig. 5. First implementation of the gateway-GUI, view of the community representative.

Figure 5 shows the implementation of the gateway dashboard to plot data stored in the Blockchain. In this version of the gateway are different power flows displayed, like current power consumption or production ("power") what amount of power was transferred to a *family community* as a subset of the community[10] ("toLFC") and how much power was transferred to the remainder ("toCEC"). The "settings" area allows to set user preferences concerning, e.g., the preferred trading algorithm of the smart contract. In this example, the user could either prefer to maximize self consumption first and transfer only the excess generated power to the community or vice versa to primarily meet the needs of the community.

Privacy-Related Implementation Aspects. A special feature in this system is the start of a new Blockchain after each accounting period. This aspect complies with the principles of data minimization and storage limitation, since data is stored on the Blockchain for one accounting period only. This also facilitates the enforcement of the rights of rectification and erasure. In case of a participant's revocation of its membership to the community, a supplementary statement is added to the Blockchain, while no data of this participant will be available on the next chain. Nevertheless, Blockchains of expired accounting periods need to be archived in a separate database at the sealer nodes and the full nodes (*Archive DB* in Fig. 4) as it may be legally required to keep the archives for some years according to civil and tax law regulations. The first transaction in the new Blockchain stores necessary linking information of the old Blockchain, such as the hash value of its last block to prevent later manipulations of the previous Blockchain. Access to those old Blockchains is even more restricted to achieve a feasible tradeoff between the obligation to archive and the data subjects rights of the GDPR.

Implemented Smart Contracts. Within the Blockchain system of the *Blockchain Grid* project, two smart contracts have been implemented:

The first smart contract is responsible for calculating energy flows within the community as well as the charging/discharging power of the community battery, based on surplus and demand information as well as the state-of-charge of the battery. Therefore, customer information about surplus or demand is provided to the smart contract in a one-minute-resolution over the measurement devices and their Blockchain clients. Based on calculation specifications, energy flows between different customers, between customers and the battery as well as between customers and energy suppliers are calculated, which are then used to calculate the corresponding monetary transactions for all participants. For this smart contract, which simulative results are presented in the Subsect. 5.2 and Subsect. 5.3, special energy prices within the community and reduced grid fees and loss fees are used.

---

[10] The *Blockchain Grid* project also investigated different kinds of relationships between the participants, such as members of one family within a community that want to trade energy between them without revenue.

The second smart contract is one special use case of the *Blockchain Grid* project in which the local DSO is one of the community's stakeholders. The smart contract is responsible to ensure a grid capacity management to avoid an overloading of grid resources like cables or transformers due to community operations. It takes the demand of the community customers including devices such as public charging stations into account and checks the compliance with the grid limits (power and voltage) provided by the DSO as model data. If grid elements are in danger of overloading, e.g., due to a charging station planning to load with its rated power, the smart contract detects the violation and resolves this situation, e.g., by reducing the loading power of the charging station. A detailed description of the model and the implementation is provided by *Rao et al.* [48].

5   Profitability of Energy Communities

While the legal definition of both types of energy communities claim the main purpose to 'provide environmental, economic or social community benefits rather than financial profits', the latter ones cannot be neglected for the applicability and acceptance of those concepts [15]. Thus, participation in a community needs to be profitable for all of its members, i.e., for producers and consumers.

5.1   Energy Costs

The main focus will be laid on the consumer side, whose costs can be divided into three components, that are in Austria currently responsible for about one third of the final costs each:

1. Energy costs
2. Grid costs (System charges), they are further divided into the
   - the system utilization charge,
   - the charge for system losses,
   - the system admission charge,
   - the system provision charge,
   - the system services charge,
   - the metering charge, and
   - the charge for supplementary services.
3. Taxes and fees, which consist of
   - the electricity tax,
   - several surcharges, for example, for the promotion of renewable electricity, and
   - the value-added-tax (VAT).

Energy costs are defined by each vendor itself in a deregulated market, while grid costs (as the grid itself continues to be a natural monopoly), taxes and fees are defined by law or by an authority such as the energy regulator authority. While a certain amount of the energy will be taken from the energy community, each consumer will still require an energy vendor for those energy amount that cannot be satisfied by the community. For instance, there are still questions on the cost-effectiveness of energy storage systems [19] as well as whether they can meet the whole demand, e.g., in the evenings, when the attached photovoltaic units no longer produce energy.

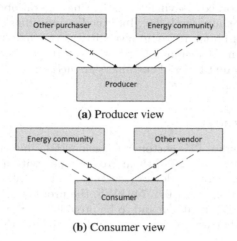

(a) Producer view

(b) Consumer view

Fig. 6. Possibilities for producers to sell their energy and for consumers to purchase energy [15]. The energy flow is shown in a dashed line, the cash flow using a continuous line.

For a high acceptance of the community concepts, financial profits for producers and for consumers are necessary. According to Fig. 6 it is required, that

- a producer receives more money for selling energy to the community than to another producer, i.e., $y > x$,
- a consumer pays less money for purchasing energy from the community than from another vendor, i.e., $b < a$,
- the energy community is not required to make a profit; however, at least cost break-even is expected, i.e., $y < b$.

Various models to determine the costs (b, y) have been enumerated by *Long et al.* [42]. However, it is in fact unlikely that the energy purchased from the community can continuously be offered at a significant lower price than by an energy vendor [15]. Therefore, it is necessary to establish financial promotions on grid costs, taxes and fees by reducing those legally defined costs for the amount of energy consumed from the community. In fact, it is also thinkable that while energy costs decrease for energy community members, and especially for prosumers, they might eventually increase for traditional consumers [45].

In Austria, grid costs are reduced for RECs' members by utilizing the proximity aspects [14,18]. Those grid costs traditionally include the costs of higher voltage grid levels that could be eliminated due to the restriction to operate only over certain low voltage grid levels (cf. Sect. 3.4). Naturally, cost savings will thus be higher for communities that span only over grid levels 6 and 7 rather than including higher voltage grid levels. Furthermore, taxes and fees are reduced by waiving the energy tax and parts of the surcharges; all of those only for the amount of energy that was indeed consumed from the community [18].

First simulations on cost savings investigating several operational scenarios have been done in previous work [50]. Intermediate results showed possible savings for consumers of about 10%. However, it was concluded that the outcome very much depends on the community setup and further simulations with larger communities and different types of customers are necessary, which will be carried out in the next section.

5.2 Simulative Study

The simulation includes 125 customers (residential, industrial, agricultural) based on real customer data; 20 of them are equipped with a photovoltaic unit, 105 do not have any generation device (see Table 2). In total, the overall community energy consumption was 1 072 749 kWh, the production was 236 373 kWh, resulting in 836 376 kWh final demand to be provided by the superior grid. Two different community battery models were used within the study:

i) a small community battery with a total capacity of 100 kWh, and
ii) a larger community battery with a capacity of 1000 kWh.

In both cases, the battery capacity per customer was not limited but the stored energy is reserved for the customer for a maximum of 36 h (battery release time).

Table 2. Overview of community customers and their annual energy balance (total, minimum, maximum and average values).

Type	Count	Total energy [kWh]	Min. energy [kWh]	Max. energy [kWh]	Avg. energy [kWh]
Residential customers (H0 profile)	81	395.577	326	23.843	4.884
Industrial customers (Gx profile)	21	388.900	706	92.698	18.519
Mixed customers (H0-Gx profile)	3	91.607	11.381	61.504	30.536
Agricultural customers (Lx profile)	15	196.665	1.273	62.389	13.111

Simulation Scenarios. To evaluate the most promising concept in terms of energy and cost savings from a customer perspective, six different scenarios were investigated – they are described in detail in the following and illustrated in Fig. 7.

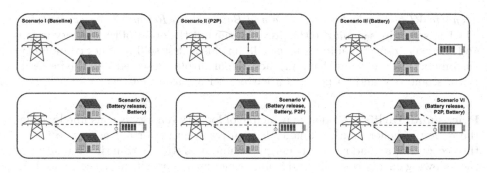

Fig. 7. Overview of different simulation scenarios.

Scenario I – Baseline Scenario (Grid). This scenario represents the current situation for grid customers which buy energy from their contracted retailer. Their surplus (after serving their own consumption) is sold to the contracted retailer. No additional storage or other devices and systems (e.g., Energy Management System) are available.

Scenario II – Peer-to-Peer Trading (P2P). This scenario extends the baseline scenario by energy trading capabilities between customers. Within the community, all surplus is distributed to the customers with demand (based on the demand/surplus share of each customer). For the peer-to-peer trading one energy price is used for all customers within the community.

Scenario III – Battery Usage (Bat2P_V1). The third scenario extends the baseline scenario by a community battery. Community members can store their surplus energy for later use and finally, for increasing their self-consumption.

Scenario IV – Battery with Release Time (Bat2P_V2). This scenario is based on the previous one. Additionally, a battery release time is included: The Blockchain technology allows to flag each kWh which is transferred and thus, also each kWh which is stored into the battery. This flag contains the origin as well as the transaction time and its price. After a configured time (e.g., 36 h in the simulation scenarios), the energy must be released from the battery. Before the release time expires, the owner of the energy needs to use it for serving its own consumption. Additional energy will be sold to other community customers and to the retailer if there are not enough recipients within the community. This strategy allows a fair usage of the battery and avoids situations in which customers only store their surplus energy without obtaining it, resulting in a fully charged battery without any possible interaction with the other community members in the worst case.

Scenario V – Battery with Release Time and Peer-to-Peer Trading (Full_Bat2P). The fifth scenario extends the previous one by adding the peer-to-peer trading as a last step. Surplus which cannot be stored in the battery is sold to community customers with demand.

Scenario VI – Peer-to-Peer Trading and Battery with Release-Time (Full_P2P).
The last scenario is similar to the previous one but the order of the battery usage
and the peer-to-peer trading is inverted. Surplus is first sold to other community
customers (if there is any demand), additional surplus is stored into the battery.
Both, scenario V and VI perform a battery release as a first step.

Prices and Tariffs. Beside the principle of locality (energy is consumed within
the region of generation), a financial incentive is an important aspect to foster
the acceptance and adoption of energy communities [15]. Within the simulations,
the following energy costs (to and from retailer as well as within the community),
grid costs (reduced tariffs for energy transfer within the community including
storage utilization), tax and other fees are used. The total costs and revenues
(from the customer perspective) for each transaction are illustrated in Fig. 8.

- Selling energy to community customers: 6.08 €ct/kWh
- Selling energy to the retailer: 5.02 €ct/kWh, 2.78 €ct/kWh, 2.75 €ct/kWh
  (staggered)
- Buying energy from community customers: 13.01 €ct/kWh
- Buying energy from the retailer: 17.40 €ct/kWh
- Battery charging: 0.385 €ct/kWh
- Battery discharging: 2.654 €ct/kWh

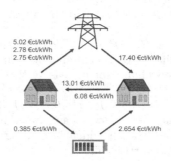

Fig. 8. Energy price (including tax and grid tariffs) for trading within the community,
using the battery, and selling to or buying from the retailer.

5.3 Results

The simulation was performed for a time period of one year with 15 min time
intervals resulting in 35040 time steps. The total costs aggregated for all community members (including energy costs, grid fees, loss fees, taxes) and all scenarios
are shown in Fig. 9 (left), both for using a 100 kWh battery storage and 1000 kWh
battery storage. Additionally, the average costs for the community customers are

shown in the right part of the figure. Obviously, the baseline scenario (*grid*) has the highest total costs. Depending on the scenario, the total and average costs can be reduced up to 6%. These savings are based on reduced fees and taxes for intra-community energy flows and community energy costs which are beneficial for customers with surplus as well as for customers with demand (compared to transactions with the retailer).

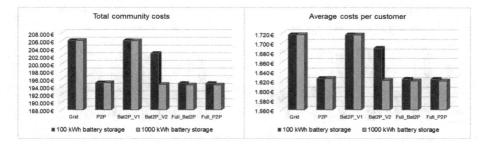

Fig. 9. Community results.

Figure 10 illustrates the average costs per customer, based on the customer type (residential customers, industrial customers, mixed customers, agricultural customers). This figure illustrates a high deviation between potential savings for customer types, based on the used storage system – residential customers benefit more than industrial and agricultural customers in the last two scenarios when using the smaller storage system; industrial and agricultural customers can save more in these two scenarios when using the larger storage system.

Additionally, the battery capacity as well as the release time (36 h in the simulation) have a high impact on the community results. The higher the battery capacity, the higher the release time could be set aiming to have a high battery utilization without blocking customers surplus feed-in due to a high state-of-charge.

To sum up, it was shown that energy sharing within an energy community as well as utilizing a community storage can have positive impacts on the total costs for each customer. The amount depends on the energy flows, the used battery storage system (with or without battery release) and especially on the composition/structure of the customer and generation types inside the community (cf. [50]). For example, if the amount of consumption and generation among community members has similar values for similar times, it is obvious that most energy can be utilized locally. Results shown here are based on a community with a dominance in consumption compared to generation. Furthermore, only PV generation was investigated, which has a rather clear and predictable power output over time. Further studies and investigations with more varying scenarios to retrieve important indicators for the constellations and behavior of energy communities via sensitivity analysis and stochastic simulation approaches have to be done in the future.

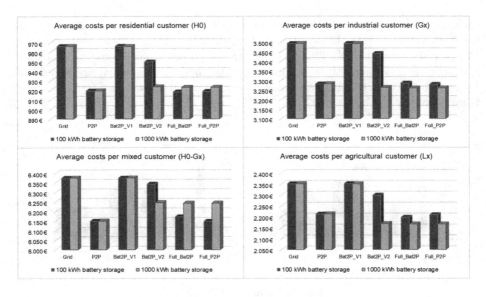

Fig. 10. Community results.

6   Conclusion and Outlook

This article explains the concept of energy communities in Europe, the legal framework and the definition of Renewable Energy Communities (RECs) and Citizen Energy Communities (CECs) as well as their participants structure. Within the European Union's Clean Energy Package, RECs and CECs are defined and the legal background is provided, whereas the Renewable Energy Directive (EU) 2018/2001 (RED) and the Electricity Directive (EU) 2019/944 (ED) are of main interest.

The Blockchain with a high level of automation, transparency, and data immutability is one possible option for implementing technical solutions for energy communities to provide mechanisms for energy trading and accounting. Several legal aspects such as privacy and data protection aspects have to be considered in the solutions as personal data are processed – in this case consumption or generation data with the opportunity to infer to (community) customers. Smart Contracts contain source code and pre-defined rules for their automated execution and contract conclusion – for example, between community participants when exchanging energy. As many legal definitions can be used only on human beings, several open questions still have to be clarified for fully-automated Smart Contract-based solutions for energy communities.

Within the Austrian research project *Blockchain Grid*, Blockchain-based solutions for energy-trading and self-consumption optimization for a REC in Styria, Austria have been developed, deployed, and validated within a several months field trial phase. The trading algorithms as well as the utilization of a available community battery storage system are implemented by using Smart

Contracts. Special energy price, reduced grid fees and loss fees as well as reduced taxes are used for energy trading within the community or when using the community battery for increasing the self-consumption of the customers. In parallel, simulation models have been used for assessment of the economical potential for community customers. A digital representation of the Styrian community was simulated and a total cost reduction of up to 6% (on average per customer) could be achieved with the implemented solution.

For successful implementation of energy communities all over Europe, several social, legal and regulatory aspects have to be clarified in order to enable the already partly available technical solutions – either on Blockchain technology or based on classical I(o)T-systems. Multi-country research projects – such as the European project *CLUE* – could help to work on transnational solutions and recommendations for legal, regulatory and technical frameworks enabling the implementation of economic communities.

Acknowledgments. The presented work is conducted in the projects *SonnWende+* (no. 861621) and *Blockchain Grid* (no. 868656), both funded by the Austrian Climate and Energy Fund (KLIEN) and the Austrian Research Promotion Agency (FFG) as well as in the project *CLUE* (no. 872286), funded by partners of the ERA-Net SES 2018 joint call RegSys and the European Union's Horizon 2020 research and innovation programme.

References

1. Ahl, A., et al.: Exploring blockchain for the energy transition: opportunities and challenges based on a case study in Japan. Renew. Sustain. Energy Rev. **117**, 109488 (2020). https://doi.org/10.1016/j.rser.2019.109488
2. Alladi, T., Chamola, V., Rodrigues, J., Kozlov, S.: Blockchain in smart grids: a review on different use cases. Sensors **19**(22), 4862 (2019). https://doi.org/10.3390/s19224862
3. Andoni, M., et al.: Blockchain technology in the energy sector: a systematic review of challenges and opportunities. Renew. Sustain. Energy Rev. **100**, 143–174 (2019). https://doi.org/10.1016/j.rser.2018.10.014
4. Article 29 Data Protection Working Party: Opinion 1/2010 on the concept of 'controller' and 'processor' (WP 169) (2010)
5. Article 29 Data Protection Working Party: Opinion 05/2014 on anonymisation techniques (WP 216) (2014)
6. Article 29 Data Protection Working Party: Guidelines on Data Protection Impact Assessment (DPIA) and determining whether processing is "likely to result in a high risk" for the purposes of regulation 2016/679 (WP 248) (2017)
7. Article 29 Data Protection Working Party: Guidelines on automated individual decision-making and profiling for the purposes of regulation 2016/679 (WP 251) (2018)
8. Ateniese, G., Magri, B., Venturi, D., Andrade, E.: Redactable blockchain - or - rewriting history in bitcoin and friends. In: 2017 IEEE European Symposium on Security and Privacy (EuroS&P), pp. 111–126, April 2017. https://doi.org/10.1109/EuroSP.2017.37

9. Barinov, I., Baranov, V., Khahulin, P.: POA network whitepaper. Technical report (2018). https://github.com/poanetwork/wiki/wiki/POA-Network-Whitepaper. Accessed 11 Sept 2020
10. Brilliantova, V., Thurner, T.: Blockchain and the future of energy. Technol. Soc. **57**, 38–45 (2019). https://doi.org/10.1016/j.techsoc.2018.11.001
11. Casino, F., Dasaklis, T., Patsakis, C.: A systematic literature review of blockchain-based applications: current status, classification and open issues. Telematics Inform. **36**, 55–81 (2019). https://doi.org/10.1016/j.tele.2018.11.006
12. Cejka, S., Zeilinger, F., Veseli, A., Holzleitner, M., Stefan, M.: A blockchain-based privacy-friendly renewable energy community. In: 9th International Conference on Smart Cities and Green ICT Systems (SMARTGREENS), pp. 95–103, May 2020. https://doi.org/10.5220/0009391300950103
13. Cejka, S.: Energiegemeinschaften im Clean Energy Package der EU. ecolex - Fachzeitschrift für Wirtschaftsrecht, pp. 338–341, April 2020. in German
14. Cejka, S., Frieden, D., Kitzmüller, K.: Implementation of self-consumption and energy communities in Austria's and EU member states' national law: A perspective on system integration and grid tariffs. In: 26th International Conference on Electricity Distribution (CIRED), p. 857, September 2021
15. Cejka, S.: Legal measures to aid profitability for energy communities and their participants. In: IEEE Zooming Innovation in Consumer Technologies International Conference 2020 (ZINC 2020), May 2020. https://doi.org/10.1109/ZINC50678.2020.9161787
16. Cejka, S., Einfalt, A., Poplavskaya, K., Stefan, M., Zeilinger, F.: Planning and operating future energy communities. In: CIRED Workshop, p. 213, September 2020
17. Cejka, S., Knorr, F., Kintzler, F.: Privacy issues in Smart Buildings by examples in Smart Metering. In: 25th International Conference on Electricity Distribution (CIRED) (2019). https://doi.org/10.34890/819
18. Cejka, S., Kitzmüller, K.: Rechtsfragen zur Gründung und Umsetzung von Energiegemeinschaften. In: 12. Internationale Energiewirtschaftstagung (IEWT), September 2021. in German
19. Comello, S., Reichelstein, S.: The emergence of cost effective battery storage. Nat. Commun. **10** (2019). https://doi.org/10.1038/s41467-019-09988-z
20. Dileep, G.: A survey on smart grid technologies and applications. Renew. Energy **146**, 2589–2625 (2020). https://doi.org/10.1016/j.renene.2019.08.092
21. Energy Community Regulatory Board (ECRB): Prosumers in the energy community - legal and regulatory framework for support and treatment of small-scale generators, March 2020. https://energy-community.org/dam/jcr:abacd12d-283c-492a-8aa4-6da5797d044a/ECRB_prosumers_regulatory_framework_032020.pdf. Accessed 11 Sept 2020
22. EU Blockchain Observatory and Forum: Blockchain and the GDPR (2018)
23. European Commission: 2030 climate & energy framework (2019). https://ec.europa.eu/clima/policies/strategies/2030_en. Accessed 11 Sept 2020
24. European Commission: 2050 long-term strategy (2019). https://ec.europa.eu/clima/policies/strategies/2050_en. Accessed 11 Sept 2020
25. European Parliamentary Research Service, Panel for the Future of Science and Technology: Blockchain and the general data protection regulation. Technical report (2019)
26. Falduto, C., Rocha, M.: Aligning short-term climate action with long-term climate goals: opportunities and options for enhancing alignment between NDCs and long-term strategies. OECD/IEA Climate Change Expert Group Papers (2020)

27. Fina, B., Fechner, H.: Transposition of European guidelines for energy communities into Austrian law: A comparison and discussion of issues and positive aspects. Energies **14**(13), (2021). Article no. 3922. ISSN 1996-1073. https://doi.org/10.3390/en14133922

28. Finck, M.: Blockchains and data protection in the European union. Eur. Data Prot. Law Rev. **4**(1) (2018). https://doi.org/10.21552/edpl/2018/1/6

29. Finck, M.: Blockchain Regulation and Governance in Europe. Cambridge University Press, Cambridge (2019)

30. Finck, M.: Smart contracts as a form of solely automated processing under the GDPR. Int. Data Priv. Law **9**(2), 78–94 (2019). https://doi.org/10.1093/idpl/ipz004

31. Fleischhacker, A., Auer, H., Lettner, G., Botterud, A.: Sharing solar PV and energy storage in apartment buildings: resource allocation and pricing. IEEE Trans. Smart Grid **10**(4), 3963–3973 (2018). https://doi.org/10.1109/TSG.2018.2844877

32. Francisco, K., Swanson, D.: The supply chain has no clothes: technology adoption of blockchain for supply chain transparency. Logistics **2**(1), 2 (2018). https://doi.org/10.3390/logistics2010002

33. Frieden, D., Tuerk, A., Neumann, C., d'Herbemont, S., Roberts, J.: Collective self-consumption and energy communities: Trends and challenges in the transposition of the EU framework (2020). https://www.rescoop.eu/uploads/rescoop/downloads/Collective-self-consumption-and-energy-communities.-Trends-and-challenges-in-the-transposition-of-the-EU-framework.pdf. Accessed 30 Sept 2021

34. Greveler, U., Justus, B., Loehr, D.: Multimedia content identification through smart meter power usage profiles. In: Computers, Privacy and Data Protection (CPDP) (2012)

35. Guegan, D.: Public blockchain versus private blockhain. Documents de travail du centre d'economie de la sorbonne (2017)

36. Harikrishnan, M., Lakshmy, K.: Secure digital service payments using zero knowledge proof in distributed network. In: 2019 5th International Conference on Advanced Computing & Communication Systems (ICACCS), pp. 307–312. IEEE (2019). https://doi.org/10.1109/ICACCS.2019.8728462

37. Holzleitner, M., Burgstaller, K., Cejka, S., Veseli, A.: Electricity trading via blockchain in an energy community from a data protection point of view. Eur. Energy Clim. J. (EECJ) **2020**(2 & 3), 33–43 (2020)

38. Holzleitner, M., Reichl, J.: Legal problems for the protection of smart grids from cyber threats. Eur. Energy J. (EEJ) **20**, 53–61 (2016)

39. Intergovernmental Panel on Climate Change (IPCC): Climate Change 2014: Mitigation of Climate Change. Contribution of Working Group III to the Fifth Assessment Report of the Intergovernmental Panel on Climate Change (2014)

40. Joint Research Centre: Blockchain now and tomorrow. Publications Office of the European Union (2019)

41. Kotilainen, K., Valta, J., Systä, K., Mäkinen, S., Järventausta, P., Björkqvist, T.: Exploring the potential of blockchain as an enabler for three types of energy communities. In: 2019 16th International Conference on the European Energy Market (EEM), pp. 1–6 (2019). https://doi.org/10.1109/EEM.2019.8916261

42. Long, C., Wu, J., Zhang, C., Thomas, L., Cheng, M., Jenkins, N.: Peer-to-peer energy trading in a community microgrid. In: 2017 IEEE Power Energy Society General Meeting, pp. 1–5 (2017). https://doi.org/10.1109/PESGM.2017.8274546

43. Lowitzsch, J., Hoicka, C., van Tulder, F.: Renewable energy communities under the 2019 European clean energy package - governance model for the energy clusters of

the future? Renew. Sustain. Energy Rev. **122**, 109489 (2020). https://doi.org/10.1016/j.rser.2019.109489
44. Martinez, J., Ruiz, A., Puelles, J., Arechalde, I., Miadzvetskaya, Y.: Smart grid challenges through the lens of the European general data protection regulation. In: Siarheyeva, A., Barry, C., Lang, M., Linger, H., Schneider, C. (eds.) ISD 2019. LNISO, vol. 39, pp. 113–130. Springer, Cham (2020). https://doi.org/10.1007/978-3-030-49644-9_7
45. Milčiuvienė, S., Kirčienė, J., Doheijo, E., Urbonas, R., Milčius, D.: The role of renewable energy prosumers in implementing energy justice theory. Sustainability **11**, 5286 (2019). https://doi.org/10.3390/su11195286
46. Plaza, C., Gil, J., de Chezelles, F., Strang, K.: Distributed solar self-consumption and blockchain solar energy exchanges on the public grid within an energy community. In: 2018 IEEE International Conference on Environment and Electrical Engineering and 2018 IEEE Industrial and Commercial Power Systems Europe (EEEIC/I&CPS Europe), pp. 1–4. IEEE (2018). https://doi.org/10.1109/EEEIC.2018.8494534
47. Politou, E., Casino, F., Alepis, E., Patsakis, C.: Blockchain mutability: challenges and proposed solutions. IEEE Trans. Emerg. Top. Comput. 1 (2019). https://doi.org/10.1109/TETC.2019.2949510
48. Rao, B.V., et al.: Grid capacity management for peer-to-peer local energy communities. In: 2020 IEEE PES General Meeting, August 2020
49. Resch, G., Totschnig, G., Suna, D., Schöniger, F., Geipel, J., Liebmann, L.: Assessment of prerequisites and impacts of a renewable-based electricity supply in Austria by 2030. In: Uyar, T.S. (ed.) Accelerating the Transition to a 100% Renewable Energy Era. LNE, vol. 74, pp. 99–111. Springer, Cham (2020). https://doi.org/10.1007/978-3-030-40738-4_4
50. Stefan, M., Zehetbauer, P., Cejka, S., Zeilinger, F., Taljan, G.: Blockchain-based self-consumption optimisation and energy trading in renewable energy communities. CIRED - Open Access Proc. J. **2020**, 371–374. Institution of Engineering and Technology (2021). https://doi.org/10.1049/oap-cired.2021.0061
51. Tang, G., Wu, K., Lei, J., Xiao, W.: The meter tells you are at home! Non-intrusive occupancy detection via load curve data. In: 2015 IEEE International Conference on Smart Grid Communications (SmartGridComm), pp. 897–902, November 2015. https://doi.org/10.1109/SmartGridComm.2015.7436415
52. Truby, J.: Decarbonizing bitcoin: law and policy choices for reducing the energy consumption of blockchain technologies and digital currencies. Energy Res. Soc. Sci. **44**, 399–410 (2018). https://doi.org/10.1016/j.erss.2018.06.009
53. United Nations Framework Convention on Climate Change (UNFCCC): The Paris Agreement (2016). https://unfccc.int/process-and-meetings/the-paris-agreement/the-paris-agreement. Accessed 11 Sept 2020
54. University of Cambridge: Cambridge bitcoin electricity consumption index (2020). https://www.cbeci.org/. Accessed 11 Sept 2020
55. Vranken, H.: Sustainability of bitcoin and blockchains. Curr. Opin. Environ. Sustain. **28**, 1–9 (2017). https://doi.org/10.1016/j.cosust.2017.04.011
56. de Vries, A.: Bitcoin's growing energy problem. Joule **2**(5), 801–805 (2018). https://doi.org/10.1016/j.joule.2018.04.016
57. Zyskind, G., Nathan, O., Pentland, A.: Decentralizing privacy: using blockchain to protect personal data. In: 2015 IEEE Security and Privacy Workshops, pp. 180–184 (2015). https://doi.org/10.1109/SPW.2015.27

Correlation of Weights in an Evaluation Model for Smart City Proficiency with Less Than 50,000 Inhabitants: A Greek City Case Study

T. Tounta[✉], E. Strantzali, C. Nikoloudis, and K. Aravossis

Sector of Industrial Management and Operational Research, School of Mechanical Engineering, National Technical University of Athens, Iroon Polytechniou 9, 15780 Athens, Greece
{tetounta,lenast,nikoloudisc}@central.ntua.gr,
arvis@mail.ntua.gr

Abstract. New canny advancements are viewed as a vital factor in battling against environmental change and improving the sustainability in urban communities. A smart city is where administrations utilize progressed data and correspondence advances. According to literature, a smart city includes actions for 6 principle spaces: economy, environment, governance, living, mobility and people. The aim of the current study is to look at four alternative techniques for an all-encompassing smart city positioning model for urban areas with populace under 50,000 inhabitants, applicable in the context of Greece. Based on the European guidelines, 25 essential elements have been resolved and 68 indicators have been embraced for the improvement of the assessment model. The instance of Region of Elefsina is analyzed with these four techniques and a final model is recommended. The proposed model will assist urban communities with comparable qualities (under 50.000 inhabitants) assess their status in the field of "smart cities" to develop programs and strategies.

Keywords: Smart cities · Smart economy · Smart mobility · Smart governance · Smart environment · Smart living · Smart people · Smart city's footprint

1 Introduction

A city is the centre for all sustainable urban development strategies. Today, more than half of the world's population live in cities, and it is predicted that by 2050 urban areas will occupy 70% of the population [11]. Nowadays there has been observed a shift in a new city pattern based on smart targets instead of only sustainability goals. Smart city provides better urban services based on the use of advanced Information and Communication Technologies (ICT). Although the dominant part of the smart cities profile is the infrastructure, the involvement of people and citizens is, also, crucial [12].

As the exact definition of a smart city does not exist, the smart city concept contains several dimensions: Smart Economy, Smart Mobility, Smart Environment, Smart People, Smart Living and Smart Governance. These smart characteristics have been identified through a literature review: [2, 3, 6, 8, 10–12, 15]. Smart economy is driven

© Springer Nature Switzerland AG 2021
C. Klein et al. (Eds.): SMARTGREENS 2020/VEHITS 2020, CCIS 1475, pp. 31–45, 2021.
https://doi.org/10.1007/978-3-030-89170-1_2

by economic competiveness, entrepreneurship and innovation. Smart mobility refers to local accessibility, safe transport systems and availability of ICT [15]. The smart environment is related to the quality of environment, including the attractiveness of nature, lack of pollution and sustainable resource management. Smart people refers not only to the level of education of the citizens but, also, to the key role of people in developing a smart city. Smart living includes factors all around quality of life. Smart governance comprises aspects of political participation, public services and e-governance.

A smart city is a city well performing in these six smart characteristics [7]. In the literature, there are a few studies that have proposed ranking models to examine the performance of a smart city: Giffinger et al. [7] ranked 70 European smart cities by adopting a set of 74 indicators under the above analysed six dimensions. All the examined cities had population between 100,000 and 500,000 inhabitants and their data have been aggregated and standardized with z-transformation. Lazaroiu and Roscia [10] used z-transformation and fuzzy logic for evaluating 10 Italian cities, by adopting 18 crucial indicators. Alibegović and Šagovac [3] implement a ranking methodology for Croatian large cities by using indicators in strategic decision-making [12] developed an evaluation model of smart city performance specialized for China. The evaluation process has been carried out by applying entropy method and the multicriteria method, TOPSIS. Akande et al. [2] ranked 28 European capital cities on how smart and sustainable they are, by using 32 indicators. Their methodology has been based on hierarchical clustering and principal component analysis (PCA). Finally, Milošević et al. [11] incorporated 35 key indicators for the assessment of Serbian smart cities. Their approach has been based on a hybrid fuzzy multicriteria decision making model.

In summary, all the above mentioned papers focused their research on metropolises with more than 100,000 inhabitants. Furthermore, their methodologies are based on multicriteria decision anlysis. So, it appears that there is no existing study examining smart city performance for cities with population less than 50,000 inhabitants. The aim of this study is to propose a holistic smart city ranking model, based on multicriteria analysis, for cities with population less than 50,000 inhabitants and, at the same time, recommend actions for improving the smart city performance. The majority of Greek municipalities cover this feature, as 95% of Greek municipalities have less than 50,000 inhabitants, and an evaluation process for smart cities' profile has not been carried out in Greek cities until now. A representative case study has been selected and so the proposed methodology has been implemented for Municipality of Elefsina.

The remainder of this paper is structured as follows: Sect. 2 presents the methodology of the study as far as the weights of the model are concerned. Section 3 contains the analysis results for the performance of Municipality of Elefsina. Finally, Sect. 4 concludes the study including, also, future thoughts.

2 Research Methodology

The approach adopted in this research comprises of four steps. Firstly, the selected set of smart city indicators are presented. Secondly, the evaluation methodology is described. In the third step, a questionnaire is developed according to the selected indicators in order to determine their values and in the fourth step, the classes of a smart city footprint are presented.

2.1 Smart City Indicators

As smartness of a city is not easily measurable, a European or International agreement on smart city indicators does not exist [10]. The overall goal is to improve sustainability with the help of technology. It should meet the needs of the population and is composed of several smart characteristics that interact with each other [11].

According to literature each smart characteristic (Smart Economy, Smart Mobility, Smart Environment, Smart People, Smart Living and Smart Governance) is defined by a number of factors. Furthermore, each factor can be broken into relevant indicators, which reflect the most important aspects of every smart characteristic [7, 8]. The research team has identified 36 factors and 136 indicators through the literature review process.

In this study, the evaluation indicators have been selected by applying a hybrid research methodology including literature review and structured interviews. The significance of each candidate indicator is examined with the aid of local stakeholders. A questionnaire has been developed which is addressed to the municipalities, based on the European guidelines for smart cities. The selection of the factors and their indicators has been based on their applicability in cities with population less than 50,000 inhabitants. In total, 25 crucial factors have been selected and 68 indicators were elicited (Table 7, Appendix). These factors with their relevant indicators are based on the European trends for smart cities and the local needs.

2.2 Evaluation Process (Previous Model)

The problem has been modelled using multicriteria analysis [1]. The aim of multicriteria analysis is to solve complicated problems taking into consideration all the criteria that affect the decision process. In the current study, the criteria are the selected indicators.

All factors have their internal impact reclassified to a common scale so that it is necessary to determine each criteria's (indicator's) relative impact. Weight is assigned to the criteria-indicators to indicate its relative importance. Different weights could influence directly the results and it is necessary to obtain the rationality and veracity of criteria-indicators weights [9, 16].

The method of equal weights has been adopted in the proposed methodology. The criteria weight in equal weights method is defined as:

$$p_i = \frac{1}{n} i = 1, 2, \ldots, n, \ (n : indictors) \tag{1}$$

This method is very popular and is applied in many decision-making problems since Dawes and Corrigan argued that the obtained results are nearly as good as those optimal weighting methods [5].

All the values of the indicators have been normalised from 0 to 1, as the standardization of indicators is required, in order to compare them.

The ranking is obtained through the additive value model. The formula describing the additive value model is the following:

$$u(g) = \sum_{i=1}^{n} p_i u_i(g_i) \tag{2}$$

$$u_i(g_{i*}) = 0, u_i(g_i^*) = 1, i = 1, 2, \ldots, n \tag{3}$$

$$\sum_{i=1}^{n} p_i = 1 \tag{4}$$

$$p_i \geq 0 \; for \; i = 1, 2, \ldots, n \tag{5}$$

where $g = (g1, \ldots, gn)$ is the performance of each smart characteristic based on n indicators, $u_i(g_{i*})$ and $u_i(g_i^*)$ are the least and most preferable levels of indicator g_i, respectively, $u_i(g_i), i = 1, \ldots, n$ are non-decreasing marginal value functions of the performances $g_i, i = 1, \ldots, n$. p_i is the relative weight of the ith function $u_i(g_i)$. Thus, for a candidate city α, $g(\alpha)$ and $u[g(\alpha)]$ represent the multicriteria vector of performances and the global value of the alternative solution (in case that there are more than one city to be compared and evaluated), respectively [4, 13, 14].

The results have been aggregated on all levels without further weighting [7, 10]. The aggregation has been done additive but divided through the number of values added.

2.3 Questionnaire for Previous Model

The development of the questionnaire is based on literature and the special features of Greek cities. Zong et al. [18] developed an evaluation indicator system of green and smart cities studying ten aspects: resource utilization, environmental governance and environmental quality, green and smart medical care, green and smart facilities, network security and citizens' experience. A similar questionnaire relative to the selected 68 indicators has been developed. It is addressed to the authorities, in order to answer the questions with their existing actions towards smart cities, and so the score for each factor and therefore for each smart characteristic has been calculated.

2.4 Questionnaire for Weights in New Model

A questionnaire is used in this case to collect measurable data that can be statistically processed, regarding the indicators of the "Smart Cities" evaluation model. According to the basic principles of using questionnaires in research, a series of individuals, called "sample", answer the same set of questions, which are asked in the same predefined order. The main advantages of the questionnaires over the other data collection methods are their flexibility and adaptability to the questions asked in the sample, the analysis and processing of their data is standardized and does not pose a risk of subjective judgment of the researcher, it is the least method and finally has lower implementation costs compared to other methods.

This questionnaire is a closed-ended questionnaire (or structured questionnaire), i.e. with specific, precise questions aimed at obtaining clear answers in order to collect quantitative data. The questionnaire is divided into a total of eight parts. The first part gives the context in which the research is conducted and then the respondent is asked for his Demographic Data. In the second part, a general definition is given regarding the "Smart Cities" through which the six central Pillars emerge. They are asked to fill in their preferences, while the participant is given the possibility of multiple choices. In the third to the eighth part, the questionnaire is structured on the same pattern. Each part is the unit for each of the six central Pillars. As already mentioned, each Pillar is divided into certain Sectors and they in turn are divided into certain Indices. Therefore, in each part the participant is first asked to choose his preferences first between the Sectors of each Pillar and then between the Indices of each Sector. In all the above cases, multiple choices are possible.

Based on the model used, in the pilot sample of 30 people where the confidence interval was set to the test and a satisfactory percentage of 95%, the probability of finding a problem is 0.10 or 10% [19].

Taking into account standard research practices [20] regarding the reliability of results on general issues (eg. non-laboratory measurements where high accuracy of sample results is required), an error margin of 5% and a confidence interval of 95% are taken into account. Given this, the minimum sample size from which safe conclusions can be drawn regardless of population size is 385 people.

2.5 SIMOS Method

The original Simos method [13] consists of the following three steps, concerning the interaction with the decision maker (DM) and the collection of information:

1. The DM is given a set of cards with the name of one criterion on each (n cards, each corresponding to a specific criterion of a family F). A number of white cards are also provided to the DM.
2. The DM is asked to rank the cards/criteria from the least to the most important, by arranging them in an ascending order. If multiple criteria have the same importance, she/he should build a subset by holding the corresponding cards together with a clip.
3. The DM is finally asked to introduce white cards between two successive cards (or subsets of ex aequo criteria) if she/he deems that the difference between them is more extensive. The greater the difference between the weights of the criteria (or the subsets of criteria), the greater the number of white cards that should be placed between them. Specifically, if u denotes the difference in the value between two successive criteria cards, then one white card means a difference of two times u, two white cards mean a difference of three times u, etc.

The information provided by the DM is utilized by the Simos method for the determination of the weights, according to the following algorithm: i. ranking of the subsets of ex aequo from the least important to the most important, considering also the white cards, ii. assignment of a position to each criterion/card and to each white card, iii. calculation of the non-normalized weights, and iv. determination of the normalized weights.

The least qualified card is given Position 1, while the most qualified one receives Position n. The non-normalized weight of each rank/subset is determined by dividing the sum of positions of a rank, by the total number of criteria belonging to it. The non-normalized weights are then divided by the total sum of positions of the criteria in each rank (excluding the white cards), in order to normalize them. The obtained values are rounded off to the lower or higher nearest integer value.

2.6 SIMOS 2 Method Alteration

The Alterated SIMOS method, consists of the following three steps:

1. The DM is given a set of cards with the name of one criterion on each (n cards, each corresponding to a specific criterion of a family F). A number of white cards are also provided to the DM.
2. The DM is asked to rank the cards/criteria from the least to the most important, by arranging them in an ascending order. At this point, if multiple criteria have a 5% difference we considered that they do not have a significant difference and we ranked them together.
3. The DM is finally asked to introduce white cards between two successive cards (or subsets of ex aequo criteria) if she/he deems that the difference between them is more extensive. The greater the difference between the weights of the criteria (or the subsets of criteria), the greater the number of white cards that should be placed between them. Specifically, if u denotes the difference in the value between two successive criteria cards, then one white card means a difference of two times u, two white cards mean a difference of three times u, etc.

The information provided by the DM is utilized by the Simos method for the determination of the weights, according to the following algorithm: i. ranking of the subsets of ex aequo from the least important to the most important, considering also the white cards, ii. assignment of a position to each criterion/card and to each white card, iii. calculation of the non-normalized weights, and iv. determination of the normalized weights.

The least qualified card is given Position 1, while the most qualified one receives Position n. The non-normalized weight of each rank/subset is determined by dividing the sum of positions of a rank, by the total number of criteria belonging to it. The non-normalized weights are then divided by the total sum of positions of the criteria in each rank (excluding the white cards), in order to normalize them. The obtained values are rounded off to the lower or higher nearest integer value.

2.7 The Footprint of a Smart City

The aim of the proposed approach is for each city to be able to rank itself. The proposed footprint of a smart city includes 9 classes, from I to H (Fig. 1). The range of scores in the higher classes is smaller than the range in the lower classes. As a result, the candidate city is obligated to implement more actions towards smart cities strategy when it is in the lower classes. The classification is elicited by aggregating the score from each separate Smart Characteristic. The result is aggregated on all levels by using equal weights and the method of additive value model (Model 1), Questionnaire, Simos Method and Simos 2 Method Alteration (Table 1).

3   The Case of Municipality of Elefsina

The municipality of Elefsina is in West Attica, Greece, situated about 18 km northwest from the centre of Athens. The municipality Elefsina was formed at the 2011 local government reform by the merger of the following two former municipalities that became municipal units: Elefsina and Magoula. The municipality has an area of 36.589 km^2, the municipal unit 18.455 km^2 and a population of 29.902. Elefsina is a major industrial centre, at least 40% of the industrial activity of the country is concentrated there, with the largest oil refinery in Greece. On 11 November 2016 Elefsina was named the European Capital of Culture for 2021 (Wikipedia).

3.1   Smart City Performance Across 6 Different Characteristics

The aim of this step is to record all the actions, fulfilling the requirements of each indicator, that Municipality of Elefsina has, already, implemented towards the smart city concept. The necessary information has been collected from the developed questionnaire and the individual interviews, addressed to the responsible Departments of the Municipality (Department of revenues, IT Department, Department of Economics, Department of Transparency Programming and Department of Environment). All the answers have been matched with the selected indicators and their values have been normalized from 0 to 1. The total score for each smart characteristic is calculated following the additive value model. Based on these data, the evaluation process has indicated the following results:

Smart Economy: The indicators in the group of smart economy measure the performance of productivity, innovation, entrepreneurship and the integration with international markets. The total score in this smart characteristic is 0.224 using Model 1, 0.245 using questionnaire, 0.310 using SIMOS Method and finally 0.313 using SIMOS 2 Method (Table 1).

Smart Environment: Indicators in the group of smart environment addresses the issues related to the energy saving in public buildings, ecological awareness, sustainable resource management, air pollution and attraction of natural conditions. Municipality of Elefsina has already implement some actions in this direction and the total score in the field is 0.171 using Model 1, 0.425 using questionnaire, 0.432 using SIMOS Method and finally 0.438 using SIMOS 2 Method (Table 1).

Smart Governance: The indicators in the group of smart governance are associated with transparency in governance: municipality expenditure, e-government online availability, political strategies and perspectives and participation in decision making. In this field municipality of Elefsina has its higher score, 0.409 using Model 1, 0.448 using questionnaire, 0.511 using SIMOS Method and finally 0.519 using SIMOS 2 Method (Table 1).

Smart Living: Smart Living improves the quality of life and it is measured by the following indicators: educational and cultural facilities, individual safety and health conditions. The total score in this Characteristic is 0.268 using Model 1, 0.261 using questionnaire, 0.295 using SIMOS Method and finally 0.299 using SIMOS 2 Method (Table 1).

Smart Mobility: Smart Mobility indicators refer to local accessibility, touristic attractivity, availability of ICT infrastructure, public database and in general sustainable, innovative and safe transport systems. Here the score is very low, 0.194 using Model 1, 0.169 using questionnaire, 0.131 using SIMOS Method and finally 0.135 using SIMOS 2 Method (Table 1).

Smart People: Lifelong learning, level of qualification and participation in public life are the indicators that determine the Characteristic of "Smart People". The score is, also, high in comparison to the other fields, 0.310 using Model 1, 0.314 using questionnaire, 0.323 using SIMOS Method and finally 0.313 using SIMOS 2 Method (Table 1).

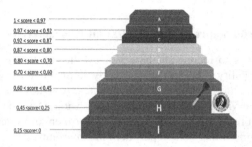

Fig. 1. Municipality Elefsina's smart footprint [1].

3.2 Overall Performance for Municipality Elefsina

Figure 1 gives the overall smartness of Municipality Elefsina for all the Characteristics and Fig. 1 shows its smart footprint. It is classified in level H (aggregated total score 0.265 using Model 1, 0.314 using questionnaire, 0.373 using SIMOS Method and finally 0.364 using SIMOS 2 Method (Table 2).

Therefore, its overall smart city performance is poor. The aggregate scores from all the Characteristics are low, even under 0.5, with a slight promotion of smart governance and smart people among the rest ones. The domains of smart environment and smart mobility have the lowest scores. It is obvious that the authorities are working towards the direction of smart cities, but more effort is needed. In that direction, a set of indicative actions will be recommended in order to improve their smart footprint.

3.3 Percentage Change Among the Four Methods

The Percentage Change Calculator (% change calculator) will quantify the change from one number to another and express the change as an increase or decrease. The formula describing the percentage change is the following:

$$\frac{(V_2 - V_1)}{|V_1|} \times 100 \tag{6}$$

Where Percentage change equals the change in value divided by the absolute value of the original value (V1), multiplied by 100.

Table 1. Weights and scores for Municipality of Elefsina using all four methods.

Characteristics/ Factors	Model 1		Questionnaire		SIMOS		SIMOS 2	
	Weights	Scores	Weights	Scores	Weights	Scores	Weights	Scores
I) Smart Economy	0.17	0.224	0.1595	0.245	0.0952	0.310	0.0952	0.313
Innovation	0.25	0.100	0.3237	0.104	0.4872	0.113	0.4557	0.112
Entrepreneurship	0.25	0.094	0.2358	0.117	0.1538	0.139	0.1646	0.138
Productivity	0.25	0.700	0.2616	0.700	0.3333	0.700	0.3417	0.700
Integration with International Markets	0.25	0	0.1789	0	0.2570	0	0.380	0
II) Smart Environment	0.17	0.185	0.1808	0.425	0.2857	0.432	0.2619	0.438
Attraction of Natural Conditions	0.20	0	0.1922	0	0.1918	0	0.1849	0
Air Pollution Integrated index	0.20	0.286	0.1798	0.600	0.1370	0.610	0.1370	0.600
Sustainable Resource Management	0.20	0.240	0.2146	0.496	0.2329	0.605	0.2466	0.598
Ecological Awareness	0.20	0.400	0.2400	0.400	0.3150	0.400	0.2945	0.400
Energy Saving in Public Buildings	0.20	0	0.1734	0.660	0.1233	0.66	0.1370	0.660
III) Smart Governance	0.17	0.409	0.1646	0.448	0.1905	0.511	0.1905	0.519
Participation in Decision Making	0.25	0.710	0.3192	0.693	0.4565	0.694	0.4778	0.698
Political Strategies & Perspectives	0.25	0.643	0.2256	0.676	0.1522	0.738	0.1444	0.736
E-Government online availability	0.25	0.285	0.2847	0.262	0.3478	0.235	0.3444	0.229
Municipality Expenditure	0.25	0	0.1705	0	0.4350	0	0.3340	0
IV) Smart Living	0.17	0.268	0.1775	0.261	0.2381	0.295	0.2619	0.299
Cultural Facilities	0.25	0.020	0.2086	0.018	0.1714	0.014	0.1471	0.014
Health Conditions	0.25	0.550	0.3104	0.629	0.3571	0.763	0.3603	0.748
Individual Safety	0.25	0	0.2293	0	0.2144	0	0.2279	0
Educational Facilities	0.25	0.500	0.2517	0.248	0.2571	0.077	0.2647	0.105
V) Smart Mobility	0.17	0.194	0.1549	0.169	0.0476	0.131	0.0952	0.135
Touristic Attractivity	0.20	0.429	0.1696	0.430	0.9620	0.043	0.762	0.430
Local Accessibility	0.20	0.066	0.2779	0.070	0.4615	0.079	0.4667	0.075
Availability of ICT Infrastructure	0.20	0.473	0.1882	0.409	0.1539	0.345	0.1905	0.351
Sustainable, Innovative & Safe Transport Systems	0.20	0	0.2019	0	0.2115	0	0.1905	0
Public Database	0.20	0	0.1624	0	0.7690	0	0.7610	0
VI) Smart People	0.17	0.310	0.1627	0.314	0.1429	0.323	0.0952	0.313
Participation in Public Life	0.34	0.600	0.3864	0.600	0.4889	0.600	0.4574	0.600
Level of Qualification	0.34	0.330	0.2295	0.367	0.6670	0.442	0.852	0.448
Affinity to Lifelong Learning	0.34	0	0.3841	0	0.4444	0	0.4574	0

Table 2. Elefsina's score and ranking.

	Model 1	Questionnaire	SIMOS	SIMOS 2
City Score	0,265	0,314	0,373	0,364
City Ranking	H	H	H	H

By using the original value the one from Model 1 the results are the following (Table 3):

Table 3. Original value model 1.

Percentage Change to MODEL 1	Model 1	Questionnaire	SIMOS	SIMOS 2
Smart Economy	0,224	9,37	38,48	39,92
Smart Environment	0,185	129,62	133,43	136,46
Smart Governance	0,409	9,47	24,86	26,69
Smart Living	0,268	-2,31	10,15	11,83
Smart Mobility	0,194	-12,58	-32,53	-30,48
Smart People	0,310	1,95	4,13	0,83
City	0,265	18,42	40,77	37,50

By using the original value the one from Questionnaire the results are the following (Table 4):

Table 4. Original value questionnaire.

Percentage Change to Questionnaire	Model 1	Questionnaire	SIMOS	SIMOS 2
Smart Economy	-8,564	0,245	26,618	27,937
Smart Environment	-56,451	0,425	1,657	2,978
Smart Governance	-8,652	0,448	14,057	15,726
Smart Living	2,363	0,261	12,757	14,474
Smart Mobility	14,395	0,169	-22,817	-20,473
Smart People	-1,912	0,316	2,142	-1,097
City	-15,557	0,314	18,872	16,106

By using the original value the one from SIMOS Method the results are the following (Table 5):

Table 5. Original value simos method.

Percentage Change to SIMOS	Model 1	Questionnaire	SIMOS	SIMOS 2
Smart Economy	-27,786	-21,022	0,310	1,041
Smart Environment	-57,160	-1,630	0,432	1,300
Smart Governance	-19,910	-12,324	0,511	1,464
Smart Living	-9,218	-11,314	0,295	1,523
Smart Mobility	48,213	29,562	0,131	3,037
Smart People	-3,970	-2,098	0,323	-3,172
City	-28,963	-15,876	0,373	-2,327

Finally, by using the original value the one from SIMOS2 Method Alteration the results are the following (Table 6):

Table 6. Original value Simos 2 method alteration.

Percentage Change to SIMOS 2	Model 1	Questionnaire	SIMOS	SIMOS 2
Smart Economy	-28,530	-21,836	-1,030	0,313
Smart Environment	-57,710	-2,892	-1,283	0,438
Smart Governance	-21,065	-13,589	-1,442	0,519
Smart Living	-10,580	-12,644	-1,500	0,299
Smart Mobility	43,844	25,743	-2,948	0,135
Smart People	-0,824	1,110	3,276	0,313

4 Conclusions

Cities are examined as a piece of the answer for a considerable lot of the present financial social and ecological issues [2]. The smart city represents the future challenge. A viable all-encompassing assessment model on the presentation of a smart city is of most extreme significance. In contrast to past examinations, this study endeavors to assess small smart cities with regards to Greece. In this article, a keen city positioning model has been proposed for urban communities with under 50,000 inhabitants, including 25 factors and 68 indicators, and the contextual analysis concerned a Greek city, Region of Elefsina. The selected indicators fall into the most critical areas for the assessment of a small smart city.

The multicriteria method, Additive Value Model, and the questionnaire for weights have been selected for the evaluation process. The combination of these two methods simplified and summarized a complex concept into a manageable form. The smart footprint of a city is introduced as a result of the evaluation process.

Although it seems that Municipality of Elefsina has already taken small steps towards the smart cities, its overall score is very poor. It is remarkable its low score on smart environment, as the development of actions for improving the local environmental conditions should be a prime objective of the authorities.

It was observed that the smart environment assumes a vital part in the inhabitants, since statistically it had the greatest change contrasted with the first model. Also important to mention is that in none of the 4 methods did the city change the ranking category, which means that the results in all 4 cases were very close to each other and thus to our previous model.

The contribution of the research is indicated by two areas: the proposed evaluation methodology for small smart cities and the implemented case study for a Greek city. Future research could focus on testing the methodology in more than one case studies, its holistic application will be improved. The presented model could be further enhanced with the evaluation of more Greek cities and the ranking of their results using multi-criteria analysis. Furthermore, the comparison with other cities will enable the share of experience and effective actions could be formulated for the development of smart city in the whole country.

Appendix

The proposed model includes 25 crucial factors and 68 relative indicators, shown in Table 7:

Table 7. The selected factors and their indicators.

Factors	Indicators
I) Smart economy	
Innovation	Public Expenditure on R&D
	Funded projects
Entrepreneurship	New businesses registered
	Promotion of digital adoption
	Entrepreneurship Programs
Productivity	Unemployment rate
Integration with international markets	Research grants funded by international projects
II) Smart environment	
Attraction of natural conditions	Green space
Air pollution integrated index	CO_2 emissions
	Air Pollutants

(continued)

Table 7. (*continued*)

Factors	Indicators
Sustainable resource management	Waste separation and disposal
	Annual thermal energy consumption
	Street lighting
	Electricity consumption
	Renewable resources
	Intelligent management of waste and recycling products
	Smart resource management
Ecological Awareness	Ecological consciousness
Energy Saving in Public Buildings	Public Schools
	Town hall and office buildings
	Museums/Theatres
	Sports Facilities
	Library
III) Smart governance	
Participation in decision-making	City representatives per inhabitant
	Political activity of inhabitants
	Share of female city representatives
Political strategies & perspectives	Communication of economic and community development to the outside world
	Strategies for economic & social development
E-Government on-line availability	Employment services
	Online Payments
	Social services
	Public cultural and sporting activities
	Services for disabled people
	Safeguard system
	Public Health
	Urban management
	Public security
	E-commerce
Municipality expenditure	Bridging the digital divide

(*continued*)

Table 7. (*continued*)

Factors	Indicators
IV) Smart living	
Cultural facilities	Theatres/Cinemas
	Culturally active citizens
	Technologies for cultural facilities
	Museums and historic monuments
	Public Libraries
Health conditions	Public care facilities
	Doctors
Individual safety	Safety at playgrounds
	Safety at sport facilities
	Safety at parks
	Safety at pools and beaches
	Safety at public buildings
Educational facilities	Public lessons
	Quality of educational system
V) Smart mobility	
Touristic attractivity	Municipality's site
Local accessibility	Availability of public transport
	Quality of public transport
	Cycle paths
Availability of ICT infrastructure	Internet facilities
	Wireless networks
Sustainable, innovative and safe transport systems	Green mobility share
	Use of economical cars
Public Database	Urban infrastructure database
	Urban economy and society database
VI) Smart people	
Participation in public life	Voters
Level of Qualification	Computer skills
	Foreign language lessons
	After school study
Affinity to lifelong learning	Book loans

References

1. Nikoloudis, C., Strantzali, E., Tounta, T., Aravossis, K.: An evaluation model for smart city performance with less than 50,000 inhabitants: a Greek case study. In: Proceedings of the 9th International Conference on Smart Cities and Green ICT Systems, pp. 15–21 (2020)
2. Akande, A., Cabral, P., Gomes, P., Casteleyn, S.: The Lisbon ranking for smart sustainable cities in Europe. Sustain. Cities Soc. **44**, 475–487 (2019)
3. Alibegović, D.J., Šagovac, M.: Evaluating smart city indicators: a tool for strategic decision-making for Croatian large cities. In: SmartEIZ – H2020-TWINN, 1–22. Zagreb, Crotia (2015)
4. Androulaki, S., Psarras, J.: Multicriteria decision support to evaluate potential long-term natural gas supply alternatives: The case of Greece. Eur. J. Oper. Res. **253**, 791–810 (2016)
5. Dawes, R.M., Corrigan, B.: Linear models in decision making. Psychol. Bull. **81**, 95–106 (1974)
6. Petrova-Antonova, D., Ilieva, S.: Smart cities evaluation – a survey of performance and sustainability indicators. In: 44th Euromicro Conference on Software Engineering and Advanced Applications (SEAA), 29–31 August, Prague, pp. 486–493 (2018)
7. Giffinger, R., Fertner, C., Kramar, H., Kalasek, R., Pichler-Milanovic, N., Meijers, E.: Smart cities ranking of European medium-sized cities. Final Report. Vienna UT: Centre of Regional Science, 1–25 (2007)
8. Giffinger, R., Haindlmaier, G.: Smart cities ranking: an effective instrument for the positioning of cities? J. Centre Land Policy Valuations 7–26 (2010)
9. Jia, J.M., Fisher, G.M., Dyer, J.S.: Attribute weighting methods and decision quality in the presence of response error: a simulation study. J. Behav. Decis. Mak. **11**, 85–105 (1998)
10. Lazaroiu, G.C., Roscia, M.: Definition methodology for the smart cities model. Energy **47**, 326–332 (2012)
11. Miloševic, M.R., Miloševic, D.M., Ste-vić, D.M., Stanojević, A.D.: Smart city: modeling key indicators in Serbia using IT2FS. Sustain. **11**, 1–28 (2019)
12. Shen, L., Huang, Z., Wong, S.W., Liao, S., Lou, Y.: A holistic evaluation of smart city performance in the context of China. J. Clean. Prod. **200**, 667–679 (2018)
13. Siskos, E., Askounis, D., Psarras, J.: Multicriteria decision support for global e-government evaluation. Omega **46**, 51–63 (2014)
14. Strantzali, E., Aravossis, K., Livanos, G.A., Chrysanthopoulos, N.: A novel multicriteria evaluation of small-scale LNG supply alternatives: the case of Greece. Energies **11**, 1–20 (2018)
15. Tahir, Z., Malek, J.A.: Main criteria in the development of smart cities determined using analytical method. J. Malaysian Inst. Planners **14**, 1–14 (2016)
16. Wang, J.J., Jing, Y.Y., Zhang, C.F., Zhao, J.H.: Review on multi-criteria decision analysis aid in sustainable energy decision-making. Renew. Sustain. Energy Rev. **13**, 2263–2278 (2009)
17. Wikipedia. https://en.wikipedia.org/wiki/Eleusis
18. Zong, J., Li, Y., Lin, L., Bao, W.: Evaluation guide for green and smart cities. IOP Conf. Ser. Earth Environ. Sci. **267**, 1–7 (2019)
19. Perneger, T.V., Courvoisier, D.S., Hudelson, P.M., Gayet-Ageron, A.: Sample size for pretests of questionnaires. Qual. Life Res. **24**(1), 147–151 (2014). https://doi.org/10.1007/s11136-014-0752-2
20. Turner, A.: Sampling strategies (2003)

PUNTOnet Prototypes: Innovative Urban Services Supporting Healthy and Sustainable Behaviours

Ilaria Fabbri$^{(\boxtimes)}$ ⓘ and Gabriele Lelli ⓘ

Department of Architecture, University of Ferrara, 36 Via Della Ghiara, Ferrara, Italy
fbblri@unife.it

Abstract. This paper describes the objectives and the outputs of a University-Industry research project, with the aim to innovate household waste collection and other urban services, through the design and development of prototype multifunctional station, in line with the principles of circular economy. It begins by presenting the potential of ordinary garbage bins to become an urban interface with the support of technology. In order to meet European recycling targets and optimize operational costs, trash containers need to achieve a greater intelligence, recognize users' identity, record the type and the quantity of delivered waste. The specialisation and improvement of such a widespread service give the possibility to reinvent collection points as a smart and sensing zones, sharing their sophisticated technology equipment with other urban facilities.

The essay then looks at possible additional services for the city and displays the research group proposal dealing with mobility infrastructure. Finally, the paper closes with the description of the content of an experimental urban dashboard gathering all data coming from the prototypes, developed by the local utility group for the demo site, a small smart city of 10 000 inhabitants.

Keywords: Waste management · Prototype development · Small smart city

1 Introduction

When it comes to smart city, innovation may affect different fields and different scales, with the common objective of improving life quality:

1) large infrastructures, roads, public spaces and buildings;
2) urban objects, standing or moving in the built environment, including public services, furniture, and vehicles as well;
3) citizens' behaviour, in response to new relationships both with others and with the city itself.

Thanks to technology advance, each one of these domains may potentially become more effective and sustainable, especially when in synergy with the other two. The collection

C. Klein et al. (Eds.): SMARTGREENS 2020/VEHITS 2020, CCIS 1475, pp. 46–65, 2021.
https://doi.org/10.1007/978-3-030-89170-1_3

and the elaboration of real time data enable easier and quicker connections between demand and supply, whatever sphere.

This paper presents PUNTOnet prototypes, addressing circular economy model and the goals of urban sustainability; designed, developed and tested in a real world environment, these urban objects are a part of a complex set of actions deployed by the research group in a small smart city of less than 10 000 inhabitants.

On the occasion of the 9th International Conference on Smart Cities and ICT Systems, the main results and experiences gained from the agreements between HERA Group, one of the leading Italian multi-utility operating in environmental, energy and water services, and Next City Lab, an interdisciplinary research group at Architecture Department University of Ferrara, were firstly presented.

Smartgreens2020 paper proceedings [1] primarily described Italian waste management background and recycling targets, and how the developed prototypes sought to address urban waste collection, through different prototype releases.

In the frame of the same University-Industry research, this paper is more focused on user experience and behavioural insight applied to specific policy issues, not only waste management, but also environmental awareness, health and mobility; moreover, it widens the description of the developed models and displays the possible advantages of combining innovative waste disposal and smart mobility infrastructure.

The main authors of this research and inventors, as appointed in the patent applications are, from the side of Hera Group, Eng. Enrico Piraccini, head of development & innovation and Eng. Simone Allegra, innovation central direction; from University side MSc associate prof. Gabriele Lelli, head of Next City Lab research group, MSc Walter Nicolino and MSc PhD(c) Ilaria Fabbri.

2   Strategies to Improve Waste Management

2.1   Waste Collection Challenges

In 2016 CFR – Consorzio Futuro in Ricerca, and specifically Next City Lab, were commissioned by Hera Group to develop an innovative research with a twofold purpose:

1. Ameliorate household waste collection, both in terms of user experience and containers' compliance with regulations and European recycling targets;
2. Identify and develop innovative services supporting sustainability and healthy environments the Company could add to their consolidated supply.

This section analyses the first part, in particular the conceptual premises to the subsequent material models.

When the project started, the local utility was facing high pressure due to the definition of specific responsibilities of actors in the waste management system at national level; the objectives set by the European Union Waste Framework Directive (2008/98/EC; EC European Commission, 2008), transposed into national law by Decree 205/2010 impacted both the way the Group collected waste and the way they tax users. In particular, Ronchi's Decree (law 22/1997) introduced a shift from undifferentiated taxation for waste production to a more equitable system based on a simple principle: "the more you pollute, the more you pay". With a document published on November 2018, the European Environment Agency (EEA) highlighted that "pay-as-you-throw" (PAYT) schemes are effective instruments that drive recycling up households to recycle their waste.

In line with the findings of EEA briefing, and with several practices supporting PAYT systems, many countries in Europe adopted a user-specific waste rate proportional to the weight and/or the volume of the delivered garbage. In 2010 Italy abolished the flat-rate tax (TARSU) and it is gradually setting a target to complete the shift to a variable rate, directly depending on citizen's recycling behaviour.

Because of the upcoming variable rate, traditional waste containers should achieve a greater intelligence in order to recognize users, measure their garbage and identify the type, as differentiated tariffs make residual waste more expensive than selectively collected waste streams, as an economic incentive for households to recycle more accurately.

2.2 Criticalities of Existing Volumetric Caps

Before this University-Industry research started, Hera Group was piloting a particular system of waste containers addressing "Pay as You Throw" schemes. In this transitional system, the bins only open when the user is identified, thanks to an RFID reader of the personal card on the lid, but, while recycling streams present an ordinary opening with no volume limitation, unsorted waste is collected in a traditional 3200-L container with a "volumetric drum" on the top, fixing the quote of 15 L per delivery. This electro-mechanical locking device with identity identification records users' frequency and the transmission of these data is performed via GPRS.

The more citizens use the slot to deliver non-recycled material the more expensive will be the bill.

This scheme – in theory – would drive recycling up. Actually, volumetric drums introduced many unexpected criticalities, and primarily:

1. Customers dislike measuring caps, requiring too many actions before throwing the garbage bag away; with such devices, waste delivery is a complex and time-consuming process, rather than an automatic, effortless act. Bad user experience finally exacerbates littering next containers.
2. A dedicated system for unsorted rubbish increased wrong delivery. As putting materials into recycling receptacles is cheaper, a percentage between 8% and 10% of customers tried to cheat the system inserting unsorted waste into inappropriate receptacles for recycled waste streams, with the consequence of a lower quality of separate collection and higher rises operational costs.
3. Accessibility is even penalized with volumetric drums than it was with standard foot-operated waste containers. The cap lever is too high and its functionality unintuitive for a wide range of users, not only for protected class.

The considered challenging aspects put high pressure on the local utility and force Hera Group to invest in the development of tangible alternatives to this type of waste collection system.

To meet the first goal of the research – a better user experience and PAYT system compliance – Next City Lab firstly reviewed worldwide trends and targets (Fig. 1).

Fig. 1. The three main criticalities of standard volumetric cap: time-consuming process, with frequent mechanical disrupt and limited accessibility.

3   PUNTOnet Waste Containers Evolution

The last version of PUNTOnet multifunctional station, displayed on June 2019 at Hera group headquarters in Bologna, during the conference "Re-inventing the city: smartness and resilience to face new challenges", is the result of gradual prototype refinements; next paragraphs describe the main stages of this process.

The name "PUNTOnet" chosen by the research group anticipates the network created among collection points in the city; in the Italian language, net also recalls something neat, tidy and clear-cut.

3.1 Conceptual Design

The negative experience with "volumetric caps" showed that technology advancements in waste management do not guarantee a better user experience, and a more sophisticated system may also penalize household every-day actions when containers' design is just the by-product of complex waste sorting regulations [2]. For these reasons, the research group set five mandatory features of innovative waste containers as primary goal of the project:

The system should be:

- Easy and quick. Increase the ease is one of the most effective behavioural lever to tackle waste policy issue according to Dessart et al. [3]. Upcoming waste regulation should not affect people during waste delivery and not cause them additional work.
- Clean experience. Levers or pedals should be avoided, and the configuration of the opening lid should minimize the physical contact with the rubbish and hide as much as possible the view of the inner content during delivery.
- Rewarding, associating a material payoff to consumers' achievements. The tangible form of recognition is being studied as well; it could be a discount on collection bill or, more interestingly, the free access to other services dispensed by the local utility.
- In safe condition, according to car flow, sidewalks depth and other features of urban environment. Moreover, a scarcely considered element in the design of waste disposal but with remarkable urban impact is the container's height. PUNTOnet is not taller than 1,60 m, for a complete visibility beyond the container. To balance the reduction of the maximum height, several studies were carried out in order to optimize the inner volume and avoid unfavourable pile of rubbish.
- Accessible to a wider target of users, including children, elderly and frail people, wheelchair users included. The project took into account different forms of disabilities, beyond physical limitations.

3.2 Opening Mock-Ups

In the first step the research group deeply focused on the opening mechanism, which should be the simplest possible, in order to simplify maintenance and cleanability, suitable for both loos garbage and bags, and the shape of the lid (Fig. 2).

Different types of opening lids were studied in shape and cinematic through 1:2 scale timber mock-ups.

16 types of openings were compared through a specific evaluation matrix taking into account 5 groups of criteria:

1. User experience
2. Adherence to individual tariff requirements
3. Optimization of inner capacity

| Closed system | Log-in | Unlocking lid | Loading | Locking lid |

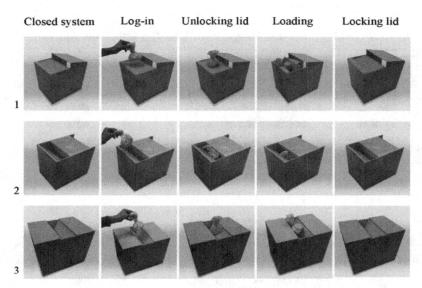

Fig. 2. Three wooden mock-ups used to test waste cinematic.

4. Realization and maintenance
5. Emptying process
6. Urban impact
7. Compatibility with the collection of different materials.

The discordance or the compliance with each criterion allowed to evaluate the potential success or deficiency of each one of the proposed opening lids. With this method the group identified the three most promising solutions to be developed in full scale (Fig. 3).

3.3 Full-Scale Indoor Prototype

In partnership with Sbarzaglia mechanical factory in Faenza (Italy), the research group realized 1:1 scale indoor prototype of the three most promising options of containers, and a mock-up of a smart totem, an innovative element integral part of the waste collection station; the synergy between the two elements (bin and totem), supported by technology, is the condition for the desired user experience and the application of PAYT law (profiling and measuring).

Each container features an interface strip, where the user can log in with a personal NFC card or using the smartphone; once logged, the chosen bin unlocks. The design of the lid allows a very easy delivery, and with even the lighter material, it opens for gravity and closes back, no need to touch the rubbish, just throwing it away (Fig. 4).

Weight and volume calculation of the delivered waste are recorded thanks to technologic equipment.

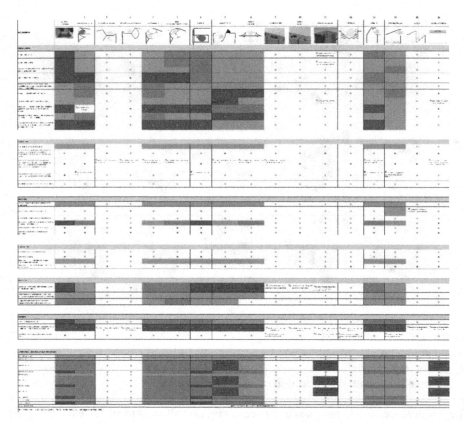

Fig. 3. Evaluation matrix comparing different opening systems.

Fig. 4. Indoor prototype completed at workshop Sbarzaglia Faenza (RA). In Smartgreens 2020, [1].

The main innovation lies in the volume measurement: on board the smart totem there are stereoscopic cameras that activates as soon as someone logs with the NFC card. The cameras take stereographic images during the release of waste and an experimental software, specifically created for this research with RETINAE srl, processes them and determines the volume of the delivered waste.

For weight calculation, small but very accurate scales are set up at the base of each container.

With the combination of volume and weight information (that the scales send to the totem intelligence), the software can display in real time the containers' filling degree, and consequently modify the itinerary of waste collection vehicles with the expected consequence of fuel saving and atmospheric pollution reduction. Furthermore, the system can detect eventual cheating or wrong delivery from users, bringing together weight and volume numbers and the used type of container (the waste fraction specific weight).

A delocalized dashboard collects the data generated by the waste station informing the utility not only about containers' filling level, but also users' inserting, eventual disruption, presence of garbage bags or loose rubbish next to the containers.

This system, including smart totem, containers and waste collection process, is patented (Fig. 5).

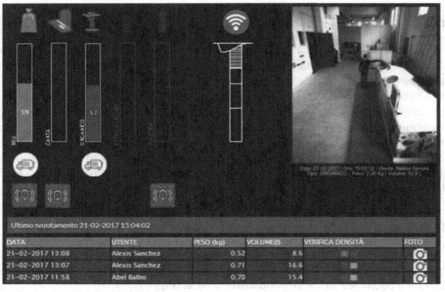

Fig. 5. The experimental software specifically created with Retinae srl for this research, processing stereoscopic images and is able to determine the volume of the submitted waste.

Fig. 6. Outdoor prototype for private test. In Smartgreens 2020, [1].

3.4   Full-Scale Outdoor Prototype (Private Tests)

At the end of 2017 Next City Lab and Hera Group, working with the mechanical engineers of Forghieri workshop in Maranello (Italy), completed the first prototype suitable for outdoor environment and fully functioning (Fig. 6). During the private test, the prototype was connected to the internet to verify the functionality of all the components, also the ones being remotely installed. Outdoor weather conditions and actual waste emptying process highlighted the need of several detail improvements, including the waterproofing of the exterior shell, whose graphic is borrowed from well-known work of art.

To maximize the system accessibility and the comprehensibility of the digital interface, the research group teamed up with valuable members from CERPA Italia Onlus (The European Centre for the promotion of Inclusion).

3.5   Full-Scale Outdoor Prototype (Public Tests)

At the end of the outdoor test in a private environment and the related refinements, the research group launched the production of the second outdoor prototype, specifically meant for a public test in a real world urban context (Fig. 7).

The demo site is the municipality of Castel Bolognese, an Italian town at roughly 10.000 residents willing to test smart urban solutions developed by the team.

PUNTOnet version for public test presents implemented features to involve citizens in the experimentation.

The most important are:

Gamification Through Funny Audio Communication. Learning from the "Deepest bin in the world" developed by the Swedish agency DDB, that proved how well gamification of environmental-friendly actions works [4], PUNTOnet reacts to user identification and waste disposal with greetings or other funny sounds that may be customized for specific audience.

Community Feedback. The research group created a Community Broadcast chat with WhatsApp, opened to the citizens testing smart waste containers, with the purpose to monitor users' difficulties during the test and support them in case of temporary breakdown, to give answers about the appropriate waste sorting, to collect citizens' opinions and suggestions. The Broadcast chat shown itself to be particularly effective enhancing a positive sense of recognition among those who participate in the experimentation, preferred to the formal Freephone number for 24/24 h communications.

Stimulation of Users' Commitment Through Text. The infographic on the containers' shell clearly discloses the imperfect nature of the prototype, saying "I'm just a prototype: help me to improve myself. Your suggestion will make the difference!". Users are invited to be more indulgent in case of malfunctioning and flaws to be fixed.

Use of Intriguing Graphics and Uncommon Materials. The physical environment can substantially affect individual decision-making, especially in contexts in which choices are made spontaneously, on the basis of automated mechanisms and habits [2], so the research group evaluated several strategies to visibly change the physical environment of the waste collection point. A set of visualisations displaying different graphics, from contemporary artworks, to abstract patterns and colour blocks, served to control and choose the most promising drawing for the external envelope of PUNTOnet. The appointed graphic for Castel Bolognese prototype is an elaboration of Peter Kogler's work of art. Experimenting with innovative materials is another strategy to intrigue and engage testers: for this reason, the wooden platform at the base of the prototype is paved with photo luminescent pigments produced by the Italian firm Reglow, which absorb sunlight during the day and glow at night.

Reward and Punishment Schemes. Mont, Lehner and Heiskanen [5] listed "stick and carrot" approach among the most effective behavioural levers to generate positive habits through material payoff to consumers' achievement. In this case, local utility, public administration and shop keepers in agreement offered grocery discount vouchers to all the sample group, as a recognition for their time in testing an early version of an experimental system.

From October 2018 to October 2019, 40 families of Castel Bolognese tested the first prototype of PUNTOnet; at the end of the experimentation the research group submitted a scientific survey that assessed a general satisfaction with smart containers innovative features.

Fig. 7. Outdoor prototype for public test. In Smartgreens 2020, [1].

4 From Waste Disposal to Urban Interface for the City

The sophisticated technology equipment on the smart containers, if primarily introduced to improve waste management and meet European targets, is consequently transforming ordinary garbage bins into innovative urban interfaces, with huge potential, especially due to the capillary diffusion of waste disposal in the built environment. The research team studied and designed the implementation of additional services for the city, in synergy with the planned technology infrastructure.

One of the first example in this sense are the smart bins installed in London for the 2012 Olympic Games by the UK Renew Startup. Equipped with wi-fi and LCD screens, they were able to send tailored advertising opportunities to the passer-byes smartphones using their wi-fi connection. These urban objects, even though interesting, were not meant for large volume of household waste, neither designed to comply with "Pay as you Throw" schemes.

In terms of electronic devices, PUNTOnet waste station and in particular the smart totem may host different services for the city:

- environmental sensors (air quality and sound pollution);
- device charging, including a suitable area where people with physical disability using electric vehicle may stop and charge it up;
- broadband wi-fi connection;
- video surveillance cameras, able to detect anti-social behaviour like littering alongside waste containers; in that case, an alert notification would appear on the general urban dashboard controlled by the multi-utility.
- A digital projector that during the night casts on the street recycling scores made by each community, and real time feedbacks on waste performance. Sometimes citizens may have little social motivation to participate in environmentally-friendly waste sorting, since this private behaviour is not socially visible and thus not rewarded by

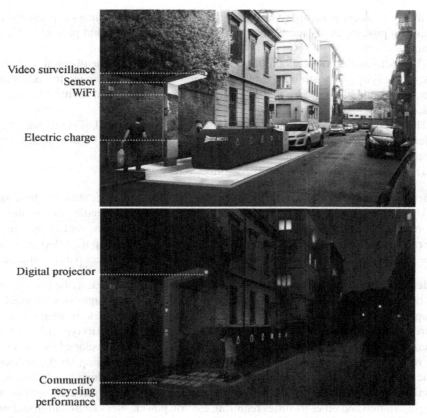

Video surveillance
Sensor
WiFi

Electric charge

Digital projector

Community
recycling
performance

Fig. 8. Conceptual visualization of the waste collection point in a specific urban environment.

social recognition or subjected to social disapproval [3]. This device, whose study is ongoing, has the potential to encourage positive competition between neighbourhoods and make community efforts visible.

More than just a waste collection station, PUNTOnet becomes a community interface, a reference site for data collection and urban services (Fig. 8).

5 The Combination of Smart Waste Containers With Facilities Supporting Sustainable Mobility

5.1 Compatibility and Synergies Between Waste Management and Smart Mobility

The innovation of urban waste collection, Hera group's core business, was the starting point of the research; jointly, the multi utility was interested in widening the services they can offer to the city, going beyond group's usual company fields. Next City Lab was therefore asked to identify viable and promising areas for business expansions and to develop prototypes of smart urban interfaces the company could present to Public Administrations.

The additional services should match with the innovative waste disposal, and, possibly, create synergies with smart containers' technology and equipment; this advocated synergism would also balance the necessary investments deployed to make the station work.

The research group highlighted favourable compatibility of PUNTOnet waste collection points with eco-friendly transport facilities (such as bus and bike shelters, electric charging station, bicycle sharing systems).

The affinity between the two urban services refers to:

Dimensions and Modularity. Standard parking space served as module for the design of PUNTOnet containers, that occupy one or more car parks, depending on the number of separately collected fractions of waste; similarly, the size of bus shelters and urban bike racks often are a multiple of parking spaces (such as Cyclehoop Bike Port, an iconic cycle parking solution that provides for 10 bicycles in a standard car parking space).

Underlying Utilities and Technical Infrastructure. As widely described in the first part of this essay, the upcoming application of user-specific garbage rates imposed by European targets implies that future waste disposal should be able to identify users, record collection frequency, and measure the amount of garbage and its type (if recyclable materials or refuse). The prototypes of smart waste containers developed by Next City Lab research group are equipped with sensors to control the filling level, connected to the cloud to upload their status and notify any possible breakdown: such system of underlying utilities, equipment and fittings could be productively shared with e-bike charging station and other facilities requiring electric power, user identification and may benefit from video surveillance.

Urban Concentration. Generally, for an adequate network of waste containers within an urban area, there should be a collection point for every 250–350 inhabitants, and the distance between them should not be excessive, as citizens are more likely to deliver garbage in the appropriate container if they have it nearby. So, the ideal distance between users and waste sorting points should be in a range of 250–400 m.

In designing additional services of smart waste stations, we identified analogies with bus stop spacing and bike solutions. There is a great number of guidelines about the optimal spacing of consecutive bus stops and a variety of standards are followed in various parts of the world, in relation to the population density and the type of housing. Peter White, for instance, has shown that different opposing aspects about bus stop location (user's convenience and access time on the one hand, and bus operating speed and costs on the other hand) are best in balance when distance between stops is about 550. Again, the UITP Guidance on Bus Stop Spacing suggest 400 m for urban areas with high density.

Street Connection. Both urban waste disposal and mobility infrastructure (bike shelters or bus stops) need to be clearly visible and easily accessible from public roads; however, it is important to consider car flow for users' safety. If located in place of parallel parking, along the traffic lane, waste containers should be exploitable only from the sidewalk, while e-bike charging or bus stop generally need to be oriented towards the street.

5.2   The Potential of Improving Eco-friendly Transportation Facility in a Small City

The reality of Castel Bolognese, where the testing stage of smart containers was carried out, influenced the exploration of possible urban services in synergy with waste collection and highlighted the potential of combining environmental services and small transportation infrastructure in the same multifunctional station.

Castel Bolognese is particularly suitable as a case study for applied research on sustainable mobility, thanks to its favourable geographical position, in an almost flat area with good infrastructure connections (railway and motorway nearby), and the proximity to larger towns as Faenza and Imola attracting a great number of local citizens for working and recreation. Even if the distance from both cities is shorter than 10 km, the major number of commuters tends to use their private car; to worsen the deeply rooted reliance on individual vehicles, in smaller centres digital services supporting bike sharing and public-facing projects promoting sustainable mobility are in general less common than they are in larger cities (Fig. 9 and 10).

Fig. 9. Frequency scheme of work trips with private cars from Castel Bolognese.

Lack of lighting and video surveillance at public bike racks area, derelict bus-stop and unattractive appearance of shelters merely, are just few examples of common conditions that penalizes everyday choice in terms of mobility.

Therefore, Next City Lab research group proposed to develop a new system of multifunctional bus and bike shelters to be combined with the prototype of smart waste, with the aim to improve citizens' travel experience using eco-friendly transportation, and promote tangible alternative to private cars in small centres.

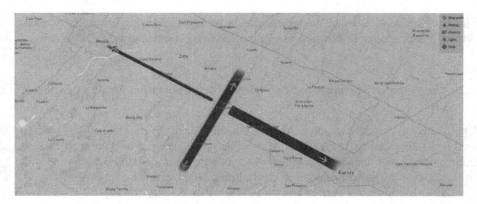

Fig. 10. Frequency scheme of leisure travels from Castel Bolognese.

5.3   Prototype of Smart Urban Interfaces Supporting Sustainable Mobility

To a great degree, the current approach to sustainable transportation by bike and by public transport significantly emphasizes quantity of travel over the "qualitative" or experiential component of travel [6].

The primary goal of recent mobility planning studies is the increase of quantity and length of non-motorized and public transportation trips, while many aspects of the trip itself are often unsuccessfully integrated.

Next City Lab research group explored a set of experiential factors that may have a great impact on everyday travel choices, such as exposure to emissions and noise, quality of wait time at bus stop, perceived safety, incentives, combination of mobility points with other services. Transportation infrastructure may play a significant role and greatly affect travelling experience, one of the key elements for liveable cities and communities. Therefore, it appeared worth investigating as an advantageous additional service Hera Group could develop next smart waste containers.

The main objectives of our prototypical transportation facilities are the following.

Improving Smart Mobility Experience. For a long time, urban furniture connected to transportation have remained unchanged: bus shelter, for instance, have traditionally provided sitting covered space used while awaiting transit, as well as the support for timetable display and advertising. With the diffusion of new modes of transport such as electric bikes and technologies, it is crucial to reinvent transportation facilities in order to increase the appeal of sustainable mobility.

Looking back to 1991, the symbol of Curitiba's transport revolution is effectively its futuristic glass-tube stop, though which public transit became aesthetically pleasant, fully accessible comfortable and attractive.

Recently, there is a growing number of worldwide practices showing the transformation of mobility infrastructures and shelters in something more.

In Dubai, the first air-conditioned bus stops protect users from summer temperatures and offer a wide range of complementary services, tiny shops, free wi-fi, electronic kiosks and recycling garbage containers as well. The need to cope with extreme weather inspired also Architecture studio Rombout Frieling Lab and Research Institutes of Sweden in the design of a prototype bus stop in Umeå, Sweden. Made of local timber, this shelter offers rotating pods rather than seating, designed to protect passengers from the wind and provide privacy; technology here is subtle and appears through the delicate lights on the roof, changing colour according to the destination of the approaching bus.

Enjoying the surrounding and relax is instead the goal of COBE's green oasis charging station, a meeting place where waiting for the completed becomes secondary.

Measuring Travel Experience. New technologies make it possible to measure not just the distance travelled in a more sustainable way, but other aspects shaping the travel experience, such as local emission, noise, light and humidity levels, surrounding cleanness, disorders and anti-social behaviour.

Everyday urban furniture evolved into sensing urban interfaces able to gather information about the city.

Our prototype aims to collect data from different fields and bring together information sets rarely examined in combination, such as detailed travel patterns and environmental data.

For public administrations and utilities, this means mapping the locations that are particularly critical and planning specific interventions (in terms of pollution, noise exposure, safety concerns…); while citizens can benefit from a better service and hopefully be rewarded for their sustainable behavioural change, as it is in real time recorded by the service itself.

5.4 PUNTOnet Bike and Bus Smart Structures

The developed prototype consists of a steel frame shelter, simply built and self-standing, with transparent roof made of special coloured photovoltaic glass, a protected meeting point with many possibilities.

The structure can be declined in two forms, BUS and BIKE, that can be gradually upgraded from the basic line to high-tech version. Seats, electric device charging, e-bike sharing, parcel locker, environmental sensor, RGB interactive lights are just a few examples of the possible equipment whose integration the research group designed. The common features are, in short:

- contemporary design, suitable for different locations;
- compatibility with urban spaces, fitting parallel parking lots;
- Simply built and easy to maintain;
- Self-standing without foundation;
- Modularly extensible services and equipment;
- Wide accessibility and intuitive operation;
- Rewarding approach, that connect the use of sustainable mobility to other urban services (waste tariff discount, for instance, is being evaluated)

These models of bus and bike shelter, modularly combinable with the innovative waste system described above, have recently obtained patents (Fig. 11 and 12).

Fig. 11. PUNTOnet BUS with environmental sensor coloured roof and RGB light.

Fig. 12. PUNTOnet BIKE, with coloured photovoltaic glass, parcel locker and e-bike sharing system

In the last version of PUNTOnet station (Fig. 13), the roof of the shelter offers itself as the support for the technology equipment previously packed in the smart totem – including stereoscopic cameras, wi-fi and environmental sensors. According to the specific location needs the totem might be completely substituted by PUNTOnet bus shelter or PUNTOnet bike sharing. This solution, adjustable in parallel parking lots or in a wider public space facing a road, provides an optimization of resources allocation in the same area, with a greater specialization of a smart urban point.

The research team is currently developing new versions of PUNTOnet bike shelter, adjusted and tailored for remote locations outside built environment; these releases are specifically studied for mountain municipalities willing to promote safe and enjoyable electric bike trips.

Fig. 13. Full-optional PUNTOnet station with parcel locker, e-bike sharing and smart waste containers. The shelter roof accommodates sensors and cameras previously packed in the smart totem.

6   A Model of Small Smart City at 10. 000 Inhabitants

The experimentation around innovative urban services and on-site validations do not complete the description of the prototypal system developed within the frame of the present research. Further aspects were made possible thanks to the particular location chosen for the tests.

Firstly, Castel Bolognese boasts a proactive and open-minded political background, a real opportunity for easier and innovative planning, approval, and funding decisions; the policy makers set the goal to build up a global innovation strategy on the municipal territory with the support of different local actors and utilities, and the scientific oversight of the University.

Secondly, the city, at roughly 10 000 inhabitants, features a favourable geographical position, a positive economic balance and a strong local cohesion, usually helpful to align citizens around smart city initiatives.

In this promising context, Hera Group promoted the elaboration of an experimental real time dashboard collecting data from different sources.

Urban dashboards are becoming increasingly popular as an effective mean to assess and guide daily operational practices across public services and provide wider information to policy makers [7]. However, the use of centralized operating systems of this kind is still infrequent in small areas, which, instead, may likely adopt smart city solutions faster than their large city counterparts.

Castel Bolognese dashboard displays five kind of services: environmental passport, energetic maps, satellite map, environmental monitoring, urban service network (Fig. 14).

Compared to other more complex city dashboards, the tentative platform developed here is particularly interesting because directly brings together dataset coming from the local utility: the composite visualization of gas, water, electricity consumptions highlights specific needs of energy rehabilitation for public and private buildings. The platform also allows city managers to monitor how innovative urban services (as waste containers, bike sharing and smart bus shelter) are performing and used.

This experiment may act as an inspiration to other small cities around the country that struggle to gather the resources to develop new digital services and public-facing projects found in larger cities, already known for their "smart" initiatives.

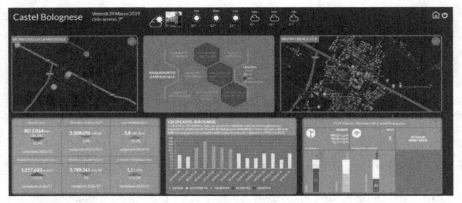

Fig. 14. Pilot urban dashboard for a 10 000-inhabitant town, Castel Bolognese. In Smartgreens 2020, Fabbri et al., 2020.

7 Conclusions

Starting from the local utility need to innovate household waste management, this paper describes the development of a multifunctional, modularly extensible, accessible station with a variety of applications and possibilities.In our design intention, PUNTOnet can be used in different urban environments, but it appears particularly suitable for small centres.

In general, the density of urban services is proportional to urban density: the first ones become less frequent at the border of large cities, until thinned-out in small villages, where, conversely, there is a closer connection to vegetation and cultivation.

When the population is spread around many small settlements rather than concentrated in larger ones, the costs of providing basic services like public transport, healthcare and commerce are much higher [8].

Acting on everyday urban services rather than consolidated and larger infrastructures may be a cost-effective solution for the improvement of life quality in small towns, in line with specific environmental requirements.

Along with the development and supply of innovative services, an appropriate digital infrastructure should be put in place, for a better management of the proposed interfaces.

In this essay we have presented a system of innovative services and a tentative urban dashboard for a small smart city that turns on a new dialogue between city and its inhabitants; this scheme has the potential to activate the re-use, the re-generation and re-interpretation of existing urban structure with limited investments, even in small centres and low densely populated areas.

References

1. Fabbri, I., Lelli, G., Nicolino, W.: PUNTOnet: innovative prototype of urban trash containers improving waste sorting and widening the services offered to the city. In: Proceedings of the 9th International Conference on Smart Cities and Green ICT Systems, pp. 29–37 (2020). https://doi.org/10.5220/0009470400290037. ISBN 978–989–758–418–3. ISSN 2184–4968
2. Using behavioural insights to improve waste management and resource efficiency. In: Tackling Environmental Problems with the Help of Behavioural Insights. OECD Publishing (2017)
3. Dessart, F.J., Lourenço, J.S., Almeida, S.R., Ciriolo, E.: Behavioural insights applied to policy - application to specific policy issues and collaboration at EU level. Publications Office of the European Union, Luxembourg (2016)
4. Alter, A.: Irresistible: Why We Can't Stop Checking, Scrolling, Clicking and Watching. Random House (2017)
5. Mont, O., Lehner, M., Heiskanen, E.: Nudging – A tool for sustainable behaviour? Stockholm: Swedish Environmental Protection Agency (2014)
6. Mondschein, A.: Healthy transportation. a question of mobility or accessibility. In Beatley, T., Jones, C., Rainey, R. (eds) Healthy Environments, Healing Spaces. Practices and Directions in Health, Planning and Design, pp. 11–30. University of Virginia Press (2018)
7. Kitchin, R., Maalsen, S., McArdle, G.: The praxis and politics of building urban dashboards. Geoforum **77**, 93–101 (2016)
8. ENRD. Smart Villages. Revitalising Rural Services. Publications Office of the European Union, Luxembourg (2018)

Information Systems Security Management for IoT Adoption in Smart Cities: A Review

Zarina Din$^{(\boxtimes)}$, Dian Indrayani Jambari , Maryati Mohd Yusof ,
and Jamaiah Yahaya

Faculty of Information Science and Technology, Universiti Kebangsaan Malaysia, 43650 Bangi,
Selangor, Malaysia
P90639@siswa.ukm.edu.my, {Dian,maryati.yusof,jhy}@ukm.edu.my

Abstract. Sustainable urban development contributes to cities evolving into
Smart Cities (SC) by utilizing the Internet of Things (IoT) technology. The major
trend towards IoT involving SC motivates significant improvements in management methods of Information Technology (IT). The strong adoption of IoT in
SC creates information security complexity that is to be handled by Information
Systems (IS). IS Security Management Strategy revise according to existing organisational structure. Hence, there is a critical demand to perform an evaluation of
IS security management in the IoT to know key concepts in managing IS security
in IoT towards SC. This paper aims to study IS security management in SC in the
adoption of IoT technology. This study also discusses and classifies five comparison criteria as dimensions for managing IS security in an IoT-enabled SC that were
explored in the literature. The five criteria consist of governance, integrity, interoperability, personalisation, and self-organisation. These dimensions will form the
IS security management conceptual framework towards realising SC enabled by
IoT technology. Document analysis was carried out to review key concepts from
seven security management frameworks and relevant research reports. The review
will help security executives and top management of any organisation to prepare
for SC to address the five identified dimensions.

Keywords: IS security management · IoT security management · Smart city ·
Governance · Cyber-attack

1 Introduction

SC is a citizen-centric urban project that is competitive and progressive through IT to
make life better, productivity, ongoing urbanisation, and knowledge of present and future
people. The idea of "smart city" leads to the creation of an urban environment which
government, industry, and people constantly use digital technology to gather and examine
information and share information in order to build and sustain a "smart person's"
successful life. Yigitcanlar and Kamaruzzaman [1] describe that when a city begins to
aggressively utilize digital technology in all aspects, it becomes "smart". Accessibility
by the community in using such technologies raises the need for high-quality service
providers in both the public and private sectors.

© Springer Nature Switzerland AG 2021
C. Klein et al. (Eds.): SMARTGREENS 2020/VEHITS 2020, CCIS 1475, pp. 66–92, 2021.
https://doi.org/10.1007/978-3-030-89170-1_4

Two methods are applied by cities in the practice of come to be SC including [2]: (i) Conversion of current cities into SC through the application of existing infrastructure technologies to facilitate smart services, as example at Barcelona, Santander and Seoul, and (ii) Setting up a SC from start, as is the case with Masdar City in Abu Dhabi and United Arad Emirates. The transformation of a town into a SC transforms a device into an intelligent machine [2]. It will benefit people as it will provide real-time access to information and create informed decisions within simple and free access to information. The seamless and ease of access to available information on a single information channel makes it at simple for citizens to search for specific information. This also allows decision-makers to have clearly understand what effect this will have on the entire city system.

IoT is an enabler to develop a smarter society by applying it to critical public service sectors such as healthcare, transport, agriculture, energy, and security. IoT technology consists of numerous of devices, such as cameras, smart cards and networked sensors to communicate with each other [3]. These devices not only transfer information immediately, but they will also manage the transfer information. IoT can come with three features; first, IoT is easy to respond with using Radio Frequency Identification (RFID) and sensor technology, such as two-dimensional code to capture object access information all the time and anyplace. Second, IoT is a secure transmission, and real time object information is reliably transmitted through the interaction of telecommunications networks and internet. Third, IoT is an intelligent method using cloud computing fuzzy identification and other intelligent computing technologies, using large data and information processing to obtain smart control [3].

Gartner estimated that by 2022 the number of IoT devices entering households would rise more rapidly from nine devices per household to 500, with IoT interconnection bundled into product [4]. Together with the expectation that 70% of the global population may live in cities by 2050, this discovery drives the conceptualisation of IoT-enabled SC. Gartner's Survey Analysis 2016 on the Backbone of Internet of Things found that safety is a key obstacle to IoT progress, supported by the difficulty of deployment and adoption, privacy issues, possible risks and responsibilities and the technology itself is immature [5]. Organisations need to be able to stay up to date with IoT innovations that influence their IoT initiatives. They need to pursue IoT technology and solve those difficulties to ensure the success of IoT programmes.

City platforms which are built on IoT and other intelligent devices must be secured from hackers or illegal users. Internet usage has allowed IoT to acquire the same vulnerabilities as any other computer system, likely to become a target for cyber-attack. Any threat on a connected computer can cause serious damage to a SC network and major vulnerability problems. In addition, sensitive information can also be reached over the network from any connected computer. Any threat on a connected computer can cause serious damage to a SC network and major vulnerability problems. In addition, sensitive information can also be reached over the network from any connected computer [6]. Security must be highlighted and improved to ensure a successful SC development. Thus, the public sector needs to develop its operational management, facilities, systems functionality, information exchange and collaboration and alignment of business processes. This shows that restructuring of IS management in public sector organisations is important, despite the challenges.

This study aims to propose main factors for managing IS security in SC by adopting IoT technology to achieve secure and reliable IS. Then, the result has been visualised in a comprehensive conceptual framework for IS security management for IoT-enable SC. The conceptual framework for SC serves as the basis for a systematic and realistic approach to support a more effective IS security management. This conceptual framework is built from examining seven existing frameworks of IS Security management in SC enabled by IoT and documents on relevant published articles and reports. The analysis aims to provide a thorough and critical evaluation of various IS and IoT security frameworks in SC. Nowadays, the recent advent of IoT has resulted in the need to develop the existing IS security management approach at SC. Therefore, a detailed study must be undertaken to classify the different between security framework for IS and IoT in SC and to discover the influencing components and elements for IS security management in SC by adopting IoT. The methods must take into consideration the characteristics of IS and IoT security; only certain measures developed for the IS and IoT security model have been considered. In this chapter, the study query concentrates on discovering existing security frameworks or model which were built for IS and IoT, and establishing the components and elements of IS security management in IoT-enabled SC. Thus, the development of conceptual framework is form on five components: (i) governance; (ii) integrity; (iii) interoperability; (iv) personalisation; and (v) self-organisation to accomplish secure and reliable IS [7].

1.1 Information System Security Management

IS safety in an IoT-enabled SC includes technology, software, infrastructure and information that are influenced by IoT's evolving integration, led to intense communication, high difficulty and interdependency. Cybersecurity is complicated by the complexity of maintaining end-to-end security through a broad and interdependent IS, involving numerous stakeholders, and incompatible application data standards and formats. Relevant IS security issues with IoT applications in SC, including data confidentiality attacks, data integrity threats [6, 8, 9], resource misuse, network loss, battery or device degradation, untrusted access [10–12], authentication threats and Denial of Service (DoS).

In addition, the features of SC need higher interaction rate, continuous involvement among various organizations and an effective governance agenda [13], like the standard [3, 6, 13–19], responsibility [3, 6, 10, 13], and policy compliant [3, 6, 10, 13, 17]. However, different types of information from various SC technologies and processing platforms have also increased the criticality in maintaining information integrity and protection of systems [20]. Quick and accurate technology [6, 11, 21, 22] and information integration communication among different organisations also impact IS connectivity as integration is complicated. The establishment of SC demands the IoT's IS security control to fix issues of unauthorized users to confidential information related to cyber-attacks. The protection of the information must follow the requirements of confidentiality, integrity, and availability. In addition, the citizens were also emphasized with reliability, availability, and real-time information [23].

1.2 Internet of Things Security Management

Security aspects such as communication confidentiality [6, 10–12], authenticity [6, 10–12], the trustworthiness of communication partners [10, 24], message integrity, and other requirements need to be emphasised in IoT. The difficulties in the implementation of IoT are the protection and privacy of citizens as IoT platforms gathered and analysed their personal and private information. Thus, managing the way in which customers and service providers can monitor the information and how it is presented to third-party applications is critical [25]. Connection to some resources is important or prevents them from interacting with other items in IoT [24].

Furthermore, authorities as service providers have to evaluate their goal, define the hardware and software needed for computing, and incorporate these heterogeneous subsystems. The presence of such infrastructure, numerous smart devices, and the requirement of a suitable work in partnership structure among IS can be a massive challenging mission for the IoT-based IS [26]. Such complexity in IS interaction in the IoT setting is challenging for IS interoperability because of the different standard of IS interface [18]. In addition, each kind of intelligent object in IoT has diverse information, processing, and transmission capabilities, and is subject to various conditions such as availability of energy and the appropriate communication bandwidth. Common standards are necessary to streamline communication and collaboration of these objects [24].

Thus, the IoT security management must take into account two dimensions which are personalisation and self-organisation. The personalisation need gain access to the private and individual information of citizens from numerous IS systems that handle the information collected and managed by IoT tools [3, 6, 10, 14, 16–18, 26–29]. As broad connected devices of citizens instantly produce a huge amount of information [11], the potential of cyber-attacks including Distributed Destruction of Service (DDoS) attack on public infrastructure are potentially increasing. Such threats highlight the challenge of managing safe exchange of information during multiple IS communication and integration to allow citizen-centric services [30].

The self-organisation feature would allow direct machine-to-machine (M2M) communication over the Internet through IoT devices. The self-organisation function would give authorization to direct machine-to-machine (M2M) interaction by IoT devices over the Internet [16]. Self-organisation is the management of the acceptance, processing and dissemination of information without human intervention using automated M2M [18, 24, 31]. Machines will be run independently or integrated with humans in order to produce customer-oriented output that works continuously to sustain itself and be made available at all times [6, 10, 18, 24, 31, 32]. Hence, the machines become independent entities that capable to collect and analyse data and provide analysis-based advice [31] that poses a risk to IS integrity. Risk is an essential aspect of IS security management in IoT-enabled SC [3, 11, 21, 28] that recognises assets, risks, and vulnerabilities. Another vital aspect is availability, which is to ensure IS performed entirely at all the time, of an authenticated user detected [10]. The safety and protection must make sure that the equivalent resources are available if any IS operation fails and must allow M2M operations as an added assurance. Using IoT technology that allows machines to handle information would improve IS protection in the SC as against leaks of information.

1.3 Influencing Factors on Information System Security Management in Smart City Enabled by IoT Technology

A study by Ijaz [33] proposed the influencing factors on information security in SC which is mainly reliant on three aspects, namely, governance, socio-economic and technological aspects, as depicted in Fig. 1.

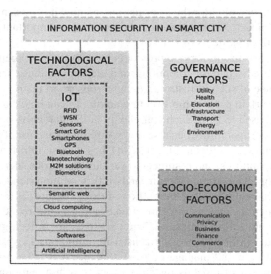

Fig. 1. Influencing factors on information security in smart city. Source: [33].

The governance and socio-economic factors rely on the technological aspects as these are applied in a SC by technology. These aspects are combined to affect information safety problems in a SC, which can be controlled again with technology as it is a primary driver in SC. Thus, the function of technology in security management and IS concerns in integrating of all technology needs a significant focus.

Governance factors are SC's biggest concern that needs to include all the approaches to sustain entire infrastructure and management problems, however, inadequate implementation may result in attacks and fraud. Therefore, there are conditions to be explored to resolve this issue:

i.   The need to conduct security testing on governance systems purchased by the authorities. Stakeholders prioritise checking the technology's functionality and are less bothered to concentrate on the safety tests. The knowledge among authorities of legitimate safety problems is a key necessity.

ii. Risks to the critical infrastructure where modifying one operation in a crucial system can affect critical services to be delayed or loss [34]. Therefore, the importance of a critical infrastructure of an SC to retain its protection, strength, and data accuracy is highlighted. The health sector is an essential kind of critical infrastructure as if it is vulnerable to security risks. It may not only contribute to a patient's privacy concerns [35] but can also present dangers to his lifetime as the attacker can change important information.

iii. Smart mobility guarantee and confidentiality conditions. Smart mobility can trigger confidentiality issues as disclosure of private information may occur while gathering, publishing, and make use of trace data. Localisation techniques which involve GPS, WiFi, Bluetooth, and RFID as centric servers need to know device IDs [36]. Information delivered and collected from machines used in smart mobility networks can be topic to malicious incidents that can affect incorrect traffic flow in satellite routing applications.

iv. Power and utility optimization. Power and utility systems progressively rely on smart grids that make use of two direction communication with the users to control the allocated electricity effectively. Data protection and confidentiality continue major concerns for utilities and users who are experiencing a major obstacle in smart grid implementation.

Another aspect is social and economic factors in an SC which comprise interaction, personal identity, banking, and finance. All of these are a vital component in an SC and exposed to security and privacy issues. There are some features that need to be highlighted:

i. Challenges in smart communication. Recent years have witnessed the growth in the popularity of smartphones that they have become the hackers' keen target [37]. Wireless networking, Bluetooth, cloud computing, IoT, practically every one of ICT technologies perform their role in smart communication, and safety issues considered as smart solutions are built.

ii. Individual Privacy. Individuals in an SC use various services and communicate via the latest technologies connected by various networks and applications, which are the object of hackers who intend to interfere with their privacy and thereby block them of their rights [38]. The role of social networking in terms of privacy and information security should be considered. The privacy issues related to social networking depend on the degree to which the user, the recipients define the information given and how it can be applied. Those public networking providers who agree not to reveal their user's identity can still offer sufficient information to detect the profile of the personal [39].

iii. Banking, finance, and industry are elements of a smart economy and is a key part of an SC for economic development and improved banking and business services, however this aspect of an SC is highly exposed to safety risks because it can be targeted for individual commercial usage. The hackers aim to destroy the financial system of some organisations or an entire town.

Finally, technical considerations are where the SC depends entirely on technology to give good quality services to the government and residents. SC guarantees people smarter economic growth, smarter governance, and more intelligent services across integrated and latest technology [33]. Therefore, these three aspects including governance, socio-economic, and technological factors should be considered in the development of IS security management in SC by using IoT technology.

Other than that, the evaluation on the willingness of the IS execution in IoT-enabled SC shows that the current IS management method for handling IS security in SC business is inappropriate or unsuitable [18]. Managing IS protection is troublesome in many ways: (i) IS is incapable of managing continuing cyber-attack risks because it is prone to information leaks and access violations [40]; (ii) IS is weakly created for IoT-enabled SC, as safety procedures are not well established [41]; and (iii) The application of IoT threatens IS integration, especially with regard to IoT technology's inconsistency with traditional IS which remains critical to operation [17, 18]. The complexity security issues indicate the multiple perspectives for IS protection in IoT-enabled SC. Current studies have concentrated on IS protection research and technological security solutions, although research on the management perspective is minimal [16]. Lam and Ma [18] proposed that IS security management must be handled by governance by setting acceptable and transparent IS security management requirements, and effective strategies for cyber-attacks and corrective plans.

Irshad [3] reviewed a comparison of four IoT security frameworks and identified some findings connected to information protection frameworks in IoT. Organisations that have chosen to incorporate IoT adoption must look into three steps: (i) Defines IoT's benefits, risks and implements security threat management processes. Information security risk management policies should follow the IT guidelines and principles of an organisation to protect the privacy, integrity, and accessibility of safety frameworks. IoT review is to assess the IoT plans and to analyse the historical security status, (ii) Carry out an IoT risk analysis by defining the assets, risks, and vulnerabilities, and (iii) Implement risk assessment by evaluating security incidents, and then implementation of risk management plans. Follow-up actions are needed as portion of a complete and constant assessment. In addition, it is proposed for OSCAR to pursue a new method to IoT's E2E security issue [3]. This is based on the principle of protection for objects which implement protection within the payload application. In OSCAR, confidentiality is used to provide capacity-based access management and oversight security throughout communication, authorisation, and verification issues for restricted ecosystems that have been discussed separately.

2   Existing Frameworks on Information System Security Management for IoT in Smart City

This section discusses the literature on seven frameworks for handling IS security and IoT security in SC due to security issues becoming a major concern. These frameworks have been selected as the most appropriate frameworks which focus on IS and IoT safety management in an SC environment. Subsequently, comparison and analysis of seven frameworks were made based on the comparison criteria to identify the dimension and elements for managing IS security in SC enabled by IoT technology.

2.1   Comparison of IS Security Management for IoT Frameworks

Seven existing frameworks and model have been critically analysed which include Integral Framework for Information Systems Security Management, Framework of Information Security System in Smart City, Model Cisco Security Framework for IoT, Object

Security Framework for Internet of Thing (OSCAR) Security Framework, Constrained Application Protocol (CoAP) Framework, Floodgate Security Framework, and Generic Smart City IoT based Framework. The frameworks were selected based on its appropriate context and its relation to the IS security management, focusing on the adoption of IoT technology within the smart city setting. Each framework is discussed as follows and concluded with a comparative analysis across all the frameworks to present the dimension of IS security management in SC by adopting IoT technology which contributes to the development of a conceptual framework.

Integral Framework for Information Systems Security Management. Trček [14] proposed IS security management to effectively manage E-business system security through integration of relevant areas. This framework focuses on three perspectives which consist of technological, organisational, and legislative as illustrated in Fig. 2.

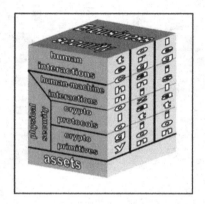

Fig. 2. Integral framework for information systems security management. Source: [14].

An organisation must start identifying threats related to business and assets to protect information. The first emphasis is threat analysis which begins with protection protocols and implementation of security services related to human-machine interaction. The technology perspective identifies Public Key Infrastructure (PKI) to address various issues such as: (i) Operational procedures with registration, initialisation, authorisation, generation, key improvement and negotiation, key update and expiration, cross-certification, and cancellation; (ii) Supporting protocols cover operating, management, and time stamping procedures; (iii) Staff-related matters in terms of awareness and preparation; (iv) Hardware and software-related concerns pertaining to flexibility, scalability, user-friendliness, costs, integration, and stability; and (v) Consultancy for individual matters connected includes space organisation, certificated paths, trust models, and etc.

Besides, the organisational viewpoint of view indicates that information security control is accountable for beginning, enforcing, or maintaining the security of an entity. Originally, there must be an information security officer or information security unit which is liable for setting up, maintaining, and revising security policy. These policies must be developed and independently reviewed by an external expert in an organisation. The policy is based on management dedication and specified by processes that define an organisation's approach to managing security. From a legislative perspective, several legal problems are yet to be addressed in IS security management. The general guidelines and details that explained the legal issues which organisations need to address within specific legislation as stated: procedures on cryptography, digital signatures, confidentiality rights, intellectual property rights and service provider obligations. However, the development of this framework is more focused on IS security management and it did not consider IoT characteristics.

Framework of Information Security System in Smart City. The Framework of Information Security System in SC identifies three aspects of IS management in an SC including management, technology, construction and operation [28] as depicted in Fig. 3.

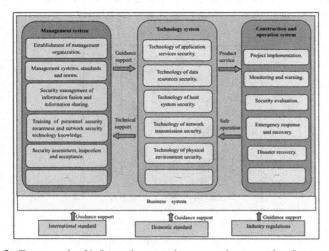

Fig. 3. Framework of information security system in smart city. Source: [28].

The construction management system is based on global and local-related standards. The management aspect sets out clear requirements regarding security management system, product description, security threat evaluation, personal information security training and others [42]. A collection of programmes and regulations is developed to manage information security effectively in an SC.

Another factor is technology which is a collection of IS technology to secure the physical environment, network communication, host security, data supplies, and application services. The physical environment is designed to avoid exposure or harm to physical equipment under unauthorised circumstances and ensure hardware protection [42]. Mechanism for access management is developed to perform security certification and manage of sensing nodes and base stations to avoid a sensing device by unauthorised users. Besides that, the network is the extremely exposed environment to be targeted and may be unlawfully stolen during the information communication activity [43]. Data encryption technology is implemented to avoid disclose during the network transmission and increase the security and reliability of information. SC host security technology refers to the problem of host security technology in the cloud computing ecosystem [44]. In this security framework, a new security approach was highlighted in identity verification, sensitive labelling, access management, security inspection, interference prevention, and malicious code prevention. Moreover, the protection of data resources in terms of safety measures and confidentiality is a main task in improving security, strengthening and transforming the application, and providing a incorporated support network for protection purposes [45].

The system of construction and operation includes two levels of meaning. First, it means locating, securing, and removing security incidents such as intruder attacks on the network or application through process and maintenance. Secondly, security process and maintenance facilities should be performed, for instance supervising, alerting, reaction, evaluation, crisis recovery, and disaster recovery. Overall, this framework is focused on IS system security management and emphasise on IoT characteristics.

Cisco Security Framework for IoT. Figure 4 shows the safety effects proposed by Cisco for IoT/M2M security framework that can be the basis for security implementation in IoT settings [3, 46].

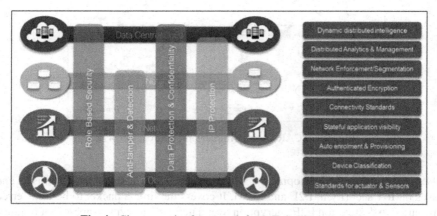

Fig. 4. Cisco security framework for IoT. Source: [3, 46].

This proposed framework may possibly be applied in procedure and product improvement. Besides, strategy implementation in operating situations is appropriate for application and infrastructure. The incorporated endpoint layer consists of highly restricted apps and has constrained the malware development to this layer. IP-based sensor progress is the equivalent of attacking surface growth. This emphasises the need for additional security procedures and recognition methods, and IoT endpoint safeguard needs to align with its improved capabilities. IoT poses additional challenges for network and security architects. Smarter security systems need to evolve which involve managed risk detection, anomaly detection, and analytical analysis [3]. Thus, the CISCO security framework is appropriate for both application and infrastructure security.

Object Security Framework for Internet of Thing (OSCAR) Security Framework.
OSCAR has been developed for the IoT to offer End-to-End (E2E) protection across
networks and transport layers [47]. This framework is derived from the principle of
item protection, which implements protection within the payload of the application as
visualised in Fig. 5. Nevertheless, separate privacy and trust validity domains were
considered. Privacy is applied during interaction to give access control and safeguard
against spying. This security framework defends against repetition attacks by using
duplicate detection to couple the information encryption key. OSCAR also demonstrated
the concept's feasibility by testing in the M2M transmission scenario wherever both sides
are resource constraints.

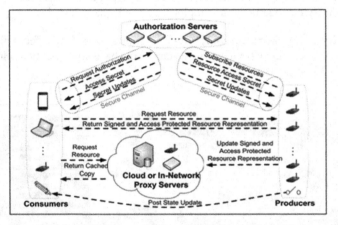

Fig. 5. OSCAR security framework. Source: [46, 47].

OSCAR is useful in developing SC where it can cater to a huge number of users and
focuses on IoT security in E2E and M2M. It covers the time a packet to be transferred
from source to destination E2E encryption over a network, a cryptographic that requires
data protection between two communicating entities without interruption. OSCAR can
also be used for M2M which allows communication between two computer platforms.
In addition, the system specifications must be defined according on the main framework
criteria: rules, standards, procedures, and guidelines.

Constrained Application Protocol (CoAP) Framework. The Constrained Application Protocol (CoAP) is a specialised for web transmission procedure providing flexibility, low latency, Machine-to-Machine (M2M) and Machine-to-Customer (M2C) communications. The CoAP protocol applies an interactive model among application endpoints
that cover a request and response model [48]. The framework consists of various modules
for handling IoT environment security and trust issues. The CoAP operates on application
layers to protect the IoT where it is mainly concerned with developing and transferring
lightweight variants to restricted devices. It uses a pocket protection approach to ensure
successful data transmission security. This framework is most appropriate for application
security [46, 49].

Floodgate Security Framework. Floodgate Security Framework offers engineers with a complete protection solution to develop embedded devices that allow to construct safe, validated, and reliable devices. IT security procedures need authentication, trust, and secure management of endpoints before they can operate on the corporate network. This framework fits best for infrastructure level security [46]. Convergence of information technology (IT)/operational technology (OT) and the advent of safety requirements in different industries allow embedded devices to have the same protection capabilities as IT devices. Its architecture includes integrating IT/OT convergence management system to ensure the device's security capabilities are secured from an attack in different industries and allows embedded devices to have the equal protection ability as IT devices. This safety framework also complies with safety standards like Embedded Device Security Assurance (EDSA), ISA/IEC 62443, and Cybersecurity guidelines for the National Institute of Standards and Technology (NIST) [50]. A framework combined with the MCU gives IoT developers the instruments required to safeguard their devices as per Fig. 6.

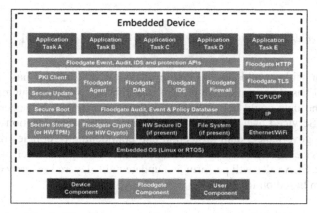

Fig. 6. Floodgate security framework. Source: [46, 50].

Therefore, this security framework helps to protect IoT tools compared to today's cyber risks and potential risks that will arise during the device's lifetime which is a crucial challenge for embedded developers. Low-end IoT devices need a customised solution, constructed to meet up the memory and performance needs of these resource limited environments [3].

Generic Smart City IoT Based Framework. This framework aims to ensure security and protect the privacy of people for SC by proposing a multi-layered security framework for disseminated IoT fog and cloud ecosystems involving data governance, data protection and confidentiality, network security and identity and access management. The firewall had been used to guarantee physical security in the network to avoid access by cyber-attackers from other unsafe SC facilities. Applications with High Level Security Requirements (HLSR), file systems, and database must be encrypted to protect the data integrity, confidentiality, and user privacy, [6]. The interaction channels should be secured, and data exchange must be based on encrypted user token for verification purposes. The implementation of the analytics cycle of all data should be anonymised as shown in Fig. 7.

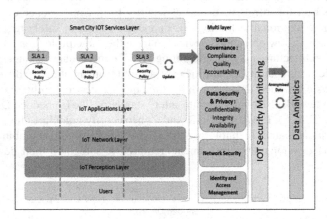

Fig. 7. Generic smart city IoT based framework. Source: [6].

Application either middle or low-level safety measures, has execute the login/password-based authentication process to verify user. Firewall can make sure network safety, and data could be substituted with no encryption. All security structure depend on the Service Level Agreement (SLA) applied between functions in SC. SLA will drive data governance, data protection and confidentiality policies reliant on the Quality of Service (QoS), such as the reaction time for a given level of service and safety. As such, SLA rules will perform and update multi-layered security conditions in the SC platform based on IoT.

3   Method

A qualitative method was adopted in this study. The aim of this research is to discover the key concepts for IS security management in an IoT-enabled SC through document analysis. The process was carried out to accomplish the objective including:

i.   Collection of Documents.
     A Review was performed by using published and unpublished documents on IS security management and IoT security management. The documents include journals, proceedings, research theses, established reports, the government's official documents, paperwork, and official web portals.
ii. Search Criteria.
     Queries were done on online databases and e-journal repositories such as Web of Science, Scopus, Science Direct, IEEE, and Springer Link. The government's web portals of chosen SCs and news articles were also discovered to obtain perceptions

and views on the subject being studied. Keywords such as "IS security management", "IoT security management", "smart city", "governance", and "cyber-attack" were applied throughout the searching procedure.

iii. Data Analysis.

The study identified 60 relevant papers from online databases and e-journal repositories by using the keywords "information security management", "IoT security management", "smart city", "governance", and "cyber-attack". The chosen documents refer to the seven frameworks of IS Security management by using IoT and related research. Next, a content review of each paper was conducted. The analysis involves defining and coding data into groups, analysing and interpreting data. Coding was done through an identification process by interpreting and categorising data into relevant and specific units of information. The document analysis in IS security management and information security for IoT found factors that are frequently seen as key concepts to the effective implementation of IS security management for IoT in SC environment. Subsequently, five key factors consist of governance, integrity, interoperability, personalisation, and self-organisation were generated to represent the basic meaning of data by iterative comparison. The well-defined categories were applied to classify the content into same categories. These activities were carried out continuously through the study to collect the common factors that guarantee the successful management of IS security in an IoT-enabled SC.

4   Result and Discussion

Based on the IS dan IoT security management scenario, the influencing factors on IS security management in SC and the reviewed seven frameworks, frameworks for IS security management for IoT in SC were compared with the identified comparison criteria as demonstrated in Table 1. The comparison criteria were based on the frequent issues discussed in previous studies.

Table 1 shows six criteria were identified as comparison criteria among seven frameworks [6, 14, 28, 46, 47, 49, 50] which consist of (1) framework applicability, (2) managing and monitoring IS security operational, (3) identifying and mitigating threat, (4) collaboration and integration of applications, (5) managing personal data profiling, and (5) capability to perform IS operational automatically (M2M). A summary of the framework comparison for IS Security Management in the adoption IoT for an SC is detailed in Table 2.

As a result, the comparison criteria from C2 until C6 can be classified into five dimension including C2:Governance, C3:Integrity, C4:Interoperability, C5:Personalisation and C6: Self-organizing which will become as important dimensions that need to be tackled in managing IS security using IoT in an SC. The description of each dimensions is as follows:

Table 1. The comparison of frameworks for information system security management for IoT in smart cities.

Comparison criteria	Security framework						
	Integral Framework for Information Systems Security Management [14]	Framework of Information Security System in Smart City [28]	Cisco Security Framework for IoT [3, 46, 51]	Object Security Framework for Internet of Thing (OSCAR) security framework [3, 46, 47]	Constrained Application Protocol (CoAP) framework [3, 46, 49]	Floodgate Security Framework [3, 46, 50]	Generic Smart City IoT based framework [6]
C1: Framework applicability	Information system security management	Information system security management	IoT security management	IoT security management	IoT security management	IoT security management	IoT security management
C2: Managing and monitoring IS security operational	• Information Security Policy and Legislation (encryption law, digital signature, privacy right, Intellectual Property Right, Public Key Infrastructure) • Accountability (Provider right and responsibilities) • Auditability (compliance)	• Management (organisation, system, standard) • Security management (information sharing) • Training and awareness • Security assessment, (inspection, and acceptance)	• Operational policy (application and infrastructure)	• Policy, standard, and guidelines	• IoT smart objects protocol suites • Fully support application requirements	• Compliance with EDSA, ISA/IEC 62443, and NIST Cybersecurity guidelines	• SLA policies • Compliance to SLA • Quality of service • Accountability

(continued)

Table 1. (*continued*)

Comparison criteria	Security framework						
	Integral Framework for Information Systems Security Management [14]	Framework of Information Security System in Smart City [28]	Cisco Security Framework for IoT [3, 46, 51]	Object Security Framework for Internet of Thing (OSCAR) security framework [3, 46, 47]	Constrained Application Protocol (CoAP) framework [3, 46, 49]	Floodgate Security Framework [3, 46, 50]	Generic Smart City IoT based framework [6]
C3: Identifying and mitigating threat	• Asset Classification and control • Physical, environment and personal control • Communications and operations security • Access control • Non-repudiation	• Identify, protect and eliminate (virus, hackers attack) • Safety operations and maintenance (monitoring, warning, response, assessment, emergency, and disaster recovery)	• Threat detection (virus attack, fraud)	• Threat detection (Denial of service) Integrity	• CoAP message layer ensures the quality of data (avoid messages that are out of order, lost, or duplicated)	• Security capabilities (ensuring device is protected from cybercrime (fraud, virus, Trojan, Worms) • Runtime Integrity Validation (RITV) • Applications Guarding APIs Internet Security	• Integrity
C4: Collaboration and integration of applications	• General interdependency (measuring risk, managing interdependencies, technological change, appropriate governance, adopting integrated system) • Trusted	Security protection: • Physical environment • Network transmission • Host system • Data resources • Applications services	• Risk of confidentiality • Security assurance • Data protection and security (exchange data) • Network security	• Analysed and extracted risk • Trusted	• Trusted • Controlling the transmission of information between two endpoints • Packet protection • Duplicate detection	• Management system integration for IT/OT convergence • Software-based vTPM for legacy system • Trusted devices	• Network security

(continued)

Table 1. (*continued*)

Comparison criteria	Security framework						
	Integral Framework for Information Systems Security Management [14]	Framework of Information Security System in Smart City [28]	Cisco Security Framework for IoT [3, 46, 51]	Object Security Framework for Internet of Thing (OSCAR) security framework [3, 46, 47]	Constrained Application Protocol (CoAP) framework [3, 46, 49]	Floodgate Security Framework [3, 46, 50]	Generic Smart City IoT based framework [6]
C5: Managing personal data profiling	None (This framework did not support IoT characteristics. Therefore, it does not consider the security aspect for managing personal data profiling which is one of IoT characteristics)	• Confidentiality • Authentication • Access Control (prevent illegal access)	• Authentication • Role-based access – authorisation access to personal data	• Privacy • Access Control • Confidentiality • Authentication	• Datagram Transport Layer Security (DTLS) will maintain the confidentiality and integrity of the information • Public key cryptography was used for authenticated identity of individuals	• Authentication process for ensuring all access is authorised • Support Public Key Infrastructure (PKI) client	• Identity and access management • Confidentiality
C6: Capability to perform IS operational automatically (M2M)	None (This framework did not support IoT characteristics, so it does not reflect M2M criteria, which is one of the IoT characteristics)	• Availability • Reliability (resources and services) • Monitoring and early warning of information security risk	• M2M operational • Smarter Security System for managing threat detection, anomaly detection, and predictive analysis	• Availability • E2E security • M2M operational	• Support M2M requirements by using User Datagram Protocol (UDP), Universal Resource Identifier (URI), and content-type	• Ensuring all communications between known and trusted devices are secured • Support PKI client	• Availability

Table 2. Summary of comparison of frameworks for information system security management for IoT in smart cities.

Criteria	Description	Source						
		[14]	[28]	[3, 46, 51]	[3, 46, 47]	[3, 46, 49]	[3, 46, 50]	[6]
C1	Framework capability: • Information system security management	/	/					
	• IoT security management			/	/	/	/	/
C2	To manage and monitor IS security operational by performed elements as follows: • IS and IoT security management policy and guidelines for applications and infrastructures • Accountability contains roles and responsibilities of individuals and organisations in SC • Compliance for policy/standard identified in SC operational must be fulfilled by SC authorities by implementing a scheduled auditing	/	/	/	/	/	/	/
C3	To ensure the integrity and accuracy of information by consider non-repudiation to avoid the arrival of out-of-order message, lost or duplicated information	/	/	/	/	/	/	/

(*continued*)

Table 2. (*continued*)

Criteria	Description	Source						
		[14]	[28]	[3, 46, 51]	[3, 46, 47]	[3, 46, 49]	[3, 46, 50]	[6]
C4	Collaboration and integration of applications by considering the following elements: • Managing and assessing risk at every level of information process, i.e. receiving and transmitting information. It is important to minimise a threat • Emergence of technology must be emphasised to increase trust on IS among SC stakeholders	/	/	/	/	/	/	/
C5	To manage personal data profiling by considering the following elements: • Confidentiality • Privacy • Authentication • Authorisation • Access control	x	/	/	/	/	/	/
C6	To perform IS operational automatically (M2M) including: • Availability of the resources • Ensuring all communications between known and trusted devices are secured	x	/	/	/	/	/	/

4.1 Governance

Governance is the anchoring principle for enhancing IS security management for IoT-enabled SC. Governance needs to be reviewed for IS integrity, interoperability, personalisation, and self-organization according to the SC's features. Governance requires procedures, policies and structures that direct organisations to ensure productive IS management to support organisational objectives and goals [17]. This was highlighted in order to ensure cooperation among various stakeholders in order to protect participants' rights and interests [18]. Besides that, it can resolve the diverse range of IS protection levels from various integrated SC organisations. Three elements are related to this study: security policy/standard, accountability, and auditability.

i. Security policy/standard: IS security standard/policy refers to a document which includes information security requirements and requirement standardisation to ensure information protection in SC through the use of IoT technology. Compliance with the policy and standards is critical in ensuring interoperability and minimising risk-taking [6, 14–18]. In an SC approach, the global security strategy must ensure data protection and privacy because IoT attacks will cause significant damage to the SC ecosystem. With this, IoT-connected attackers can access all Smart City's platform.

ii. Accountability: Accountability refers to the person or system responsible for producing and processing the information. Accountability assurance may help determine which device has produced which data and which device has managed which data in the heterogeneous IoT setting [10, 52]. It is a capability to ensure that users are held liable for their actions. Accountability can be self-assured using the right devices detection method. Most ground-level devices will use RFID or NFC technologies to communicate, while edge-level devices will receive an IP address based on IPv6 as an identifier [10].

iii. Auditability: Auditability is relate the capacity of a device to track all actions continuously and reliably refer to the ability of a system to perform continuous and consistent monitoring of all actions [10, 52] such as collecting, processing, and transmitting information. As information securing management become common practice, standard for auditing becomes essential. As the most important practical guideline, the International Standard ISO/IEC 27001, explicitly in the "Information technology-protection-technique-information security management systems-Requirements" were recommended to be the auditing standard. ISO/IEC 27001 is complemented by the implementation guideline within ISO 27002 [53].

4.2 Integrity

Managing IS Integrity is important for a SC to ensure correct decision-making in terms of quality information. Integrity consist of four attributes, i.e. completeness, timeliness, accuracy, and validity of the information managed by IS [8, 54]. This prohibits unauthorised users from modifying even a single bit of contact data to ensure completeness and accuracy [10, 52]. In the IoT, integrity become critical when it comes to changing information in important everyday activities such as medical records, financial transactions, and so on. Therefore, integrity issues will become crucial. The non-repudiation element was discovered to affect the integrity dimension.

i. Non-repudiation: Non-repudiation is described as verification behaviour of a system, whether or not an incident has occurred. It to avoids things from refuse. The policy on the occurrence of events must be strictly applied [10, 52]. Non-repudiation in the IoT scenario ensures that the sensor can not deny sending the message to other nodes requesting or experience the message from another node in the network.

4.3 Interoperability

Other impacted IS security management is interoperability. Interoperability is the ability of the IS to facilitate the exchange of information, and knowledge sharing business processes [11]. An organisation must be able to efficiently communicate and move data by using various IS in terms of infrastructure, geographical area and culture [55]. Interoperability is complex in its many aspects including layers and governance. This contains multiple stakeholders, perspectives, norms, and principles which are different. Solutions to complex problems request an extra exploratory, experimental, and reflexive approach [56]. Simultaneously, the readiness of organisations to use IoT technology is still low and needs an interconnected link between various devices, services and applications due to the use of various IS provider technologies. This study proposed the risk evaluation and technology as elements affecting IS security control for IoT in SC.

i. Risk Assessment: This means to identify, estimate, and prioritise risks to SC operational, organisational and individuals, resulting from IoT in IS. The risk analysis of IoT is performed by identifying the assets, threats, and vulnerabilities [3, 28]. The identified risks were then analysed to classify the IS and IoT security objectives of the city authorities.
ii. Technology: Technology need a series of information security technology to perform security protection of the physical environment, network transmission, host system, data resources, and application services in an SC [21, 22]. The SC relies solely on technology to provide people with improved systems for smarter economic development, smarter governance, and more intelligent services through integrated and up-to-date technology [33].

4.4 Personalisation

The services are given in a unique and precise way, depending on the application and the individual needs [11]. Thus, the personal information of individual is becoming vulnerable to attacks. This study uses confidentiality, privacy, authentication, authorisation and control of access to represent an aspect of personalisation.

i. Confidentiality: Confidentiality refers to ensuring that the information is accessed only by approved users and that the information must be transmitted confidentially from sensor systems to storage [10, 52]. Devices gather different confidential user information in IoT. Unknown users can then monitor the identity and specifics of the information. Different symmetric and asymmetric encryption algorithms will achieve confidentiality. There are resource-constrained tools for the IoT, and attackers can use various algorithms such as Elliptic curve cryptography-based encryption algorithms [10].

ii. Privacy: Privacy can be described as 'not even a single bit of a person's information will be released to someone else without the owner's permission.' In the IoT, most sensors that are part of public services collect personal information, but to whom personal information should be shared, the owner will determine [10]. Individuals in an SC use different services and communicate through the latest technology linked through various networks and systems, which are the target of hackers who intend to interfere with their individual privacy and deprive them of their personal rights. The privacy concerns with public networking rely on the individual's level, the recipients' recognition of the information supplied and how it can be used [33].

iii. Authentication: Authentication requires the exchange of communications between the parties using the authenticated equivalents. An effective authentication system ensures information is secure, accurate, and accessible. IoT authentication becomes important because of the variability in the number of devices involved [57]. Each device transmits data or requires access to other devices, so user must authenticate to obtain access from the sensors. Authentication is challenging since it typically needs adequate authentication infrastructures and servers that achieve their goal by exchanging messages among the nodes.

iv. Authorisation: Authorisation is to guarantee access to the information that is controlled by authorising only legitimate users. It is linked to the permission of the users or IoT devices to access confidential information in a SC area. Authentication would allow approved users to access the data[6]. For instance, in Amazon Web Services IoT, the authorisation is policy-based and can be implemented by matching authored rules and policies. This requires that only devices or applications listed within these rules may have access to the system [58].

v. Access control: Only authorised users or devices are able to access data and devices from other individuals [57]. IS protection management must make sure information is correct by preventing unauthorised users from changing the information. Access control may be split into two groups which are organisation's internal members and external members or third parties. For internal members, only designated workers with established positions may access sensitive information. Although access to third parties should be based on a structured contract which includes a general security policy, service description should be made accessible with physical and logical access control [14].

4.5 Self-organisation

IoT technology enables the acquisition, processing and dissemination, without human intervention, of personal information. Information system interaction is computerized via machine-to-machine (M2M) without having to wait for individual directions [18, 24, 31]. M2M procedures will be applied to set interaction rules for at least two network nodes for M2M communication. The Internet Protocol (IP) has come to be the standard for interaction reasons [33]. It is also vulnerable to hacking despite a rise in productivity. Integrating to more computers adds to the vulnerabilities. This research identified two elements in the self-organising dimension which influence IS security management for IoT in SC.

i. Trust: Trust can be described as maintaining full faith and confidentiality of the services and information accepted by the people and devices involved in the IoT system [52]. Trust protection requires accurate data collection, secure combination of data and processing, and improved privacy for users. IS must being accurate on the data in real time [59]. Effective IS security trust will ensure IoT services are of high quality.
ii. Availability: This relates to the guarantee that, when requested by an authorised user, all facilities are accessible and run in the complete system without fail [10, 52]. Safety availability can be ensured by adequate resources if it is necessary to use parallel availability of resources if any other fails.

5 Conclusions

Many IoT tools or information could be uncovered to information safety risks and weaknesses. It will become an obstacle for the development of secure IoT ecosystems if it does not possess adequate protection. However, the IS security investigation using IoT in SC is more focused on the technical perspective, while the management side has not been sufficiently investigated. Selected security frameworks covering IS were presented and compared by using IoT in SC and established the knowledge of important concepts for managing IS security in IoT towards SC development. Thus, the huge literature review and comparison of seven different frameworks had been verified. As a result, the proposed conceptual framework of IS security management for IoT-enable SC was created based on the five dimensions for handling IS security for IoT in SC consisting of governance, integrity, interoperability, personalisation, and self-organisation. These dimensions will become a dimension for IS security management for an IoT-enabled SC. Each identified dimension is illustrated in Fig. 8.

Future work is already scheduled for constructing a comprehensive framework and validation based on the empirical work of this study. The outcome will guide SC authorities and agencies that were created for service delivery to improve their IS security management in an IoT-enabled SC.

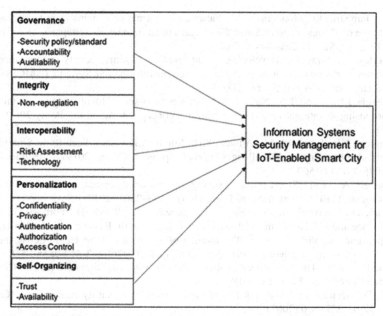

Fig. 8. Conceptual framework for information system security management for Internet of Things (IoT)-enable smart cities. Source: [7].

Acknowledgements. This study is supported by the Fundamental Research Grant Scheme (FRGS/1/2019/ICT04/UKM/03/2), 2019, Malaysian Ministry of Education, and The National University of Malaysia.

References

1. Yigitcanlar, T., Kamruzzaman, M.: Does smart city policy lead to sustainability of cities? Land Use Policy **73**, 49–58 (2018)
2. Muvuna, J., Boutaleb, T., Mickovski, S.B., Baker, K.J.: Systems engineering approach to design and modelling of smart cities. In: 2016 International Conference for Students on Applied Engineering ICSAE 2016, pp. 437–440 (2017)
3. Irshad, M.: A systematic review of information security frameworks in the Internet of Things (IoT). In: Proceedings - 18th IEEE International Conference on High Performance Computing and Communications. 14th IEEE International Conference on Smart City. 2nd IEEE International Conference on Data Science and Systems HPCC/SmartCity/DSS 2016, pp. 1270–1275 (2017)
4. Nuttall, N.: The evolution of IoT and its impact on adopters and technology providers: a Gartner Trend Insight Report. Stamford USA (2018)
5. Ganguli, S., Friedman, T.: IoT technology disruptions : a Gartner trend Insight Report. Stamford USA (2017)
6. Witti, M., Konstantas, D.: A secure and privacy-preserving Internet of Things framework for Smart City. In: ICIT, pp. 145–150 (2019)

7. Din, Z., Jambari, D.I., Mohd Yusof, M., Yahaya, J.: Information systems security management for Internet of Things : enabled Smart Cities conceptual framework. scitepress – Sci. Technol. Publ. Lda, No. Smartgreens 44–51 (2020)
8. Dunkerley, K., Tejay, G.: Developing an information systems security success model for eGovernment context. In: American Conference on Information Systems (AMCIS) 2009 Proceedings. vol. 346., pp. 59–60 (2009)
9. Gil-Garcia, J.R., Pardo, T.A., Nam, T.: What makes a city smart? Identifying core components and proposing an integrative and comprehensive conceptualization. Inf. Polity **20**(1), 61–87 (2015)
10. Hassanien, A.E., Elhoseny, M., Ahmed, S.H., Singh, A.K. (eds.): Security in Smart Cities: Models, Applications, and Challenges. LNITI, Springer, Cham (2019). https://doi.org/10.1007/978-3-030-01560-2
11. Gharaibeh, A., et al.: Smart cities: a survey on data management, security, and enabling technologies. IEEE Commun. Surv. Tutor. **19**(4), 2456–2501 (2017)
12. Zedadra, O., Guerrieri, A., Jouandeau, N., Spezzano, G., Seridi, H., Fortino, G.: Swarm intelligence and IoT-based smart cities: a review. In: Cicirelli, F., Guerrieri, A., Mastroianni, C., Spezzano, G., Vinci, A. (eds.) The Internet of Things for Smart Urban Ecosystems. IT, pp. 177–200. Springer, Cham (2019). https://doi.org/10.1007/978-3-319-96550-5_8
13. Ruhlandt, R.W.S.: The governance of smart cities: a systematic literature review. Cities Int. J. Urban Policy Plan. **81**, 1–23 (2018)
14. Trček, D.: An integral framework for information systems security management. Comput. Secur. **22**(4), 337–360 (2003)
15. Theodorou, S., Sklavos, N.: Chapter 3 - blockchain-based security and privacy in smart cities. Smart Cities Cybersecurity and Privacy, pp. 21–37. Elsevier, Greece (2019)
16. Whitmore, A., Agarwal, A., Da Xu, L.: The internet of things—a survey of topics and trends. Inf. Syst. Front. **17**(2), 261–274 (2014). https://doi.org/10.1007/s10796-014-9489-2
17. Laudon, K.C., Laudon, J.P.: Management Information Systems : Managing The Digital Firm, 15th edn. Pearson Education Limited, London (2018)
18. Lam, P.T.I., Ma, R.: Potential pitfalls in the development of smart cities and mitigation measures: an exploratory study. Cities **91**, 146–156 (2018)
19. Bull, R., Azennoud, M.: Smart citizens for smart cities: Participating in the future. In: Proceedings of the Institution of Civil Engineers – Energy, vol. 169, no. 3, pp. 93–101 (2016)
20. Gichoya, D.: Factors affecting the successful implementation of ICT project in government. Electron. J. E Gov. **3**(4), 175–184 (2005)
21. Harrison, C., et al.: Foundations for smarter cities. IBM J. Res. Dev. **54**(4), 1–16 (2010)
22. Nam, T., Pardo, T.A.: Conceptualizing smart city with dimensions of technology, people, and institutions. In: Proceedings of the 12th Annual International Conference on Digital Government Research, vol. 12, pp. 282–291 (2011)
23. Giffinger, R., Fertner, C., Kramar, H., Meijers, E.: City-ranking of European medium-sized cities 2007. http://www.smartcity-ranking.eu/download/city_ranking_final.pdf. Accessed: 15 Jan 2019
24. Mohammeda, Z.K.A., Ahmed, E.S.A.: Internet of Things applications, challenges and related future technologies. World Sci. News. **67**(2), 126–148 (2017)
25. Moreno, M.V., et al.: Applicability of big data techniques to smart cities deployments. IEEE Trans. Ind. Inf. **13**(2), 800–809 (2017)
26. Arasteh, H., et al.: IoT-based smart cities: a survey. In: EEEIC 2016 - International Conference on Environment and Electrical Engineering (2016)
27. Ferraz, F.S., Ferraz, C.A.G.: Smart city security issues: depicting information security issues in the role of an urban environment (2014)
28. Dong, N., Zhao, J., Yuan, L., Kong, Y.: Research on information security system of smart city based on information security requirements. J. Phys. Conf. Ser. 1069(1) (2018)

29. Elmaghraby, A.S., Losavio, M.M.: Cyber security challenges in smart cities: safety, security and privacy. J. Adv. Res. **5**(4), 491–497 (2014)
30. Aldairi, A., Tawalbeh, L.: Cyber security attacks on smart cities and associated mobile technologies. Procedia Comput. Sci. **109**, 1086–1091 (2017)
31. Sung, T.K.: Industry 4.0: a Korea perspective. Technol. Forecast. Soc. Change **132**, 40–45 (2018)
32. Mohanty, S.P., Choppali, U., Kougianos, E.: Everything you wanted to know about smart cities. IEEE Consum. Electron. Mag. **5**(3), 60–70 (2016)
33. Ijaz, S., Ali, M., Khan, A., Ahmed, M.: Smart cities: a survey on security concerns. Int. J. Adv. Comput. Sci. Appl. 7(2) (2016)
34. Abouzakhar, N.S.: Critical infrastructure cybersecurity: a review of recent threats and violations. In: 12th European Conference on Cyber Warfare and Security. Semantic. Transformational Smart Cities Cyber Security Resilience, pp. 1–11 (2013)
35. Solanas, A., et al.: Smart health: a context-aware health paradigm within smart cities. IEEE Commun. Mag. **52**(8), 74–81 (2014)
36. Pan, G., Qi, G., Zhang, W., Li, S., Wu, Z., Yang, L.: Trace analysis and mining for smart cities: issues, methods, and applications. IEEE Commun. Mag. **51**(6), 120–126 (2013)
37. Leavitt, N.: Mobile security: finally a serious problem? Comput. **44**(6), 11–14 (2011)
38. Martínez-ballesté, A., Pérez-martínez, P.A., Solanas, A.: The pursuit of citizens' privacy: a privacy-aware smart city is possible. IEEE Commun. Mag. **51**(6), 136–141 (2013)
39. Gross, R., Acquisti, A., Heinz, H.J.: Information revelation and privacy in online social networks. In: WPES'05 Proceedings of the 2005 ACM Workshop on Privacy in the Electronic Society, pp. 71–80 (2005)
40. Wahab, M.A., Jambari, D.I.: Service level agreement parameters for drafting public sector information system contract. J. Pengur. **52**, 153–167 (2018)
41. Mah, P.: Lessons from the Singapore exchange failure. Singapore Exchange Board Committee of Inquiry (2015)
42. Bharat, V., Shubham, S., Jagdish, D., Amol, P., Renuka, K.: Smart water management system in cities. In: Proceedings 2017 International Conference on Big Data Analytics and Computational Intelligence ICBDACI 2017, pp. 267–271 (2017)
43. Zou, X., Cao, J., Guo, Q., Wen, T.: A novel network security algorithm based on improved support vector machine from smart city perspective. Comput. Electr. Eng. **65**(3), 67–78 (2018)
44. Klonari, V., Toubeau, J.-F., Lobry, J., Vallée, F.: Photovoltaic Integration in Smart City Power Distribution. In: 2016 5th International Conference on Smart Cities and Green ICT Systems, pp. 166–178 (2016)
45. Zhang, K., Ni, J., Yang, K., Liang, X., Ren, J., Shen, X.S.: Security and privacy in smart city applications: challenges and solutions. (2017)
46. Kuruwitaarachchi, N., Abeygunawardena, P.K.W., Rupasingha, L., Udara, S.W.I.: A systematic review of security in electronic commerce-threats and frameworks. Glob. J. Comput. Sci. Technol. **19**(1), 33–39 (2019)
47. Vucinic, M., Tourancheau, B., Rousseau, F., Duda, A., Damon, L., Guizzetti, R.: OSCAR: object security architecture for the Internet of Things. Ad Hoc Netw. **11**(12), 1–14 (2014)
48. Rathod, D., Patil, S.: Security analysis of Constrained Application Protocol (CoAP): IoT Protocol. Int. J. Adv. Stud. Comput. Sci. Eng. **6**(8), 37–41 (2017)
49. Rahman, R.A., Shah, B.: Security analysis of IoT protocols: A focus in CoAP. In: 2016 3rd MEC International Conference on Big Data and Smart City, ICBDSC 2016, pp. 172–178 (2016)
50. Icon Labs.: Floodgate Security Framework | Icon Labs. Icon Labs, 2019. http://www.iconlabs.com/prod/product-family/floodgate-security-framework. Accessed 12 May 2019

51. Cisco: Securing the Internet of Things: A proposed framework - Cisco. CISCO, 2013. http://www.cisco.com/c/en/us/about/security-center/secure-iot-proposed-framework.html. Accessed 12 May 2019
52. Nia, A.M., Jha, N.K.: A comprehensive study of security of IoT. IEEE Trans. Emerg. Top. Comput. **6750**, 1–19 (2016)
53. ISO IEC 27001: ISO/IEC 27001 2013, pp. 1–30 Switzerland (2013)
54. Flowerday, S., von Solms, R.: Real-time information integrity = system integrity + data integrity + continuous assurances. Comput. Secur. **24**(8), 604–613 (2005)
55. van der Veer, H., Wiles, A.: Achieving technical interoperability. France (2008)
56. Kouroubali, A., Katehakis, D.G.: The new European interoperability framework as a facilitator of digital transformation for citizen empowerment. J. Biomed. Inform. **94**, 103166 (2019)
57. Liu, J., Xiao, Y., Chen, C.L.P.: Internet of things' authentication and access control. Int. J. Secur. Netw. **7**(4), 18–21 (2012)
58. Ammar, M., Russello, G., Crispo, B.: Internet of Things: a survey on the security of IoT frameworks. J. Inf. Secur. Appl. **38**, 8–27 (2018)
59. Shwe, H.Y., Jet, T.K., Chong, P.H.J.: An IoT-oriented data storage framework in smart city applications. In: 2016 International Conference on Information and Communication Technology Convergence ICTC, pp. 106–108 (2016)

Comparison of Energy Performance Metrics of Photovoltaics Using IPAT Sustainability Model

T. J. Abodunrin[1]([✉]) [iD], M. E. Emetere[1], and O. O. Ajayi[2]

[1] Department of Physics, Covenant University, P.M.B. 1023, Ota, Nigeria
temitope.abodunrin@covenantuniversity.edu.ng
[2] Department of Mechanical Engineering, Covenant University, P.M.B. 1023, Ota, Nigeria

Abstract. Energy security is an imminent problem since natural crude oil resources seem to have maintained a production peak in most recent years, inclusive of expected further discoveries. It is therefore imperative that, alternative energy sources contribute to existing grid. Global greenhouse gas (GHG) emissions which have also risen as a consequent of fossil sources need to be checked to curtail their negative externality. In this work, IPAT (I = P x A x T) is used as an investigation tool for photovoltaic prone solution to energy crisis, owing to its pragmatism and uncomplicatedness. This is in with a view of providing some insights or circumventing environmental hazards resulting from the use of toxic materials in the process of manufacturing photovoltaic technology.

1 Introduction

Environmentally benign resources are the vital future for approval of the right support and economic development required for increased life expectancy [1]. The ultimate price for industrialization has been, exploitation of resources, gaseous pollutants, indiscriminate wastewater discharge and solid wastes [2–4]. A vicious cycle therefore exists, it necessitates striking a balance between increasing income and better quality of life in both developing and developed countries, as both entail the employment of more natural resources [5]. All of the unprecedented expansion we have witnessed in this decade; enlargement of numerous industrial sectors, are consequent of severe resource extraction and consumption, raising growing concern over public health [6]. This study examines emergy analysis on IPAT perspective; Photovoltaic-Impact, Population, Affluence and Technology equation to elucidate the affiliation between photovoltaic- population dynamics, human well-being and competing energy consumption uses. In this paper, temporal analysis is used to uncover the driving forces, of our proposed econometric forecasting technique based on three central themes revolving around national wealth, population, and technological development in the application of photovoltaics respectively [7]. Quite a lot of related research has ensued under the same driving forces centered on changing landscapes, hydrological resources and GHG emissions under climatic change impact [8–10]. Under such circumstances, several models were employed to evaluate emergy analysis for proper sustainable development strategies. Research

© Springer Nature Switzerland AG 2021
C. Klein et al. (Eds.): SMARTGREENS 2020/VEHITS 2020, CCIS 1475, pp. 93–101, 2021.
https://doi.org/10.1007/978-3-030-89170-1_5

models reflected a tendency to decompose from monocrystalline silicon solar cells to a macrocosm of bio-compatible options, influencing emergy factors based on actual relationship between population, economy, technology and the environment [11–13]. The future research order requires maintenance of the energy balance in this scenario, considering that in real time, mobilization bias requirement of 1.5 planets is currently required for Earth's sustenance-a somewhat surreal solution [15]. A prognostic approach resides in the appropriate use of technology, whose performance efficiency can significantly lessen throughput and consequently, offset the effects of industrial growth, using photovoltaic population and energy consumption. Thus, IPAT formulation prescribes simple views, hereby de-limiting growth from system perspectives; consumption of non-renewable natural resources population, photovoltaic production, pollution, and global health issues. The system analysis identifies that a crucial further ingredient to sustainability is aggregate of carbon intensity in the economy as the 'emergy–health balance' [13–15]. Consequently, based on specific technological assessments, climate impacts are likely to continue to grow not solely attributable to new GHGs but largely due to the inertia in the climate system and mankind's past energy choices. Future climatic indexes will definitely tilt towards demographic changes and decadal changes owing to present stock of physical photovoltaic infrastructure, as this study indicates.

2   Materials and Method

Stoichiometric quantities of C.papaya, P.dulcis and C.longa plants dried extract were milled, and mixed in ratio 1:1 methanol proportion. This was constituted into a slurry comprising of a suspension of three separate dye extracts with conc. nitric acid additive placed on a glass substrate. The slurry spread on the substrate to form a thin layered sheet upon drying. A continuous relative movement between the blade and the substrate established the doctor blade, the speed of operation was 0.024 ms^{-1}. This sweeping process was continued until a coat substrate range of wet film thicknesses of 100 microns was obtained. The same process was repeated for each of three separate titanium frameworks assembled on the indium doped (ITO) conducting slides following standard procedures described in previous researches for photoanode preparation [16, 17]. High temperature sintering of the photoanode was carried out to create a strong framework for articulation with other dye solar cell components. A counter electrode with same ITO dimensions as the photoanode was prepared by using platinum-free deposition of conformal soot coat over a naked blue Bunsen flame, inside a low-pressure chamber. Consequently, an assemblage comprising of a photoanode and counter electrode was secured together with clasps, 2 ml hypodermic needles were used to insert three drops of aqueous electrolyte in-between the resulting ITO sandwich. Excess electrolyte seeped through the interface but was noted for any substantial effect on energy-environmental balance. Three units of ITO were connected in turn in parallel to a variable load, digital multimeter with the multi-flex wires to obtain photovoltaic parameters. Photovoltaic parameters such as open circuit voltage V(oc), short circuit (Isc), fill factor (ff), maximum power (Pmax) and efficiency were obtained from the experimental set-up. This apparatus was taken outdoors for readings under standard airmass conditions of 1 atmosphere. The indoor air quality on introduction of concentrated nitric acid into the slurry mixture, calcination and kinematics of reaction were determined by assigned values relevant to IPAT analysis. Phytochemical screening of the extracts identified the chromophores present in each dye and were values based on their effect in charge transport and environmental diffusion and reaction times [18, 19]. Ultraviolet-Visible spectroscopy of each dye was used in this study to gauge peak absorbances and their effect in specific regions of the electromagnetic spectrum and possible discharges into the environment. Elemental composition of these specimens was given by scanning electron microscopy where the energy dispersive spectrum was used to model vital statistics for computation of IPAT values.

3 Results and Discussion

3.1 Phytochemical Screening

The Impact (I) will be evaluated using presence or absence of definite chromophores which influences the population of charges involved in charge transport as illustrated by Table 1.

Table 1. Phytochemical results of the three Organic Extracts.

	Ch	Ta	Sa	Fl	Al	Qu	Gl	Ca	Te	Ph	St
C.papaya	1	0	1	1	1	0	0	1	0	1	0
P.dulcis	0	1	1	1	1	0	0	1	0	1	0
C.longa	1	0	1	1	1	0	0	1	0	0	0

Legend: Al-(Alkaloid), Ca- (Cardiac Glycoside), Ch-(CHO), Fl-(Flavonoid), Gl- (Glycoside), Ph-(Phenol), Qu-(Quinone), Sa-(Saponin), St-(Steroid), Ta-(Tannin), Te-(Terpenoid). 1 represents presence, 0 means absence of a chromophore

3.1.1 The Impact and Population (P) of C.Papaya and P.Dulcis Are Both Assigned Values Equal to 6 While C.Longa Has 5, Adapting IPAT Equation Transforms to Eqs. 1–4 and Fig. 1 [13]

$$I_n = P_n \times A_n \times T_n \tag{1}$$

$$= P_0(1 + P)^3 \times A_0(1 + a)^3 \times T_0(1 - t)^3 \tag{2}$$

$$= I_0[(1 + P)(1 + a)(1 - t)]^3 \tag{3}$$

$$I = D \times T \tag{4}$$

Where D represents demand and T is total consumption.

3.1.2 Impact (I) of Ultraviolet-Visible Spectroscopy of Organic Photovoltaics

P.dulcis and C.papaya record their peak absorbance within the visible region, the values are 0.404 and 0.254 a.u respectively. They both exhibit negative eternality of 0.066 and 0.089 respectively, the implication is that, since absorbance can only have positive

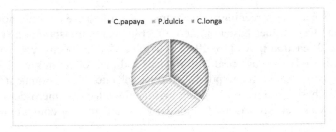

Fig. 1. Composition of chromophores used in photovoltaic charge transport.

values defined as the natural logarithm of the ratio of incident and transmitted light intensities i.e. I_0/I_t. A negative value implies a log function less than 1, which is at variance with Lambert-Beer law. For in that case, the incident light intensity < transmitted light intensity. Nevertheless, inserting this negative value into the equation gives a positive concentration value. This is corroborated by C.longa showing the highest absorbance of 1.824 a.u but, this is in the ultraviolet region as illustrated by Figs. 2, 3 and 4 respectively. Thus, the absorbances would be rated for their intrinsic value, the signs would be disregarded with respect to this IPAT analysis.

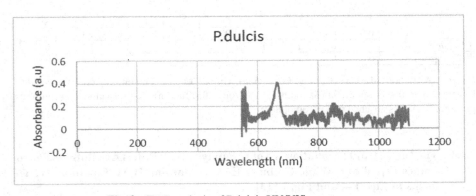

Fig. 2. IPAT analysis of P.dulcis UV/VIS spectroscopy.

3.2 Assessing IPAT Population (P) and Affluence (a)

This will be assessed following the region of absorption multiplied by the absorbance units, buttressed by Table 2. Rapid population and gross domestic product offsets use of energy due to improvement of technology. IPAT Population theme will be addressed from perspective of first, second and third World Countries, first world countries are characterized by relatively clean technologies and stable population, but the problem here is affluence (A_1). Second World Countries have very minimal affluence but dirty technologies (T_2), and at times population (P_2). Third World Countries have little affluence, some dirty technology and high population (P_3). This can be re-written as Eqs. 5–8, [19]:

$$\text{First Countries}: (1 + P)(1 + a)(1 + t) > 1 \tag{5}$$

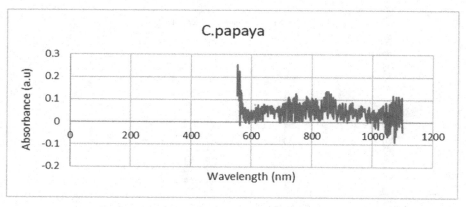

Fig. 3. IPAT analysis of C.papaya UV/VIS spectroscopy.

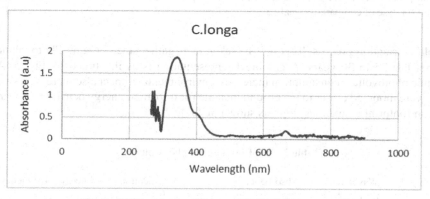

Fig. 4. IPAT analysis of C.longa UV/VIS spectroscopy.

$$\text{Second Countries}: (1 + P)(1 + a)(1 - t) = 1 \qquad (6)$$

$$\text{Third Countries}: (1 + P)(1 + a)(1 - t) < 1 \qquad (7)$$

$$D = P \times A \qquad (8)$$

Where P stands for population of photovoltaics, this is relative to human population and A represents affluence.

3.2.1 Impact of Externality Factor Organic Photovoltaics Using Technology (T)

The externality of organic photovoltaics is classified into the positive factor based on the advantage of reduced CO_2 emissions. The impact of manufacturing CO_2 is dependent upon energy return of organic Photovoltaics ERoEI which diverges from 0–1, because of the high temperature sintering and other input and output factors investment to the

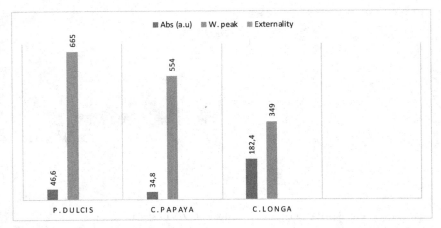

Fig. 5. Externality FACTOR of UV/Vis of organic photovoltaics. Note: abs*100 values were plotted for ease of comparative analysis.

whole fabrication process. This will be taken as negative since organic Photovoltaics do not last 25 to 30 years. A graphical representation is as illustrated by Fig. 5. As organic photovoltaic consumption increases, environmental impact also increases, since they were mounted closer to the ground than the rooftop, their energy density is low and carbon footprint is relatively high as shown in Table 2.

Table 2. ERoEI of organic photovoltaics.

	Wavelength Peak (nm)	Absorbance (a.u)	Degradation	Energy Efficiency (%)
P.dulcis	665	0.404	5	20
C.papaya	554	0.254	5	10
C.longa	349	1.824	10	40

Degradation is on a scale: 1–10, scale 10 depicts highest degree of degradation, ultraviolet radiation degrades faster than visible light.

The ERoEI of C.longa has the highest value of 30–40% while, P.dulcis has the least. The energy efficiency (E.E) is greater than the degradation value and lie within 20–30% and 10–20% respectively, as shown in Fig. 6.

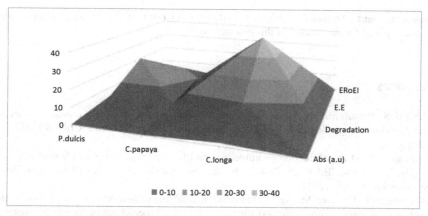

Fig. 6. Bi-pyramidal energy flux of organic photovoltaics EroEI.

3.2.2 Impact of Energy Dispersive Spectrum (EDS) of Organic Photovoltaics on Technology (T)

Choice of technology can either enhance or harm the environment, manufacturing of the organic photovoltaics required high temperature, addition of toxic chemicals, such as concentrated nitric acid and volatile electrolytic liquids as electrolytes which eventually contributes to waste on expiration. Indium is moderately toxic to humans when ingested through direct inhalation, this was observed in P.dulcis extract as shown in Fig. 7. Chlorine is corrosive and gas which causes irritation to the respiratory tract and eyes. Applying Eq. 4 to EDS (I) = Wt (%) x σ.

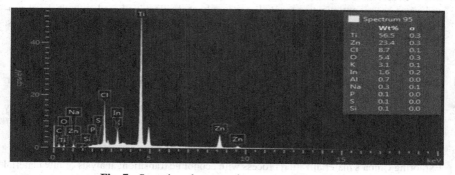

Fig. 7. Scanning electron microscopy of Dye Slurry.

4 Conclusion

The IPAT modelling shows that discarding harmful materials may not be feasible but, emergy defines the transitional processes which may nullify their toxic effect.

Acknowledgement. The authors are grateful to Covenant University for providing an appropriate ambience required for the success of this research work.

References

1. Abdoli, S., Pamulapati, M., Kara, S.: An investigation into the role of PV industry in meeting the growing energy demand towards absolute sustainability. Procedia CIRP **90**, 383–387 (2020)
2. Fthenakis, V., et al.: Methodology guidelines on life cycle assessment of photovoltaic electricity, 2nd edition, IEA PVPS Task 12. In: International Energy Agency Photovoltaic Power systems Programme (2011)
3. Abodunrin, T., Emetere, M., Ajayi, O.: Environmental impact assessment (eia) of ph and other factors on organic photovoltaic performance output. In: Proceedings of the 9th International Conference on Smart Cities and Green Energy (2020)
4. UNESCAP, ADB and UNEP, Green growth, resources and resilience: environmental sustainability in Asia and the Pacific. 978–92–1–120635–7, United Nations and Asian Development Bank Publication, Bangkok. ST/ESCAP/2600, RPT124260 (2012)
5. Song, M., Wang, S., Yu, H., Yang, L., Wu, J.: To reduce energy consumption and to maintain rapid economic growth: analysis of the condition in China based on expended IPAT model. Renew. Sustain. Energy Rev. **15**(9), 5129–5134 (2011)
6. Cui, Z., Liu, X.: Urban building energy consumption forecast based on the IPAT theory. Adv. Mater. Res. **689**, 482–486 (2013)
7. Liu, G., Ming, W.U., Jia, F., Fan, X., Dong, H.: IPAT-based analysis/forecast of water consumption for a city. J. Liaoning Shihua Univ. **1**, 5–8 (2014)
8. Wang, Q., Li, S., Li, R.: Forecasting energy demand in China and India: using single-linear, hybrid-linear, and non-linear time series forecast techniques. Energy **161**, 821–831 (2018)
9. Chen, Y., He, L., Guan, Y., Lu, H., Li, J.: Life cycle assessment of greenhouse gas emissions and water-energy optimization for shale gas supply chain planning based on multi-level approach: case study in Barnett, Marcellus, Fayetteville, and Haynesville shales. Energy Convers. Manag. **134**, 382–398 (2017)
10. Turner, G.M.: Energy shocks and emerging alternative technologies. Aust. J. Int. Affairs **66**(5), 606–621 (2011)
11. Victor, P.A.: Managing without Growth: Slower by Design, Not Disaster. Edward Elgar, Cheltenham, UK (2008)
12. Gan, Y., Zhang, T.Z., Liang, S., Zhao, Z.G., Li, N.: How to deal with resource productivity relationships between socioeconomic factors and resource productivity. J. Ind. Ecol. **17**(3), 440–451 (2013)
13. Wang, H.M., Tian, X., Tanikawa, H., Chang, M., Hashimoto, S., Moriguchi, Y., et al.: Exploring China's materialization process with economic transition: analysis of raw material consumption and its socioeconomic drivers. Environ. Sci. Technol. **48**(9), 5025–5032 (2014)
14. Ding, G.K.: Sustainable construction—the role of environmental assessment tools. J. Environ. Manag. **86**(3), 451–464 (2008)
15. Gan, Y., Zhang, T.Z., Liang, S., Zhao, Z.G., Li, N.: How to deal with resource productivity relationships between socioeconomic factors and resource productivity. J. Ind. Ecol. **17**(3), 440–451 (2013)
16. Abodunrin, T.J., Emetere, M.E., Ajayi, O.O., Uyor, U.O., Popoola, O.: Investigating the prospect of micro-energy generation in S. Anisatum Dyesensitized solar cells (DSCs). J. Phys. Conf. Ser. **1299**(1), 012028 (2019)

17. Abodunrin, T.J., Boyo, A.O., Usikalu, M.R., Ajayi, O.O.: Investigation of effect of batch-separation on the micro-energy generation in M.indica L. dye-sensitized solar cells. Procedia Manuf. **35**, 1273–1278 (2019)
18. Abodunrin, T.J., Boyo, A.O., Usikalu, M.R., Emetere, M.E.: Investigating the Influence of Selective Co sensitization of Two N719 Dyes on the Micro-Energy Generation from Dye-sensitized Solar Cells. J. Phys. Conf. Ser. **1299**(1), 012027 (2019)
19. Hosenuzzaman, M.: Global prospects, progress, policies, and environmental impact of solar photovoltaic power generation. Renew. Sust. Energ. Rev. **41**, 284–297 (2015)

Analysis of Software Defined WSN and Related Network Re-orchestration Down-Time

Indrajit S. Acharyya$^{(\boxtimes)}$ and Adnan Al-Anbuky

Sensor Network and Smart Environment Research Centre, Auckland University of Technology, Auckland, New Zealand
iarchary@aut.ac.nz

Abstract. Re-orchestration is a crucial operational requirement secured by Software-Defined Wireless Sensor Networks (SDWSN). Herein, WSN flexibility involves functional identification, definition, modularization, and virtualization. These components support sensor network software-control and allow for dynamically redefining the network topology and operational behavior. This paper reflects the core ideology behind the proposed cloud-based cyber-physical organizational structure. This utilizes the virtualization and testing of the functionalities that edge towards desired re-orchestrations. The physical implementation of re-orchestration process, however, may cause network operational disruption for a brief period of time. This research work reflects the parameters involved in network re-orchestration process. Analysis of an example performance indicator that influences the downtime in SDWSN during re-orchestration is offered. Clarity of these involvements can offer significant help in supporting planning for reducing this 'down time'.

Keyword: SDWSN · Network virtualization · Re-orchestration latency

1 Introduction

Re-orchestration of wireless sensor network organizations tends is a key requirement for reflexive adaptation towards dynamic service demands [1–6]. A system solution involving operation of a 'Software-defined wireless sensor network' (SDWSN) under the aegis of a Cyber-Physical System (CPS) organization serves as a viable approach towards offering support for such operational flexibility in a dynamic manner [1–4, 7–15]. One of the approaches for software redefinition is that of 'Reconfigurability'. Here, the physical devices could be re-configured to certain roles or possibly even assume multiple functional roles simultaneously [3, 4]. The presence of requisite 'logical software modules' residing within the code with which they were initially configured allows for assuming multiple configurable status. This approach requires the 'program' or 'code' (with which the devices are configured) to comprise of requisite conditional statements as well as 'well-defined', 'logical' modules that could be assumed (in accordance with conditional execution within the program) during run-time. Prior to embarking upon establishment of such a 'modular' software defined sensor network, it is deemed imperative to reflect certain essential pre-requisites that could arguably be entailed by such

C. Klein et al. (Eds.): SMARTGREENS 2020/VEHITS 2020, CCIS 1475, pp. 102–119, 2021.
https://doi.org/10.1007/978-3-030-89170-1_6

organizations from a formalization standpoint. These pre-requisites pertain to identification and definition of the integral functional components associated with any sensor network formation, modularization of the functions so identified (based on their definitions) and subsequently paving the way for their virtualization [3, 4].

It is deemed conceivable to assert that any sensor network is composed of the three generic functions viz., 'Gateway', 'Leaf' and 'Routing' [3, 4]. By means of including certain examples of possible topological orientations that a sensor network could resort to (by virtue of SDWSN re-orchestration), a specific portion of the preceding work [4] brings to the fore the integrity of the elementary functionalities in regard to any sensor network organization. The motive behind ensuing upon modularizing and virtualizing of the three key functionalities (so identified and defined) is to render them as re-usable virtual modules that could be subjected to soft-trials within the cloud-hosted virtualization environment. Such virtualization-abetted 're-orchestration planning' could lend itself towards significant expedition of the re-orchestration implementation process. The scope of the re-orchestration implementation process, however, may yet entail a certain amount of latency that could prove to be detrimental to its ongoing processes [3, 4].

The research work documented within the previous work [4] highlighted the ideological basis (along the lines of Industry 4.0) leading to the proposed modular architectural organization for software-defined sensor network. Furthermore (by means of certain example cases of network re-orchestration), it also highlighted the efficacy of a virtual environment towards 'planning' the desired re-orchestrations as well as gaining an insight into the key performance measure of the 'downtime' or latency experienced by the network whilst undergoing re-orchestration. In furtherance to the research work documented within [4], this paper vies to put forth the pseudo codes for each of the core WSN functions, outlining the operational activities associated with each, and thereby attempting to explore how 'software manipulation' of certain of these key network parameters viz., MAC protocol employed, data communication rate, etc. could influence network 're-orchestration downtime'. Besides, certain research work pertaining to network downtime has also been included as part of the literature review herein.

In furtherance to the state-of-the-art pertaining to SDN-facilitated topological re-orchestration of WSNs documented within [4], literature review revolving around the time elapsed as a result of a network undergoing re-orchestration has been considered within this paper. Zhou et al. [16] seek to undertake an approach directed towards effectively eliminating any re-orchestration-induced downtime via partitioning the network into multiple subsets and allowing for each of them to undergo re-orchestration sequentially i.e. one subset at a time. For this purpose, the authors ensue upon formulating the problem of partitioning the sensor network in subsets and proving the same to be 'Non-deterministic polynomial time. Subsequently, heuristics pertaining to downtime free system migration are presented and compared.

Szczodrak et al. [17] propose a 'Fennec Fox', a framework that allows for flexible WSN reconfiguration via offering supporting for different applications that could be dynamically switched to, at different time instants (based on the network service requirements). Each such application is based on separate MAC and network protocol specifications. Network re-orchestrations are brought about by means of broadcasting of 'control messages' amongst the (relevant) nodes in a sort of peer-to-peer fashion. The authors utilize the 'Finite State Model' computation model in a bid to model such re-orchestrations undergone by the network. Based on experimentation conducted, authors mention that adoption of such an approach results in a reconfiguration delay of the order of milliseconds and that it (reconfiguration delay) is dependent on factors such as distance between the nodes, radio-duty cycling, etc. and that as the reconfiguration delay decreases, so does the percentage of the number of nodes that successfully get configured.

2 Main WSN Functional Modules

As alluded to within the earlier section, the three key functions that enable a WSN to perform its tasks satisfactorily pertain to sensing and data acquisition (Sensing function), routing (Router function) and escalation of data aggregated by a sink node (Gateway function) [3, 4]. The core and auxiliary activities associated with each of these three core functions is depicted in Fig. 1 [3, 4].

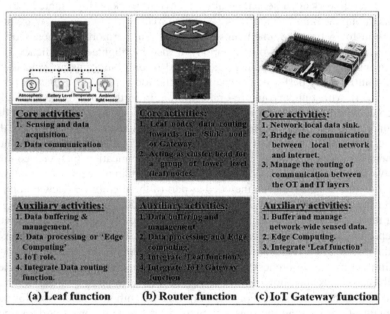

Fig. 1. Core and non-core activities associated with the main WSN functional modules (a) Leaf node function (b) Router node function and (c) IoT-based WSN Gateway node function [3, 4].

Such clear segregation of the main WSN functions on the basis of the unique core activities associated with each of them paves the way for rendering them as reusable modules [3, 4]. Such independent functional modules could be assumed one at a time or simultaneously (provided the hardware employed is able to encompass and execute multiple tasks at the same time. Modern day SoCs-based wireless sensor transceivers are capable of accommodating for edge-computing-based tasks.). These (definition and modularization) pave the way for enhanced flexibility from the node-operational stand-point. Such node-level flexibility may implicate on the flow of data within the network, in some cases altering the topology of a given network (network-level flexibility). In this regard, consider Fig. 2 wherein certain different possible (typical) network topological arrangements are presented [4]. Herein, the CC538 Evaluation Module (EM), along with the Raspberry Pi that have been utilized for implementation purposes within this research have been depicted. Most of the CC2538 EMs have been configured to play the role of leaf nodes whereas a few have been configured to execute the role of routers. The gateway function, however, has been realized by means of employing the Raspberry Pi which acts as protocol converter and escalates the sensed data over to the cloud [3, 4].

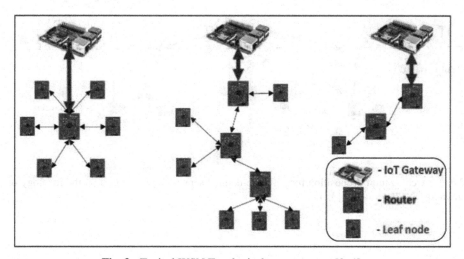

Fig. 2. Typical WSN Topological arrangements [3, 4].

Contiki software (IDE) has been employed for developing and compiling of codes as well as configuration of the physical hardware nodes (using the codes so developed and compiled). By virtue of its network simulator platform of Cooja, Contiki also provisions for network virtualization (since the same codes utilized for hardware nodes can be used to create and/or configure virtual nodes), typically within the cloud server. Besides monitoring of the underlying physical WSN, such a virtualization platform can be availed for soft trialing of numerous re-orchestration scenarios, prior to implementation on the physical network.

3   SDWSN Proposed Architecture

Based on the ideology prescribed by the Industry 4.0 paradigm, the architectural proposition herein consists of two layers viz., 'Operational Technology (i.e. OT)' layer and 'Information Technology (i.e. IT)' layers, as depicted in Fig. 3. The upper layer of IT hosts the three main components of the 'Virtualization unit', 'Data and Knowledge

Repository' and the requisite 'Operational software' that act as facilitators for trialing and figuring out the necessary re-orchestrations to be applied to the lower layer of OT which hosts the physical hardware nodes [3, 4].

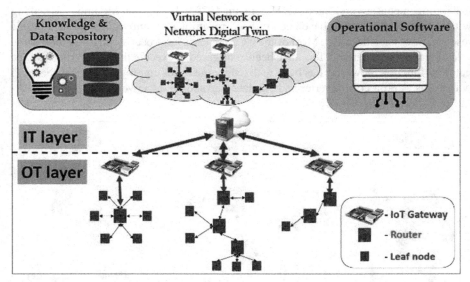

Fig. 3. Architectural proposition for software-defined sensor network based on the ideology of the Industry 4.0 paradigm [3, 4].

3.1 IT Layer

Besides monitoring, the component of virtualization unit facilitates plays a key role towards planning of the suitable re-orchestration scenarios that could be assumed by the underlying physical layer. Such suitable re-orchestrations are attained through running soft trial of re-orchestration scenarios and observing the implications on the network performance for the same. Besides cutting costs, such hardware-independent testing reduces the time required for working out the 'customized' or 'most pertinent' re-orchestrations, allowing for the system to better cope with the real-time re-orchestration service demands [3, 4].

The virtualization unit however, requires interaction with both the OT layer (to fetch the necessary parametric information required for the 'planning' of the 're-orchestrations) as well as with the 'Data and Knowledge Repository' present within the IT layer.

In a bid to assist the process of figuring out of the most suitable re-orchestrations via both augmenting the options of flexibilities available for incorporation as well as storing of re-orchestration solution applied for previous service demands, it was deemed reasonable to establish a single repository consisting of reusable virtual software modules and capable of evolving with historical experiences. Such a repository that could be readily accessed by the virtualization unit whenever required could lend itself towards tackling re-orchestration demands in a time-efficient manner [3, 4].

The 'operational software' unit refers to the requisite tools that allow for the development of the necessary codes pertaining to the network functionalities, as well as the necessary re-orchestration service specific knowledge components. Contiki IDE, for instance has been employed for the purposes of development, compilation, and configuration of codes for both virtual and physical nodes. Besides, software tools as MATLAB that allow for data analytics, data processing, data computation, etc. could also prove to be of vital assistance during the 'Re-orchestration planning' phase [3, 4].

3.2 OT Layer

The 'Operational Technology' (i.e. OT) layer comprises of the physical wireless nodes deployed across the monitored area for capturing real-world data and escalate it to IT layer over the internet [3, 4]. The wireless network formed by these sensor nodes could either be clustered or non-clustered based on the application or 'service requisites. Furthermore, each cluster (or the non-clustered physical WSN as a whole) could be centralized or decentralized. Centralized constituent clusters could be arranged in accordance with star, tree, or mesh topological frameworks (depending upon the application and/or operational requirements) whereas decentralized networks would be arranged in accordance with the mesh topological framework. Depending upon their capability and resourcefulness, codes for (certain advanced) modern day wireless transceivers (such as the Texas Instruments CC2538 SoC) could be written in such a way that they could dynamically configured to switch form their existing role of say, a leaf node to that of a router node (or vice-versa) via directing them to do so by means of an external command (as part of a re-orchestration process). Such modern SoCs could also be similarly re-configured to execute edge-computing based tasks.

4   Example WSN Re-orchestration Scenarios

4.1   WSN Topological Manipulation

An example case of network topological manipulation involving reconfiguring the individual node's functional level so to alter overall network behavior in terms of flow of data within the network [4] has been depicted within this sub-section. Consider Fig. 4a wherein a virtual three-node multi-hop network has been implemented within Cooja. Herein, the data transmitted by the node configured to act as the leaf node. In this case, node 1 reaches node 3 (the Gateway node) via the intermediate node 2 (the router node). The 'network window' and 'mote output' screenshots for the same are depicted within Figs. 5a and 5b respectively.

By means of directing (the intermediate) node acting as a router i.e. node 2 to assume leaf node function and by manipulation of the MAC protocol so as to enable the network to operate as per TDMA scheme, the same three-node network undergoes re-orchestration from the network i.e. topological standpoint and operates as a star topology based network. The 'network window' and 'mote output' screenshots for this star

108   I. S. Acharyya and A. Al-Anbuky

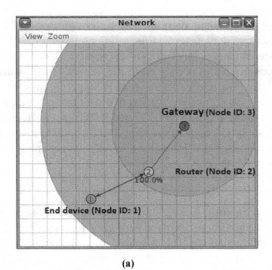

(a)

(b)

Fig. 4. (a) Screenshot of the 'Network window' depicting a 3-node multi-hop network (in operation) within Cooja; (b) Screenshot of the 'Mote output window' obtained from Cooja for the multi-hop network [4].

topological behavior exhibited by the re-orchestrated virtual network are depicted within figures _a and b respectively.

This example case of network re-orchestration performed at the virtual level demonstrates the implications of subjecting a single node within a network, on the overall dataflow or topology of the network in some cases. Such re-orchestrations could prove to be handy towards resolving network fragmentations caused by departure of mobile node beyond the communication range of the gateway. It also aptly implies the efficacy of adopting a software-defined approach (i.e. one involving separation of data plane from

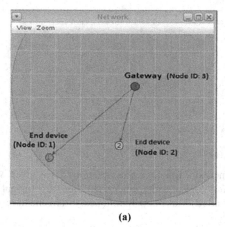

(a)

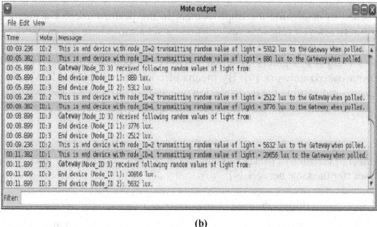

(b)

Fig. 5. (a) Screenshot of the 'Network window' depicting the re-orchestrated 3-node star network (in operation) within Cooja; (b) Screenshot of the re-orchestrated 'Mote output window' obtained from Cooja for the re-orchestrated star network [4].

the control plane) for conduction of soft-trials within a virtualization environment prior to ensuing upon complex network re-orchestrations at the physical level.

4.2 Further Complexity in WSN Re-orchestration Scenarios

WSNs is required to be capable of re-assuming their behavior through re-orchestrating the network through both node functional behavior and network-topological standpoints in order to cope with the dynamic 'service' or 're-orchestration' demands in a satisfactory way. Software-defined network re-orchestrations could pave the way for a host of topological adaptations, as illustrated within Fig. 6. These examples reflect the possible formations through the manipulation of the core functions outlined in our work [4].

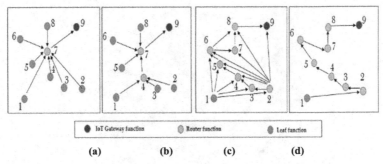

Fig. 6. Typical example network topological adaptations for a given WSN as a result of SD re-orchestration (a) Star Topological arrangement; (b) Tree Topological arrangement, (c) Mesh Topological arrangement and (d) Multi-hop Topological arrangement respectively [4].

As a means to determine the improvement in the performance of a network upon undergoing network re-orchestration, consider a scenario wherein a network, initially configured to operate as a multi-hop network (as depicted in Fig. 6d) is re-orchestrated via software control to operate as a star network (as depicted in Fig. 6a) within the virtual (Cooja-based) network [4]. By means of considering 'packet loss' as a performance measure and varying the transmission rate, the performance of the two topological arrangements are compared. Results of the simulation experiment are presented within Table 1.

Table 1. Effect of variation of packet communication rate on packets lost for multi-hop and star topology cases (for the same network [4]).

Packet communication rate	Packets dropped		
	Star Topology (TDMA)	Star Topology (CSMA)	Multi-hop Topology
1 PPS	0 Packets	0 Packets	0 Packets
5 PPS	0 Packets	0 Packets	3 Packets
10 PPS	0 Packets	0 Packets	5 Packets
15 PPS	0 Packets	0 Packets	8 Packets

From Table 1, it can be seen that as the transmission rate is increased, network tends to lose far fewer packets when operating as 'star' network as opposed to when operating as a multi-hop network. Moreover, implementation of TDMA scheme for the re-orchestrated star network results in no packet losses (at least up to '25' samples per second) whereas four packets are lost for the same when operating under the CSMA scheme.

This simple example too, highlights the significance of conduction of soft trials within the virtual environment to foresee the implications of network re-orchestrations prior to implementation onto the actual hardware nodes present in the physical (OT) layer.

5   WSN Re-orchestration Downtime

The process of sensor network re-orchestration can largely be said to encompass the three separate stages of 'Data Analysis' and 'Event Identification', 'Planning' and finally the 'Implementation or 'Execution'. The latency of the re-orchestration process as well as the actual downtime suffered by the network when undergoing re-orchestration are identified to be important performance measures that necessitate requisite analyses via experimentation [4].

For this purpose, an example case of network fragmentation caused due to departure of a router node was elaborately detailed within [4] and has been briefly discussed here. The virtual representation of the network is as shown in Fig. 7.

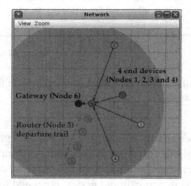

Fig. 7. Virtual representation of a 6-node network due to undergo network re-orchestration (owing to fragmentation caused by departure of router node i.e. node 5) [4].

Based on a dedicated knowledge component set apart for constantly monitoring the 'radio signal strength' between the gateway node and the router node, a trigger is raised during the initial stage of 'Data Analysis' and 'Event Identification'. This results in initiation of the second stage of the re-orchestration process i.e. 'Planning' stage wherein another dedicated knowledge component (as per a suitable fitness model), gathers the requisite information form the underlying layer and determines the most suitable leaf node among all the participant leaf nodes (the ones capable of assuming the functional role of a router and act as a cluster-head for the all remaining leaf nodes). Finally, the 'execution' stage involves the implementation of the 're-orchestrations' foreseen within the 'planning' stage.

Figure 8 below presents the various messages that are exchanged between the nodes for all the three stages of re-orchestration [4].

Based on the results obtained within Cooja, it was found that the actual 'downtime' suffered by the network as a result of the re-orchestration process was equal to that entailed by 'six messages', although the overall re-orchestration process entailed much

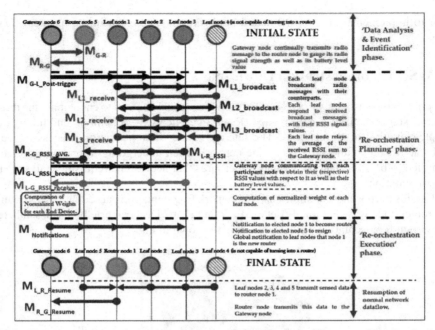

Fig. 8. Messages exchanged among the various constituent nodes of the network during the three stages of network re-orchestration [4].

higher latency. As mentioned in [4], such results tend to be highly relative in nature. For a more accurate estimate of the downtime caused due to re-orchestration, factors such as the MAC protocol implemented, influence of the dynamics of the physical world on the communication amongst the constituent nodes, etc. need to be considered.

6   Example Network Functions Implementation

As a means to offer better elucidation on the three core WSN functionalities of Gateway function, Leaf function and router functions, this section puts forth the pseudo code associated with each of them. These (Contiki-pertinent) Pseudo codes (written specifically in regard to configuration of the Texas Instruments CC2538 microcontroller) outline sample operational activities encompassed by each of the functionalities in a logical way, thereby laying the ground for the functional execution of each, as a whole. While each of the operational activities specified within the three pseudo codes expressed within the subsequent sub-sections can be tweaked as desired via 'Contiki-software' control, certain of them viz., MAC protocol, 'sampling' rate, etc. have been accessed and manipulated via Contiki software for performance evaluation purposes (in regard to the above network re-orchestration scenario i.e. to observe the implications of doing so on network re-orchestration latency) presented within the latter sub-sections.

- Selection of requisite sensor(s): Select one or more sensor variables (e.g. RSSI, temperature, light, etc. via Contiki)

```
light=adc_sensor.value(ADC_SENSOR_ALS);
temperature = adc_sensor.value(ADC_SENSOR_TEMP);
rssi=packetbuf_attr(PACKETBUF_ATTR_RSSI);
```

- Buffering: Storing the data sensed within an array say, 'k' before transmission

```
k[0]=Node_ID_number;
k[1]=light;
k[2]=temperature;
k[3]=rssi;
```

- Communication Addressing type:
Activating one of the three communication addressing types viz., Broadcast, Multicast or Unicast.

- Channel Allocation:
```
#ifndef CC2538_RF_CONF_CHANNEL
#define CC2538_RF_CONF_CHANNEL  <Any channel value from '11' to '26'>
```

- Communication scheme:
Enabling any of the communication protocols viz., TDMA, CSMA, etc.

-Radio Frequency (Output) Transmission Power:
Set the desired (hexadecimal) value within the requisite '*cc2538_rf_power_set*' function via contiki

```
cc2538_rf_power_set(uint8_t new_power)
{
  REG(RFCORE_XREG_TXPOWER) = new_power;
  return (REG(RFCORE_XREG_TXPOWER) & <hex_value>);
}
```

- Setting the Transmission rate: Set the desired value (say,) 'r' within the 'etimer' i.e. 'event timer function' via Contiki

```
etimer_set(&et, CLOCK_SECOND*r);
```

- Transmission (of sensed data):   Transmission of the array to requisite node acting as a 'sink' node.

```
packetbuf_copyfrom(&<array_name>, sizeof(<array_name>));
broadcast_send(&bc);
```

-Radio Duty Cycling: Manipulation of the low power mode (i.e. 'LPM' function within Contiki) to configure the Contiki- ported CC2538 to run on one of the following four power modes viz., 'PM0', 'PM1', 'PM2' and 'PM3'.
```
}
```

Fig. 9. Pseudo code for 'Leaf function'.

6.1 Leaf Function Pseudo Code

The pseudo code expressed for the leaf function in Fig. 9 highlights the execution of its core intrinsic operational activities pertaining to 'sensing', 'data acquisition', buffering, data communication, etc. in a logical way. It commences with the flexible select-ability of one or more sensors (e.g. 'ambient light', 'temperature', or 'RSSI') available at disposal by means of retaining the requisite 'sensing function' within the code (and disregarding the ones not needed). The various sensing functions have been specified corresponding to the 'ambient light', 'temperature', or 'RSSI variables have been specified within the pseudo code. 'Buffering' of the single or multiple sensor variables so sensed involves declaration of an array of certain size, say 'k', depending upon the quantity of the sensed variables to be stored. Prior to data communication of the sensed variables stored within the array so declared, parameters such as 'the communication addressing type', 'channel allocation', 'communication scheme' as well as the 'output radio transmission power' must be configured. Herein, firstly, one of the three communication addressing types viz., 'broadcast', 'multicast' or 'unicast' is selected and activated. This is followed by selecting one of the channels (15 in total for the TI CC2538 SoC transceivers) available to be accessed (via specifying the number corresponding to the 'macro' specified within the pseudo code). The communication scheme could then be realized by means of requisite conditional statements followed by configuration of the 'output transmission' power (via specifying the hexadecimal value corresponding to one of the 13 'power output values' available for selection. Finally, the desired rate of transmission could be specified within the 'etimer_set' function as a numerical value prior to transmitting it in accordance with the 'communication addressing type' (e.g. 'packetbuf_copyfrom' function along with 'broadcast_send(&bc)' function, when employing the 'broadcast' 'communication addressing' type).

6.2 Router Function Pseudo Code

As outlined within the pseudo code for the 'router function' shown in Fig. 10, declaration and initialization of requisite arrays of certain sizes, (say 'n',) to accommodate for the incoming data emanating from the group of 'leaf' nodes governed by it forms the first part of the router node program. By virtue of the 'broadcast_recv' function, the data reported by 'x' nodes within its cluster are accumulated within the respective arrays within the router node. Another array 'd' (of size equal to the number of values to be transmitted) is declared firstly for aggregation of the data received by the leaf nodes as well as transmission over to the Gateway, router or sink node. As stated within the Subsect. 6.1, certain parameters viz., the type of 'communication addressing', 'channel', 'scheme of communication' as well as the 'power of output transmission' can be configured through software control (as explained in Subsect. 6.1). Subsequently, the transmission rate can be easily adjusted by specifying the value in the 'etimer_set function' before utilizing the 'packetbuf_copyfrom function', together with the 'broadcast_send(&bc)' function), to transmit the array consisting of values to be transmitted (i.e. 'd' in this case) whilst employing 'broadcast mode' of communication (Fig. 10).

Initialization of Arrays:

Declaring and initialization of arrays of size say, 'n' so as to accommodate for incoming sensed data from 'n' nodes

```
light_v[n]        ={0_1,0_2,....0n};
temperature_v[n] ={0_1,0_2,....0n};
rssi_v[n]         ={0_1,0_2,....0n};
```

Reception of incoming sensed variables:

-Reception and storage of sensed data

```
int16_t *datapointer_tem;
datapointer_tem= (int16_t *)packetbuf_datapointer();
x =datapointer_tem[0];
light_v[x]           =datapointer_tem[1];
temperature_v[x] =datapointer_tem[2];
rssi_v[x]            =datapointer_tem[3];
```

- *Aggregation of received sensed data within an array 'd'*

```
d[0]= node_ID_number;
d[1]= light_v;
d[2]= temperature_v;
d[3]= rssi_v;
```

- **Communication Addressing type:**

Activating one of the three communication addressing types
- Broadcast
- Multicast
- Unicast

- **Setting the MAC Protocol:**
                -CSMA
                -TDMA

FORWARDING OF RECEIVED DATA:

Setting the Transmission rate: Set the desired value (say,) 'r' within the 'etimer' i.e. 'event timer function' via Contiki

```
etimer_set(&et, CLOCK_SECOND*r);
```

- *Transmission (of sensed data):*   Transmission of the array to requisite node acting as a 'sink' node.

```
packetbuf_copyfrom(&<array_name>, sizeof(<array_name>);
broadcast_send(&bc);
}
```

Fig. 10. Pseudo code for 'Router function'.

6.3   Gateway Function Pseudo Code

The code for the gateway function too commences with both 'declaration' and 'initialization' of the arrays to receive and store the incoming sensed data, as present with the pseudo code for the same (shown in Fig. 11). Upon reception, the data values are firstly assigned within another array (declared along with the reception arrays) prior to being subjected to 'protocol-conversion' (e.g. 802.15.4 or Zigbee to an IP-based protocol) []. This enables the gateway to 'escalate' the sensed data received by it over to a (remote) server over internet. Besides, the gateway also ensues upon 'management' (processing, edge-computing, filtering, compression, etc.) of the 'upstream' data or exercising some form of control over the 'downstream' commands [18, 19].

Initialization of Arrays:
    Declaring and initialization of arrays of size say, 'n' so as to accommodate for incoming sensed data from 'n' nodes

```
light_v[n]        ={0₁,0₂,....0n};
temperature_v[n] ={0₁,0₂,....0n};
rssi_v[n]         ={0₁,0₂,....0n};
```

Reception of incoming sensed variables:

    -Reception and and storage of sensed data

```
int16_t *datapointer_tem;
datapointer_tem= (int16_t *)packetbuf_datapointer();
x =datapointer_tem[0];
light_v[x]         =datapointer_tem[1];
temperature_v[x] =datapointer_tem[2];
rssi_v[x]          =datapointer_tem[3];
```

    - Aggregation of received sensed data within an array 'd'

```
d[0]= node_ID_number;
d[1]= light_v;
d[2]= temperature_v;
d[3]= rssi_v;
```

Conversion of Protocol:
                    - From 'Zigbee' to 'TCP/IP' &
                    - From 'HTTP' to 'CoAP' proxy

Management of 'dataflow' and 'commands':
            -management of flow of 'data'
            -Processing of the 'downstream' commands

Fig. 11. Pseudo code for 'Gateway function'.

6.4   Factors Influencing Network Re-orchestration Latency

Parameters such as the 'data communication rate', 'total number of nodes', total numbers of messages exchanged amongst the various (requisite) nodes, MAC communication scheme employed, duration of the time slot (if TDMA scheme has been implemented for the network), contributes to the overall latency. In a bid to gain an estimate the 'extent' to which such parameters tend to influence network re-orchestration latency, experiments could be conducted within the virtual platform of Cooja. One such experiment involving variation of data communication rate has been outlined within the sub-section below.

This experiment has been conducted in furtherance the re-orchestration example case considered in [4] (briefly described within Sect. 5) wherein a network of 6 nodes suffers fragmentation owing to the departure of the router node (node 5) as depicted in Fig. 7.

6.5 Effect of 'Data Communication Rate' on 'Re-orchestration Latency'

As a means to determine the effect of variation of the 'Data communication rate' of the constituent nodes on the overall network re-orchestration latency, certain factors viz., network topology, number of nodes, communication scheme (TDMA, CSMA, etc.) were kept constant (This experimental scenario however was trialed for both the communication schemes (i.e. TDMA and CSMA independently).

Table 2. Effect of varying sampling rate on Overall Re-orchestration Latency.

Data communication rate (Packets Per Second i.e. PPS)	Overall Re-orchestration Latency (Star Topology)	
	CSMA (Seconds)	TDMA (Seconds)
10	0.1	0.398
8	0.125	0.497
5	0.2	0.798
4	0.25	0.997
2	0.5	2
1	1	4
0.75	1.33	5.329
0.5	2	8
0.25	4	15.997
0.2	5	19.998

Table 2 clearly indicates that increase in transmission rate results in decrease in the overall re-orchestration latency and vice versa, for both TDMA and CSMA cases. For lower values of data communication rates, overall re-orchestration latency tends to be significantly higher when TDMA scheme is implemented for the network (as opposed when CSMA is adopted for the same).

7 Conclusion

A cyber-physical architectural framework (consisting of reusable modular functionalities) that allows for virtualization and testing of the underlying physical sensor network is deemed viable towards realizing the objective of SDWSN. The approach pertaining to 'conditional execution' of the functional modules (pre-defined within the code with which the constituent resource-rich physical transceivers are configured) by means of requisite external radio signal messages is one of the ways to achieve flexible re-orchestration and has been adopted for this work. Several other approaches, most notably, OTAP-based approaches or fuzzy logic-based approaches, could be adopted to attain the objective of SDWSN in a more effective manner. Re-orchestrations occurring within such SDWSNs tend to be accompanied by some amount of 'network downtime' that may prove to be partially or massively detrimental to its ongoing operational processes. Such 'downtime' tends to be dependent on certain network parameters like 'data communication rate', 'number of nodes, etc. within the tree structure of the SDWSN.

References

1. Acharyya, I., Al-Anbuky, A.: Towards wireless sensor network softwarization. In: IEEE NetSoft Conference and Workshops NetSoft, Seoul, Korea Republic, pp. 378–383 (2016)
2. Ezdiani, S., Acharyya, I., Sivakumar, S., Al-Anbuky, A.: Wireless sensor network softwarization: towards wsn adaptive QoS. In IEEE Internet of Things Journal 4(5), 1517–1527 (2017)
3. Acharyya, I., Al-Anbuky, A., Sivakumar, S.: Software-Defined Sensor Networks: Towards Flexible Architecture Supported by Virtualization. In: Global IoT Summit GIoTS, Aarhus, Denmark, pp. 1–4 (2019)
4. Acharyya, I., Al-Anbuky, A.: Software-defined wireless sensor network: WSN virtualization and network re-orchestration. In: Proceedings of the 9th International Conference on Smart Cities and Green ICT Systems SMARTGREENS 2020, LNCS, vol. 1, pp. 79–90 (2020)
5. Krasteva, Y., Portilla, J., De la Torre, E., Riesgo, T.: Embedded Runtime Reconfigurable Nodes for Wireless Sensor Networks Applications. In IEEE Sensors Journal 11(9), 1800–1810 (2011)
6. Eronu, E., Misra, S., Aibinu, M.: Reconfiguration approaches in wireless sensor network: issues and challenges. In: IEEE International Conference on Emerging and Sustainable Technologies for Power and ICT in a Developing Society NIGERCON 2013, Owerri, pp. 143–142 (2013)
7. Aslam, M., Hu, X., Wang, F.: SACFIR: SDN-Based Application-Aware Centralized Adaptive Flow Iterative Reconfiguring Routing Protocol for WSNs. Sensors 17, 2893 (2017)
8. Huang, M., Yu, B.: Towards general software-defined wireless sensor networks. In: Proceedings of the 4th IEEE International Conference on Computer and Communications ICCC 2018, Chengdu, China, pp. 923–927 (2018)
9. Oliveira, B., Margi, C.: Distributed control plane architecture for software-defined Wireless Sensor Networks. In: IEEE International Symposium on Consumer Electronics ISCE 2016, Sao Paulo, pp. 85–86 (2016)
10. Kobo, H., Abu-Mahfouz, A., Hancke, G.: A Survey on Software-Defined Wireless Sensor Networks: Challenges and Design Requirements. In IEEE Access 5, 1872–1899 (2017)
11. Kobo, H., Hancke, G., Abu-Mahfouz, A.: Towards a distributed control system for software defined Wireless Sensor Networks. In: In 43rd Annual Conference of the IEEE Industrial Electronics Society IECON 2017, Beijing, pp. 6125–6130(2017)

12. Kgogo, T., Isong, B., Abu-Mahfouz, A.: Software defined wireless sensor networks security challenges. In: IEEE AFRICON 2017, Cape Town, pp. 1508–1513 (2017)
13. Jian, D., Chunxiu, X., Muqing, W., Wenxing, L.: Design and implementation of a novel software-defined wireless sensor network. In: In 3rd IEEE International Conference on Computer and Communications ICCC 2017, Chengdu, pp. 729–733 (2017)
14. Ezdiani, S., Acharyya, I., Sivakumar S., Al-Anbuky, A.: An IoT environment for wsn adaptive QoS. In: IEEE International Conference on Data Science and Data Intensive Systems 2015, Sydney, NSW, Australia, pp. 586–593 (2015)
15. Ezdiani, S., Acharyya, I., Sivakumar S., Al-Anbuky, A.: An Architectural Concept for Sensor Cloud QoSaaS Testbed. In: Proceedings of the 6th ACM Workshop on Real World Wireless Sensor Networks RealWSN 2015, pp. 15–18 (2015)
16. Zhou, Y., Lyu, M.R., Liu. J.: On sensor network reconfiguration for downtime-free system migrations. In: Proceedings of the 5th International ICST Conference on Heterogeneous Networking for Quality, Reliability, Security and Robustness QShine 2008. Brussels, Belgium, Article 24, pp. 1–7 (2008)
17. Szczodrak, M., Gnawali, O., Carloni, L.: Dynamic configuration of wireless sensor networks to support heterogeneous applications. In: IEEE International Conference on Distributed Computing in Sensor Systems Cambridge, MA, pp. 52–61 (2013)
18. Baghyalakshmi, D., Kothari, S., Ebenezer, J., SatyaMurty, S.: Ethernet gateway for wireless sensor networks. In: Twelfth International Conference on Wireless and Optical Communications Networks (WOCN), Bangalore, pp. 1–5 (2015)
19. Yuan, Z., Cheng, J.: The Design and Realization of Wireless Sensor Network Gateway Node. Adv. Mater. Res. **760**, 462–466 (2013)

Vehicle Technology and Intelligent Transport Systems

Digital Infrastructure for Cooperative and Automated Road Transport

Meng Lu[1]([⊠]) [iD] and Julian Schindler[2] [iD]

[1] Dynniq Nederland B.V., Basicweg 16, 3821 BR Amersfoort, The Netherlands
wklm@xs4all.nl
[2] German Aerospace Center (DLR), Lilienthalplatz 7, 38108 Braunschweig, Germany
julian.schindler@dlr.de

Abstract. With the fast development of new technologies in the domain of ITS (Intelligent Transport Systems), it is a challenge how to pave a suitable way to high-level automated road transport for further enhancing road safety, traffic efficiency, and energy efficiency, environmental friendliness and comfort of road transport. The challenges concern multiple aspects, not only technology, but also legal, human factors, future mobility and business. This chapter focuses on the role of ICT (Information and Communications Technology) infrastructure for cooperative and automated driving. Taking into account traffic management of the transport system as a whole (and not merely from the perspective of vehicles), and targeting mature V2X (Vehicle to everything) communication technologies and their applications for future connected road transport. The chapter reviews recent research and innovation results from three selected projects (MAVEN, TransAID and C-MobILE), funded by the European Union under Horizon 2020 Framework Programme. Approaches, main outcomes and key findings are presented. In addition, the way forward towards infrastructure supported high-level automated road transport, including sophisticated traffic management and signal control in urban areas, is discussed.

Keywords: Automated driving · Road transport · C-ITS

1 Introduction

1.1 Background and Core Technologies

After around three decades of development and deployment of Intelligent Transport Systems (ITS) for improving road transport in terms of safety, traffic efficiency, energy efficiency, environmental friendliness and driving comfort, the mission has become much more ambitious, aiming at towards high-level automated driving. Driving automation levels are defined in SAE *(Society of Automotive Engineers)* Standard J3016 [1]. Traditional autonomous vehicle systems, using sensor technologies such as radar, lidar, camera, ultrasound and (absolute and relative) positioning, would not be sufficient to achieve this goal. To increase the reliability, robustness and redundancy of the whole system enabling automated driving, the stand-alone systems need to be complemented by

© Springer Nature Switzerland AG 2021
C. Klein et al. (Eds.): SMARTGREENS 2020/VEHITS 2020, CCIS 1475, pp. 123–148, 2021.
https://doi.org/10.1007/978-3-030-89170-1_7

another vehicle technology, developed since about 2006: cooperative systems. The essential technology for Cooperative Intelligent Transport Systems (C-ITS), also referred to as Connected Vehicles outside Europe, is V2X (Vehicle to everything) communication, with main components V2V (Vehicle-to-Vehicle) and V2I (Vehicle-to-Infrastructure).

Currently, two main mature communication technologies are available for V2X, direct vehicular communication based on IEEE 802.11p, and cellular network communication (3G/4G, in the future possibly 5G) [2–7]. IEEE 802.11p was the first V2X technology, and is the basis for ETSI *(European Telecommunications Standards Institute)* ITS-G5. These mature technologies have been extensively trialled and tested worldwide in cooperative applications. As cellular needs to go through the network, it has a latency impediment. A competing technology, which is not mature, is 4G LTE-V2X (Long Term Evolution - Vehicle to everything) or Cellular V2X (C-V2X). It is based on the so-called PC5 or sidelink LTE radio interface, which allows direct vehicle-vehicle and vehicle-infrastructure communications without transferring the data over the cellular network (see: 3GPP (Third Generation Partnership Project) Release 14 [8] and Release 15 [9]). According to solid research and expert analysis, compared with ETSI ITS-G5/IEEE 802.11p, LTE-V2X has in general lower performance for V2X communication, and still needs substantial development and testing for technical maturity [3–6]. A major drawback is that IEEE 802.11p and LTE-V2X are not interoperable. Careful selection of eventual technologies and business models will have a major influence on the further development towards connected, cooperative and automated road transport, and may be crucial for its success [2].

In Europe, intensive R&D on C-ITS started some fifteen years ago. Under the EU funding scheme FP6-IST (The 6th Framework Programme Information Society Technologies), the European Commission (EC) launched in 2006 three called Integrated Projects targeting cooperative systems: SAFESPOT (Co-operative Systems for Road Safety; focusing on the in-vehicle side and traffic safety) [10], CVIS (Cooperative Vehicle Infrastructure Systems; focusing on the infrastructure side and traffic efficiency) [11], and COOPERS (CO-OPerative SystEms for Intelligent Road Safety; focussing on the domain of the road operator) [12]. In early 2014, the EC decided to take a more prominent role in the deployment of connected driving by setting up a C-ITS Deployment Platform, which defined C-ITS services by 2016, with an extension in 2017 [13, 14] (see Table 1). Most of these C-ITS services were already considered since around 2005, but received little attention and interest from the end-user community. However, for high-level automated vehicles, such high quality services are a must. We assume that high-level automated vehicles shall be cooperative when they enter the market, which means that they need to be able to communicate with other vehicles and road users, the infrastructure and the network, but that different vehicle control modes, communication technologies and business models can be applied.

The CAR 2 CAR Communication Consortium (C2CCC) published in 2018 V2X application roadmap towards fully automated driving distinguishing three implementation phases. V2X communication takes place through messages, and an important component is therefore definition of message types. These are specified based on ETSI, ISO (International Organization for Standardization) and SAE standards. The three implementation phases and the related message types as used in Europe and/or the USA are:

1) Awareness Driving: *CAM* - Cooperative Awareness Message/ETSI EN 302 637–2, *DENM* - Decentralised Environmental Notification Message/ETSI EN 302 637–3, *BSM* - Basic Safety Message, *SPaT* - Signal, Phase, and Timing/ISO/TS 19091:2017, *MAP* - road/lane topology and traffic maneuverer/ISO/TS 19091:2017, *VAM* - Vulnerable Road User (VRU) Awareness Message/ETSI TS 103 300–3, *PSM* - Personal Safety Message/SAE J2735; 2) Sensing Driving: *CPM* - Collective Perception Message/ETSI TS 103 324 (draft), ETSI TR 103 562; 3) Cooperative Driving: *MCM* - Manoeuvre Coordination Message/ETSI TR 103 578 (draft), *PCM* - Platooning Control Message/ETSI TR 103 298 [15, 16].

Table 1. C-ITS services defined by the EC C-ITS Platform.

C-ITS Day-1 services	Day-1'5 services	Additional services
Hazardous location notifications	Information on fuelling & charging stations for alternative fuel vehicles	**New additional urban specific services**
Slow or stationary vehicle(s) & traffic ahead warning	Vulnerable Road User (VRU) protection	Access zone management V2I
Roadworks warning	On street parking	Public transport vehicle approaching V2V
Weather conditions	management & information	**Extended functionality of**
Emergency brake light	Off street parking information	**original list of Day-1/1.5**
Emergency vehicle approaching	Park & Ride information	**services**
Other hazardous notifications	Connected & cooperative navigation into and out of the	Access management of speed
Signage applications	city (1st and last mile,	On/off-street parking
In-vehicle signage	parking, route advice,	management
In-vehicle speed limits	coordinated traffic lights)	Temporary traffic light priority
Signal violation / Intersection safety	Traffic information & smart routing	for designated vehicles
Traffic signal priority request by designated vehicles		Collaborative perception of VRUs
Green Light Optimal Speed Advisory (GLOSA)		Collaborative traffic management
Probe vehicle data		**Additional user groups of**
Shockwave damping		**existing C-ITS Day-1/Day-1.5 services** GLOSA for cyclists V2I

This chapter targets three main issues of cooperative and automated road transport:

1) How to manage cooperative and automated vehicles in an urban environment with mixed traffic?
2) How to enable high-level automated vehicles to enter the market in a transition phase, which may have to switch to a lower automation level at certain conditions and circumstances?
3) What is the state of the art of the C-ITS deployment in Europe, and how to overcome the challenges?

The following three sections focus on some key aspects of these issues, based on the results of the selected EU-funded projects (MAVEN, TransAID and C-MobILE), in which the aforementioned two mature communication technologies have been implemented. In addition, infrastructure-supported high-level automated driving, especially using sophisticated traffic signal control and traffic management in an urban environment, is discussed before conclusions are drawn.

2 Managing Automated Vehicles in an Urban Environment

2.1 Research Scope and Main Objectives

MAVEN (Managing Automated Vehicles Enhances Network) was a three-year project funded by the European Union (EU) with a budget of around EUR 3.15 million, which ended in August 2019. The research targeted hierarchical traffic management and traffic signal control with cooperative and automated vehicles, to maximise throughput and increase traffic efficiency; and further enhancement of ADAS (Advanced Driver Assistance Systems) and C-ITS applications. Platooning and CACC (Cooperative Adaptive Cruise Control) on arterial roads in urban areas with mixed traffic and signalised intersections are illustrated in Fig. 1.

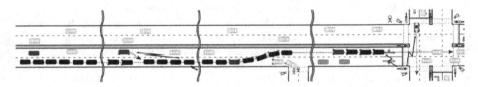

Fig. 1. An illustration of management regimes for automated driving in urban areas [17].

The main research objectives were: 1) to develop a generic multi-level system for the guidance of highly automated vehicles, and application of this system to dynamic platooning and CACC at signalised intersections and signalised corridors; 2) to contribute to the development of C-ITS communication standards, in particular message sets for V2V and V2I interactions to support platooning and CACC; and negotiation and scheduling algorithms; 3) to (further) develop and integrate ADAS techniques to prevent and/or mitigate dangerous situations taking into account VRUs (e.g. pedestrians and cyclists); 4) to develop, test, demonstrate and evaluate the developed systems for signalised intersections and signalised corridors; and 5) to produce a roadmap for future traffic management of cooperative and automated road transport.

2.2 Approach, Use Cases and Architecture

MAVEN developed concepts for *vehicle automation* and *infrastructure automation*. Important components of vehicle automation include system architecture, a general approach of the targeted cooperative sensing, and the control logic to be used. Important components of infrastructure automation include enhanced traffic signal control and cooperative road infrastructure for V2I, I2V (infrastructure to vehicle) and I2I (infrastructure to infrastructure) communication. These components are based on emerging technologies and their further development, such as V2X communication and HD (High Definition) maps for automated driving. An open-source microscopic traffic simulation SUMO (Simulation of Urban MObility) was used, and simpla was developed and released, which allows users to simulate automated vehicles in SUMO [18]. In addition to simulation, various assessment tools were applied, e.g. emulation techniques, traffic and communication modelling, system prototyping, and trials (on a real world public road, on closed roads and at test sites, respectively). Moreover, new data elements have been introduced, such as *number of occupants, distance to following vehicle, distance to preceding vehicle, platooning/CACC state, desired speed, current lane,* and *route information.*

Sixteen use cases (see Table 2) were identified and assessed, from technical, functional, impact and user perspectives [19]. The following scenarios were considered: 1) intersection priority management; 2) queue estimation (note: this information can improve queue model accuracy, leading to more optimal solutions for GLOSA negotiation and signal timing); 3) signal optimisation and intersection priority; 4) queue estimation and GLOSA negotiation; 5) lane advice; and 6) queue estimation, signal optimisation and GLOSA.

Table 2. MAVEN use cases.

Platooning/CACC management	Longitudinal and lateral management	Signal optimisation	Intersection and other road user management
Initialisation Joining Travelling Leaving Break-up Termination	Speed change advisory (GLOSA) Lane change advisory Emergency situations	Priority management Queue length estimation Local level routing Network coordination (green wave) Signal optimisation	Intersection negotiation Detect non-cooperative road users

A simulation architecture (see Fig. 2) was developed keeping maximal compatibility with and re-use of real-world systems, while enabling retrieving sensor information from the simulation environment and changing states of traffic lights and vehicles according to the actuator outputs. Components that are identical to the real-world implementation are marked in grey, simulation specific components are marked in orange and adapted elements are marked in grey/orange hatch. The interfaces to the grey elements should stay the same. The vehicle and the intersection have a shared Local Dynamic Map (LDM), as the communication units have been removed, saving a lot of computational time for encoding and decoding messages. Systems connected to this LDM will not notice a difference, the same data is still present in the same format [20].

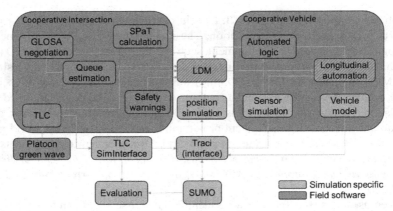

Fig. 2. High-level simulation architecture. (Note: LDM - Local Dynamic Map, TraCI - Traffic Control Interface, TLC - Traffic Light Controller, GLOSA - Green Light Optimal Speed Advisory, SPaT - Signal Phase and Timing, SUMO - Simulation of Urban MObility).

2.3   Main Results and Key Findings

The MAVEN research has provided scientific and technical contributions for a sophisticated urban road transport and cooperative systems infrastructure for highly automated vehicles [21]. A generic multi-level system for the guidance of highly automated vehicles was developed (see Fig. 3). This enables cooperative and automated vehicles to have route plan, speed advice and lane advice, in addition to conventional GLOSA (see Fig. 3a), as well to have lane change advice for a re-arrangement of vehicle clusters for passing an intersection efficiently and in an optimal way, and even to support the creation of green waves of vehicle clusters at a network level (see Fig. 3b).

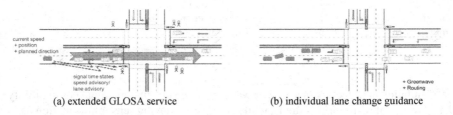

(a) extended GLOSA service   (b) individual lane change guidance

Fig. 3. A generic multi-level system for the guidance of cooperative and automated vehicles.

To enable cooperative and automated driving solutions, V2X communication schemes and message sets have been developed. These include several contributions: for the cooperative infrastructure, an I2V Lane Change Advisory service and a dedicated profiling of the *SPaT* and *MAP* messages for lane-specific GLOSA were developed. For the cooperative automated vehicles, extensions of standard *CAM* (for *Awareness Driving)* message have been designed, to allow for interaction with cooperative intersections and to support management and control of platoons. Finally, the currently under standardisation *CPM* (for *Sensing Driving)* message service has been adapted to support applications of cooperative and automated vehicles aiming at increasing the safety of VRUs and vehicle drivers. The developed schemes are backward compatible as required by automotive industry. Definitions and detailed message data specifications are described in ASN.1 (Abstract Syntax Notation One) and with open access. The communication schemes were tested in test benches, the technical functionality of the developed solutions from a communication point of view were evaluated, and their suitability for integration in infrastructure and vehicle prototypes were thereby established. MAVEN actively contributed to the ETSI standardisation process, especially for the collective perception definitions [22].

Moreover, specific ADAS functions for VRU and driver protection were developed, for use in cooperative and automated vehicles. Firstly, it was decided not to consider ADAS solutions based on retrofitting VRUs with C-ITS technology to let them cooperatively advertise their presence. Due to positioning limitations of these retrofitting solutions, the resulting ADAS applications would not be reliable and create uncertainty in the reactions of the automated driving algorithms. Secondly, it was considered that ADAS functions in the context of automated driving cannot be treated as separate functions, but have to be integrated in the overall algorithms for environmental perception and path planning. For example, ADAS functions relying on cooperative sensing (collective perception) can be seen as complementing extensions of functions relying on on-board sensors: system reactions will directly influence the path planning (e.g. slow down and braking) when the confidence of the advertised detected object is good enough to justify this, but have no effect when the advertised object was not yet present in the environmental perception module databases because no local sensor has detected it yet. The techniques to prevent and/or mitigate dangerous situations are presented in Fig. 4.

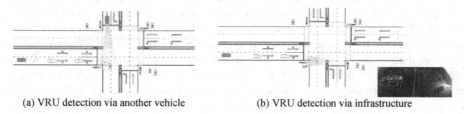

(a) VRU detection via another vehicle   (b) VRU detection via infrastructure

Fig. 4. Illustration of techniques for conflict prevention and/or mitigation between cooperative and automated vehicles and VRUs.

Furthermore, HD (High Definition) maps and their usage to optimally support the defined use cases have been investigated. Commercially available HD map databases of the designated test sites have been evaluated. Based on these databases, additional requirements for vehicle automation in terms of map format extensions for highly automated driving were identified. In particular, the project detected the need for a "corridor" representation for road intersections as a pair of "virtual lane boundary lines" that connect the lane boundary markings of in-bound lanes to the lane boundary markings of outbound lanes. This information is necessary for automated driving software because it indicates the boundaries to be respected when performing a given intersection crossing manoeuvre to avoid invading zones where conflicting situations with other road users can occur. With the MAVEN extensions embedded in the reference HD maps, an evaluation of the impact of the resulting map accuracy on the automated vehicle trajectory and control calculation was performed, by comparing the results obtained with the new extended format with those obtained with the original format. This evaluation demonstrated that the resulting extended maps for highly automated driving are suitable, as they permit trajectory calculation with sufficient quality. As complementary activity, a thorough investigation of the state of the art on map standardisation was performed. The extensions for the intersection corridor approach were identified to be a possible input for standardisation (see Fig. 5) [23].

(a) Ideal MAVEN intersection corridor representa- (b) MAVEN extended HAD map format for the
tion for the Braunschweig Tostmannplatz test site   Braunschweig Tostmannplatz test site (visualised
(visualised on GoogleMaps)   on GoogleMaps)

Fig. 5. Illustration of HD maps development in MAVEN.

MAVEN has conducted modelling, numerous simulation for algorithm development, testing and evaluation [24, 25], emulation, intensive real-world testing and demonstrations [25, 26], surveys and interviews [19]. Key findings of these efforts are as follows: In general, people have high expectations of the positive impact of automated vehicles, e.g. more than 80% of the respondents believe that cooperative and automated vehicles will decrease the number of traffic accidents, around 70% of the respondents expect improvements with respect to traffic congestion, and most customers would be willing to pay a bit extra, up to EUR 5,000 for a car with automated features. Furthermore, proper integration of automated vehicles into the road infrastructure has clear effects of emission reduction, travel time reduction, traffic flow harmonisation, road safety, amongst several other positive effects. Moreover, lower penetration levels have already a positive influence on travel experience, e.g. 20% penetration (studied for the effect of speed change advice and green wave optimisation) leads to reductions of 17.3% in delays, of 10.9% in queue length and of 0.4% in CO_2 emission. It also should be emphasised that different algorithms can aim at contradictory functional objective, therefore, they must be combined carefully. For instance, minimising delay does not necessarily lead to the most optimal harmonised traffic flow. In addition, during the transition phase, traffic management and traffic signal control play an important role, i.e. when the penetration rate of automated vehicles is low, it will strongly influence the (safety and efficiency) impact; other impacts of automated vehicles depend on (future) transport policies and regulations [19].

3   Enabling High-Level Automated Driving

3.1   Motivation and Concept

Although vehicle systems will increasingly become more sophisticated, high-level auto-mated driving (e.g. Level-3 and Level-4) will not be able to handle all situations. The boundaries are given through the concept Operational Design Domain (ODD), which explicitly defines under which conditions the system has to function, and its behaviour is tested and proven. The system has to monitor at all time if it is still well inside its ODD or if it is about to leave it. In the latter case, the vehicle has to bring the driver back into the loop, by performing a Transition of Control (ToC). If the ToC fails, as the driver is not responding, a Level-4 system still has to guarantee safety. If leaving the ODD is unavoidable, the vehicle therefore will perform a Minimum Risk Manoeuvre (MRM), which in most cases will be a simple stopping of the vehicle on the road. Besides some obvious system malfunctions, like when a sensor is not working anymore, the real world offers a large spectrum of possible ODD restrictions, such as limited visibility, low sensor ranges, or unclassifiable objects on the road. Most of these restrictions will be related to environment conditions, e.g. fog in valleys or on bridges, complex road or intersection topologies, or road-works situations.

Based on this, it is very likely that automated vehicles will face issues on the very same positions on the road, resulting in ToCs and possibly also in MRMs. Apart from the fact that this can be frustrating for drivers, there may be important other consequences. Each single ToC is possibly negatively impacting the traffic flow, as vehicles may reduce their speed during the ToC and as drivers may not properly react when taking over control, because they have been out-of-the-loop before. In addition, the negative impacts will certainly be much larger when ToCs will be unsuccessful and vehicles will stop on the driving lane due to MRMs. It even gets worse when there are more and more automated vehicles on the roads in the future, and when ToCs and MRMs in such "Transition Areas" (see Fig. 6) are not an exception, but rather common.

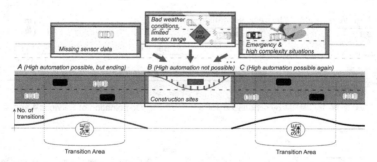

Fig. 6. Definition of a Transition Area: automated vehicles need to perform a ToC.

To enable automated vehicles on the market, it will be a key argument to offer uninterrupted automated driving though. Therefore, ways need to be found to remove Transition Areas from the roads. While the "ODD frontier" can be pushed further away by increasing system capabilities and the performance of vehicle sensors, there will still be "islands" where the system is not working. Therefore, it could be more beneficial to make the islands "automated driving ready". While this can be achieved by specific "off-line" measures, e.g. by providing correct lane markings in roadworks areas, also "on-line" measures using collective perception and communication, and temporarily adapted HD maps, will be beneficial.

This is where TransAID (Transition Areas for Infrastructure-Assisted Driving) steps in. The project, which was launched in 2017, is funded by the EU with a budget of around EUR 3.84 million. It investigates the impact of ToCs and MRMs on traffic systems at different vehicle mixes. Using this data, infrastructure-based "on-line" measures to reduce the negative impacts are developed and tested in simulation, using collective perception and V2X communication. After simulation testing, the measures are also implemented in the real world to demonstrate the feasibility of the approach.

3.2 Use Cases Definition

As there are no Level-3 and Level-4 vehicles on the road, but only several prototypical implementations of such systems, the use cases could not easily be derived from statistics. A literature study was performed accompanied by expert ratings and a stakeholder workshop with participants from automotive industry and authorities [27].

In the process, possible issues of automated vehicles were identified. Five categories of services were identified (see Fig. 7). All use cases were tested in simulation and in the real-world [28, 29]. Table 3 provides some examples of use cases.

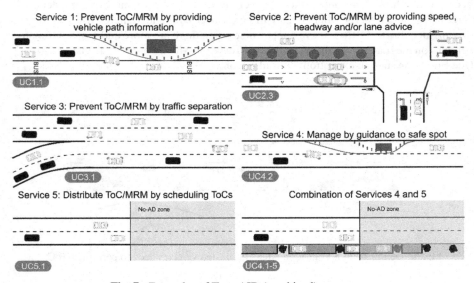

Fig. 7. Examples of TransAID (combined) use cases.

Table 3. Examples of TransAID use cases.

Service	Use case	Use case description
1 Prevent ToC/MRM by providing vehicle path information	UC 1.1: Roadworks are blocking all lanes of the road, except for a dedicated bus lane	An automated vehicle will not be able to pass the roadworks without using the bus lane, and initiates a ToC. Infrastructure supports by providing a path around the roadworks area and allowing the vehicles to drive on the bus lane in a limited area, avoiding the ToC
2 Prevent ToC/MRM by providing speed, headway and/or lane advice	UC2.3: An incident is blocking the turning lane of an intersection	Automated vehicles may not be able to turn on that intersection. Intersection can provide lane advice allowing the vehicles to perform the turn from the through-lane
3 Prevent ToC/MRM by traffic separation	UC3.1: Complex highway merging	The vehicle is not able to perform the lane change and needs to initiate a ToC on the on-ramp. This can be accompanied by a temporal traffic separation
4 Manage ToC/MRM by guidance to *safe spot*	UC4.2: Roadworks are blocking part of the road	Automated vehicles are not able to pass and will perform ToCs, resulting MRMs on the free lane. To avoid negative impacts, infrastructure is providing *safe spots* on the closed lane, which can be used in case MRMs need to be performed
5 Distribute ToC/MRM by scheduling ToCs	UC5.1: ToCs are need to be initiated at the very same position	As it will have negative impacts when ToCs are initiated at the very same position, infrastructure is distributing the ToCs on the road by providing individual ToC advice

3.3 Communication and Message Sets

Communication between infrastructure and cooperative automated vehicles is the key of this research. As Transition Areas are locally bound, it was decided to use ETSI ITS-G5 for communication. Based on this approach, existing messages were analysed, and extended where required. This especially was the case for Day-1 messages such as *CAM, DENM, SPaTEM* (SPaT Extended Message) and *MAPEM* (MAP Extended Message) [30]. *CAM* provides information about the position and speed of the vehicle. It was found necessary to include also an *AutomatedVehicle* container, which is used to provide information about the currently driven automation level and state. By this, surrounding vehicles and the infrastructure are able to identify the automation level, and if the vehicle is currently performing a MRM. *DENM* contains information about abnormal situations on the road, such as roadworks, broken-down vehicles, emergency vehicles. This message is used unchanged in TransAID. *MAPEM* contains topology information about the environment. While it is normally used for urban intersections, identifying connections between lane boundaries of inbound and outbound lanes, this is also used for roads, especially when lane types are changed or positions of *safe spots* are indicated. Accordingly, small changes concerning road types were proposed. *SPaTEM* is used to provide information about current traffic light states and phase durations, for which no changes have been proposed in TransAID.

Besides these Day-1 messages, two further aspects of infrastructure support have been investigated: collective perception and manoeuvre coordination. Both aspects require new message definitions, which are currently part of standardisation activities in Europe, and are influenced by TransAID results. *CPM* contains information about sensors and objects detected by those, including positions, dimensions and further attributes like velocities. The message can be provided by vehicles and infrastructure. It is also used to share information about unequipped vehicles or detected blockages [31]. MCM is recently designed for the coordination of movements of cooperative and automated vehicles. In the message, the currently planned and the desired trajectories are included, allowing a V2V negotiation about the planned behaviour, e.g. for cooperative lane changes. In TransAID, this idea has been extended by the inclusion of infrastructure, which is now able to give specific speed, distance and lane advice to individual vehicles. On top, infrastructure may advice ToCs and explicit *safe spot* positions to cooperative automated vehicles.

As not only the message content, but also the reliability of message transmissions is very important, several tests have been performed analysing Packet Delivery and Channel Busy Ratios. In this light, also different compression techniques have been investigated [32]. To reduce negative impacts at Transition Areas in general, and considering that not all vehicles are equipped with communication technology, further research was done to explore possibilities to also inform unequipped vehicles about incidents and countermeasures. As result, two major components have been identified to provide this information: 1) Variable Message Signs (VMS) have the potential to provide very specific warnings about possible ToCs and their reasons [33]; 2) it was found that automated vehicles should inform also non-automated vehicles in their surroundings in case an MRM is performed. A Virtual Reality (VR) study has revealed that the use of external HMIs (eHMI) improves the understanding of behaviour of cooperative automated vehicles, and has the potential to also improve traffic [34].

3.4 Modelling and Simulation

To investigate the impact of Transition Areas, a first step was to identify prospective numbers for the different vehicle types on the road. These types consist of vehicles performing manual driving, vehicles driving partially automated, and vehicles with conditional automation. Partial automation here means that the vehicles are driving automated, but drivers need to be able to instantly take over control when requested corresponding to SAE Level-1 and Level-2. Consequently, there is no MRM implemented in those vehicles. Conditional automation is an enabled automation which includes ToCs and MRMs in case of transition failures, and therefore includes vehicles of Level-3 and above. While manual driving occurs with and without Day-1 connectivity, it is assumed that all automated vehicles are also cooperative, see Table 4.

Table 4. Vehicle mixes used in TransAID simulations.

Vehicle mix	Manual driving	Manual driving + Conn	Partial autom	Partial autom. + Conn	Cond autom	Cond autom. + Conn
1	60%	10%	-	15%	-	15%
2	40%	10%	-	25%	-	25%
3	10%	10%	-	40%	-	40%

Another important aspect of the simulation activity is the definition of the simulated traffic demand. Traffic demands corresponding to Levels of Service (LoS) A, B and C was first chosen, as it was forecasted that higher demand levels will have insufficient reserve capacity to manage traffic due to a high risk of traffic jams and a high variability of results. But the simulation revealed that LoS A is not providing a lot of insights and that traffic conditions did not substantially deteriorate for LoS C. Therefore, it was decided to also include LoS D in the simulations, and the results of capacity (vehicle per hour per lane) and LoS are presented in Table 5.

The automation functionality was also modelled. Automated driving in the context of TransAID consists of speed and distance keeping (longitudinal) and automated lane changes (lateral). While on the longitudinal side the SUMO ACC model was parametrised, laterally the default lane change model (LC2013) was used [35].

In order to model transition of control, a new ToC model was implemented, which is able to include adapted behaviour during the ToC, the MRM, and also during a phase of reduced driver performance when the driver takes over, as the driver needs to recover to full situation awareness (see Fig. 8). All use cases were implemented in SUMO and a first round of baseline simulations was performed. The baseline simulations showed that unmanaged MRMs can cause severe traffic disruption, even when the driver is quickly

Table 5. Traffic demand chosen for TransAID simulations.

Facility type	Capacity (veh/h/l)	Level of service (LoS)			
		A	B	C	D
Urban (50km/h)	1500 veh/h/l	525	825	1155	1386
Rural (80 km/h)	1900 veh/h/l	665	1045	1463	1756
Motorway (120 km/h)	2100 veh/h/l	735	1155	1617	1940
Intensity/Capacity (IC) ratio		0.35	0.55	0.77	0.92

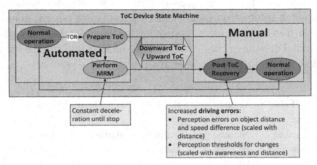

Fig. 8. ToC model implemented in SUMO [35].

responding to MRMs by taking over. But also successful ToCs can cause significant disruption if the number of cooperative and automated vehicles is high [35]. While automated driving leads to a more homogeneous traffic flow, the more conservative behaviour of automation functions will reduce traffic throughput. Furthermore, it has been found that the conservative behaviour of cooperative and automated vehicles will possibly increase the number of safety-critical events.

The aforementioned countermeasures have been applied to the use cases. The simulations revealed that congestions are reduced drastically and that throughput is increased. As consequence, safety-critical events were reduced up to 75%. Also the average travel time, shockwaves, lane change intensity and the number of Take-Over Requests (TOR) are reduced, as well as CO_2 emissions in most cases [36].

After simulating the use cases including the measures with SUMO, more sophisticated simulations including communication simulation have been performed. Here, the already existing iTetris framework was used as platform, which allows coupling of SUMO simulations with different communication simulations and applications [37]. In the TransAID setup, communication simulations have been performed first with a simple "LightComm" approach where all messages are simply forwarded at once. In a second round of simulations, ns-3 (network simulator) was used for communication, allowing detailed analysis of communication aspects. Here, it turned out that communication aspects normally do not negatively impact the results. Even at higher packet losses, the traffic management algorithms reacted in a robust way [38]. Only in motorway conditions a significant increase of critical events could be revealed, as shown exemplarily for UC5.1 ToCs need to be initiated at the very same position (under Service 5 Distribute ToC/MRM by scheduling ToCs) in Fig. 9.

The reason for the negative impact in this use case is that messages including the ToC advice are only sent once. If the message is not received, vehicles tend to perform the ToC late, just in front of the zone where automated driving is not possible, and therefore similar to the baseline case. Therefore, it was found that additional protocols for reliable communication should be investigated. TransAID also evaluated in detail possible measures for reliability, and proposes a context-based broadcast acknowledgement mechanism which is in line with and therefore relevant for the future standard IEEE 802.11bd [32].

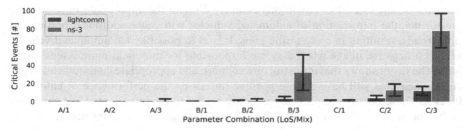

Fig. 9. Impact of communication on the number of critical events in UC5.1 ToCs are need to be initiated at the very same position.

3.5 Real-World Implementations

In order to further assess the feasibility of the traffic management measures and the communication techniques, real-world implementations have been conducted. The tests have been performed using: 1) two DLR test vehicles (the FASCarE, a fully electric Volkswagen Golf, and the ViewCar2, a Volkswagen Passat GTE, both equipped with a large set of sensors, a Cohda Wireless MK5 OBU and the possibility to drive fully automated); 2) one road side infrastructure pole, equipped with a Cohda Wireless MK5 RSU, an ACTi camera for object detection and tracking, and an application PC, on which the infrastructure software was running; 3) one mobile variable message sign able to display an appropriate advice to other vehicles.

Initially limited tests were performed at the test track at the former aerodrome Peine-Eddesse in Germany, for which virtual lanes were created on the runway and added to the map, to investigate urban and motorway scenarios. A set of requirements for each scenario was set up and validated [39]. Later, also full-scale tests were performed, both at Peine-Eidesse and on public road. As result, three different assessments were made: 1) Detailed tests of all use cases in a set of 26 scenarios on the Peine-Eddesse test track. In the full-scale tests, additional vehicles were driving on the test track, allowing a more realistic assessment. In addition, the algorithms react to dynamic situation changes, e.g. blocked *safe spots* or lane changes of unequipped vehicles; 2) The use case highway merging assist has been tested on a public highway in The Netherlands. Here, the traffic is monitored using a camera and data of existing induction loops. An emulated automated vehicle equipped with ITS-G5 is entering the highway and receiving online speed and lane change advice using MCM; 3) A combination of use cases for managing and distributing ToC/MRM services was tested with an automated car on the closed test track.

3.6   Key Findings and Next Steps

A detailed analysis of Transition Areas was performed. It was found that a detailed investigation of those areas is required and should be further addressed to allow a smooth integration of automated vehicles. Although it may still take some time before reaching 80% or even 50% penetration of automated vehicles on the roads, it is important to emphasise the role of C-ITS in this context. Without the appropriate infrastructure investments, the introduction of automated vehicles will cause additional bottlenecks on the roads, resulting in more traffic jams. It is even possible that automated vehicles may get a negative image when they are responsible for more and more issues on the roads. The result shows that infrastructure support, and appropriate communication and sensing measures will have a large positive impact on the performance of automated vehicles. These positive impacts are not only bound to the investigated use cases, but can be considered valid for completely different use cases of the identified services as well. The developed messages and measures are extensible. Furthermore, the defined and used new messages MCM and CPM are already being dealt with in standardisation activities. In addition to performing some still remaining tests, TransAID is going to provide a roadmap and guidelines for stakeholders, addressing how infrastructure can be extended to best cope with Transition Areas in the future.

4   C-ITS Deployment in Europe and Challenges

4.1   Objective and Approach

In addition to C-ITS projects under the C-ROADS Platform, C-MobILE (Accelerating C-ITS Mobility Innovation and depLoyment in Europe) was launched in 2017 with a total project budget above EUR 15 million. It aims to stimulate large-scale and interoperable C-ITS deployments across Europe. The following C-ITS deployment sites are directly involved: Barcelona (ES), Bilbao (ES), Bordeaux (FR), Copenhagen (DK), Newcastle (UK), North Brabant, especially Helmond and Eindhoven (NL), Thessaloniki (GR) and Vigo (ES). The C-MobILE approach is presented in Fig. 10.

C-MobILE mainly focuses on three aspects: 1) Connectivity - Enabling C-ITS services to support in-vehicle applications and bi-directional communication, based on appropriate data access and sharing; 2) Interoperability - Enabling interoperability across systems by testing and validation, and by contribution to standards; 3) Deployment - Demonstration, assessment and evaluation of the benefits of C-ITS.

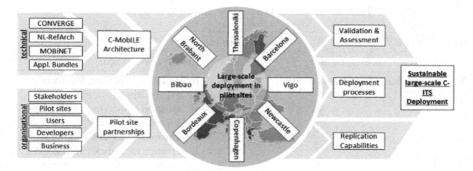

Fig. 10. C-MobILE approach [39].

4.2 Deployable Services and Use Cases

Use cases under twenty C-ITS services were defined within C-MobILE [41] (see Table 6) and were or will be implemented by the C-ITS deployment sites. For the implementation of each use case, both technical and non-technical requirements were analysed, and technical specifications were detailed [42]. In addition, operational procedures and C-ITS implementation guidelines for authorities were provided [43], and business models for C-ITS services were analysed [44].

C-MobILE has conducted a C-ITS survey to gain insight into the requirements and expectations of stakeholders of the following four categories: Drivers, VRUs, Public Authorities, and Private Companies, and to validate the service definitions and use cases [45]. The results of ranking of the service importance (using a 5-point Likert scale from not important to highly important) are presented in Fig. 11. Drivers considered *traffic jam ahead warning* and *flexible infrastructure* important. Private companies ranked *roadworks warning, road hazard warning, traffic jam ahead warning* and *emergency vehicle warning* as important. Public Authorities considered *Green Priority* and *GLOSA* important. VRUs only considered *pedestrian warning system* important [41].

Figure 12 presents the raking results of the extent (on a 5-point Likert scale from strongly disagree to strongly agree), to which the service influences four impact areas: road safety, traffic efficiency, environmental protection, and comfort. All services are considered to significantly contribute to at least one of the impact areas. The services that involve warnings (e.g. *road hazard warning, roadworks warning, signal violation warning, motorcycle approaching indication/warning*) were regarded as the key means to improve road safety. Furthermore, some services that contribute mostly to traffic efficiency, such as *mode & trip time advice, green priority*, and *in-vehicle signage* were deemed to have the most significant contributions when all dimensions are considered together [41].

Table 6. Services and use cases defined in C-MobILE.

ID	Service	Use case
1	Rest-time management	UC1.1 - Rest time indication
2	Motorway parking availability	UC2.1 - Information on parking lots location, availability and services via internet UC2.2 - Information on parking lots location, availability and services via I2V UC2.3 - Information on a truck parking space UC2.4 - Reservation of a truck parking space UC2.5 - Guide the truck in a port/terminal (truck parking)
3	Urban parking availability	UC3.1 - Information on a vehicle parking space UC3.2 - Reservation of a vehicle parking space UC3.3 - Information about on-street parking availability for urban freight (loading zones) UC3.4 - Information about on-street parking availability for private car drivers
4	Roadworks warning	UC4.1 - Roadworks warning for 4 situations
5	Road hazard warning (incl. traffic jams)	UC5.1 - Hazardous location notification UC5.2 - Traffic condition warning UC5.3 - Weather condition warning
6	Emergency vehicle warning	UC6.1 - Emergency Vehicle Warning for 3 situations
7	Signal violation warning	UC7.1 - Red traffic light violation warning
8	Warning system for pedestrian	UC8.1 - Warning Signage to drivers about pedestrians
9	Green priority	UC9.1 - Green Priority for Designated Vehicles
10	GLOSA	UC10.1 - Optimised Driving with GLOSA
11	Cooperative traffic light for pedestrian	UC11.1 - Cooperative Traffic Light for Designated VRUs UC11.2 - Cooperative traffic light based on VRU detection
12	Flexible infrastructure (peak-hour lane)	UC12.1 - Flexible infrastructure as in-vehicle signage
13	In-vehicle signage (e.g. dynamic. speed limit)	UC13.1 - In-vehicle signage, dynamic traffic signs
14	Mode & trip time advice	UC14.1 - Mode and trip time advice for event visitors UC14.2 - Mode and trip time advice for drivers
15	Probe vehicle data	UC15.1 - Basic probe vehicle data UC15.2 - Extended probe vehicle data

(continued)

Table 6. (*continued*)

ID	Service	Use case
16	Emergency brake light	UC16.1 - Emergency electronic brake lights
17	CACC	UC17.1 - CACC vehicles approaching urban environment UC17.2 - CACC vehicles approaching semi-urban environment UC17.3 - Truck platooning UC17.4 - Cooperative Adaptive Cruise Control
18	Slow or stationary vehicle warning	UC18.1 - Slow or stationary vehicle warning
19	Motorcycle approaching indication (including other VRUs)	UC19.1 - Approaching two-wheeler warning (V2V) UC19.2 - Approaching two-wheeler warning (V2V, V2I)
20	Blind spot detection/warning (VRUs)	UC20.1 - Digital road safety mirror

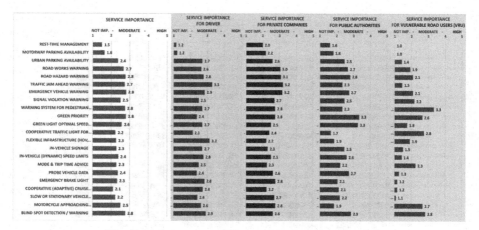

Fig. 11. Survey results: C-ITS service importance [41].

Concerning business aspects, business value, time to value, usefulness and willingness to pay were ranked in the survey using a 5-point Likert scale from strongly disagree to strongly agree, and the results are presented in Fig. 13. In general, C-ITS services were considered to be useful, with adequate business value. However, willingness-to-pay for these services is low. The survey results are consistent with the results from other C-ITS projects [41].

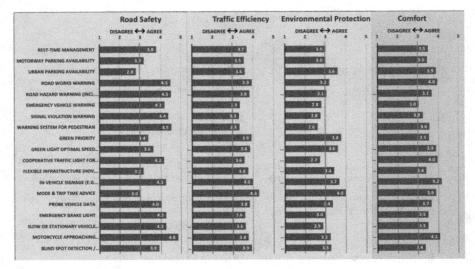

Fig. 12. Survey results: C-ITS service impacts [41].

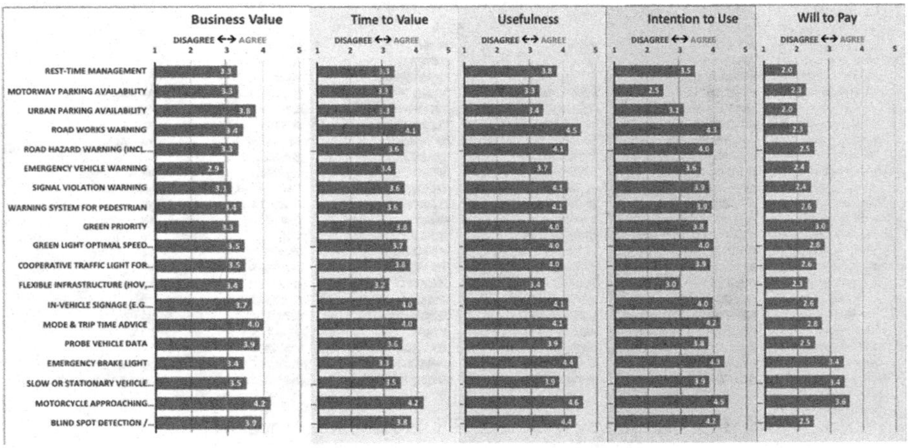

Fig. 13. Survey results: Business aspects, including willingness-to-pay [41].

4.3 Open Architecture for C-ITS Services

Based on analysis of existing architectures [46], architecture frameworks and architecture patterns, C-MobILE has developed a *Reference Architecture*, a *Concrete Architecture* and an *Implementation Architecture* supporting the architectures of deployment sites.

Key perspectives for implementing C-ITS services are: interoperability, security, performance, usability, reliability, availability and adaptability. Within C-MobILE two available and mature communication technologies are deployed: short-range communication based on IEEE 802.11p/ETSI ITS G5 and 3G/4G cellular communication. The former has as it main challenge the extent of the standardised messages, i.e. the substantial amount of optional elements, and possibility (and risk) of differences in interpretation of some elements. Within C-MobILE, interoperability is achieved through harmonisation of message profiling. The latter is not practical and in fact rather inefficient from an end-user perspective, as each user may have to use many different apps. Another disadvantage is fragmentation of services. C-MobILE also contributes to interoperability for internet-based cellular solutions.

Technical development also includes relevant features of an open and broker-centric architecture for connecting local systems using short-range communication to an infrastructure server, which uses an information broker (Fig. 14). For the client side, a topic structure inside the broker facilitates an efficient method for geocasting. On top of this functionality, a combination of certification, web tokens and transport layer security is developed to ensure security. A link of the architecture to the relevant business models is made to demonstrate that the two are compatible. The architecture elements enable service providers to both compete and complement each other in an efficient way at an international scale for providing attractive and seamless services to end users [47].

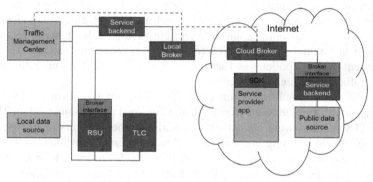

Fig. 14. Connection to local data sources. [47] (Note: RSU - Road-Side Unit, TLC - Traffic Light Controller, SDK - Software Development Kit).

5 Discussion

In the past years, the development of automated vehicles became a topic of much attention. Several promises have been made, drafting a wonderful, safe and efficient future of mobility. In 2020, the promises became much more realistic and several companies retreated from their vaulting ambitions. One of the reasons for this is that automated driving is a very complex task, and that having "real" vehicle automation requires that automation functionality is available during the whole trip, from origin to destination, for each travel. Since it is already common sense that Level-5 automation (based on the definition of SAE J3016) is a scenario of the far future, the current goal is to strive for Level 3 and Level-4 functionality, where automated driving is at least possible on long stretches of the road (e.g. highways) and where people at least benefit from longer periods during which they do not have to control the operation of the vehicle.

Recent research results provide the contours of a traffic management system and a cooperative infrastructure (V2V, V2I, I2V, I2I) for sophisticated urban road transport using highly-automated vehicles. Solid methods for evaluation and modelling of automated driving prototypes, and of driver behaviour, have been developed. Assessment of the impacts on road safety, traffic (network) efficiency, environment and comfort has been conducted. ICT infrastructure-based management procedures and protocols, V2X message sets, and communication protocols have been developed. Monitoring and detection systems have been enhanced. Cooperative and automated driving supported by integration with the traffic management system has been intensively tested, validated, evaluated and demonstrated. Furthermore, stakeholder guidelines and roadmaps for automated road transport have been developed.

In addition to the technical challenges of sensor and communication technologies, high-level automated driving generates requirements for enhanced traffic management. In general, the current traffic signal control and traffic management systems are not well connected and coordinated, and are instead operating in a rather fragmented way. Moreover, traditional traffic management does not take into account cooperative and automated vehicles, although cooperative vehicle-infrastructure communication technologies are feasible. Future traffic management will cope with all types of vehicles (passenger cars, public transport, heavy duty vehicles, coaches), different modes of operation (including remote control), and different business models. A major requirement for success is that authorities at all levels (cities, regions, countries and the EC) develop and implement cohesive policies and actions, at strategic, tactical and operational levels, for future traffic control and management.

The C-ITS survey results show that the C-ITS services have convincing importance, impacts (on safety, efficiency, environment, and comfort) and business value. The benefits of C-ITS services were also studied in various other projects in Europe. As an example, roadworks warning and road hazard warning may contribute to 9% fatality reduction; signal violation warning may contribute to 7% injury reduction; and green priority may contribute to 9% travel time reduction, 17% fuel-consumption reduction, and 5% CO_2-emission reduction [48]. However, the survey results with respect to willingness to pay clearly indicate a need to have well-thought and well-structured business models for large-scale service implementation.

Business models and security are important parameters for the establishment of an open architecture for pan-European C-ITS applications. The resulting C-ITS architecture provides a secure, pragmatic, cost-effective, and easy-to-operate basis for authorities to implement C-ITS services. Very important is that it allows neutral brokers to operate, and avoids vendor-lock-in situations. It is even possible to have multiple brokers of different vendors in parallel, and internet brokers competing through a free market. A security model was developed enabling at the same time competition and cooperation between business entities. JWT (JSON Web Tokens) can indicate that a user has the right to receive data for a number of services. The service provider that supplies the app to the end user has a contract with the internet provider, but is not involved in the real-time data exchange. An architecture with JWT allows an app provider to buy services at different internet providers, which is good for roaming.

6 Conclusion

Cooperative and automated road transport has a high potential for future mobility and quality of life. The automotive industry has made substantial technical developments for sustainable road transport, from different perspectives: social (safety, health), environmental (emissions, recycling), and economic (efficiency, cost-effectiveness).

However, it would be naive to expect that fully automated vehicles (Level-5) will be on the market in the near future, as many issues still need to be solved, which will take a substantial amount of time, if it will not appear to be impossible at all. There are many challenges, not only from a technical perspective (communication and positioning), but also from legal, human-factors, and social-economic perspectives. Therefore, strong cooperation between industry, authorities (at different levels) and academia in countries worldwide is a must for the successful further development and eventual implementation of high-level automated road transport, with harmonisation and interoperability as key determinants.

ICT infrastructure will play an important role for enabling the use of high-level automated vehicles on public roads, for supporting safe driving and operation, for protecting VRUs, and for enhancing road network efficiency. Future traffic signal control and traffic management systems will have to be well connected, to be able to cope with cooperative and automated vehicles, benefiting all road users (not just one or more vehicles under certain circumstances and certain conditions). Recent R&D (research and development) has demonstrated solid results, and provides guidance for the implementation of digital infrastructure. During the process towards high-level automated road transport, road users will experience increasing benefits, in terms of safety, comfort, energy efficiency, traffic efficiency, air quality, economic growth and job creation.

Acknowledgements. The chapter presents some main research results of three projects MAVEN (Managing Automated Vehicles Enhances Network), TransAID (Transition Areas for Infrastructure-Assisted Driving) and C-MobILE (Accelerating C-ITS Mobility Innovation and depLoyment in Europe), funded by the European Commission Horizon 2020 under Grant Agreement No. 690727, No. 723390 and No. 723311 respectively. The authors especially thank the partners of the consortia for their technical contributions.

References

1. On-Road Automated Driving committee: Taxonomy and definitions for terms related to on-road motor vehicle automated driving systems. SAE Standard J. **3016**, (2018), USA
2. Lu, M. (Ed.): Cooperative Intelligent Transport Systems: Towards High-Level Automated Driving. IET (Institution of Engineering and Technology), London (2019)
3. Molina-Masegosa, R., Gozalvez, J., Sepulcre, M.: Comparison of IEEE 802.11p and LTE-V2X: an evaluation with periodic and aperiodic messages of constant and variable size. IEEE Access **8** (2020). https://doi.org/10.1109/ACCESS.2020.3007115
4. Shimizu, T., Lu, H., Kenney, J., Nakamura, S.: Comparison of DSRC and LTE-V2X PC5 Mode 4 performance in high vehicle density scenarios. In: World Congress on Intelligent Transport Systems, Singapore (2019)

5. Dynniq Nederland, B.V.: Volkswagen Golf supports Car2X via ITS-G5, but the EU Member States are Still Divided on Which C-ITS Standard to Use: How to Move Forward? Dynniq Press Release, Amersfoort (2019)
6. Turley, A., Moerman, K., Filippi, A., Martinez, V.: C-ITS: Three Observations on LTE-V2X and ETSI ITS-G5 - A Comparison. NXP B.V., The Netherlands (2018)
7. Wevers, K., Lu, M.: V2X communication for ITS - from IEEE 802.11p towards 5G. IEEE 5G Tech Focus 1(2), 5–10 (2017).
8. 3GPP TR 21.914V0.8.0 (2017–09) 3rd Generation Partnership Project; Technical specification group services and system aspects; Release 14 description; Summary of Rel-14 work items (Release 14) (2017)
9. 3GPP TR 21.914 V0.5.0 (2018–12) 3rd Generation Partnership Project; Technical specification group services and system aspects; Release 15 description; Summary of Rel-15 work items (Release 15) (2018)
10. SAFESPOT Consortium: Technical Annex. SAFESPOT (Co-operative Systems for Road Safety Smart Vehicles on Smart Roads, Brussels (2005). (restricted)
11. CVIS Consortium: Technical Annex. CVIS (Cooperative Vehicle Infrastructure Systems; focusing on the infrastructure side and traffic efficiency), Brussels (2005). (restricted)
12. COOPERS Consortium: Technical Annex. COOPERS (CO-OPerative SystEms for Intelligent Road Safety), Brussels (2005). (restricted)
13. C-ITS Platform: Platform for the deployment of cooperative intelligent transport systems in the EU (E03188) C-ITS Platform final report. European Commission DG MOVE (Directorate-General for Mobility and Transport), Brussels (2016)
14. C-ITS Platform: Platform for the Deployment of Cooperative Intelligent Transport Systems in the EU (C-ITS Platform) Phase II Final Report. European Commission DG MOVE (Directorate-General for Mobility and Transport), Brussels (2017)
15. CAR 2 CAR Communication Consortium (C2CCC): Position roadmap: services & sample use cases. C2CCC (2018)
16. CAR 2 CAR Communication Consortium (C2CCC): Position paper on road safety and road efficiency spectrum needs in the 5.9 GHz for C-ITS and cooperative automated driving, C2CCC (2020).
17. MAVEN Consortium: Description of Action. MAVEN (Managing Automated Vehicles Enhances Network), Brussels (2002). (restricted)
18. DLR: SUMO (Simulation of Urban MObility). German Aerospace Center (DLR), Germany
19. MAVEN Consortium: Deliverable D7.2 Impact assessment - technical report. MAVEN (Managing Automated Vehicles Enhances Network) (2019)
20. MAVEN Consortium: Deliverable D2.2 System architecture, specifications and verification criteria. MAVEN (Managing Automated Vehicles Enhances Network) (2017)
21. Lu, M., Blokpoel, R.: A sophisticated intelligent urban road-transport network and cooperative systems infrastructure for highly automated vehicles. In: Proceedings: World Congress on Intelligent Transport Systems, Montréal (2017). Paper ID EU-TP0769
22. Rondinone, M., Walter, T., Blokpoel, R., Schindler, J.: V2X communications for infrastructure-assisted automated driving. In: Proceedings: IEEE International Symposium on a World of Wireless, Mobile and Multimedia Networks (WoWMoM), Chania (2018)
23. MAVEN Consortium: Deliverable D5.2 ADAS functions and HD maps. MAVEN (Managing Automated Vehicles Enhances Network) (2018)
24. MAVEN Consortium: Deliverables D3.3 Cooperative manoeuvre and trajectory planning algorithms. MAVEN (Managing Automated Vehicles Enhances Network) (2019)
25. MAVEN Consortium: Deliverables D4.4 Cooperative adaptive traffic light with automated vehicles. MAVEN (Managing Automated Vehicles Enhances Network) (2018)

26. MAVEN Consortium: Deliverables D6.4 Integration final report. MAVEN (Managing Automated Vehicles Enhances Network) (2019)
27. Vreeswijk, J., et al.: Deliverable 8.1 Stakeholder consultation report. TransAID Consortium (2019)
28. Wijbenga, A., et al.: Deliverable 2.1 Use cases and safety and efficiency metrics. TransAID Consortium (2019)
29. Wijbenga, A., et al.: Deliverable 2.2 Scenario definitions and modelling requirements. TransAID Consortium (2019)
30. Rondinone, M., et al.: Deliverable 5.1: Definition of V2X message sets. TransAID Consortium (2019)
31. Correa, A., et al.: Deliverable D5.2 V2X-based cooperative sensing and driving in Transition Areas. TransAID Consortium (2019)
32. Coll Perales, B., Thandavarayan, G., Sepulcre, M., Gozalvez, J., Correa, A.: Deliverable D5.3 Protocols for reliable V2X message exchange. TransAID Consortium (2020)
33. Schindler, J., Zhang, X., Wijbenga, A., Mintsis, E., Herbig, D.: Deliverable D5.4 Signalling for informing conventional vehicles. TransAID Consortium (2020)
34. Schindler, J., Herbig, D., Lau, M., Oehl, M.: Communicating issues in automated driving to surrounding traffic. In: The 22nd International Conference on Human-Computer Interaction (HCII) (2020) Accepted
35. Mintsis, E., et al.: Deliverable D3.1 Modelling, simulation and assessment of vehicle automations and automated vehicles' driver behaviour in mixed traffic. TransAID Consortium (2019)
36. Maerivoet, S., et al.: Deliverable 4.2 Preliminary simulation and assessment of enhanced traffic management measures. TransAID Consortium (2019)
37. Lücken, L., et al.: Deliverable 6.1 An integrated platform for the simulation and the assessment of traffic management procedures in Transition Areas. TransAID Consortium (2018)
38. Lücken, L., et al.: Deliverable 6.2 Assessment of traffic management procedures in Transition Areas. TransAID Consortium (2019)
39. Schindler, J., et al.: Deliverable 7.2 System prototype demonstration (iteration 1). TransAID Consortium (2019)
40. C-MobILE Consortium: Description of Action, C-MobILE (Accelerating C-ITS Mobility Innovation and depLoyment in Europe), Brussels (2017). (restricted)
41. C-MobILE Consortium: Deliverable D2.2 Analysis and determination of use cases. C-MobILE (Accelerating C-ITS Mobility Innovation and depLoyment in Europe) (2018)
42. C-MobILE Consortium: Deliverable D2.3 Requirements and specifications for C-ITS implementation. C-MobILE (Accelerating C-ITS Mobility Innovation and depLoyment in Europe) (2018)
43. C-MobILE Consortium: Deliverable D2.4 Operational procedures guidelines. C-MobILE (Accelerating C-ITS Mobility Innovation and depLoyment in Europe) (2018)
44. Turetken, O., Grefen, P., Gilsing, R., Adali, O.E., Ozkan, B.: Business-model innovation in the smart mobility domain. In: Lu, M. (Ed.) Cooperative Intelligent Transport Systems: Towards High-Level Automated Driving. IET, London (2019)
45. Lu, M., Turetken, O., Adali, O.E., Castells, J., Blokpoel, R., Grefen, P.: C-ITS (cooperative intelligent transport systems) deployment in Europe - challenges and key findings. In: Proceedings: The 25th World Congress on Intelligent Transport Systems, Copenhagen (2018). Paper ID EU-TP1076
46. Havinoviski, G.N.: Architecture of cooperative intelligent transport systems. In: Lu, M. (ed.) Cooperative Intelligent Transport Systems: Towards High-Level Automated Driving. IET, London (2019)

47. Lu, M., Blokpoel, R., Fünfrocken, M., Castells, J.: Open architecture for internet-based C-ITS Services. In Proceedings: The 21th IEEE International Conference on Intelligent Transportation Systems (ITSC), Hawaii, pp. 7–13. IEEE Xplore (2018)
48. C-MobILE Consortium: Deliverable D2.1 Ex-ante cost-benefit analysis. C-MobILE (Accelerating C-ITS Mobility Innovation and depLoyment in Europe) (2018)

A Two-Stage Approach for Traffic Sign Detection with Arrow Signal Recognition Using Convolutional Neural Networks

Tien-Wen Yeh, Huei-Yung Lin[(⊠)], and Mu-Yun Tsai

Department of Electrical Engineering, National Chung Cheng University,
168 University Rd., Chiayi 621, Taiwan
lin@ee.ccu.edu.tw

Abstract. In this work, a two-stage traffic light detection and recognition technique based on convolutional neural networks is developed. The object detection in the first stage utilizes the information provided by the HD map. To deal with the traffic lights at different ranges, two cameras with various focal lengths are adopted. For the traffic light recognition in the second stage, the detector is combined with a classifier to distinguish different light states. It is specifically important for the identification of challenging arrow signal lights in common Taiwan road scenes. Moreover, the overall computation time is reduced by the implementation of the end-to-end network with shared feature maps. In the experiments, two public datasets (LISA and SKTL) and our own dataset collected from two routes with urban traffic scenes are used to demonstrate the effectiveness of the proposed technique.

Keywords: Traffic light detection · Arrow signal recognition · Convolutional neural network · Advanced driver assistance system

1 Introduction

At present, the advanced driver assistance systems (ADAS) or autonomous driving vehicles have achieved fairly well results in simple environments such as highways and closed parks. To further improve the capability of autonomous driving, more complicated traffic scenarios such as the urban roads need to be considered. In these cases, it is necessary to have the ability to perceive the dynamic traffic conditions. One of the important issues is to detect the traffic signals and realize their states for driving instructions. Although the vehicle positioning by GPS combined with GIS mapping can provide the rough road junction information, the exact locations and states of the traffic lights are not guaranteed to be precisely marked in the HD maps. Thus, online detection and recognition of traffic signals are essential for driving assistance and autonomous vehicles.

Traffic light detection approaches are mainly divided into two categories. One is to make traffic lights have the capability to communicate with nearby vehicles through the V2I (Vehicle-to-Infrastructure) communication framework [1]. The other is to detect the positions and light states of the traffic lights by the onboard sensors of the vehicles.

C. Klein et al. (Eds.): SMARTGREENS 2020/VEHITS 2020, CCIS 1475, pp. 149–164, 2021.
https://doi.org/10.1007/978-3-030-89170-1_8

In general, these two approaches have both pros and cons. However, the former needs to be installed with the replacement of basic equipment and infrastructure. This is more expensive compared to the sensing based methods adopted by individual vehicles.

The traffic light detection and recognition techniques using the onboard sensors of vehicles have been investigated for many years [9]. In the early research, the main approaches usually combine image processing and computer vision algorithms to analyze the videos captured by the in-vehicle camera. Recently, the techniques based on deep learning have become more popular because of the public availability of the large collection of driving data [4,17,22]. However, the detection accuracy is still not satisfactory due to many disturbance factors in the outdoor environment. A few issues for the image-based traffic light detection methods are as followings.

- Images with hue shift and halo interference due to other light sources.
- (Partial) occlusion due to other objects or oblique viewing angles.
- Incomplete light shape due to sensing malfunction.
- False positives from reflection, billboard, pedestrian crossing light, etc.
- Dark light state due to unsynchronized light duty cycle and camera shutter.

In general, these problems are very difficult to solve by conventional computer vision algorithms. But with the success of deep learning and the use of convolutional neural networks (CNN) for traffic light detection [24], it is expected to have more powerful feature extraction capability to deal with these issues.

In this work, we propose a traffic light detection system for Taiwan road scenes based on deep neural networks. There are two technical challenges in our application scenarios. First, the traffic lights we are dealing with are arranged horizontally, which are different from the traffic lights in most public datasets. Second, the arrow signals are very common in Taiwan's traffic scenes, but most existing works use classifiers to recognize the circle lights only. These problems requires the solution of creating a self-collecting dataset. Moreover, the lack of enough arrow light images leads to the data unbalance among multiple classes. This makes the network training more complicated and difficult. Thus, a new method by combining the object detector and classifier for light state recognition is proposed. This two-stage approach first detects the light position, followed by the classification on the types of the arrow lights. Finally, the traffic light detection network is integrated to an end-to-end model with feature maps sharing [25]. Compared to the previous works, the experiments we carried out on the public LISA and SKTL datasets and our own dataset have reported better performance.

2 Related Work

2.1 Classical Traffic Light Detection

The early developments of image-based traffic light detection are mostly based on conventional computer vision techniques [6]. The input images are converted to different color spaces, and various features such as color, shape, edge and gray-level intensity are used for detection. In the later machine learning based approaches [10], image features such as HoG or Harr-like operators are adopted for SVM or AdaBoost classification techniques. There also exist techniques using multiple sensor inputs. Fregin *et al.* presented a method to integrate the depth information obtained using a stereo camera for traffic light detection [7]. Alternatively, Müller *et al.* presented a dual camera system to increase the range of traffic light detection with different focal length settings [16]. They used a long focal length camera to detect the far away traffic lights, while a wide-angle lens camera is adopted to detect the close by traffic lights.

2.2 Traffic Light Detection Using CNN

In the past few years, many techniques based on deep neural networks have been proposed to predict the positions of traffic lights. DeepTLR [24] and HDTLR [23] proposed by Weber *et al.* used convolutional neural networks for the detection and classification of traffic lights. Sermanet *et al.* presented an integrated framework, OverFeat, for classification, localization and detection [21]. They have shown that the multi-scale and sliding window approach can be efficiently implemented in a convolutional network structure. Recently, general object detection networks are successfully adopted and specifically modified for traffic light detection. Behrendt *et al.* presented a deep learning approach to deal with the traffic lights using the YOLO framework [3, 18]. Since the traffic lights might appear very small in some images, one common approach is to reduce the stride of the network architectures to preserve the features. Müller and Dietmayer adapted the single network SSD approach [14] and emphasized on the small traffic light detection [15]. Bach *et al.* presented a unified traffic light recognition system which is also capable of state classification (circle, straight, left, right) based on the Faster R-CNN structure [2, 20].

For the traffic light recognition, recent approaches are divided into two categories. One is to detect the traffic light, crop the traffic light region, and send it to a classifier for the light state recognition [3]. The other approach simultaneously detect the traffic light position and recognize the light state [2, 15]. When the object location is predicted with a confidence and the bounding box, one more branch is used to predict the light state. For general traffic light recognition, except for the recognition of basic circular lights, it is also required to deal with various kinds of arrow lights in many countries. In the existing literature, this issue is only covered by a limited number of research [2, 23]. A two-stage approach is usually adopted with first the light color classification, followed by the arrow type classification.

2.3 Map Assisted Traffic Light Detection

One major drawback of image-based traffic light detection is the false positives caused by the similar features in the background. To reduce the incorrect detection, a simple method is to restrict the ROI in the image for traffic light search. Alternatively, the location of the traffic light on the map or from other input sources can also provide additional information for more accurate detection. This intends to improve, rather than replace the image-based methods. In this map-based traffic light detection approach, the idea is to utilize the fact that traffic lights are located at fixed locations in normal conditions. GPS or LiDAR are commonly used to establish the HD map and annotate the traffic light positions in the route [5, 8]. When the vehicle is driving, the map and localization information is used to calculate the traffic light appeared in a small image region. Moreover, it can also provide the verification about which traffic light to follow if there exist more than one at a junction.

3   Dataset

Although several public datasets are available for traffic light detection and evaluation, they are not suitable for network training for Taiwan road scenes due to the different appearance. In this work, we cooperate with Industrial Technology Research Institute (ITRI) and collect our own dataset for both network training and performance evaluation.

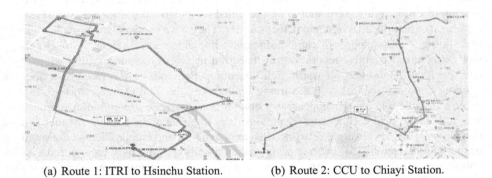

(a) Route 1: ITRI to Hsinchu Station.   (b) Route 2: CCU to Chiayi Station.

Fig. 1. The routes for collecting data to create our own dataset. Route 1 is from ITRI to THSR Hsinchu station, and route 2 is from CCU to THSR Chiayi station. The distances are 16 km and 39 km, respectively.

Figure 1 shows the two commuter routes for data collection. One route is from the ITRI campus to Hsinchu High Speed Railway Station, and the other is from National Chung Cheng University to Chiayi High Speed Railway Station. These routes contain the driving distances of 16 km and 39 km, and the recording time of 40 min and 50 min, respectively. Two cameras with the focal length of 3.5 mm and 12 mm are mounted below the rear view mirror of a vehicle for image acquisition. The image sequences are captured at 36 fps with the resolution of 2048 × 1536. The LiDAR data are also recorded (by Velodyne Ultra Puck VLP-32C) and used for the segmentation of rough traffic light regions in the images.

The first route is recorded three times, and the second route is recorded once. We sample 5 images per second for processing, labeling the position of the traffic light and the class of the light state. The labeled data contain 26,868 image frames and 29,963 traffic lights. Only the traffic lights with clear light states are labeled, and there are totally 14 classes of light state combination in the dataset. Due to the lack of left arrow lights in our collected image data, we have picked additional 784 images from South Korea Traffic Light (SKTL) dataset. As shown in Fig. 2, the SKTL dataset contains the traffic light boxes with the lights arranged horizontally, which are similar to the layout of traffic

(a) The images from South Korea Traffic Light dataset.

	Frames	TLs	Composition			
			Green	Red	Green Left	Red Left
Train	15555	45081	27456	13537	1775	2313
Valid	5185	15243	9381	4471	610	781
Test	5142	14931	9084	4519	599	729
Total	25882	75255	45921	22527	2984	3823

(b) The layout and quantity of traffic lights in South Korea Traffic Light dataset.

Fig. 2. Some information of South Korea traffic light dataset.

lights in Taiwan. One major difference is that the left arrow light appears next to the green light in the SKTL dataset, but it is next to the red light in Taiwan road scenes.

As shown in Fig. 3, the traffic lights in LISA dataset [9] are arranged vertically, which is very different from the ones arranged horizontally in Taiwan. Furthermore, the available light states are also different. Only a single light can be displayed at a time in LISA dataset (see Fig. 3(a)), but there exist many combinations with various types of arrow lights in the Taiwan road scenes (see Fig. 3(b)). Figure 4 shows our dataset collected using the cameras with 3.5 mm lens (in blue color) and 12 mm lens (in orange color) in terms of the cropped traffic light image size and the number of traffic lights in different classes. The dataset contains much more circular lights, but only a limited number of arrow lights. For the traffic light ROI size, LISA dataset mainly consists of the image regions in the range of 15–30 pixels. In our dataset, the images captured with 3.5 mm and 12 mm lenses have the traffic light regions in the ranges of 10–20 pixels and 15–50 pixels, respectively.

4   Approach

This work integrates the map information for traffic light detection and recognition. We use the pre-established HD map with the traffic light annotation which contains ID, position, horizontal and vertical angles. The position between the vehicle and traffic lights can be determined by the LiDAR data and HD map during driving. This information is used to crop the image for a rough traffic light position (see Fig. 5). Due to the characteristics of the LiDAR data and the registration with images, it is not possible to identify the traffic lights accurately. The cropped ROI is then fed to the neural networks for precise location detection and light state recognition.

(a) The traffic scene in LISA dataset.

(b) The traffic lights in LISA dataset.

(c) The images captured with our 3.5/12 mm lens cameras.

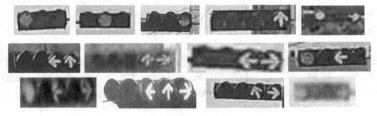

(d) Examples of traffic lights collected in our dataset.

Fig. 3. The traffic light images in the LISA dataset and our dataset captured using the cameras with 3.5 mm and 12 mm lenses [25].

The proposed traffic light detection and recognition technique is a two-stage approach, with the first stage for the traffic light detection and the second stage for the light state recognition. In the first stage, several popular object detection networks including Faster R-CNN, SSD, YOLO have been tested. In the traffic light detection application, the computation load is one of the major concerns. YOLOv3 [19] provides the best accuracy vs. processing time trade-off in the experiments, and is adopted for our detection framework. In the second stage, we propose a new method which combines the

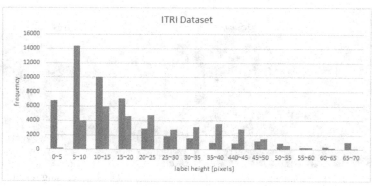

(a) Traffic light size vs. number.

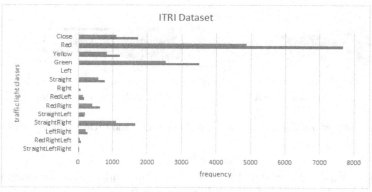

(b) Traffic light class vs. number.

Fig. 4. The statistics of our dataset in terms of the traffic light size and class. The blue and orange colors indicate the numbers from 3.5 mm and 12 mm lenses, respectively [25].

object detection and classification. The light states are detected by YOLOv3-tiny [19] and classified to four classes: RedCircle, YellowCircle, GreenCircle and Arrow, followed by the classification of Arrows into LeftArrow, StraightArrow and RightArrow using LeNet [12]. As an example, if there is a Red-Left-Right light state, YOLOv3-tiny will detect one RedCircle and two Arrows, and LeNet will recognize the two Arrows as LeftArrow and RightArrow. The final traffic light state is then provided by combining the results of two networks.

This approach is expected to mitigate the unbalanced data problem. Furthermore, it is also flexible in that detecting less common light states can be performed with a slight modification to LeNet and prediction classes.

4.1 Detection Network

Network Architecture. The proposed detection and classification technique consists of three cascaded network structures. It takes more time to train and inference if all

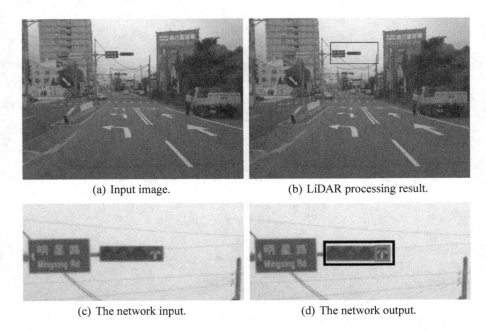

(a) Input image.   (b) LiDAR processing result.

(c) The network input.   (d) The network output.

Fig. 5. The results of traffic light detection combining image and LiDAR data in the experiments [25].

three networks are independent. Thus, in the implementation, they are integrated to a single end-to-end network with shared feature maps. Better detection and classification results are obtained, and the speed of network training and inference is also improved. The unified network architecture is shown in Fig. 6. Because the subnets share the same feature map, the architecture of the second and third subnets have changed. Feature extraction of the network is removed, which leaves only the prediction part. The subnet inputs are also changed from images to the feature maps coming from the FPN of the previous subnet.

Loss Function and ROI. The loss of the unified network is the error summation of the three subnets. It is expected that the network can back-propagate based on the overall task error. We use the original loss functions for YOLOv3 and YOLOv3-tiny, and the cross entropy loss for LeNet. The network training of the second and third subnets is not based on the detection results of the previous subnet, but directly from the groundtruth. This is due to the initial training of each subnet is not good enough to accurately identify the traffic lights or light states. Only when inferencing for evaluation, the network runs based on the detection results of the previous subnets.

Training Image and Data Augmentation. Our detection network is based on the cropped image, so the training data are also cropped to simulate the LiDAR processing, as shown in Fig. 7. Each traffic light image is cropped 3 times, and the traffic light positions are randomly shown in the cropped image. The dataset mainly contains six

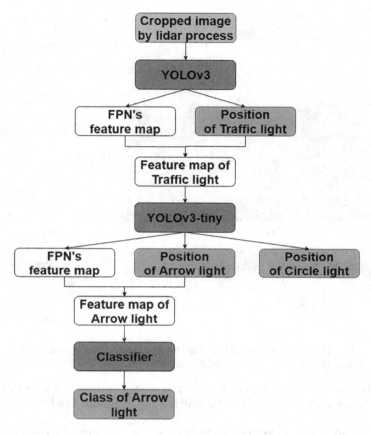

Fig. 6. The flowchart of the proposed network architecture. The subnet inputs are the shared feature maps from the FPN (feature pyramid network) [25].

classes: Red, Yellow, Green, Straight and StraightRight. Thus, data augmentation is carried out to generate more training data by rotating the Arrow light images (see Figs. 7(a) and 7(b)).

5 Experiments

5.1 Evaluation Criteria

We adopt three indicators for the evaluation of machine learning models: precision, recall, and F1-score.

– Precision: The ability to classify negative samples. If the precision is higher, the ability to classify negative samples is stronger, i.e.,

$$Precision = \frac{TP}{TP + FP} \tag{1}$$

Fig. 7. Examples of the training images [25]. (a) Original image, (b) cropped with LiDAR data, (c) training image, (d) data augmented 1, (e) data augmented 2.

Table 1. The results obtained using our dataset. Three network structures are compared and one with data augmentation. The table shows the mAP and the computation time [25].

Network	YOLOv3 + AlexNet	YOLOv3 + YOLOv3-tiny+LeNet	Unified Network	Unified Network
Data augmentation	✗	✗	✗	✓
mAP	0.36	0.55	0.57	0.67
Speed (ms)	31	52	40	40

- Recall: The ability to classify positive samples. If the recall is higher, the ability to classify positive samples is stronger, i.e.,

$$Recall = \frac{TP}{TP + FN} \tag{2}$$

- F1-Score: A combination of precision and recall. If the F1-Score is higher, the classifier is more robust, i.e.,

$$F1 - Score = \frac{2 \cdot Precision \cdot Recall}{Precision + Recall} \tag{3}$$

Two indicators are used to evaluate the object detection results: the precision-recall curve (PR curve) and the mean average precision (mAP).

- PR curve: Different thresholds have different precision and recall. The precision-recall curve is given by drawing all the precision and recall. The trend of this curve represents the quality of a classifier.
- AP (average precision): It represents the area under the PR curve (AUC), which indicates the robustness of a classifier. If the area is larger, the classifier is stronger.
- mAP: AP only represents one class, but the models often detect many classes. So mAP is used to represent the average AP of all classes.

Table 2. The LISA daytime dataset test result (mAP using IoU 0.5). The results of columns 1, 2, 3 are from [9]. The results of columns 4, 5, 6, 7 are from [13].

Method	Stop	StopLeft	Go	GoLeft	Warning	WarningLeft	All
Color detector							0.04
Spot detector							0.0004
ACF detector							0.36
Faster R-CNN	0.14	0.01	0.19	0.001			0.09
SLD	0.08		0.10				0.09
ACF	0.63	0.13	0.40	0.37			0.38
Multi-detector	0.72	0.28	0.52	0.40			0.48
Ours	0.70	0.40	0.88	0.71	0.52	0.24	0.66

5.2 Training and Testing on LISA Dataset

For the performance comparison with other techniques, the LISA daytime dataset is used for training and testing. As shown in Table 2, the conventional detectors do not provide good results due to the complex scenes in the dataset. The low accuracy results obtained from Faster R-CNN are mainly due to the small traffic light regions, and it is difficult to detect after the layer-by-layer convolution [13]. The proposed method has achieved the best results as shown in the last row, which include the circular lights and arrow lights.

5.3 Training and Testing on Our Dataset

In Table 1, we compare the accuracy and computation speed of different network structures on our dataset. The first one uses YOLOv3 to detect the traffic lights and AlexNet [11] to classify the light states. The second method is the 'YOLOv3+YOLOv3-tiny+LeNet' combination proposed in this work, but with three independent networks. The last one is the unified network structure containing the integration of the three subnets. All networks are trained and tested on the same dataset. As shown in the table, the mAPs of the proposed methods are better than 'YOLOv3+AlexNet' at the cost of more computation time. Comparing the first two network structures, the one with LeNet for arrow light classification has a better mAP but requires more computation time. For the proposed methods, the unified network (the last two columns in the table) has an improvement in mAP compared to the one without integration (the second column in the table). Furthermore, the computation speed is also faster due to the use of shared feature maps.

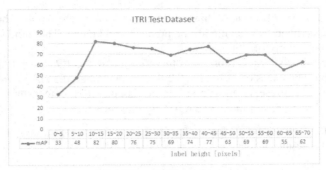

(a) mAP vs. traffic light size

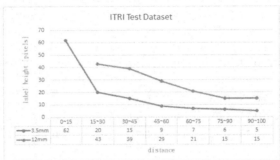

(b) Traffic light size vs. distance.

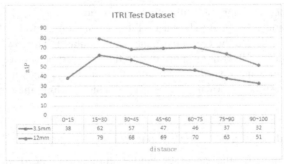

(c) mAP vs. distance.

Fig. 8. The relationship among the mAP, the traffic light size in the image, and the distance of the traffic light in our dataset [25].

5.4 Comparison on Different Distance

The images taken from different distances contain the traffic lights with different ROI sizes. This will apparently affect the detection and recognition results. In the experiments, the cameras with 3.5 mm and 12 mm lenses are used for image acquisition. Figures 8(a), 8(b) and 8(c) show the mAP of different traffic light ROI size (height in pixel), the size of traffic lights at different distance, and the mAP of different distance, respectively. In Figs. 8(a) and 8(b), the traffic lights taken by 12 mm lens are larger than taken by 3.5 mm lens. It is reasonable that larger traffic lights provide better detection results. Figure 8(c) shows the detection results for 12 mm lens are better than 3.5 mm for all distances. However, the short focal lens camera can still be used to cover the close range scenes.

In the experiments, we find that some traffic lights in the 3.5 mm lens dataset are too small for the proposed network. Thus, we restrict the size of traffic light between 10×10 and 30×30 pixels for training and testing on this dataset. When the lights are larger than 30×30 pixels, they are usually too close to the camera physically and appear near the top image border. In this case, the traffic lights are oblique and becomes too dark to perceive. It is also found that the mAP of red lights in 3.5 mm lens dataset is much lower than the mAPs of yellow and green lights. This is mainly due to the similarity of red and yellow traffic lights acquired by the cameras as shown in Fig. 9.

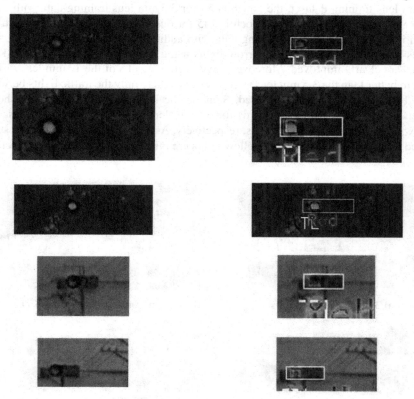

Fig. 9. Some red lights that are similar to yellow lights in 3.5 mm lens test images. (Color figure online)

5.5 Detection Results in Each Stage

Our approach consists of three stages for traffic light detection, initial light state classification, and arrow type recognition. Table 3 shows the mAPs of 3.5 mm lens and 12 mm

Table 3. The mAPs of 3.5 mm lens and 12 mm lens testing results with and without the training data from the SKTL dataset.

Class	Traffic light	Red	Yellow	Green	Left	Straight	Right
3.5 mm lens	0.97	0.74	0.92	0.97	0.80	0.83	0.84
3.5 mm lens (with SKTL)	0.96	0.76	0.90	0.97	0.87	0.85	0.91
12 mm lens	0.98	0.95	0.97	0.90	0.97	0.94	0.95
12 mm lens (with SKTL)	0.98	0.97	0.94	0.91	0.98	0.91	0.95

lens testing results with and without the training data from the SKTL dataset. It emphasizes the state classification with three types of arrow lights (left, straight, and right). Some training parameters are as follows: the batch size is 8, the epoch is 273 for our 3.5 mm lens training dataset, the epoch is 50 for 3.5 mm lens training data with additional SKTL dataset images, the epoch is 145 for our 12 mm lens training dataset, the epoch is 100 for 12 mm lens training data with additional SKTL dataset images. The results indicate that the mAPs of arrow lights using the training data with the SKTL images are clearly improved. Moreover, the detection results of the 12 mm lens testing data are better than the 3.5 mm lens testing results, where only the traffic lights between 10×10 and 30×30 are considered. Some traffic light detection results are shown in Figs. 10(a) ,10(b), 10(c) and 10(d) for 3.5 mm lens and 12 mm lens datasets, and with/without SKTL training samples, respectively. As seen in the experimental results, the red lights which are similar to yellow lights are much easier to have false detection.

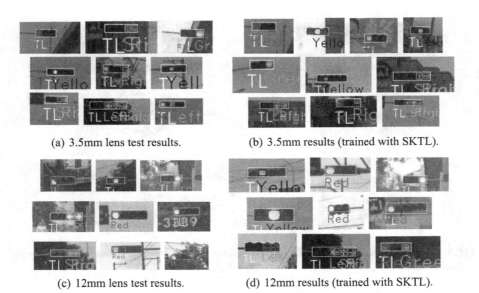

(a) 3.5mm lens test results.   (b) 3.5mm results (trained with SKTL).

(c) 12mm lens test results.   (d) 12mm results (trained with SKTL).

Fig. 10. Some traffic light detection results for 3.5 mm lens and 12 mm lens datasets, and with/without SKTL training samples.

6   Conclusion

In this work, a traffic light detection and recognition technique based on convolutional neural networks is developed. It is a two-stage approach with the first stage for the detection of the traffic light positions, followed by the second stage for the light state recognition. The network is specifically designed to deal with the arrow signal lights commonly seen in Taiwan road scene. In the traffic light detection stage, the information from the HD map is utilized to facilitate the detection by restricting the ROI. Two cameras with different focal lengths are used to capture the near and far scene images. In the recognition stage, a method combining the object detection and classification is presented. It is used to cope with the problem of multiple light state classes in many urban traffic scenes. The training and inference computation costs are reduced by our end-to-end unified network with shared feature maps. In the experiments, the public datasets and our own datasets are tested to demonstrate the feasibility of our method.

Acknowledgments. The support of this work in part by the Ministry of Science and Technology of Taiwan under Grant MOST 106-2221-E-194-004, is gratefully acknowledged.

References

1. Abboud, K., Omar, H.A., Zhuang, W.: Interworking of DSRC and cellular network technologies for V2X communications: a survey. IEEE Trans. Veh. Technol. **65**, 9457–9470 (2016)
2. Bach, M., Stumper, D., Dietmayer, K.C.J.: Deep convolutional traffic light recognition for automated driving. In: 2018 21st International Conference on Intelligent Transportation Systems (ITSC), pp. 851–858 (2018)
3. Behrendt, K., Novak, L., Botros, R.: A deep learning approach to traffic lights: detection, tracking, and classification. In: 2017 IEEE International Conference on Robotics and Automation (ICRA), pp. 1370–1377 (2017)
4. Caesar, H., et al.: nuscenes: a multimodal dataset for autonomous driving. arXiv preprint arXiv:1903.11027 (2019)
5. Fairfield, N., Urmson, C.: Traffic light mapping and detection. In: 2011 IEEE International Conference on Robotics and Automation, pp. 5421–5426 (2011)
6. Fregin, A., Müller, J.M., Dietmayer, K.C.J.: Feature detectors for traffic light recognition. In: 2017 IEEE 20th International Conference on Intelligent Transportation Systems (ITSC), pp. 339–346 (2017)
7. Fregin, A., Müller, J.M., Dietmayer, K.C.J.: Three ways of using stereo vision for traffic light recognition. In: 2017 IEEE Intelligent Vehicles Symposium (IV), pp. 430–436 (2017)
8. Hirabayashi, M., Sujiwo, A., Monrroy, A., Kato, S., Edahiro, M.: Traffic light recognition using high-definition map features. Rob. Auton. Syst. **111**, 62–72 (2019)
9. Jensen, M.B., Philipsen, M.P., Møgelmose, A., Moeslund, T.B., Trivedi, M.M.: Vision for looking at traffic lights: issues, survey, and perspectives. IEEE Trans. Intell. Transp. Syst. **17**, 1800–1815 (2016)
10. Kim, H.K., Park, J.H., Jung, H.Y.: Effective traffic lights recognition method for real time driving assistance systemin the daytime (2011)
11. Krizhevsky, A., Sutskever, I., Hinton, G.E.: Imagenet classification with deep convolutional neural networks. Commun. ACM **60**, 84–90 (2012)
12. LeCun, Y., Bottou, L., Bengio, Y., Haffner, P., et al.: Gradient-based learning applied to document recognition. Proc. IEEE **86**(11), 2278–2324 (1998)

13. Li, X., Ma, H., Wang, X., Zhang, X.: Traffic light recognition for complex scene with fusion detections. IEEE Trans. Intell. Transp. Syst. **19**, 199–208 (2018)
14. Liu, W., Anguelov, D., Erhan, D., Szegedy, C., Reed, S., Fu, C.-Y., Berg, A.C.: SSD: single shot multibox detector. In: Leibe, B., Matas, J., Sebe, N., Welling, M. (eds.) ECCV 2016. LNCS, vol. 9905, pp. 21–37. Springer, Cham (2016). https://doi.org/10.1007/978-3-319-46448-0_2
15. Müller, J.M., Dietmayer, K.C.J.: Detecting traffic lights by single shot detection. In: 2018 21st International Conference on Intelligent Transportation Systems (ITSC), pp. 266–273 (2018)
16. Müller, J.M., Fregin, A., Dietmayer, K.C.J.: Multi-camera system for traffic light detection: about camera setup and mapping of detections. In: 2017 IEEE 20th International Conference on Intelligent Transportation Systems (ITSC), pp. 165–172 (2017)
17. Ramanishka, V., Chen, Y.T., Misu, T., Saenko, K.: Toward driving scene understanding: a dataset for learning driver behavior and causal reasoning. In: Conference on Computer Vision and Pattern Recognition (2018)
18. Redmon, J., Divvala, S.K., Girshick, R.B., Farhadi, A.: You only look once: unified, real-time object detection. In: 2016 IEEE Conference on Computer Vision and Pattern Recognition (CVPR), pp. 779–788 (2016)
19. Redmon, J., Farhadi, A.: Yolov3: an incremental improvement. CoRR arXiv:1804.02767 (2018)
20. Ren, S., He, K., Girshick, R.B., Sun, J.: Faster R-CNN: Towards real-time object detection with region proposal networks. IEEE Trans. Pattern Anal. Mach. Intell. **39**, 1137–1149 (2015)
21. Sermanet, P., Eigen, D., Zhang, X., Mathieu, M., Fergus, R., LeCun, Y.: Overfeat: integrated recognition, localization and detection using convolutional networks. In: Bengio, Y., LeCun, Y. (eds.) 2nd International Conference on Learning Representations, ICLR 2014, Banff, April 14–16, Conference Track Proceedings (2014). http://arxiv.org/abs/1312.6229
22. Waymo: waymo open dataset: an autonomous driving dataset (2019)
23. Weber, M., Huber, M., Zöllner, J.M.: HDTLR: a CNN based hierarchical detector for traffic lights. In: 2018 21st International Conference on Intelligent Transportation Systems (ITSC), pp. 255–260 (2018)
24. Weber, M., Wolf, P., Zöllner, J.M.: DeepTLR: a single deep convolutional network for detection and classification of traffic lights. In: 2016 IEEE Intelligent Vehicles Symposium (IV), pp. 342–348 (2016)
25. Yeh, T., Lin, H.: Detection and recognition of arrow traffic signals using a two-stage neural network structure. In: Berns, K., Helfert, M., Gusikhin, O. (eds.) Proceedings of the 6th International Conference on Vehicle Technology and Intelligent Transport Systems, VEHITS 2020, Prague, May 2–4, pp. 322–330 SCITEPRESS (2020). https://doi.org/10.5220/0009345203220330

Open Your Eyes: Eyelid Aperture Estimation in Driver Monitoring Systems

Juan Diego Ortega[1,2]([✉]) [iD], Paola Cañas[1] [iD], Marcos Nieto[1] [iD],
Oihana Otaegui[1] [iD], and Luis Salgado[3] [iD]

[1] Vicomtech Foundation, Basque Research and Technology Alliance (BRTA),
San Sebastian, Spain
{jdortega,pncanas,mnieto,ootaegui}@vicomtech.org
[2] Departamento de Señales, Sistemas y Radiocomunicaciones, ETSIT,
Universidad Politécnica de Madrid (UPM), Madrid, Spain
[3] GTI, Information Processing and Telecommunications Center (IPTC) and ETSIT,
Universidad Politécnica de Madrid (UPM), Madrid, Spain
luis.salgado@upm.es

Abstract. Driver Monitoring Systems (DMS) operate by measuring the
state of the driver while performing driving activities. At the gates of the
arrival of SAE-L3 autonomous driving vehicles, DMS are called to play
a major role for guarantee or, at least, support safer mode transfer transitions (between manual and automated driving modes). Drowsiness and
fatigue detection with cameras is still one of the major targets of DMS
research and investment. In this work we present our eyelid aperture
estimation method, as enabling method for estimating such physiological status, in the context of two main use cases. First, we show how the
technique can be integrated into a DMS system, along with other outside-
sensing components, to showcase SAE-L3 demonstrations. Second, we
adopt the DMD (Driver Monitoring Dataset) open dataset project with
a twofold purpose: evaluate the quality of our method compare to other
state-of-the-art techniques, and to contribute to the DMD with ground
truth labels about drowsiness concepts.

Keywords: Eyelid aperture · Blink detection · Drowsiness · Driver
monitoring · ADAS · Datasets

1 Introduction

According to the World Health Organization (WHO), traffic accidents are the
eighth leading cause of death in the world [55]. Driving a car is a very complex
task, requiring the person behind the wheel to correctly coordinate different
cognitive and psychomotor functions at once. Crashes can be the consequence of
many different factors, which can be classified into three categories: the road, the
vehicle, and the driver. Despite all other factors at play on the road, human error
is still the deadliest factor. In fact, 90% of traffic accidents are caused by human
error [35]. Human error can be attributed to different causes being fatigue and

© Springer Nature Switzerland AG 2021
C. Klein et al. (Eds.): SMARTGREENS 2020/VEHITS 2020, CCIS 1475, pp. 165–189, 2021.
https://doi.org/10.1007/978-3-030-89170-1_9

drowsiness one of the most prevalent cause in traffic accidents. In fact, in the EU, 20% of truck-involved fatal crashes were related with fatigued drivers [47]. Therefore, the efficient detection and prevention of driver drowsiness must be considered as a high priority road safety issue.

Over the past years, automotive research scientists have developed Advanced Driver Assistance Systems (ADAS) with the focus on preventing such accidents by improving vehicle safety. These type of systems usually sense the outside of the vehicle and vehicle movement to determine possible threads with respect to other vehicles, pedestrians, lanes, etc. However, developing techniques to sense the driver state has demonstrated to have an enormous effect in reducing traffic accidents[1].

Along with the advances in ADAS, the research community have pushed forward the development of autonomous driving systems with the main objective of reaching SAE-L4 and SAE-L5. Nevertheless, such type of systems is still far to be available commercially. In this transition through SAE-L4 L5 there will be a paradigm shift in terms of driver responsibility and function [46] (see Fig. 1). The driving task will become a shared activity with both machine and human agency involved. For this to be successful, the estimation of driver behaviour and state will need to factored in.

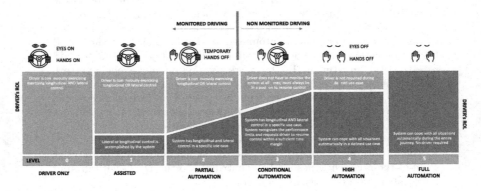

Fig. 1. SAE Levels for autonomous driving. The gap between L2 and above mainly relies on the need to release the driver from certain driving tasks, but also monitor the driver to return to manual driving when the AD function exits its Operational Design Domain (ODD).

Proposed Driver Monitoring Systems (DMS) methods that determine fatigue and distraction take different types of inputs from the driver. Traditional DMS had relied on vehicular features to determine driver inattention (e.g. steering wheel angle, pedal action, lane deviation, etc.) [8]. However, these features will not be available when using highly autonomous vehicles, since the driver is not manipulating the vehicle, which makes it difficult to continuously monitor the driver state and behaviour.

---

[1] STRIA Roadmap on Connected and Automated Transport: Road, Rail and Waterborne.

Other works studied biological features of the driver (e.g. heart, brain, skin signals) [7] using devices attached to the driver. These methods require expensive intrusive sensors which make them unfeasible for real applications in vehicles.

Drivers also exhibit certain observable behaviour such as eyelid and head movements that correlate significantly with distraction and drowsiness. Besides, the advances in computer vision research have made it possible to robustly extract observable features from the driver face with unobtrusive sensors [50].

This paper represents a continuation of the work presented in [39], where an eyelid aperture detection method was presented. In this manuscript we report new work in the same line. The main new contributions within this manuscript are the following:

- Integration of the eyelid aperture estimation method into a DMS (Driver Monitoring System) in the VI-DAS project vehicle and simulation set-ups under the real-time multisensor framework RTMaps (see Fig. 2).
- Contribution to the DMD (Driver Monitoring Dataset) open project with labelling effort of drowsiness-related concepts
- Evaluation and comparison of the proposed method with the DMD labelled material

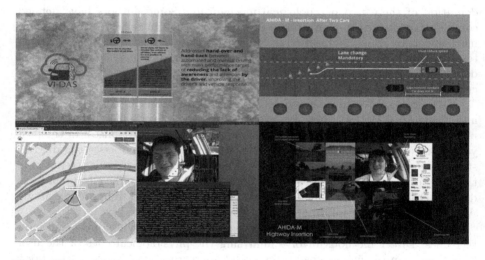

Fig. 2. Driver Monitoring System integrated into the VI-DAS vehicle, and demonstrated at the ITS Europe Congress 2019, with the DMS connected to the (Bottom-left) IoT solution and the decision making system (Bottom-right).

It is particularly relevant the utilisation of the DMD (Driver Monitoring Dataset) [40] as a valuable open dataset project where our proposed method can be evaluated. In particular, in this work we have contributed to the DMD by using the available labelling tool to produce drowsiness-related labels (eye-state: open, closing, close, opening, gestures: yawning, etc.) so that other researchers can use the same material for fair comparison.

The remaining of the paper is organised as follows: Sect. 1 (new section compared with previous paper) presents an introduction to the topic; Sect. 2 (new section) shows an overview of the state-of-the-art in DMS and related topics; Sect. 3 (same as in previous paper) describes the proposed eyelid aperture detection method; Sect. 4 (new section) details the new contributions on the DMD project and the integration into the RTMaps-based DMS component. Section 5 (new section) presents accuracy results of the implementation against the labelled DMD material.

2 Related Work

2.1 Driver Monitoring Systems

There is a lack of consensus to define driver's state, which causes a number of problems. First, it can make the interpretation and comparison of research findings across studies difficult, or even impossible. Secondly, similar works may be measuring slightly different constructs and measuring different outcomes. Usually driver state has been related to driver inattention and driver distraction. In the same way, the works found in the literature show inconsistency in the definition of these two psychological mechanisms. Some authors have defined complex taxonomies to characterise driver inattention in terms of the different mechanisms by which inattention may arise [43]. Many definitions of driver inattention have been proposed and had evolved throughout the years. A common definition of inattention is given as "insufficient, or no attention, to activities critical for safe driving" [42].

Variation in driver state can be produced by two main causes: (a) distraction and (b) fatigue. Both of them are grouped into the driver's inattention mechanisms which can show different physical and physiological responses. In the past years, different attempts have been made to understand and asses the driver's state through a variety of objective and subjective methods in order to mitigate the effect of human errors and reduce accident fatalities [27]. The efforts made to develop Driver Monitoring Systems (DMS) have contributed to improve existing ADAS and In-Vehicle Information Systems (IVIS).

The in-cabin human state can be analysed first by observing direct and indirect cues. Direct methods involve analysing the physiological cues of the user to obtain features such as head pose, eyelid aperture, gaze direction, feet, body and hand pose, brain activity, heart and skin parameters, etc. (see Fig. 3); either using intrusive or unobtrusive sensors [38]. Indirect methods involve extracting the activity of on-board sensors such as vehicle's dynamics, phone, smart watches, or GPS. Then, based on the direct and indirect measures, it is possible to infer and predict the human state and behaviour [16].

Subjective approaches are used to directly ask the users about their fatigue, attention and workload levels, which are easier to implement but non-automatic. However, these type of systems are usually not suitable for commercial DMS, because they are generally measured before or after the driving activity by means

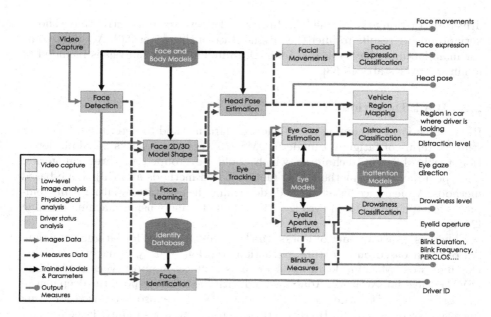

Fig. 3. DMS operates by defining modular components that solve shared requirements for different driver feature extraction: face detection, tracking, landmark extraction, eyelid aperture estimation, behaviour analysis, etc.

of self-reporting. Therefore, they cannot provide driver state reference for real-time systems. One of the most used metric to measure fatigue is the Karolinksa Sleepiness Scale (KSS) which can categorise the driver's fatigue and drowsiness in 9 levels [25].

Moreover, other types of methods have also been studied which imply the use of intrusive physiological measurements such as heart rate (pulse detection), brain activity (electroencephalography), eyelid closure and blinks (eyelid sensor) or skin conductance (electrodes) [34]. To obtain a measure of driver state (fatigue, distraction, cognitive workload and stress) different correlations between these indicators and the current driver state is performed. However, the intrusive typology of these sensors makes them difficult to implemented in commercial applications.

Other methods use computational algorithms to sense and predict the state of the driver. Computer vision and machine learning such as gaze-tracking [21], eye tracking [15], body and head pose [36] are promising approaches to solve this problem as they use unobtrusive sources of multitude information of driver condition. By analysing visual-based metrics that describe various characteristics of the physiological state of the human, the method is capable of predicting the temporal relationship of the data to generate a driver state model [30].

Face and eye movement features (e.g. head pose, eye blinks, gaze direction, yawning, etc.) are typically considered for deriving driver cognitive states, such as driver distraction and fatigue [11]. In particular, eye-related metrics have shown very promising results to infer the fatigue state of the driver [50]. Actually, some car manufacturers have released basic DMS in which eye analysis is included to monitor driver state [45,53].

2.2 Blink Detection

Blink detection is becoming one of the standard method to determine the driver state in terms of fatigue in modern DMS [23]. Scientific works on blink detection tackle different techniques which could be grouped in three categories: (i) appearance-based methods, (ii) motion-based methods and (iii) shape-based methods. Appearance based methods determine the eye state by either using templates for open and closed eyes [22] or trained classifiers using machine learning [24,32].

There is a vast amount of works which suggest methods for fatigue detection. All of them based on a feature extraction step followed by a machine learning classifier step. Machine learning algorithms such as Support Vector Machines (SVM), Bayesian Network, Adaboost and with the recent hype of the deep neural networks. These Deep Learning (DL) approaches have also been used for blink detection systems [29,30]. However, these types of systems require large amount of annotated data to reach high results. Acquiring such datasets for driver state estimation imply large efforts to store and annotate the data.

Moreover, motion-based methods typically require to detect the face and eye regions within the image by means of statistical classifiers. Then, by using optical flow strategies, the motion of the eyelids can be obtained [12,14]. Finally, a decision is made whether the eyes are not covered by the eyelids or not.

Since one of the most reliable physiological indicator for determining the driver status is the eyelid aperture level [9], methods which exploit this features have shown good results [3,39]. The eyelid aperture level is the basic measure to obtain more complex and discriminative indicators such as blink duration, blink frequency or PERCLOS. The latter being widely used in the literature [26] to determine the fatigue state of the driver.

To obtain the eyelid aperture level, shape-based methods are found appropriate in the context of blink detection. These methods obtain the contour of the eyelid borders and compute an indicator of the degree of eye aperture. Traditionally, thresholds for the eyelid aperture [48] have been applied to determine whether the eyes are closed or opened. In other works classification algorithms [51] or rule-based methods [3] are used to detect blinks.

The signals to compute the contour of the palpebral fissure can be obtained by image processing algorithms such as the adjustment of an Active Shape Model (ASM) [56] or a Regression Landmark Model [23]. These methods are suitable and practical for real DMS solutions where face landmark detection are required for other functions, such as blink analysis, head pose estimation, or gaze estimation refinement [15,21].

The computation of eyelid aperture can be approached by different methods. For instance, [19] approximate the upper and bottom eyelids contours by fitting two intersected parabolic functions, one per eyelid border. The eyelid aperture is estimated by using the distance from the upper and lower eyelid curves.

In [54] an 8-point eye deformable model is proposed. The eyelid aperture level degree is obtained by computing the ratio of the maximum vertical distance and the intra-ocular distance (IOD) for each eye. Eye blink detection is determined by applying an heuristic threshold determined by a set of evaluation face data. Similarly, in [56], a face tracker based on ASM is computed to obtain a first position of eye landmarks. Then the eye contour is refined by fitting a deformable template of two intersected parabolic sections to a distance map based on the distance of each pixel to the distribution of the skin colours. The final eye closure score is evaluated from the converged eye shape.

Moreover, a rule-based approach was used in [3]. The method require the input of the eye geometrical ratio. The steps to define blink features is obtained by analysing the properties of blinks. A set of standard steps are provided for regular blinks with the inclusion of some edge-cases. Nevertheless, the computation of some of the design thresholds are done taking a temporal windows of several minutes which prevents it to be used in continuous driving monitoring.

2.3 Datasets

The development of computer vision algorithms devoted to detection and classification tasks require the availability of a set of data with enough richness to perform the target task. Due to the increasing popularity of DMS in the computer vision community, a wide range of datasets were proposed targeting different zones of the driver's body: face analysis [41,44], body analysis [6,33], hands analysis [10,37].

Many datasets available in the context of DMS centre their attention in the annotation of geometrical features or temporal characteristics. Within the group of geometrical features, bounding boxes [10,49], head pose [44], face landmarks [18], body pose [5], eye gaze [13] are the most common. This data is commonly used with distraction and fatigue algorithms.

In addition, there has been a increasing interest in detecting and classifying driver actions with videos captured from in-cabin cameras. To achieve this, the image sequences need to be annotated in terms of temporal actions. Examples of such datasets include Drive&Act [33] in which sequences from different views are captured. The participants in the dataset performed several action in the context of autonomous driving. Besides, AUC Dataset [1] was defined specifically to solve the problem of distracting action classification. The dataset is comprised of images of the body from a side-view perspective.

Most of the datasets available for driver monitoring found in the literature focus either on specific parts of the drivers' body or specific driving actions. However, driver monitoring involves several human behaviour which has to be taken into consideration as a whole. Therefore, the recently published Driver Monitoring Dataset (DMD) [40] has opened room for exploration in different fields within driving monitoring as it contains sequences of drivers in real driving and simulation conditions. In this work we contribute to the expansion of the annotation and validation of the DMD in the field of blink detection since the DMD provides sequences of drivers with different blink patterns.

3   Eyelid Aperture Estimation Method

It is well known that the shape of human eye varies between individuals. Different factors such as ethnicity, age and gender can make the individuals to have this variability. Then, the method that characterises the palpebral fissure should learn from observations what is the current degree of eye aperture based on the maximum and minimum eyelid aperture levels for the opened and closed eye states, respectively. This dynamic information allows the method to normalise the eyelid aperture level to be user-agnostic.

Note that we distinguish between eyelid amplitude and normalised eyelid aperture. In this work the eyelid amplitude is referred as a value obtained from ratios of eye dimensions; while the normalised eyelid aperture, or simply the eyelid aperture is the degree of openness of an eye. It is described as a value between 0 (closed-eye) to 1 (open-eye).

3.1   Definition of Eyelid Amplitude

We choose to use facial landmarks models to extract eye dimensions. There are robust real-time facial landmark detectors available in the literature [2,28] and as open-source libraries: DLib ERT [31] or OpenFace [4] that allows to obtain the eye dimensions. Besides, the information of the facial landmarks could be used by other driver monitoring methods such as head pose estimation and gaze estimation, reducing the computational overhead of algorithms in complex systems, obtaining real-time integrated DMS applications.

Face alignment methods compute the eye shape as a connected set of feature points. Therefore, a measure of the eyelid amplitude is necessary to obtain the final eye aperture level. In the literature different methods for measuring the eyelid amplitude from landmarks are proposed.

In [52] the amplitude is measured as the mean distance between vertically corresponding landmarks. Similarly, in [20] the eye amplitude is defined as the height between eyelids. However, these methods will not tolerate changes of scale. In contrast, other authors [32,51] suggest to use scale-independent metrics where the measure involves using a ratio of a vertical and horizontal distance.

Moreover, in [3], the eye closure is obtained from the ratio between the vertical distance between eyelids and a fixed diameter of the iris. However, to obtain real dimensions of the eye this method should need to have a calibrated camera which could not be possible in all DMSs.

In our approach the eye amplitude A_t is set as the eye aspect ratio (EAR) between height and width. We take the eye contour landmarks provided by our facial landmark model and compute the eye aspect ratio using the maximum height H_t and width W_t of the contour of the facial points as shown in Fig. 4.

Fig. 4. Eye landmark fitting and estimation of the height (H) and width (W) of the eye [39].

The eye usually has an rectangular shape (i.e. the width is larger that height); therefore, to obtain values closer to one when the EAR is maximum, we propose to use the double of the EAR as the value of eye amplitude to be normalised by our method (Eq. 1).

$$A_t = min\left(1, \frac{2H_t}{W_t}\right) \tag{1}$$

The eye amplitude A_t saturates to 1 for eyes whose height is half the width, which is something that may occur for very round eyes. Depending on the physiological state and the facial physiognomy of individuals, the nominal amplitude level for opened and closed eye may be different between each others. Figure 5 illustrates this difference: we can observe that different individuals have different maximum and minimum A values.

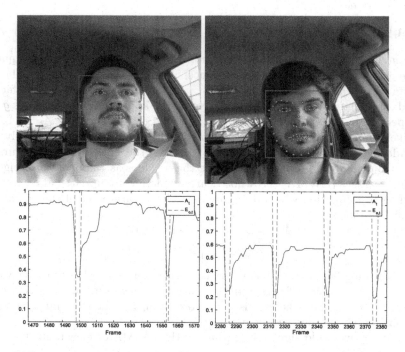

Fig. 5. Differences in eyelid amplitude for two different individuals blinking normally. The graphs below each user's frame show the corresponding amplitude A_t computed as in Eq. 1 [39].

3.2   Normalised Aperture Estimation

The eyelid amplitude A_t value (Eq. 1) should be normalised to obtain an aperture level, which is robust to changes of subject facial characteristics. The computation of the normalised eyelid aperture $A_{n,t}$, for each time frame t is achieved using an online probabilistic approach, which computes the posterior probability of the event where eye is open $E_{o,t}$ and closed $E_{c,t}$, such as $A_{n,t} = P(E_{o,t}|A_t)$.

Using the Bayesian formulation we have the following expressions:

$$P(E_{o,t}|A_t) = \frac{p(A_t|E_{o,t})P(E_{o,t})}{P(A_t)}; \tag{2}$$

$$P(E_{c,t}|A_t) = \frac{p(A_t|E_{c,t})P(E_{c,t})}{P(A_t)} \tag{3}$$

where $p(A_t|E_{o,t})$ and $p(A_t|E_{c,t})$ are the probability density functions that represent the likelihood of observing the eye in open and closed states, respectively. $P(E_{o,t})$ and $P(E_{c,t})$ are the a priori probability of each event, and $P(A_t)$ is the evidence, a normalisation factor to ensure $\sum_{s \in \{o,c\}} P(E_{s,t}|A_t) = 1$, which is computed as $P(A_t) = \sum_{s \in \{o,c\}} p(A_t|E_{s,t})P(E_{s,t})$.

The likelihood models are derived from two balanced distributions, truncated at their extremes:

$$p(A_t|E_{o,t}) = \omega_g(A_t)g(A_t|A_{o,t-1}; Var(A_{o,t-1})) + \omega_u(A_t)u(A_t|A_{o,t-1}, 1) \tag{4}$$

where $g(A_t|A_{o,t-1}; Var(A_{o,t-1}))$ is the normal distribution with mean equal to $A_{o,t-1}$ and variance equal to the variance of $A_{o,t-1}$; and $u(A_t|A_{o,t-1}, 1)$ is a uniform distribution in the interval $(A_{o,t-1}, 1)$, scaled to $g(A_{o,t-1})$. The factors ω_g and ω_u are step functions which determine the application of functions g and u, respectively: $\omega_g(A_t) = 1$ for $A_t \leq A_{o,t-1}$ and $\omega_u(A_t) = 1$ for $A_t > A_{o,t-1}$. The likelihood of A_t of event $E_{c,t}$, $p(A_t|E_{c,t})$ can be expressed analogously.

Updating the values of $A_{o,t}$ and $A_{c,t}$ makes the entire process recursive. For that purpose, we propose to estimate these values as Exponential Weighted Moving Averages (EWMA) [17] whose learning factors are updated at each frame according to a function which determines the local variability of the signal in a temporal window:

$$A_{o,t} = \omega_o \ A_{o,t-1} + (1 - \omega_o)A_t \tag{5}$$

$$A_{c,t} = \omega_c \ A_{c,t-1} + (1 - \omega_c)A_t \tag{6}$$

The learning factors, ω_o and ω_c, are not static, but defined as dynamic values to increase the impact of a new measurement A_t according to its distance to $A_{o,t-1}$ and $A_{c,t-1}$, i.e. when A_t is very close to $A_{o,t-1}$ then its impact on $A_{o,t}$ update is higher (by decreasing ω_o).

Therefore, we build signal $A_{s,t}$, which is the EWMA of measurement A_t.

$$A_{s,t} = \alpha \ A_{s,t-1} + (1 - \alpha)A_t \tag{7}$$

where α is the averaging factor of $A_{s,t}$.

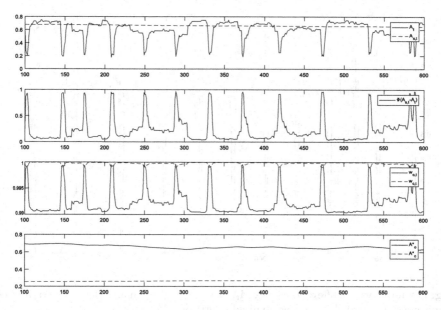

Fig. 6. Values of the different parameters involved in the computation of the normalised aperture for a sample sequence [39].

Under the hypothesis that the time eyes are open is higher than the time eyes are closed, then $A_{s,t}$ is always closer to $A_{o,t}$ than to $A_{c,t}$. Therefore, we can use $A_{s,t}$ to define the value of ω_o. A way to implement this idea, and also provide a mechanism to define ω_c is to create a sigmoid function (which returns a value between 0 and 1) on the difference between A_t and $A_{s,t-1}$ (higher values of this sigmoid corresponds to situations the eye is more likely open, and lower values correspond to closed eye measurements). The sigmoid function is defined as:

$$\Phi(A_{s,t} - A_t) = \frac{1}{1 + e^{-a(A_{s,t} - A_t - c)}} \tag{8}$$

where variables a and c can be selected to make the sigmoid function be centred at $c = (A_{o,t} - A_{c,t})/2$ (i.e. the expected mid-way between the eye amplitudes at open and closed states), and to reach a significant value at the maximum possible difference, e.g. $\Phi(A_{o,t} - A_{c,t}) = 0.95$ (note the sigmoid function asymptotically approaches to 1 but without never reaching it):

$$a = -\frac{log\left(\frac{1}{\Phi(A_{o,t} - A_{c,t})} - 1\right)}{A_{o,t} - A_{c,t} - c} \tag{9}$$

Figure 6 details the evolution of the involved functions in the computation of the normalised aperture. Note in second row, the values of the sigmoid range from 0 to 1, following the variability of A_t. In practice, this variability is counter-productive for an EWMA learning factor (i.e. it makes the EWMA not smooth). Therefore, the learning factor update equation needs to be regularised as follows:

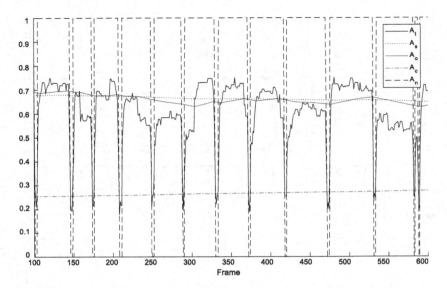

Fig. 7. Sample values of eyelid closure A_t, EWMA $A_{s,t}$, open and closed-eye estimated amplitudes $A_{o,t}$ and $A_{c,t}$, and normalised aperture $A_{n,t}$ [39].

$$\omega_o = \beta + (1 - \beta)\Phi(A_{s,t} - A_t) \tag{10}$$

$$\omega_c = \beta + (1 - \beta)(1 - \Phi(A_{s,t} - A_t)) \tag{11}$$

These learning factors leads to smoother evolution of $A_{o,t}$ and $A_{c,t}$. Parameter β is a user-defined parameter that balances the impact of Φ.

In addition, Fig. 7 illustrates the values of the computed amplitudes on a sample 500 frames sequence. As we can observe, the EWMA is slowly learning the average of A_t, while $A_{o,t}$ and $A_{c,t}$ adapt to the observed open and closed-eye amplitudes. For this example the following constants were used: $\alpha = 0.999$ and $\beta = 0.99$. It is possible to see that Φ determines how likely the measurement belongs to the open and closed states, and the learning factors ω_o and ω_c are updated according to Φ. In other words, the average closed-eye amplitude $A_{c,t}$ is updated with significant weight, assigned to the current measurement A_t proportionally to ω_c, which corresponds to the situations where the eye is likely closed.

4   Use Cases

This section summarizes the work carried out to apply the proposed eyelid aperture estimation method in practical use cases. The following subsections detail our two main interests: (i) utilisation of the DMD (Driver Monitoring Dataset) open dataset, and (ii) integration of the method into a DMS (Driver Monitoring System) in a real vehicle and simulators.

4.1   DMD: Driver Monitoring Dataset

The recent DMD dataset[2] for driver monitoring systems development was presented in [40]. It is a still-going project in which we have contributed to in this research by producing drowsiness-related annotations which we have also used to evaluate our eyelid aperture estimation method.

The DMD is committed to becoming the richest public dataset for driver monitoring applications, offering material of various driving situations that require identification to address possible threats that affect safe driving. As of this date, it possesses material that supports tasks like distracted driver detection, driver's gaze estimation, driver's hands-wheel interactions and driver fatigue or drowsiness detection. This last scenario is what we focus on in this study.

As a novelty for the state-of-the-art, the dataset presents its data in video format. The recordings are made from three perspectives, with cameras installed inside an equipped car (see Fig. 8); the position of the cameras was to capture specifically the face, hands and body of the driver. The devices used were Intel RealSense Depth Camera D400-Series, which allow the collection of three channels of information: RGB, depth and infrared. Including these three channels, different opportunities can be found for this research line, since infrared images can be helpful for driver monitoring systems in low-light conditions and depth information can enhance algorithm's capabilities to estimate 3D information of the scene.

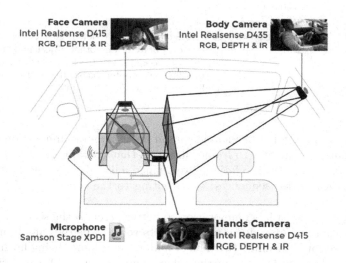

Fig. 8. Inside-vehicle camera set-up for the recordings of the DMD.

The recordings had the participation of 37 volunteers with a distribution of 27% and 73% of women and men respectively. Also, 27% of the participants

---

[2] https://dmd.vicomtech.org/.

wore glasses when driving. In total, the dataset has 40:45 h of video, of which 11% belong to scenes or situations of drivers with a certain degree of fatigue and drowsiness. For this drowsiness-related material, the participants were asked to do activities like yawning with and without covering their mouths with their hands, have micro-sleeps and, in general, perform a sleepy driving.

Table 1. Description of levels of annotation for drowsiness-related material of the DMD.

Level	Labels	Description
0: Eye state (right)	- Open - Close - Opening - Closing - Unclassified	This category of labels aim to indicate the state of the driver's right eye. Following the eye state criteria presented in Sect. 4.1
1: Eye state (left)	- Open - Close - Opening - Closing - Undefined	This category of labels aim to indicate the state of the driver's left eye. Following the eye state criteria presented in Sect. 4.1
2: Yawning	- Yawning with hand - Yawning without hand	This category is defined to establish when the driver yawns and discriminate if he/she does it covering his/her mouth with his/her hands or not
3: Camera occlusion	- Face camera - Body camera - Hands camera	An occlusion is an event that happens when above 50%–60% of the camera view is covered by the driver's own body or any other object and the scene is not recognisable. Occlusions are important to consider in computer vision, to avoid them in analysis or to learn identifying them

The DMD is intended to include spatial and temporal annotations; that is, from landmarks of the face to frames intervals that contain an action. To make use of the material related to fatigue, we defined a list of classes with annotation criteria for these video sequences, contributing to the continuous development of the DMD.

We propose a multi-label annotation to better describe the scene. Within the same annotation file of a video, many aspects want to be described; on the one hand, the cases of "Yawning" (with hand and without hand, being faithful to the actions defined in the DMD), on the other hand, the state of each driver's eye and, as a final description, the annotation of cameras occlusions is also included. All the above is annotated through frame intervals. The categories or levels of annotation that were defined are presented in Table 1, along with their labels. In this work we exploit the annotation of eye state to evaluate our eyelid aperture estimation method.

To reach an agreement between annotators and reduce ambiguity in the annotations, an annotation criteria is proposed. That is the explanation of each of the labels and the conditions in which a frame should be labelled as such. The definitions of the eye states adopted are described below:

– **"Open"**: The driver has his/her eye open and this not change in time. This means that this state is a stationary state in which the eye aperture is constant or stable. Comes after an "Opening" state.
– **"Close"**: The driver has his/her eye closed, meaning that, from the frontal camera, there is not a pixel belonging to the interior of the eye that is visible. This is also a stationary state in which the eye remains closed. Comes after a "Closing" state.
– **"Opening"**: This is a transitory state in which the eyelid moves upwards. After a "Close" state, this one starts when the interior of the eye is visible. After a "Closing" state, it starts when the eyelid stops going down to go up. Finishes when the upper eyelid has completed its upwards trajectory, passing to the next state of "Open", or when the eyelid starts going down, leaving to the next state of "Closing".
– **"Closing"**: This is a transitory state in which the eyelid moves downwards. After an "Open" state, this one starts when the eyelid starts to go down. After an "Opening" state, starts when the eyelid stops going up to go down. Finishes when the upper eyelid has completed its downwards trajectory, passing to the next state of "Close", or when the eyelid starts going up, leaving to the next state of "Opening".
– **"Undefined"**: This occurs when the eye cannot be captured correctly from the front camera and one of the previously defined states can't be assigned. It usually occurs when the driver turns his head, taking the eye off the camera view. Also, when an occlusion of the eye occurs; either due to the driver's hand or an object interferes between the eye and the camera or when lighting conditions (e.g. sun-ray) affect the camera and it is unable to capture a recognisable image.

Within the dataset video sequences, people do not blink in the same way, as it is natural. There are complete blinks in which the flow of states is normally performed: "open"-"closing"-"close"-"opening"; however, people's blink pattern is not perfect and sometimes they do not close the eye completely, so the "close" state is not included in the blinking cycle. These differences in blinking pattern make annotating eye states a complex task, hence the relevance of defining an annotation criteria.

Fig. 9. Temporal Annotation Tool (TaTo) for annotating eye states of the DMD videos.

As an extension of the DMD, the authors have created a tool for temporal annotations or TaTo (Temporal Annotation Tool). This software allows making multi-label temporal annotations, providing the option of annotating time-intervals by blocks or frame-to-frame. It offers a simple and intuitive interface (see Fig. 9), showing the annotations on a timeline through colours, and offers easy keyboard navigation. TaTo is public to the scientific community and to anyone who wants to use the DMD, create and/or change its annotations. Besides, it is possible to adapt the tool to perform temporal annotations in other domains outside of the DMD. In this work we adapted and used this tool to create the ground truth necessary for this project, making temporal annotations of the DMD's drowsiness-related material. The DMD annotations are in VCD (Video Content Description) format[3]. This is an open description language that supports spatial and temporal annotations for describing objects, actions, events, contexts and relations, of scenes or data sequences. This is the first annotation toolset compliant with the preliminary definitions of the ASAM OpenLABEL standard (to be published 2021).

4.2 Integration Setup

The proposed eyelid aperture method was implemented into a DMS (Driver Monitoring System) and integrated into an instrumented vehicle and different simulators, in the context of the EU H2020 project VI-DAS (GA 690772)[4].

The implementation of the DMS consists on a C++ library which defines modular components to address different driver monitoring functions, such as face detection, landmarks tracking, eyelid aperture, and gaze estimation

---

[3] https://vcd.vicomtech.org/.
[4] http://www.vi-das.eu/.

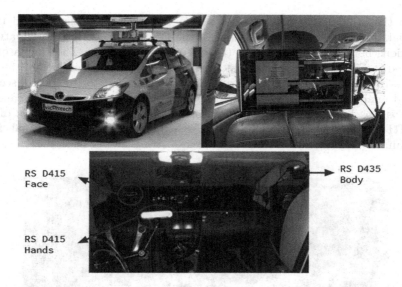

Fig. 10. Instrumented vehicle with interior cameras (Intel RealSense D400) for face, body and hands monitoring. The vehicle was instrumented also with perception and localisation devices (Velodyne HDL-32, 4 Sekonix 100° cameras, xNAV550, uBlox) and broadcasting mechanisms to send the output demo images to screens outside the vehicle.

(as depicted in Fig. 3). The library is wrapped into RTMaps framework[5] to enable interconnection with other vehicle components.

The instrumented vehicle was equipped with interior cameras monitoring the face, hands and body of the driver (Intel RealSense D400 Series Depth), while 4 external fisheye cameras were used to create a 360° surround view system as shown in Fig. 10. Lane detection and positioning systems along with risk estimation, IoT and HMI components completed the vehicle set-up. The entire system worked real-time in an Intel i7-7740X machine, with 32 GB RAM, NVIDIA GTX Titan XP GPU card, and running Ubuntu 18.04.

The demonstration took place at the ITS Europe Congress 2019, 3–6 August 2019, under the EU H2020 VI-DAS project (see Fig. 2)[6], focused on control transfer between human driver and AD function, for which driver monitoring played a major role to assess the driver is in the required physiological conditions (drowsiness, distraction).

The evaluation of the prototypes were carried out using two different set-ups: on the one hand, an IoT platform was established to capture driver signals and store them into georeferenced databases (see Fig. 2, bottom-left) with the aim of demonstrating real-time DMS and V2C capabilities.

---

[5] https://intempora.com/products/rtmaps.html.

[6] A video summary of the demo can be seen in: https://www.youtube.com/watch?v=8o3hT3H_gDU.

On the other hand, a simulation set-up was used to gather ground truth material, and to test the performance of the DMS C++ library in operational conditions before installing it into the instrumented vehicle. The simulator, as depicted in Fig. 11 was set-up to emulate the same camera locations of the test vehicle. In addition, the simulator run the PreScan simulator to control scenarios and enable Driving-in-the-Loop test runs. A bridge between PreScan and RTMaps was built by the VI-DAS consortium to enable the utilisation of the same RTMaps processing pipeline (as in Fig. 12) but with simulated signals from PreScan.

Fig. 11. Driving simulator of VI-DAS project.

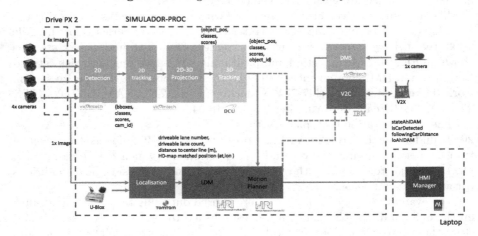

Fig. 12. Logical diagram of the VI-DAS instrumented vehicle.

5 Experiments

5.1 Dataset

To test the method for eye aperture estimation we took a subset of the DMD recordings. Since one of the objective of this work is to contribute to the annotation and validation of videos from the DMD project, our experiments consisted in, first, manually annotate recording of drivers, then apply our method for evaluating blink detection.

We select recordings for both male and female drivers in order to have a balanced evaluation set. Recordings from a total of 4 individuals were selected, being 2 female and 2 male. The recording of the DMD contain sequences of drowsy driving in which the driver shows patterns of increased periods of closed eyes, yawning and microsleeps. In addition, in other sequences the driver is performing commonly actions (using cellphone, combing hair, drinking, etc.), some of them could imply some form of distraction. In these samples the drivers are fully awake and rested. To validate the eyelid aperture estimation method, recordings form both drowsy and actions data was selected. A total of 15000 frames was used from the drowsy sequences and 12000 frames for driver actions.

To annotate the evaluation subset we used the official annotation tool for the DMD (TaTo) configured to annotate eye states. A total of 5 possible labels could be annotated: "open" and "close" for maximum and minimum eye aperture state, "opening" and "closing" for the transition between the two previous states, and "undefined" when the eye state cannot be inferred from the video either due to occlusions of other objects or large head movements. The annotation effort done in this work was also used to annotate other relevant events present in the DMD recordings, namely "yawning" and "occlusion" events. The availability of these extra annotation is very helpful for future systems which integrate different DMS algorithms such as yawning detectors. The output of this annotations will be publicly available for the research community and will contribute to the already available "driver actions" annotation of the DMD.

5.2 Results and Discussion

The evaluation of our method for eyelid aperture estimation was done applying the same approach as in [39] but expanding to a new dataset which is more challenging as the variability of illumination conditions and driver actions is richer. Although, the dataset used in the work in which this study [39] is based was collected in a driving scenario, the driver's head movements were much more controlled and the illumination conditions were clearly stable. Therefore, using the DMD dataset results in a more challenging evaluation.

The aim of this evaluation is to assess correctly the classification of open and closed states of the driver's eyes. Our method computes a normalised eyelid aperture which is a value between 0 and 1, being 0 totally closed and 1 totally open. The benefit of this method is the adaptability of eye shapes of different drivers. Therefore, it is possible to apply a simple closing threshold (e.g. eyelid below 80% are considered closed) to extract open or closed eye states. In addition, we also implemented the method for eye blink detection presented in [3] to compare with our method and the robustness against the DMD dataset. The method of Baccour et al. [3] outputs blink segments which we consider closed eye intervals which allows to apply the same evaluation methodology as with our method. We choose this method since it requires as input the same type of data (eyelid amplitude) as our method.

The classification results of open and closed eyes are presented in Table 2. As it can be seen our algorithm gets better accuracy results than other state-of-the-art methods. The overall results for our method beat the 90% accuracy reference even for a challenging dataset as DMD, confirming our method can be applied to real scenarios. The F1-score values show that there is still room for performance, however, the results are valid for implementation in combination with other DMS modules. Actually, this method was successfully integrated in a real DMS system to feed advanced decision support methods in autonomous driving (ref. Sect. 4).

Table 2. Classification results of open and closed states of our method and Baccour et al. [3]. Values of accuracy for open a closed eye states are presented. Separation for different typology video sequeces is also analysed.

Method	Data	Accuracy (%)	Acc. open (%)	Acc. close (%)	F1-score
Baccour et al. [3]	Drowsy	72.9%	76.1%	61.8%	0.519
	Actions	71.3%	72.8%	43.4%	0.334
	Male	68.0%	72.1%	44.3%	0.342
	Female	76.5%	76.8%	60.1%	0.455
	All	72.1%	74.4%	57.2%	0.387
Our method	Drowsy	**91.2%**	**91.5%**	**89.4%**	**0.763**
	Actions	80.6%	80.8%	72.6%	0.586
	Male	86.2%	86.5%	79.5%	0.758
	Female	85.5%	85.9%	80.4%	0.635
	All	**90.1%**	**90.5%**	**89.4%**	**0.755**

Moreover, we also analysed the influence of different type of data to identify possible weaknesses. In general, better results are obtained from the sequences of drowsy drivers. In these videos the time with closed eyes is larger and generally, the persons tend to reduce head movements. Therefore the detection of face and eyes is better. On the contrary, in the sequences of actions while driving, since the drivers are performing several activities, some form of noise is introduced in the input signal, therefore the lower results are consistent. An analysis according to driver gender was also performed. The results show that for our method there is not considerable effect of gender in classifying open and close eye states.

As the DMD dataset has become available, the analysis of blink detection open the possibility of more research in the field of driver monitoring systems.

The eyelid aperture estimation can feed other complex algorithms for driver monitoring so higher knowledge of the driver behaviour could be extracted. In this sense, the results of the different components of a DMS (such as in Fig. 3) could help improve the accuracy of the algorithms. For instance, our method for blink detection can benefit from head pose estimation methods. The availability of head pose could help identify large movements and filter noisy eyelid aperture signals improving the overall accuracy.

Finally, the method for eyelid aperture estimation could serve as a tool for pre-annotating the remainder of the DMD dataset. This could reduce considerably the manual annotation efforts since the annotators will only need to correct the small divergences in the boundaries between the defined eye states. With these eye state annotations, more complex features can be extracted such as microsleep events, PERCLOS, time between blinks, blinking frequency and speed. Such type of features are valuable for the development of robust fatigue monitoring systems.

6 Conclusions

In this paper we have shown our work continuing the research on eyelid aperture detection presented in our previous publication [39]. In this work we focused on applying our method into practical use cases to fully exploit its possibilities.

In particular, we have tackled the integration of the method into a fully operational DMS, deployed into different vehicle and simulator environments under the context of the demonstrations of the EU H2020-funded project VI-DAS. Live demonstrations of different SAE-L3 scenarios were carried out, including the integrated DMS component.

During the integration within the DMS system, the DMD open dataset project was launched, which provide a unique, extensive and comprehensive dataset for development of DMS. In this paper we report both our contribution to the DMD, by means of creating ground truth drowsiness-related labels (using the VCD labeling format), and by using DMD material to publish our results and make them available for other researchers.

It is our intention and future line of work to continue contributing to the DMD project, by producing more labels, and also tools to post-process ground truth labels to create drowsiness detection-related metrics, such as PERCLOS, frequency-between-blinks, etc. so they can be used along with the raw DMD material for further comparative analyses.

Acknowledgements. This work has received funding from the European Union's H2020 research and innovation programme (grant agreement 690772, project VI-DAS), and from the Basque Government under project AUTOLIB of the Elkartek 2019 programme.

References

1. Abouelnaga, Y., Eraqi, H.M., Moustafa, M.N.: Real-time distracted driver posture classification. In: 32nd Conference on Neural Information Processing Systems (NIPS 2018), Workshop on Machine Learning for Intelligent Transportation Systems (2018)
2. Asthana, A., Zafeiriou, S., Cheng, S., Pantic, M.: Incremental face alignment in the wild. In: IEEE Conference on Computer Vision and Pattern Recognition, CVPR, pp. 1859–1866 (2014)
3. Baccour, M.H., Driewer, F., Kasneci, E., Rosenstiel, W.: Camera-based eye blink detection algorithm for assessing driver drowsiness. In: IEEE Intelligent Vehicles Symposium, pp. 866–872 (2019)
4. Baltrusaitis, T., Robinson, P., Morency, L.P.: OpenFace: an open source facial behavior analysis toolkit. In: 2016 IEEE Winter Conference on Applications of Computer Vision, WACV 2016 (2016)
5. Borghi, G., Fabbri, M., Vezzani, R., Calderara, S., Cucchiara, R.: Face-from-depth for head pose estimation on depth images. IEEE Trans. Pattern Anal. Mach. Intell. **42**(3), 596–609 (2020)
6. Borghi, G., Venturelli, M., Vezzani, R., Cucchiara, R.: POSEidon: face-from-depth for driver pose estimation. In: Proceedings of the 30th IEEE Conference on Computer Vision and Pattern Recognition, CVPR 2017, pp. 5494–5503 (2017)
7. Borghini, G., Astolfi, L., Vecchiato, G., Mattia, D., Babiloni, F.: Measuring neurophysiological signals in aircraft pilots and car drivers for the assessment of mental workload, fatigue and drowsiness. Neurosci. Biobehav. Rev. **44**, 58–75 (2014)
8. Boyle, L.N., Tippin, J., Paul, A., Rizzo, M.: Driver performance in the moments surrounding a microsleep. Transport. Res. F: Traffic Psychol. Behav. **11**(2), 126–136 (2008)
9. Danisman, T., Bilasco, I.M., Djeraba, C., Ihaddadene, N.: Drowsy driver detection system using eye blink patterns. In: International Conference on Machine and Web Intelligence, ICMWI, pp. 230–233 (2010)
10. Das, N., Ohn-Bar, E., Trivedi, M.M.: On performance evaluation of driver hand detection algorithms: challenges, dataset, and metrics. In: Proceedings of the IEEE Conference on Intelligent Transportation Systems, ITSC, pp. 2953–2958 (2015)
11. Dong, W., Li, J., Yao, R., Li, C., Yuan, T., Wang, L.: Characterizing driving styles with deep learning. arXiv (2016)
12. Drutarovsky, T., Fogelton, A.: Eye blink detection using variance of motion vectors. In: Agapito, L., Bronstein, M.M., Rother, C. (eds.) ECCV 2014. LNCS, vol. 8927, pp. 436–448. Springer, Cham (2015). https://doi.org/10.1007/978-3-319-16199-0_31
13. Fang, J., Yan, D., Qiao, J., Xue, J.: DADA: a large-scale benchmark and model for driver attention prediction in accidental scenarios, pp. 1–12. arXiv (2019)
14. Fogelton, A., Benesova, W.: Eye blink detection based on motion vectors analysis. Comput. Vis. Image Underst. **148**, 23–33 (2016)
15. Fridman, L., Lee, J., Reimer, B., Victor, T.: Owl and Lizard: patterns of head pose and eye pose in driver gaze classification. IET Comput. Vis. **10**(4), 1–9 (2016)
16. Fridman, L., Reimer, B., Mehler, B., Freeman, W.T.: Cognitive load estimation in the wild. In: Proceedings of the 2018 CHI Conference on Human Factors in Computing Systems, CHI 2018, no. 1, pp. 1–9 (2018)
17. Friedrichs, F., Yang, B.: Camera-based drowsiness reference for driver state classification under real driving conditions. In: IEEE Intelligent Vehicles Symposium, vol. 4, pp. 101–106 (2010)

18. Fuhl, W., Castner, N., Zhuang, L., Holzer, M., Rosenstiel, W., Kasneci, E.: MAM: transfer learning for fully automatic video annotation and specialized detector creation. In: Leal-Taixé, L., Roth, S. (eds.) ECCV 2018. LNCS, vol. 11133, pp. 375–388. Springer, Cham (2019). https://doi.org/10.1007/978-3-030-11021-5_23

19. Fuhl, W., Santini, T., Kasneci, E.: Fast & robust eyelid outline & aperture detection in real-world scenarios. In: IEEE Winter Conference on Applications of Computer Vision (2017)

20. García, I., Bronte, S., Bergasa, L.M., Almazán, J., Yebes, J.: Vision-based drowsiness detector for real driving conditions. In: Proceedings of the IEEE Intelligent Vehicles Symposium, pp. 618–623 (2012)

21. Goenetxea, J., Unzueta, L., Elordi, U., Ortega, J.D., Otaegui, O.: Efficient monocular point-of-gaze estimation on multiple screens and 3D face tracking for driver behaviour analysis. In: 6th International Conference on Driver Distraction and Inattention, pp. 1–8 (2018)

22. González-Ortega, D., Díaz-Pernas, F.J., Antón-Rodríguez, M., Martínez-Zarzuela, M., Díez-Higuera, J.F.: Real-time vision-based eye state detection for driver alertness monitoring. Pattern Anal. Appl. 16(3), 285–306 (2013). https://doi.org/10.1007/s10044-013-0331-0

23. Gou, C., Wu, Y., Wang, K., Wang, K., Wang, F.Y., Ji, Q.: A joint cascaded framework for simultaneous eye detection and eye state estimation. Pattern Recogn. 67, 23–31 (2017)

24. Han, W., Yang, Y., Huang, G.B., Sourina, O., Klanner, F., Denk, C.: Driver drowsiness detection based on novel eye openness recognition method and unsupervised feature learning. In: IEEE International Conference on Systems, Man, and Cybernetics, SMC, pp. 1470–1475 (2016)

25. Kaida, K., et al.: Validation of the Karolinska sleepiness scale against performance and EEG variables. Clin. Neurophysiol. 117(7), 1574–1581 (2006)

26. Kaplan, S., Guvensan, M.A., Yavuz, A.G., Karalurt, Y.: Driver behavior analysis for safe driving: a survey. IEEE Trans. Intell. Transp. Syst. 16(6), 3017–3032 (2015)

27. Kashevnik, A., Lashkov, I., Gurtov, A.: Methodology and mobile application for driver behavior analysis and accident prevention. IEEE Trans. Intell. Transp. Syst. 21(6), 1–10 (2019)

28. Kazemi, V., Sullivan, J.: One millisecond face alignment with an ensemble of regression trees. In: Proceedings of the IEEE Computer Society Conference on Computer Vision and Pattern Recognition, pp. 1867–1874 (2014)

29. Kim, K.W., Hong, H.G., Nam, G.P., Park, K.R.: A study of deep CNN-based classification of open and closed eyes using a visible light camera sensor. Sensors 17(7), 1534 (2017)

30. Kim, W., Jung, W.S., Choi, H.K.: Lightweight driver monitoring system based on multi-task mobilenets. Sensors 19(14), 3200 (2019)

31. King, D.E.: Dlib-ml: a machine learning toolkit. J. Mach. Learn. Res. 10, 1755–1758 (2009)

32. Mandal, B., Li, L., Wang, G.S., Lin, J.: Towards detection of bus driver fatigue based on robust visual analysis of eye state. IEEE Trans. Intell. Transp. Syst. 18(3), 545–557 (2017)

33. Martin, M., et al.: Drive & act: a multi-modal dataset for fine-grained driver behavior recognition in autonomous vehicles. In: The IEEE International Conference on Computer Vision (ICCV), pp. 2801–2810 (2019)

34. Melnicuk, V., Birrell, S., Crundall, E., Jennings, P.: Towards hybrid driver state monitoring: review, future perspectives and the role of consumer electronics. In: IEEE Intelligent Vehicle Symposium (IV), pp. 1392–1397. IEEE (2016)

35. National Center for Statistics and Analysis: Distracted driving in fatal crashes, 2017. Technical report, National Highway Traffic Safety Administration (NHTSA) (2019)
36. de Naurois, C.J., Bourdin, C., Stratulat, A., Diaz, E., Vercher, J.L.: Detection and prediction of driver drowsiness using artificial neural network models. Accid. Anal. Prev. **126**, 95–104 (2019)
37. Ohn-Bar, E., Trivedi, M.M.: The power is in your hands: 3D analysis of hand gestures in naturalistic video. In: IEEE Computer Society Conference on Computer Vision and Pattern Recognition Workshops, pp. 912–917 (2013)
38. Ohn-Bar, E., Trivedi, M.M.: Are all objects equal? Deep spatio-temporal importance prediction in driving videos. Pattern Recogn. **64**, 425–436 (2017)
39. Ortega, J.D., Nieto, M., Salgado, L., Otaegui, O.: User-adaptive eyelid aperture estimation for blink detection in driver monitoring systems. In: Proceedings of the 6th International Conference on Vehicle Technology and Intelligent Transport Systems - Volume 1: VEHITS (2020)
40. Ortega, J.D., et al.: DMD: a large-scale multi-modal driver monitoring dataset for attention and alertness analysis. In: Bartoli, A., Fusiello, A. (eds.) ECCV 2020. LNCS, vol. 12538, pp. 387–405. Springer, Cham (2020). https://doi.org/10.1007/978-3-030-66823-5_23
41. Palazzi, A., Abati, D., Calderara, S., Solera, F., Cucchiara, R.: Predicting the driver's focus of attention: the DR(eye)VE project. IEEE Trans. Pattern Anal. Mach. Intell. **41**(7), 1720–1733 (2018)
42. Regan, M.A., Hallett, C., Gordon, C.P.: Driver distraction and driver inattention: definition, relationship and taxonomy. Accid. Anal. Prev. **43**, 1771–1781 (2011)
43. Regan, M.A., Strayer, D.L.: Towards an understanding of driver inattention: taxonomy and theory. In: Engaged Driving Symposium: Annals of Advances in Automotive Medicine, vol. 58, pp. 5–14. Association for the Advancement of Automotive Medicine (2014)
44. Roth, M., Gavrila, D.M.: DD-Pose - a large-scale driver head pose benchmark. In: IEEE Intelligent Vehicles Symposium, June 2019, pp. 927–934 (2019)
45. Saab: Saab Driver Attention Warning System (2007). http://www.saabnet.com/tsn/press/071102.html. Accessed 23 Oct 2020
46. SAE International: Taxonomy and definitions for terms related to driving automation systems for on-road motor vehicles. Technical report, SAE International (2018)
47. SafetyNet: Fatigue. Technical report, European Commission Project (2009)
48. Schmidt, J., Laarousi, R., Stolzmann, W., Karrer-Gauß, K.: Eye blink detection for different driver states in conditionally automated driving and manual driving using EOG and a driver camera. Behav. Res. Methods **50**(3), 1088–1101 (2017). https://doi.org/10.3758/s13428-017-0928-0
49. Schwarz, A., Haurilet, M., Martinez, M., Stiefelhagen, R.: DriveAHead - a large-scale driver head pose dataset. In: IEEE Computer Society Conference on Computer Vision and Pattern Recognition Workshops, July 2017, pp. 1165–1174 (2017)
50. Sikander, G., Anwar, S.: Driver fatigue detection systems: a review. IEEE Trans. Intell. Transp. Syst. **20**(6), 2339–2352 (2019)
51. Soukupová, T., Cech, J.: Real-time eye blink detection using facial landmarks. In: 21st Computer Vision Winter Workshop (2016)
52. Sukno, F.M., Pavani, S.-K., Butakoff, C., Frangi, A.F.: Automatic assessment of eye blinking patterns through statistical shape models. In: Fritz, M., Schiele, B., Piater, J.H. (eds.) ICVS 2009. LNCS, vol. 5815, pp. 33–42. Springer, Heidelberg (2009). https://doi.org/10.1007/978-3-642-04667-4_4

53. Volvo Car Group: Volvo Cars conducts research into driver sensors in order to create cars that get to know their drivers (2014). https://www.media.volvocars.com/global/en-gb/media/pressreleases/140898/volvo-cars-conducts-research-into-driver-sensors-in-order-to-create-cars-that-get-to-know-their-driv. Accessed 23 Oct 2020
54. Wang, L., Ding, X., Fang, C., Liu, C., Wang, K.: Eye blink detection based on eye contour extraction. In: Proceedings of SPIE - The International Society for Optical Engineering, vol. 7245 (2009)
55. World Health Organisation (WHO): Global status report on road safety 2018. Technical report (2018)
56. Yang, F., Yu, X., Huang, J., Yang, P., Metaxas, D.: Robust eyelid tracking for fatigue detection. In: 19th IEEE International Conference on Image Processing (ICIP), pp. 1829–1832. IEEE (2012)

A Hybrid Real and Virtual Testing Framework for V2X Applications

Michael Klöppel-Gersdorf(✉) ⓘ and Thomas Otto

Fraunhofer IVI, Institute for Transportation and Infrastructure Systems,
Zeunerstr. 38, 01069 Dresden, Germany
{michael.kloeppel-gersdorf,thomas.otto}@ivi.fraunhofer.de

Abstract. With the increasing sophistication of vehicles, more and more (automated) driving functions become available, some of which are based on Vehicle-to-Everything (V2X) communication. While every new developed functionality needs thorough testing, the need is pronounced for V2X applications as these rely on external input by other vehicles and infrastructure, thereby increasing the space of possible test scenarios. Multiple access technologies (e.g., 802.11p or Long Term Evolution (LTE)), interfaces, different interpretations of standards as well as interactions between several entities make it difficult to find and eliminate malfunction of cooperative components. The ranges and boundaries of drive and test scenarios make debugging during test drives in a real traffic environment substantially difficult, since it requires reproducible conditions. To overcome the aforementioned problems, a hybrid real and virtual testing framework for V2X applications is proposed, which allows the coupling of real entities, i.e., traffic lights with Road-Side Unit (RSU), with other connected entities either in hardware or software in order to carry out V2X application tests under controlled conditions.

Keywords: V2X · Simulation · Hardware-in-the-Loop · Software-in-the-Loop · Testing · OpenSCENARIO

1 Introduction

As Vehicle-to-Everything (V2X) communication becomes more prevalent, more and more V2X applications will appear. These range from rather simple visualisations to complex backend computations and finally also to automated driving functions. The implementation of such services requires careful testing. This is true even for the visualisations, where a wrong display of information might lead to a wrong action by the driver, e.g., crossing a red traffic light because an Human-Machine-Interface (HMI) still displayed a green phase, but becomes most prominent when considering automated driving functions.

Typically, V2X applications will initially be tested in completely virtual environments, but later stages usually necessitate the consideration of more realistic scenarios. While some of these scenarios might be contained in corresponding databases, at some point field tests are unavoidable, e.g., to verify the robustness of the solution under various external factors like weather, temperature or

© Springer Nature Switzerland AG 2021
C. Klein et al. (Eds.): SMARTGREENS 2020/VEHITS 2020, CCIS 1475, pp. 190–203, 2021.
https://doi.org/10.1007/978-3-030-89170-1_10

electromagnetic interference of other participants. Unfortunately, such studies are extremely time-consuming, expensive and may be infeasible due to safety concerns.

Surprisingly, testing V2X applications during development actually is not enough. Once deployed, these application live in an ever changing environment, e.g., due to Over-the-Air (OTA) software updates, exchange of parts of the system or degradation of sensors. This necessitates a continued monitoring of the deployed services, e.g., during the general inspection of the vehicles, which is mandatory in many jurisdictions. To do so, the vehicle under test has to be exposed to several test scenarios, which mimic the operation in real traffic. Nonetheless, these tests cannot actually be conducted in real traffic since this would require corresponding infrastructure and other communicating vehicles near every testing center, which cannot be guaranteed in practice. Furthermore, testing has to follow given standards and certain standard test cases may not be testable at every location. Obviously, a testing framework can also be used to derive evaluation scenarios for the general inspection in the first place. This is done by replacing the vehicle under test with a corresponding simulation.

To overcome the challenges mentioned above, we propose a hybrid real and virtual (i.e., simulated) test environment for testing and evaluating implementations of V2X applications. The proposed framework is building on prior research [12], which is based on the real system architecture for cooperative driving with heterogeneous communications and cloud infrastructure described in [3]. The current implementation of the testing framework is deeply embedded in the Dresden testbed. Still, the general design choices can be applied to other testing scenarios as well.

Hybrid tests of V2X communication scenarios are no new development and have also been considered in [8], where a full testing kit for developing commercial applications is described. Nonetheless, the issue of continued testing is not addressed. The authors of [15] provide a Hardware-in-the-Loop (HiL) testing environment, which is focused on Vehicle-to-Vehicle (V2V) applications. Their solution is based on a intermediate layer between V2X modem and the onboard computer. This layer can be used to rewrite message contents, i.e., the real position of the modem is overwritten with a position gained from traffic simulation, and simulate message loss.

This paper is an extended version of a previously published work [12]. This extension describes an evolution of the testing framework introduced before, addressing the organization of test scenarios as well as logging and allowing for a wider scope of possible testing scenarios. The paper organized as follows: The next section introduces the use cases we want to support with our solution, whereas the following section describes the different components, which need to be considered when implementing the test environment, as well as our proposed solution. In Sect. 4, a detailed description of the testing of a V2X lane change application is presented. The paper is concluded in the last section.

2   Exemplary Application Scenarios

In this section, three different applications to be tested with the proposed hybrid testing framework are introduced, highlighting the wide range of possible V2X applications by considering an HMI, backend and automated driving application. Still, these examples provide only a small subset of all possible testing scenarios. The first two applications are motivated by the C-ROADS Germany and C-ROADS Germany - Urban Nodes project, where so-called Day 1.0 and Day 1.5 Cooperative Intelligent Transport Systems (C-ITS) use cases are being tested in various German pilot locations, with one location being the city of Dresden. The last applications stems from the ErVast project, which investigates how advanced driving technologies, like automated or connected driving, can be tested during the general inspection and how such test scenarios can be derived in the first place. Besides describing the applications, requirements for a potential testing framework will be derived.

2.1   Green-Light Optimized Speed Advisory (GLOSA)

At signalized intersections actual and/or predicted information on the phases and timing of traffic lights can be given to road users to optimize their driving and to overcome inefficiencies, e.g., due to frequent starts/stops. The implementation of this so-called GLOSA service consists of two parts.

The first part is the service located at the traffic light controller, reading the current traffic light state and providing the information (e.g., via WLAN802.11p using Map Extended Message (MAPEM) and Signal, Phase and Timing Extended Message (SPATEM) or via LTE using a custom format) to a connected vehicle. In addition, the service also could generate predictions or consume these predictions from a third party source, e.g., the overall traffic control backend.

The second part consists of a GLOSA application running in a vehicle. If an equipped vehicle approaches such a signalized intersection, the application needs to calculate the correct next intersection, compute the right approach, extract the correct data from the information provided and display the result to the driver.

2.2   Probe Vehicle Data (PVD)

Acquisition of road traffic data is an important aspect of traffic management systems. An innovative approach is utilizing the vehicles themselves as a source of real-time traffic data, functioning as roving traffic probes. The PVD service gathers anonymized sensor data (e.g. speed, braking force and weather conditions) from passing vehicles using secure ETSI ITS G5 connections. A potential PVD application has to ingest probe data (e.g., by analyzing the received Cooperative Awareness Message (CAM)), preprocess the data (e.g., remove duplicates and ourliers) and provide a comprehensive overview over the traffic situation.

2.3   Continuous Testing of Automated Driving Functions

In the future, it is to be expected that automated driving functions also rely on information submitted via V2X communication. While these functions will be thoroughly tested during the development phase, there is the additional topic of assuring the ongoing functionality of such modules, e.g., during the general inspection, which is mandatory in several states. For instance, consider an automated driving function, which acts on the GLOSA information mentioned above, by automatically adapting the speed of the vehicle such that the intersection can be passed in an efficient manner. In addition to the tasks, which also have to be fulfilled by the GLOSA visualisation, the automated driving function has to take into account the current location (including potential location errors), safety (e.g., being able to stop in time if there is a sudden change in traffic light state) and legal considerations (e.g., no speeding).

2.4   Derived Requirements

Looking at the aforementioned V2X applications, the following requirements for a testing framework become apparent:

Logging: Even in the simple case of just providing the current traffic light phase logging is inevitable as it allows comparing the output of the real or simulated traffic light controller with the information provided by the GLOSA application. It is also of great importance when testing automated driving functions, as this allows a detailed analysis of the actual system behavior. While a system might seem to be working at a superficial level, problems might still exist, e.g., the automated driving function proposes a non-safe speed but is consequently overturned by an additional safety system.

Connecting Remote Entities: Especially in the case of the GLOSA service on the infrastructure side it might be desirable to connect to an existing traffic light controller, while still testing the service purely in software. On the one hand this requires that these infrastructure elements are actually connected to a network but on the other hand also requires common description of the information to be interchanged.

Scenario Control: While it is benefitial to test V2X applications in a real environment, it is also necessary to test them under controlled conditions, especially when debugging applications but also when considering the use case of testing applications during the general inspection.

Enabling Software-in-the-Loop (SiL) testing: As aluded before, some modules might only exist in software at the time of testing. The framework, therefore, should allow testing software implementations. In this case, the generated V2X messages might also be simulated.

Enabling HiL Testing: Besides software also completely developed hardware together with corresponding software implementations should be handled by the framework, e.g., the vehicle under test in the general inspection use case.

Central Simulation: Some data might not be available at the time of test, e.g., surrounding traffic (either because there are not enough connected vehicles in the vicinity or the vehicle under test is on a testing ground). In this case, information on additial connected vehicles or intersection may be provided by simulation. Also, certain automated driving functions might only work together with other connected vehicles, e.g., when coordinating using the Maneuver Coordination Message (MCM), currently at the phase of specification at ETSI. In this case the driving function in the other vehicles have to be simulated.

Hybrid V2X Communication: As is clear from the above, some test entities might only use simulated/virtual V2X communication, while other entities use physical communication. In the case that both types of entities are present, there has to be a way to make the information available to all participants.

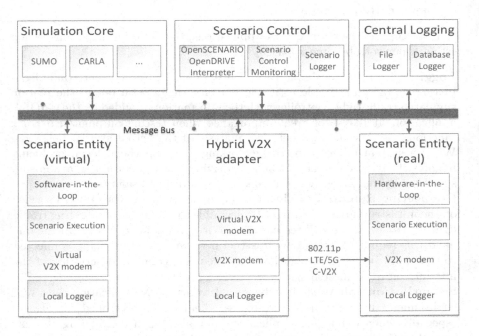

Fig. 1. Different components of our proposed solution and their connections.

3   Implementation

The proposed testing framework is based on an earlier development [12], which was extended to comprise a greater scope of applications. The extension is greatly influenced by the high level architecture [5], which is obvious from Fig. 1. Usually, the top three building blocks (Simulation Core, Scenario Control, Central

Logging) will all reside on one machine or at least on a local network and form a kind of backend, whereas the test entities might be on a local net (especially for virtual entities) or on a remote net (for real entities). Depending on this setup, the message broker needs to exchange messages only local or needs to be available from a remote network. The different building blocks will be described in the following.

3.1 Scenario Control

Scenario Control is the central unit of the proposed framework, as it coordinates the test, provides instructions to the different entities and generally monitors the flow. As such, it is responsible for the strategic decisions but leaves the minutiae to Simulation Control and the different entities. It acts on OpenSCENARIO [1] scenario descriptions and reads OpenDRIVE [2] for description of the road network. It has the ability to provide the scenario information to the Simulation Core as well as the single entities, possibly translating the instructions in a format understood by the different participants. All decisions taken by Scenario Control are logged directly at the source to allow accurate time stamping.

OpenSCENARIO is chosen as it seems to become the de facto standard for simulation and testing, at least in Europe. It is backed by most European vehicle manufacturers as well as OEMs and developers of simulation software.

3.2 Simulation Core

As described in the requirements, it may sometimes be desirable to simulate (additional) traffic and/or traffic lights. The proposed framework uses Simulation of Urban Mobility (SUMO) [13] for this task, providing the possibility for microscopic and mesoscopic traffic simulation. The network topology is usually created from OpenDRIVE, which is provided by the Scenario Control. Traffic demand and traffic light timing is also provided by Scenario Control. For more details on the SUMO simulation see [11]. The simulation is accessed using Traffic Control Interface (TraCI) using the multiclient capability introduced in the newer versions of SUMO. As SUMO usually performs simulation steps as fast as possible, Scenario Control is responsible for ensuring an accurate timing. Since this works only in the case that SUMO calculates faster than real time, it is necessary to assure that this can be done at any simulation step, e.g., by using a more powerful simulation machine or using the parallel simulation feature. Furthermore, it might also be necessary to simulate additional connected vehicles with their own automated driving functions. Here, it is proposed to use CARLA [6], which also integrates with SUMO and is able to directly act on OpenSCENARIO descriptions.

3.3 Message Broker

Non-V2X communication is carried out via Message Queuing Telemetry Transport (MQTT). In the implementation, the message broker is provided by Scenario Control using EMQX [7]. The single entities might also employ seperate

MQTT brokers based on Mosquitto [14], which offer a bridge to the central broker. These local brokers facilitate a faster local communication and ease the scenario setup, especially if the connection to the central is encrypted and secured by passwords or certificates. Also of importance is the right choice of MQTT Quality of Service (QoS). We opt for level two (every message is received only once) even though this may lead to higher latencies, as any lower QoS might lead to message loss or multiple versions of the same message being received.

3.4 Real Test Entities

In the following, examplary real test entities are introduced. These are inspired by systems existing in the Dresden Testbed. As most of the existing systems are not able to follow OpenSCENARIO directly, a translation of the OpenSCENARIO instructions into the native description (in our case a custom JSON-based description) format is necessary. These translation will be provided by Scenario Control.

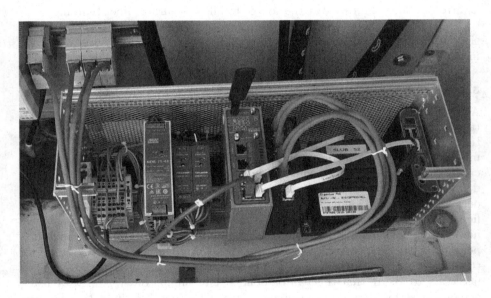

Fig. 2. Experimental setup for traffic lights, consisting, from left to right, of power supply units, LTE router, PoE switch and two processing units. The equipment is installed at an intersection in the Testbed Dresden. Not shown is the V2X modem, which is installed at the traffic light post.

Traffic Lights with RSUs. As of now, more than twenty RSUs are installed at traffic lights in the Dresden Testbed, both for productive and scientific use. The productive RSU are provided by suppliers of traffic lights, whereas the ones for scientific use are custom. Figure 2 shows an overview over the setup, a more detailed description of the RSU can be found in [3,18]. At the moment, signal control devices of different suppliers are equipped with RSUs. Some signal control devices provide a socket connection, which delivers a status message containing current signal state, traffic signal priority requests, detector status and predictions (in the case of a fixed plan) every second. The content is in Protobuf [9] format and can be ingested by the RSU. Other signal control devices at least provide signal state information and possibly also predictions if the required module is installed. Additional information might be available via the traffic management system.

Connected Vehicles with On-Board Units (OBUs) and HMIs. Test vehicles are equipped with OBUs solutions from Cohda Wireless (MK5) and Preh Car Connect (Connectivity Box (C-BOX)). Both solutions are quite similar, except that the C-BOX delivers additional WiFi and LTE connection abilities. Even applications can be shared between the two systems without the need for recompilation. The OBUs usually run a custom communication stack (see below), the backend of our HMI as well as any components required by our testing framework. If necessary, they can also connect to a central backend. An examplary setup is depicted in Fig. 3. In order to visualize V2X communication, we developed a Android-based HMI as can be seen in Fig. 4. Besides visualizing phase and GLOSA information, it is also able to communicate maneuver recommendations received via the research message formats MCM and MRM. It also aids tests drivers in real world test scenarios with driving recommendations [16].

Fig. 3. Experimental setup for vehicles, consisting of Cohda MK5 (top right), C-V2X modem (top left), power supply (bottom right) and LTE router (bottom left). The equipment is installed in a BMW i3, but can be transferred to other vehicles.

3.5   Virtual/Simulated Entities

These entities comprise all SiL components as well as the simulation of entities not covered by Simulation Core. V2X messages may use the same interface as real entities, but instead of transmitting them via V2X modem, the message contents is transported via the message broker.

3.6   Hybrid V2X Adapter

Depending on the type of communication stack used by the test entities, two different approaches to couple virtual and real entities are possible. If all real entities are equipped with our custom message stack (see below), message can directly be injected from simulation and virtual entities. On the other hand, if some of the real entities use their own stack a solution similar to [15] is employed, i.e., every virtual entity is assigned a V2X modem, which transforms the virtual communication via the message bus into a physical one. Using our own stack implementation on these modems allows a full customization of the message contents.

Fig. 4. HMI displayed on the central console of a VW Passat. The ego vehicle is depicted in white, other simulated vehicles in blue. On the left hand side GLOSA information is shown, which is derived from an existing trafficlight in the Dresden Testbed. The actual vehicle is at stand still, while its motion is simulated. (Color figure online)

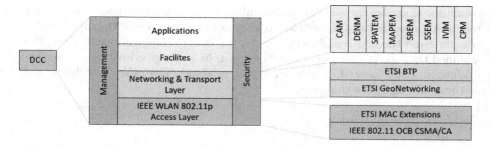

Fig. 5. ITS communication stack. C4CART is used to provide the ITS facilities. Besides the message formats shown above, additional, non-standardized message types like MCM and MRM are supported.

Custom ITS-G5 Communication Stack. We use a custom implementation of the ETSI ITS-G5 facilities called Communications for Connected and Automated Road Traffic (C4CART). This facilitates the implementation and experimentation with message types, which are not (yet) fully standardized as well as using completely standardized messages. Figure 5 shows the ITS communication stack with the message types supported by C4CART highlighted. Besides the standardized message types CAM, Decentralized Environmental Notification Message (DENM), MAPEM, SPATEM, and Collective Perception Message (CPM), C4CART also supports MCM and MRM for maneuver coordination. The communication between the application layer and the facilities layer is carried out using Lightweight Communications and Marshalling (LCM) [10], which is based on UDP multicast. The proposed solution exploits this multicast to inject messages to the application layer, which are indistinguishable from messages received via V2X communication. The ITS-G5 facilities implementation follows a hybrid approach, allowing messages not only be send via 802.11p or C-V2X but also via a LTE connection (for more details see [3]). This allows for test cases, where direct V2X communication is currently not available.

4   Application

In this section, the application of the proposed testing framework to a cooperative lane change application is described. An overview of the intended service is shown in Fig. 6. The vehicle under test closes in on an intersection equipped with a RSU. Due to the situation behind the intersection, the RSU recommends to change from the left to the right lane. Via communications and its internal sensors, the vehicle under tests detects two other vehicles on the right lane and computes that the current gap is not sufficient for a lane change. Therefore, it requests the second of the vehicles to leave a larger gap. Once the other vehicle complies and the gap is sufficiently large, the lane change will occur. Here, it is assumed that the vehicle under test is a real vehicle equipped with the described driving function located on a roller type test stand. The other vehicles as well as the traffic light are simulated.

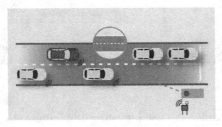 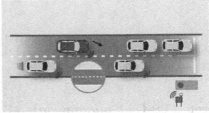

(a) RSU recommends lane change to blue vehicle via MRM.

(b) Blue vehicle communicates its intention to change lane and requests a larger gap.

Fig. 6. Example use case testing a V2X application performing an cooperative lane change. Vehicle under test is the blue one. This use case was also considered in [4], the figures are reproduced from there. (Color figure online)

The complete scenario is described in OpenSCENARIO, whereas the road topology is given in OpenDRIVE. Listing 1.1 shows an excerpt from the scenario definition. This is a simplified version, where the second vehicle on the right lane only acts on the position of the vehicle under test and does not rely on V2X communication between these two vehicles. In the given case, the two simulated vehicles are handled within CARLA, whereas the traffic light is a virtual entity. SUMO is used to simulate the movement of all three vehicles taking into account the actual velocity of the vehicle under test. Since all communication is based on C4CART, no hardware V2X adapter is necessary, instead the direct injection feature mentioned above can be used.

Listing 1.1. Excerpt from the OpenSCENARIO definition describing the action of the vehicle opening the gap such that the vehicle under test can change lane.

```
<Maneuver name="EgoBrakeManeuver">
  <Event name="EgoBrakeEvent" priority="parallel">
    <Action name="EgoBrakeAction"><PrivateAction>
      <LongitudinalAction>
        <LongitudinalDistanceAction continuous="true"
          entityRef="$owner"
          distance="$VehicleEndDistMeter"
          freespace="true">
          <DynamicConstraints maxAcceleration="2"
            maxDeceleration="4"
            maxSpeed="40" />
        </LongitudinalDistanceAction>
      </LongitudinalAction>
    </PrivateAction></Action>
    <StartTrigger><ConditionGroup>
      <Condition name="EgoBrakeCondition"
        delay="0"
        conditionEdge="rising">
        <ByEntityCondition>
          <TriggeringEntities triggeringEntitiesRule="any">
            <EntityRef entityRef="EgoAhead" />
          </TriggeringEntities>
          <EntityCondition>
            <RelativeDistanceCondition entityRef="$owner"
              relativeDistanceType="longitudinal"
              value="14"
              freespace="false"
              rule="lessThan" />
          </EntityCondition>
        </ByEntityCondition>
      </Condition>
    </ConditionGroup></StartTrigger>
  </Event>
</Maneuver>
```

Once the three vehicles arrive at a predefined position on the approach to the intersection, the MRM message to the vehicle under test is triggered. After this message arrives, the vehicles must check whether a lane change is feasible. For this, the position of the two simulated vehicles must be known, either using their simulated V2X communication (CAM) or via the sensors using sensor simulation. Given the information, the vehicle under test should request a larger gap using the MCM. Once this has been done, it has to monitor communications as well as the simulated situation on the road. If the gap is large enough, the lane change can be carried out.

The lane change application might fail the above testing scenario for various reasons, e.g., it cannot decode the MRM or does not detect that it is target of the recommendation. Further failures might occur in decoding the CAM of the other vehicles. Even non-V2X related errors are possible, e.g., the lane change is carried out before the gap is large enough.

5   Conclusions and Outlook

Prior research results [12] have shown that the proposed approach is feasible in the sense that relaying V2X information via message bus induces about the same latencies as direct V2X communication, thereby allowing to enhance real test entities with virtual entitites as well as simulated information. The proposed solution allows a multitude of testing scenarios. As such, the hybrid testing framework for V2X applications proposed above will be used to develop, test and deploy further services like Traffic Signal Priority request (TSP), Emergency Vehicle Approaching (EVA) and Vulnerable Road User (VRU).

Future work includes the development of further adapters, which translate the OpenSCENARIO description in the custom format required by the single entities. Furthermore, additional simulators should be interfaced, e.g., NS-3 [17] for network simulation.

The advantages of HiL and SiL testing for V2X applications are undeniable, since it allows the development in and debugging of complex drive and test scenarios. Furthermore, it allows the test of a multitude of interfaces, connections and devices under natural conditions, all of which can be done under reproducible scenarios. On top, it can also be used to perform stress tests with real devices and interfaces by, e.g., variation of different penetration rates.

Acknowledgements. This research is financially supported by the German Federal Ministry of Transport and Digital Infrastructure (BMVI) under grant numbers FKZ 01MM19003D (ErVast), European Regional Development Fund (ERDF) and European Union "Connection Europe Facility" (C-Roads Urban Nodes). We would like to thank Rico Auerswald for contributing to the solution architecture, Jan Günther for providing the OpenSCENARIO description and Stephan Ihrke for implementing parts of the solution.

References

1. ASAM e.V.: OpenDRIVE 1.0 (2020). https://releases.asam.net/OpenSCENARIO/1.0.0/ASAM_OpenSCENARIO_BS-1-2_User-Guide_V1-0-0.html. Accessed 09 Oct 2020
2. ASAM e.V.: OpenDRIVE 1.6 (2020). https://releases.asam.net/OpenDRIVE/1.6.0/ASAM_OpenDRIVE_BS_V1-6-0.html. Accessed 09 Oct 2020
3. Auerswald, R., et al.: Cooperative driving in mixed traffic with heterogeneous communications and cloud infrastructure. In: Proceedings of the 5th International Conference on Vehicle Technology and Intelligent Transport Systems - Volume 1: VEHITS, pp. 95–105. INSTICC, SciTePress (2019). https://doi.org/10.5220/0007682900950105

4. Auerswald, R., et al.: Heterogeneous infrastructure for cooperative driving of automated and non-automated connected vehicles. In: Helfert, M., Klein, C., Donnel-
lan, B., Gusikhin, O. (eds.) SMARTGREENS/VEHITS-2019. CCIS, vol. 1217, pp.
270–296. Springer, Cham (2021). https://doi.org/10.1007/978-3-030-68028-2_13
5. Dahmann, J.S., Fujimoto, R.M., Weatherly, R.M.: The department of defense high
level architecture. In: Proceedings of the 29th Conference on Winter Simulation,
pp. 142–149. WSC 1997. IEEE Computer Society, USA (1997). https://doi.org/
10.1145/268437.268465
6. Dosovitskiy, A., Ros, G., Codevilla, F., Lopez, A., Koltun, V.: CARLA: an open
urban driving simulator. In: Proceedings of the 1st Annual Conference on Robot
Learning, pp. 1–16 (2017)
7. EMQ Technologies Co., Ltd: EMQ X broker project page (2019). https://www.
emqx.io. Accessed 18 Dec 2019
8. Freese-Wagner, M. (ed.): A Rapid Innovation Framework for Connected Mobility Applications: High Performance Center Connected Secure Systems. Fraunhofer AISEC, EMFT & ESK. Fraunhofer ESK, München (2018). http://publica.
fraunhofer.de/documents/N-487489.html
9. Google: Protocol buffers project page (2018). https://github.com/google/protobuf.
Accessed 23 Jan 2018
10. Huang, A.S., Olson, E., Moore, D.C.: LCM: lightweight communications and marshalling. In: 2010 IEEE/RSJ International Conference on Intelligent Robots and
Systems, pp. 4057–4062, October 2010
11. Kloeppel, M., Grimm, J., Strobl, S., Auerswald, R.: Performance evaluation of
GLOSA-Algorithms under realistic traffic conditions using C2I-Communication.
In: Nathanail, E.G., Karakikes, I.D. (eds.) CSUM 2018. AISC, vol. 879, pp. 44–52.
Springer, Cham (2019). https://doi.org/10.1007/978-3-030-02305-8_6
12. Klöppel-Gersdorf., M., Otto., T.: Linked real and virtual test environment for
distributed c-its-applications. In: Proceedings of the 6th International Conference
on Vehicle Technology and Intelligent Transport Systems - Volume 1: VEHITS, pp.
377–384. INSTICC, SciTePress (2020). https://doi.org/10.5220/0009426003770384
13. Krajzewicz, D., Erdmann, J., Behrisch, M., Bieker, L.: Recent development and
applications of SUMO - Simulation of urban MObility. Int. J. Adv. Syst. Meas.
5(3 & 4), 128–138 (2012)
14. Light, R.A.: Mosquitto: server and client implementation of the MQTT protocol.
J. Open Source Softw. 2(13), 1 (2017). https://doi.org/10.21105/joss.00265
15. Menarini, M., Marrancone, P., Cecchini, G., Bazzi, A., Masini, B.M., Zanella, A.:
Trudi: testing environment for vehicular applications running with devices in the
loop. In: 2019 IEEE International Conference on Connected Vehicles and Expo
(ICCVE), pp. 1–6, November 2019. https://doi.org/10.1109/ICCVE45908.2019.
8965152
16. Otto, T., Auerswald, R.: Toolbox for test planning and test realization of scenario-
based field tests for automated and connected driving. In: Automatisiertes Fahren
2019. Proceedings, pp. 165–180. Springer, Wiesbaden (2020). https://doi.org/10.
1007/978-3-658-27990-5_15
17. Riley, G.F., Henderson, T.R.: The ns-3 network simulator. In: Wehrle, K., Gross, J.
(eds.) Modeling and Tools for Network Simulation, pp. 15–34. Springer, Heidelberg
(2010). https://doi.org/10.1007/978-3-642-12331-3_2
18. Strobl, S., Klöppel-Gersdorf, M., Otto, T., Grimm, J.: C-its pilot in Dresden -
designing a modular c-its architecture. In: 2019 6th International Conference on
Models and Technologies for Intelligent Transportation Systems (MT-ITS), pp.
1–8, June 2019. https://doi.org/10.1109/MTITS.2019.8883376

Robust IoT Based Parking Information System

Omar Makke$^{(\boxtimes)}$ and Oleg Gusikhin$^{(\boxtimes)}$

Global Data Insight and Analytics, Ford Motor Company, Michigan Avenue,
Dearborn, MI 22001, USA
{omakke,ogusikhi}@ford.com

Abstract. In this paper, we propose an adaptive parking information system. In this system, sensors and cameras monitor choke points in a parking space. Using process discovery algorithm, and by adhering to assumptions described in this paper, a Petri Net model is generated which tracks the occupancy of the parking space. This model automatically adapts to adding or removing sensors and to sensor failures. We also discuss how to detect sensor failures using relatively small amount of data. A use case is also provided which demonstrates the benefits of parking information system to smart cities.

Keywords: Smart parking · Adaptive infrastructure · IoT · Petri Nets · Mobility · Smart city · Digital twin

1 Introduction

In big cities, parking a vehicle takes significant amount of time. The average annual search time in the U.S. is 17 h, but this number is much greater for big cities. For example, in New York, the average annual time spent looking for a parking spot is 107 h, and in Los Angeles it is 85 h [4]. Assuming a sleep duration average of 7 h a day, then people spend around 1.72% and 1.37% of their awake time looking for a parking spot in New York and Los Angeles respectively. As the population and cities grow, it is natural to assume that these numbers will increase if cities do not enhance their mobility technologies. To alleviate parking issues, there have been numerous efforts to develop and deploy various parking guidance and information systems [10] for both on-street parking as well as off-street parking decks. The off-street parking information systems range from the simple gate-based counting system to the sophisticated sensor based infrastructure. However, there are still many parking structures without any information system, especially free parking municipal or corporate structures that don't have any access control and lack the opportunity to implement simple counting. Such parking structures present significant inefficiencies to smart cities as the drivers may waste substantial amount of time roaming through a fully occupied structure. As we will show in the case study, even a simple information system can benefit the city mobility by reducing time and fuel wasted roaming

© Springer Nature Switzerland AG 2021
C. Klein et al. (Eds.): SMARTGREENS 2020/VEHITS 2020, CCIS 1475, pp. 204–227, 2021.
https://doi.org/10.1007/978-3-030-89170-1_11

through a fully occupied parking structure, and can provide a compelling case for the cities to justify the investment in such system.

The emerging autonomous parking capability is another strong motivating factor for the need of parking information systems. The owners of vehicles equipped with autonomous valet parking functionality can take advantage of convenient vehicle drop-off at the entrance of the parking space, allowing the vehicle to roam through the parking space on its own in the search of available spots. However, the lack of available spots will lead to the necessity of contacting the vehicle owners to resolve this failure mode. Consequently, it will be important to provide the driver in advance information about the parking spots availability and potentially provision the coordination between the parking infrastructure and the vehicles simultaneously seeking available parking spots to minimize the parking time.

The advancements in IoT technology paved the way to the progress in the development and implementation of smart parking systems and methods. The state-of-the art parking structures utilize on-roadways (e.g. pneumatic tube, loop detector, magnetic sensor, acoustic sensor, piezoelectric sensor, etc.) and off-roadways sensors (ultrasonic sensors, infrared sensor, cameras, photoelectric barriers, etc.) to identify the occupancy of each individual spot and provide the drivers with information about the availability of parking spaces through Virtual Message Signs or vehicle connected services [10]. However, the implementation of such intelligent parking solution may be expensive and can only be afforded by limited number of commercially viable cites. A more practical approach is based on limiting the sensors installation to only few strategic choke points and special purpose parking spots (Handicap or Electric Vehicle Charging). In this case the parking system needs to integrate and consolidate the disjointed separate IoT messages into overall parking state. The efficient and effective approach is to use a digital twin approach [6]. Parking space digital twin is the virtual representation of the parking system dynamically updated by IoT messages. The digital twin can leverage analytics to estimate the current state of the parking space and project future behavior.

To develop a digital twin we propose and illustrate the use of Petri Net formalism. The approach presented is very scalable. It supports the development of low-cost infrastructure with minimum number of sensors while easily expandable to upgrade to more detailed infrastructure by gradually adding sensors. Although our original system is based purely on the camera-based recognition, the formalism allows to efficiently integrate all kind of different sensors. Furthermore, Petri Net formalism allows to easily expand the system from pure parking information to parking guidance for human drivers as well as autonomous valet.

This paper extends our previous work [14]. We describe how the process discovery algorithm works with its assumptions. We also investigate how to add/remove sensors, and how to identify sensor failures. This allows us to build a robust digital twin that is adaptive to the changes in the IoT devices of the parking space. If new cameras or sensors are added, fail, or recover, the system adjusts automatically. Furthermore, we summarize the experience and lessons learned of designing a cost-efficient parking information system for the municipal free parking structure and show results from a case study.

The paper is organized as follows. The next section explores the existing technologies and methods used in parking information systems. Section 3 discusses the Petri Net-based occupancy model and how to implement process discovery methods and adapt to changes in sensors. Section 4 provides a case study with analytics and the implementation results. Section 5 concludes the paper.

2   Smart Parking

The increased demand for parking spaces created an interest in topics which range from information services to developing new sensor technologies and detection methods as shown in [11] where the authors classified the existing approaches along three dimensions: information collection, system deployment, and service dissemination. Information collection relies on obtaining relevant information from parking sensors or from crowd-sensing. In [3], the authors categorized the sensing into 3 types: Counter-based, sensor-based, and vision-based. The counter-based systems use existing gate-arm counters, inductive loop detectors and similar sensors located at the entrances and exists. The sensor-based systems attempt to sense if spots are vacant or occupied, and can provide information regarding where to find a vacant spot. In this approach, sensors are installed at each parking space. The vision-based systems can use either dedicated cameras configured specifically to support the parking information system or leverage existing surveillance cameras. The latter method can be a cost efficient alternative, although it has a major challenge. The existing CCTV system may not provide full visibility to monitor the occupancy of all parking spots especially during high occupancy times. In most cases however, existing CCTV systems provide sufficient coverage to identify the vehicle movements within critical choke points in the parking space. Tracking vehicle movements between the parking areas and feeding the results into an adequate model helps overcome the challenge. The solution presented in the paper uses this type of approach.

In addition, a combination of counter-based, sensor-based, and vision-based systems can also be used. For example, [20] describes a parking system which utilizes BLE beacons to track the vehicles inside the parking area. The authors also used cameras located at the entrance/exit points of the parking space to account for the potential of drivers disabling their beacons.

In vision-based parking systems, there are generally two approaches to track the occupancy [9]. The first approach is based on tracking the vehicles driving through the parking to estimate the occupancy of parking areas while the second approach is based on identification of occupancy of individual spots. In the first approach, the main idea is to track how many vehicles went into a specific area, and how many vehicles left that area, and the difference between the two indicates the number of available spots. The second approach can be roughly categorized into three major types: car-oriented methods, space-oriented methods, and parking-lot-oriented methods [15], or a combination of these methods. Methods using car-oriented approach detect parked vehicles and then derive the number of available spots. Methods using space-oriented approach compare the appearance of the parking place, using a static model prepared in advance, with the current appearance of the parking space. The vacancy is then determined by analyzing the dissimilarity between the appearances. In parking-lot-oriented methods, the parking lot is modeled in a 3D program such as game engines, and the observed image is compared to the 3D model to infer the parking status. For example, in [9], the authors proposed a probabilistic method which considers lighting variations, shadows, varying perspective distortion on the image, and inter-object occlusion among parked cars. In [21], three commercial truck parking detection systems were evaluated, and their accuracy was above 95%, and exceeding 99% in some cases. However, the effect of rain and snow required further analysis. In [15], the authors introduced QuickSpot, which is an on-street parking spot detection system based on video analytics. When vision-based systems are used to identify empty and occupied spots, the required number of sensors and/or cameras is usually a scalar multiple of the number of spots. For example, one camera may be required for every 10 spots as proposed by DeepParking team, which can be found at https:// github.com/DeepParking/DeepParking. In some cases where the detection is performed in an opened parking lot, it is possible to reduce the number of required cameras by placing the cameras strategically to obtain a bird view. However, this is not possible in an infrastructure. In addition to the presence of many walls and relatively low ceiling height, vehicles can easily obscure the vision of other vehicles behind them relative to the camera. Thus, many cameras or sensors must be used in a parking infrastructure to cover all the spots. Regardless of which technology is used, the digital twin must be agnostic to the sensors and edge devices.

3 Petri Net Modeling

To implement digital twin, Petri Nets (PN) were selected to represent the parking occupancy model. Petri Nets have been proven to be a powerful framework for design, evaluation and control of discrete event systems [7]. In addition to basic PN models, there are numerous PN modifications and extensions which are used to incorporate diverse methods from different domains while sharing a common modeling approach.

A Petri Net structure is a marked bipartite graph formally defined as following [18]:

Definition 1. *A Petri Net structure N is a 3-tuple $N = (P, T, F)$ where $P = \{p_1, p_2, ..., p_n\}$ is a finite set of n places; $T = \{t_1, t_2, ..., t_m\}$ is a finite set of m transitions, $F \subseteq (P \times T) \cup (T \times P)$ is a set of arcs; $P \cap T = \phi$ and $P \cup T \neq \phi$ A marking is a function $M : P \to \mathbb{N} \cup \{0\}$ that assigns a non-negative integer number of token to each place.*

Graphically, a Petri Net is represented as the following. Places are represented by circles and transitions are represented by bars. Places and transitions are connected through directed arcs, and the tokens are represented by dots in the places. See for example Fig. 1. The dynamic behavior of PN is defined by its transition firings. Transition firings move tokens from their input place to their output place.

Petri Net models have wide range of applications in the industry, specifically in applications related to information integration and IoT-based systems. For example, in [8], the authors demonstrate how to integrate plant floor information for scheduling and control in real time. They used modified Petri Nets to represent material flow, and they tied plant floor heterogeneous messages with transitions of a PN model. They used existing process timing information to compensate for potential errors in plant floor information systems. [23] discusses PN application to IIoT, where Colored Petri Nets are used to assist in managing multiple sensors in 'Plug and Play' manner. In [22] Petri Nets have been applied to automatically compose IoT software services.

Furthermore, among the comprehensive set of analytical and simulation techniques PN provide for evaluation and control of discrete event systems, PN have developed an extensive body of research in state estimation and process mining which can be useful in development of IoT based tracking systems. PN marking estimation research deals with algorithms and methods that estimate the state of a model which combines observable and non-observable transitions and places to determine the optimal set of sensors to achieve observability [13,19].

Process discovery, a subset of process mining, focuses on automatic construction of PN models by analyzing the events log files [2]. A review of different PN-based process discovery algorithms is provided in [5]. Within the scope of IoT tracking applications, automatic generation of a PN model can substantially reduce the time for initial model development and testing. In our work, we leverage α-algorithm [1] to construct the initial parking model and/or extend it automatically.

3.1   Modeling Approach

In the context of parking application, the natural interpretations of PN is that the tokens represent vehicles, places represent areas or individual parking spots, and transitions represent entrances and exits of different parking areas. For example, [12] uses this interpretation and describes an interactive modeling process for a three story parking infrastructure controller.

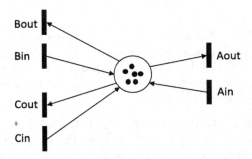

Fig. 1. Low fidelity model. The place represents the entire parking structure [14].

One of the advantages of PN is that they support evolutionary and hierarchical development of the model. A PN place can represent the entire parking space, specific parking zones, or even individual parking spots. The fidelity of the model is determined based on the available IoT infrastructure and the application logic requirements. The practical approach is to combine different levels of granularity for different zones, based on the need.

We start by using a low fidelity model of the parking infrastructure. A low fidelity PN model is shown in Fig. 1. The whole parking space is lumped into one place, and each entrance is represented by two transitions, one for entering vehicles, and the other for exiting vehicles. Despite the simplicity of this model, it can provide important insights into the dynamics of the parking space and offer a useful parking service, as we will show later.

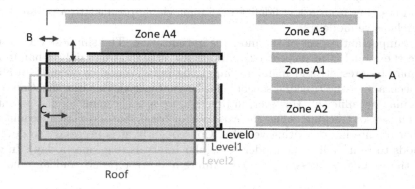

Fig. 2. Parking space. It consists of an open area and 4 parking levels, including roof. Grey area represents where vehicles can park [14].

Normally, there are enough CCTV cameras to cover critical choke points in the parking space. By selecting the cameras overseeing the choke points in the infrastructure, a medium fidelity model of the parking structure in Fig. 2 is created. This PN model is shown in Fig. 3. In this model, similar to the previous model, each camera detects vehicles transitioning from one place to another. Elaborate models as this one would also allow a guidance service to be provided due to its increased fidelity.

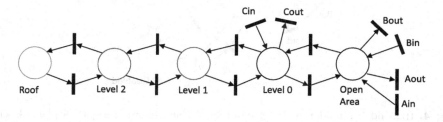

Fig. 3. Medium fidelity model. The place represents group of parking spots.

In order to provide an even more detailed model and to identify the vacancy for charging zones or disability zones, the PN model can be further enhanced as shown in Fig. 4. The requirement for a higher fidelity model may lead to a PN model with some transitions and places that are not supported by existing sensors. In lieu of using additional sensors or cameras, existing cameras can sometimes be used to detect vehicles transitioning between multiple defined places by analyzing different regions in the cameras' field of view.

It is possible to refine the model further to detect the vacancy of each spot individually in extreme cases, at an added cost. We argue that this is only required for special parking spots if the parking space is divided into sufficiently small zones. It would be enough to provide information and guidance to the zone containing an empty spot unless it is a special spot. Because this type of solution is scalable, this method can support incremental development of the system starting from a low fidelity minimum viable product to a detailed and comprehensive model.

An important aspect of the model is initialization. The simplest way to initialize the model is to inspect the parking lot at night when only a handful of cars may be present, and manually input the initial marking once. If an absolute accuracy of the tracking sensors can be guaranteed, this initialization approach may be sufficient. However, in practice, we must account for the potential errors in sensor tracking, when the cameras (or other sensors) may miscount the number of entering or exiting vehicles. Consequently, it is necessary to develop methods to re-initialize the model at regular intervals (e.g. once a day). In this case, the manual process is time consuming and error prone, and may not be

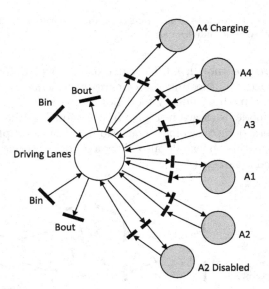

Fig. 4. High fidelity model for the ground level. Each zone is assigned a place. Each special spot is assigned a place individually [14].

(a) Image approximates the camera view during peak time.

(b) Image approximates the camera view at night.

Fig. 5. Peak time vs night time camera views [14].

adequate. One method to automate the recognition of the initial parking state is using cameras to identify the open parking spots or parked vehicles. In case of high occupancy as seen in in Fig. 5a, it may be very challenging for cameras to identify the occupied spots. On the other hand, when the parking structure is mostly empty, e.g. at night, the identification is much easier as shown in Fig. 5b. Consequently, we can initialize the model based on the vision recognition of the occupancy at the times when the parking mostly empty. Alternatively, during peak hours, the parking space gets completely filled. The indication of a completely filled parking space can be detected by examining the overflow vehicle movement pattern as will be shown later in the paper.

3.2 Process Discovery

It is possible to reduce the burden of modeling the parking space by applying techniques in process mining and process discovery. For example, α-algorithm [1] is a known method to generate a Petri Net model from event logs. To make use of the α-algorithm, we must ensure that the transitions are triggered in the correct temporal order, so that no incorrect places are inserted. For example, if a vehicle is entering the roof, and then another vehicle enters zone A1 in Fig. 4, it may appear that zone A1 can be entered from the roof level, or that both

212   O. Makke and O. Gusikhin

places are somehow parallel. To remedy this problem, a simple solution would be to track a special vehicle such as a security vehicle as it passes through the zones, and only record these transitions during an initial training phase. Here, we assume that there is only one such security vehicle present at a given time. In [14], more implementation details on how the infrastructure communicates with the digital cloud can be found.

As an example of how α-algorithm works, assume that the tracked vehicle will tour all the zones in the parking space, hence covering all the transitions to generate a complete log file. This is doable in a relatively small amount of time in parking spaces. In this example, referring to Fig. 3, the "Open Area" place will be represented by O, roof by R, Li refers to the ith level, and a transition between two places will be denoted by P1_P2 to indicate a transition between place P1 and place P2. Then the following log will generate Fig. 6

[Ai, O_L0, L0_L1, L1_L2, L2_R, R_L2, L2_L1, L1_L0, Cout]

This log file indicates that a vehicle as entered from entrance A, and went all the way to the roof, then went down to the floor level and exited the parking structure from C exit. Using this string from log file alone does not have enough information to indicate that P3 and P5, P2 and P6, P1 and P7 are actually the same place. In general, the α-algorithm struggles in finding loops of length 2 [1] even if the tracked vehicle generates the following strings:

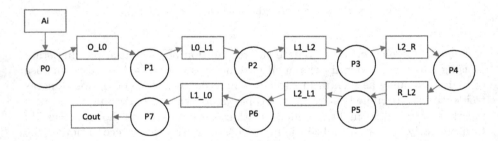

Fig. 6. First step in log file generation.

$$[..., L2\_R, R\_L2, L2\_R, ...]$$

$$[..., L1\_L2, L2\_L1, L1\_L2, ...]$$

$$[..., L2\_R, R\_L2, L2\_R, ...]$$

$$[..., L1\_L2, L2\_L1, L1\_L2, ...]$$

To solve these problem, note that in many IoT applications, sensors are used to generate complementary events, such as object is present/removed, object is close/far, object has entered/left an area, switch on/off etc. In the parking information service case, a sensor installed at a choke point between two places and can give directionality, or in other words, generate two events: "vehicle entered a place, vehicle exited a place". Due to the nature of the problem, an event "vehicle existed place p1" immediately implies that "vehicle entered place p2". Then, for two events [in, out], we know from the geometry of our problem that there is a loop of length 2 between the places connected by [in, out]. Furthermore, suppose a string in the log file contains

$$[..., e1, ..., e2, ...]$$

Then, if e1 and e2 triggers are generated from the same stationary sensor observing a choke point, we immediately know that e1 and e2 triggers form a loop of length 2 between two places. Then, given this additional knowledge of the sensors, loops are inserted as shown in Fig. 7.

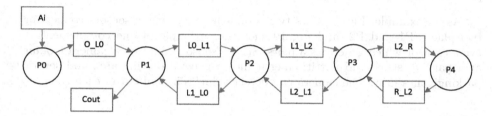

Fig. 7. Incorporating knowledge about the type of sensor and its usage.

If the security vehicle in the example generates additional log string:

$$[Cin, L0\_O, Bout, Bin, Aout]$$

then the result is shown in Fig. 8.

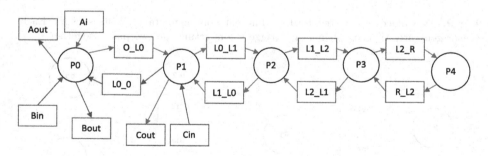

Fig. 8. Final result.

In Fig. 4, one camera may be installed to generate many triggers connecting the driving area with parking zones, in a detailed model. Although this type of sensor generates more than two events, it generates pairs of complementary events. It senses vehicles passing from one place (driving area) to many places (parking zones within the area). In general, for each pair of complementary events, it is enough to sense one transition in order to identify the places which are also connected by the complementary transition. Therefore, we can reduce the number of strings required to generate a complete log file.

It is important to note that only extra data required here is meta data describing if the sensor complementary events sensor, and the general use of the sensor (stationary, sensing a choke point). No information about the parking structure itself is required.

3.3 α-Algorithm Special Case

Definition 2. *A complementary events sensor is a sensor which generates a set of pairs where each pair consists of two triggers t_1 and t_2 which connect two places P_1 and P_2 in opposing directions to form a loop of length 2 between them.*

As an example, Fig. 9 shows two complementary events sensors connecting two places P1 and P2, and Fig. 10 shows an example of one complementary events sensor which generates 3 pairs. Such a sensor would be a camera looking at a parking space and partitioning it into a general driving area and several parking zones in it. The camera can detect vehicles in and out of each zone.

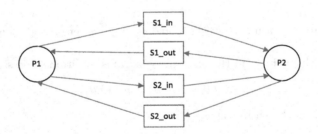

Fig. 9. Two places connected by two different complementary events sensors. Each sensor generates two complementary triggers connecting the two places together.

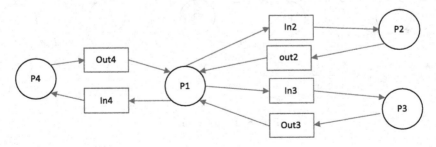

Fig. 10. A complementary events sensor consiting of many pairs.

Suppose we are modeling a problem as a Petri Net. Assume that

- The model can be represented by a state machine (each transition is restricted to having exactly one input and one output).
- All required information to build the model can be sensed (e.g. no constraints are present in the model which cannot be sensed).
- Complementary events sensors are known whenever used.
- A mapping exists between complementary events sensors and their triggers.

Given these assumptions, whenever we observe an event e in the log which connects two places P1 and P2, we immediately add its complementary trigger $\bar{e}$ connecting P1 and P2 in the opposing direction if e is generated by complementary events sensor. Although it may be argued that such triggers may not be always valid in ideal case, such as one-way lanes where the vehicle can only go in one direction, from practical point of view, it is important to consider the cases where vehicles do not follow the assigned direction, and there is no harm done by adding the complementary transition if we can, as long as we are observing vehicles and not providing any control. If we are to provide controls, we will have to distinguish between which transition can be used for control, and which is only for detection. By following these assumptions, generating complete log becomes less tedious for big parking structures.

3.4 Removing Sensor

In additional to automatic adaptation for introduction of new sensors we need to be able to adapt to the removal of arbitrary sensors. This removal may be a permanent removal of the sensor, or temporary malfunctioning of the given sensor. When a sensor failure is detected, the Petri Net model is modified by removing the failed sensor.

To illustrate the method let us go through the example in Fig. 11. Assume that we intend to remove the camera associated with transitions t5 and t6. In this case we can merge places P2 and P4 into single place P2+P4 as shown in Fig. 12. In case t5 and t6 are transitions associated with the same sensor and only one direction is switched off, we will still remove both input and output transitions to maintain integrity of the system.

The original underlying infrastructure of P2 and P4 can be maintained by the system and incorporate the probabilistic estimate of the occupancy between P2 and P4. The final result is shown in Fig. 12. In general, if a sensor fails, the two places connected by that sensor are merged into one place. If this sensor happens to be at the entrance, then the place is removed to indicate that it is merged with the "rest of the universe" outside the model.

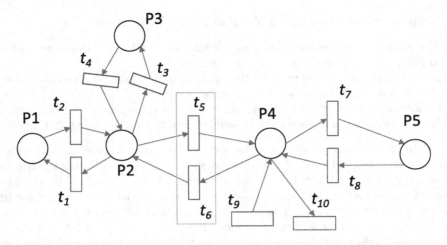

Fig. 11. Triggers inside the box represent sensors that will be removed.

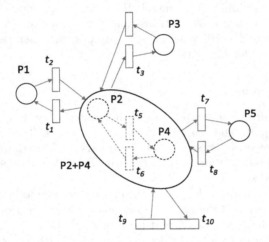

Fig. 12. Places P2 and P4 are combined to form 1 Place.

3.5 Detecting Sensor Failure

Adapting to sensor failures is critical especially if the parking information system
is provisioned to coordinate autonomous valley parking between vehicles. The
class of PN that deals with this type of models is Partially Observable Petri
Nets (POPN) that combine observable and non-observable transitions. POPN
research provides the methods to estimate the current markings from the existing
observations [13] or attempts to find a minimum set of sensors (or additional

sensors) required to achieve complete observability [19]. In order to automate the adaptation of the model to sensor failures, it is important to be able to detect these failures automatically. The failure modes of the sensors can vary from complete failure such as a camera may be damaged by rain or snow, intermittent such as object/dirt blocks the sensor partially or completely, or due to noise such as in vision based sensors. Complete failure detection is straightforward to diagnose when remote diagnostic signals are available. However, when such signals are not available, or when the failure is not electrical and is intermittent due to noise or other factors, then detecting the failure is more challenging.

It is desirable to have an algorithm which does not require large amount of data collected over long period of time. To build the algorithm, we assumed that only one sensor fails at a time. Identifying sensor failures is possible by indirectly sensing the failure using other sensors, or by relying purely on statistics when other sensors are not available or cannot sense the failure. Considering the sensors can only directly observe vehicles, identifying failed sensors relies on vehicle activities in the parking space. Then, the time required to identify a sensor failure varies based on the time of day due to variations in traffic patterns, and the higher traffic volume is, the better the detection will be.

To illustrate that, consider the case of a single place with a single sensor as shown in Fig. 13a. In such a case, the only way we can identify the sensor failure is by relying on data. Statistical metrics can be used to identify failure, such as average detection in a given time frame. If the probability distribution of vehicles entering and exiting the parking space is known, then the failure can be identified in shorter time. Assuming the parking space exists in commercial area, then a sensor failure can be identified faster during peak activity in the morning, lunch time, and the evening.

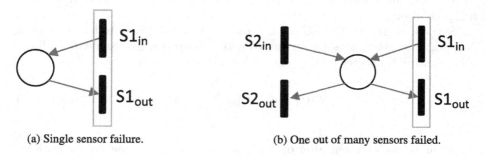

(a) Single sensor failure.   (b) One out of many sensors failed.

Fig. 13. Single place with a failed sensor.

Consider the case in Fig. 13b where a single place exists with one failed sensor, and many other sensors lumped as one sensor for analysis. As vehicles enter and exit the parking space, three scenarios may occur. First, the model may arrive to a negative number of vehicles if more vehicles leave through the choke point observed by functioning sensor than enter it. Second, the model may arrive to a number that exceeds the capacity of the place when more vehicles enter through the choke point observed by the functioning sensor than leave. Third, the model may always have a valid number. In the first two cases, assuming that the initial state of the model was correct, we can infer that a sensor has failed.

An improvement to the approach can be built as soon as data is available. Regardless of what the real distribution is for vehicles entering or exiting from choke points observed by sensors S_1 and S_2, we assume that the rate of detection $R_1(t)$ for sensor S_1, at a given time interval, is proportional to the rate of detection $R_2(t)$ of sensor S_2 at that same time, regardless of seasonality. Here $R_i(t)$ is the rate of detection over a defined period of time, such as the past 10 min.

$$R_1^{in}(t) = \bar{\lambda}^{in}(t)R_2^{in}(t) + \bar{\alpha}^{in} \tag{1}$$

Then approximate $\bar{\lambda}^{in}(t)$ and $\bar{\alpha}^{in}$ by finding λ^{in} and α^{in} which minimize E^{in} in

$$(R_1^{in}(t) - \lambda^{in}(t)R_2^{in}(t) - \alpha^{in})^2 = E^{in}(t) \tag{2}$$

Similarly, E^{out} can be found by following the same procedure for the "out" triggers. Then the error in a given time frame NT can be approximated as:

$$E_T^{in} = \sum_{n=0}^{N-1} E^{in}(t - nT) \tag{3}$$

Here, T is the defined period of time over which the rate of detection is calculated. The term α^{in} is required since in some cases the roads are one way roads. Then it would be possible that for a given place $R_1^{in}(t) > 0$ but $R_2^{in}(t) = 0$. In that case, by adding the term α^{in}, α^{in} becomes the average, and we can still find a solution.

Suppose there are N sensors. Then these calculations have to be carried out N times, where each sensor is compared with a lumped sensor comprising all the other sensors connected to the place. Then Eq. 1 becomes:

$$R_i(t) = \bar{\alpha} + \bar{\lambda_i}(t) \sum_{\substack{j=0 \\ j \neq i}}^{N-1} R_j(t) \tag{4}$$

Then for each trigger, after optimization, the expected value of the error is:

$$\left(R_i(t) - \alpha - \lambda_i(t) \sum_{\substack{j=0 \\ j \neq i}}^{N-1} R_j(t)\right)^2 = \epsilon \tag{5}$$

where R_j is the rate of vehicles in/out of a place in a defined period of time, as detected by a trigger t_j, and ϵ is the optimization error. If a place has N "in" triggers, then we have N equations to optimize for these triggers (same applies for the "out" triggers).

Suppose out of N sensors, sensor k fails. Given an arbitrary sensor $j \neq i$, if $k = i$ and k has failed, then

$$R_k^{failed}(t) = R_i^{failed}(t) < R_i(t) \tag{6}$$

To simplify the analysis, let

$$a = R_i(t) \tag{7}$$
$$c = R_i^{failed}(t) \tag{8}$$
$$a - c = d > 0 \tag{9}$$
$$b = \alpha + \lambda_i(t) \sum_{\substack{j=0 \\ j \neq i}}^{N-1} R_j(t) \tag{10}$$

Then we can rewrite and simply Eq. 5

$$(a - b)^2 = \epsilon \tag{11}$$
$$(c + d - b)^2 = \epsilon \tag{12}$$
$$c^2 + b^2 - 2bc = \epsilon + 2d(c + b) - d^2 \tag{13}$$
$$(c - b)^2 = \epsilon + 2d(c + b) - d^2 \tag{14}$$

Note that $(c - b)^2$ is the quantity which measures the sensor failure. If there is no failure, then $d = 0$. Once the sensor starts to fail, d increases, up to a value of a. As an example, we can choose $(c - b)^2 > 2\epsilon$ to be an indication of some sensor failure, which gives:

$$\epsilon + 2d(b + a - d) - d^2 > 2\epsilon \tag{15}$$

This allows us to find how large d has to be in order to detect an error. This puts the requirements on both the duration of time T for which R_i is calculated and ϵ. For example, at night when traffic volumes are low, we may not be able to detect the sensor failures depending on how large ϵ is chosen to be, unless we look into the past 12 h to calculate R_i. However, since traffic volumes are low, the need for the information system is not critical when it is difficult to identify failures using this method, and therefore this is not an issue. Note that Eq. 15 should be treated statistically, and when to actually declare a failure can depend on traffic volumes which help to improve the confidence that a sensor has failed. This demonstrates how to choose T and d and what considerations must be taken.

If on the other hand, $k \neq i$ then

$$R_k^{failed}(t) < R_k(t) \tag{16}$$

$$\left(R_i(t) - \alpha - R_k^{failed}(t) - \lambda_i(t) \sum_{\substack{j=0 \\ j \neq i \\ j \neq k}}^{N-1} R_j(t) \right)^2 = \epsilon \tag{17}$$

By repeating the same process, we also arrive to Eq. 15. Then, in order to identify which sensor failed, we note that a failing sensor's rate of firing is reduced. Then if the sensor is a, a is reduced. If the sensor part of b, b is reduced. Then, if $a > b$, it is an indication that the failure is not a, but somewhere in b. If $a < b$, then the failure is attributed to the ith trigger represented by $a = R_i(t)$.

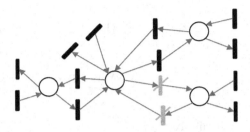

Fig. 14. General problem. Slashed sensors represents a failed sensor.

A more general case is considered as shown in Fig. 14. We can apply the same detection algorithm to identify failures in each place. When a potential sensor failure is identified between two places, it will be identified twice instead of once, thus improving the identification accuracy.

4   Case Study

4.1   Background

In the of 2018, the Ford Global Data Insight and Analytics (GDIA) team was relocated to Wagner Place. Wagner Place consists of two newly constructed buildings each is 3 stories high, and several new retail locations operate out of the first floor of these buildings. Furthermore, new shops and restaurants opened around the same time in the downtown area. To help with the increased demand for parking in the area, the City of Dearborn constructed a 373-space public parking structure next to the building as shown in Fig. 15. This structure, along with other nearby public structures, provide free parking for both Ford employees and shoppers.

The parking space consists of a ground parking lot and a 4-level parking structure where the 4th level is the structure's roof. As a free parking space, there are no gates installed, and no occupancy information is provided. Drivers usually circle around the ground level while searching for an available parking spot, and if none is found, the drivers usually proceed to go through the structure. It is beneficial to provide information on parking vacancy, especially in the structure, to the residents of Wagner Place to reduce the unnecessary time and fuel spent while scanning the parking space before resorting to an alternative parking location. The parking information will also be very useful to other Ford employees attending offsite meetings at Wagner Place by helping them to decide on whether to use their personal vehicles or to take a corporate shuttle.

To address the parking challenge, the GDIA team decided to explore the opportunity to develop a cost efficient IoT-based parking information solution. Specifically, the team considered leveraging the existing CCTV cameras in the infrastructure which cover the parking space, and connected vehicles for information delivery to the parking tenants using SmartDeviceLink (https://smartdevicelink.com/). The team created a partnership with the City of Dearborn and was able to process real time video streams from the cameras to design a parking information system at minimum cost and effort. One of the critical requirements to utilize the video stream is data privacy. The stream can only be processed on the edge, and no video or images are to be stored or accessed by the cloud. Furthermore, the system must be robust so that if new cameras or sensors are added, fail, or recover, the system must adjust automatically. An edge device is placed in the infrastructure and connects to existing CCTV cameras. This edge device is capable of processing video streams from several cameras and translates the data to labels. The edge device sends the labels to a digital twin of the parking space in the cloud. The details of this architecture can be found in [14].

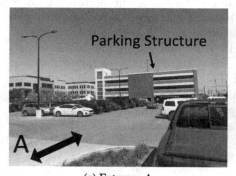
(a) Entrance A.

(b) Entrances B and C.

(c) Panoramic view of the parking space.

Fig. 15. Wagner place parking.

4.2 Parking Analytics

We captured data over a period of three months. To highlight our results, we provide analysis for the parking structure, starting from the second level and up. By lumping all the places above ground level into one place, we gain insight into the activity within the parking structure. We noticed consistent patterns across the weeks. Figure 16 shows that in general, it is easy to find a parking spot on Monday, Thursday and Friday, but it is hard to find one on Tuesday and Wednesday. Our daily experience was consistent with this result. This motivates the use of probabilistic and statistical methods for parking information systems. The reason why these curves don't reach capacity is due to the fact that businesses on the first floor were not opened until the last few weeks in our 3 months analysis.

From our experiments, we found that it takes a vehicle at least 2.5 min (average 3 min) to drive from the entry point of level-1 all the way to the roof, turn, and drive and back to the same entry point of level-1. We chose the third week of January as an example, after the businesses at Wagner Place opened, and compare the days of that week with the 3 month average, where for the most part, these businesses were closed.

The results are shown in Figs. 17 and 18. We define the occupancy curve as the *minimum* between capacity (270) and the number of both parked and moving vehicles in a place at a given time of the day. We define the "Overflow" curve as the *maximum* between the capacity (270) and the number of parked and moving vehicles. The curve "3M Average" shows the 3 months average occupancy curve of the structure above ground level. This average never exceeded capacity, and hence there was no overflow. For all the shown days except for Monday (Fig. 17a), it can be seen that the occupancy has reached capacity, and there was overflow during the day. Monday was a holiday, and therefore the capacity in the structure never exceeded capacity.

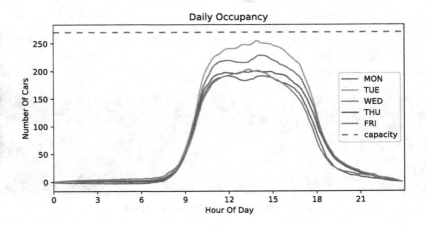

Fig. 16. Average occupancy over 3 months.

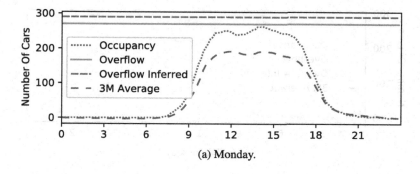

(a) Monday.

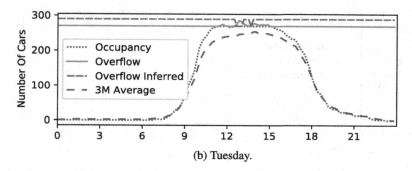

(b) Tuesday.

Fig. 17. Peak time vs night time for Monday and Tuesday.

It is also possible to infer when the parking structure reaches maximum capacity without knowing the initial marking by analyzing the vehicles entering and leaving the structure. Whenever the signal representing entering vehicles is similar to a 3 min lagged signal representing exiting vehicles, and when the volume of vehicles is not close to 0, we infer that capacity is reached, as illustrated by Fig. 19. The curve "Overflow Inferred" drops whenever it is inferred that maximum capacity has been reached. The absolute value of this line is not important, and is shown for demonstration. Using this type of detection, variations in the capacity due to construction, or due to vehicles parked incorrectly, can be accounted for, although at a delayed time.

We calculated that on Wednesday of that week, around 10.75 h were wasted trying to find a parking spot. Furthermore, for every liter of gas consumed, around 2.3 kg of CO_2 is produced, and each 10 min of idling costs 300 ml in wasted fuel for 3 L engines [16,17]. Thus we estimate that the overflow on the selected day contributes to 44.5 kg of CO_2 from around 5 gallons of gasoline.

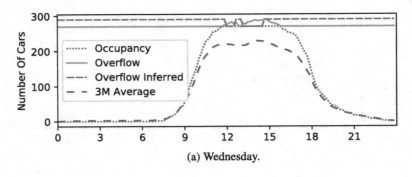

(a) Wednesday.

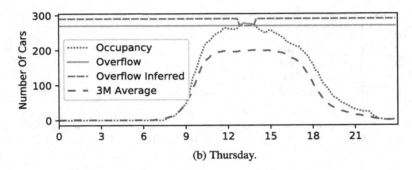

(b) Thursday.

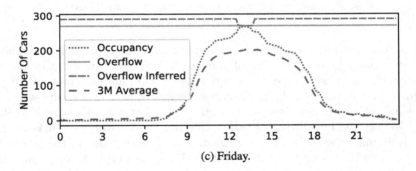

(c) Friday.

Fig. 18. Peak time vs night time Wednesday through Friday.

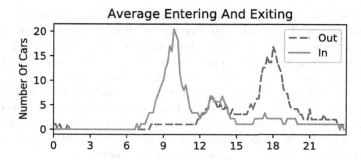

Fig. 19. Number of cars entering and exiting the parking throughout the day on the selected Wednesday.

5 Conclusion

The paper presents a robust parking information system that adapts to adding, removing or failing parking infrastructure sensors. Parking information systems can provide different levels of details to the drivers seeking a parking spot. This can range from a simple count of cars entering and exiting, count of vehicles in specific sections, and up to individual count of each and every occupied parking spot. A digital twin is the core of the parking information system that can integrate the data from disjointed IoT sensors to derive the parking occupancy information. The details of the parking information system depend on the number of installed sensors in the parking. Adding more sensors naturally leads to more detailed information. However, the addition of sensors increase the chance of sensor permanent and intermittent failures, and it is important to detect and tolerate the sensor failures and recoveries.

The development presented in this paper demonstrates how Petri Nets can be used as digital twin to implement a robust parking information system. Petri Nets can support any level of desired details, and the model can be incrementally and automatically extended to support adding, removing or failing sensors. An initial low fidelity model can be naturally extended by adding additional sensors in the parking space to reach the desired fidelity. Petri Nets provide a good foundation for parking information system analytics since the Petri Net model is an observer for the disjointed messages generated by the parking infrastructure, and it enables us to gain insights into the parking dynamics. Furthermore, we showed how process discovery algorithms in Petri Nets can be applied for automatic model generation to reduce the development efforts.

The paper also presents a case study for a cost efficient smart parking information system in which the sensors comprise existing CCTV infrastructure, where the vision processing is implemented on an edge device to ensure data privacy. A Petri Net-based digital twin is implemented in the cloud which tracks current parking occupancy. We discussed the analytics of the parking dynamics and showed that for the given parking structure, it is possible to identify unique patterns for the days of the week. The results illustrate that there is measurable waste produced by vehicles seeking a parking spot in the absence of a parking information system. The result indicates that adding a simple parking information billboard which indicates if maximum capacity has been reached can have tangible time and fuel savings. In our future work, we will focus on supporting drivers and autonomous vehicles to navigate to an empty spot. When a guidance service is available, the digital twin may communicate directly with connected vehicles in order to support the coordination of autonomous valet parking. The analysis of sensor failure detection will be extended to multiple sensors. The advantages of Petri Net extensions will be investigated, such as timed Petri Nets, Petri Nets with inhibitors, and colored Petri nets.

References

1. Van der Aalst, W.M.P., van Dongen, B.F.: Discovering petri nets from event logs. In: Jensen, K., van der Aalst, W.M.P., Balbo, G., Koutny, M., Wolf, K. (eds.) Transactions on Petri Nets and Other Models of Concurrency VII, pp. 372–422. Springer, Berlin Heidelberg, Berlin, Heidelberg (2013). https://doi.org/10.1007/978-3-642-38143-0
2. Aalst, W.V.D.: Process Mining (2016). https://doi.org/10.1007/978-3-662-49851-4
3. Almeida, P., Soares de Oliveira, Jr. L., Britto, Jr. A.S., Eunelson, J., Koerich, A.: Pklot - a robust dataset for parking lot classification. Exp. Syst. Appl. 42, 4937–4949 (2015). https://doi.org/10.1016/j.eswa.2015.02.009
4. Cai, B.Y., Alvarez, R., Sit, M., Duarte, F., Ratti, C.: Deep learning-based video system for accurate and real-time parking measurement. IEEE Internet Things J. 6(5), 7693–7701 (2019). https://doi.org/10.1109/JIOT.2019.2902887
5. van Dongen, B.F., Alves de Medeiros, A.K., Wen, L.: Process mining: overview and outlook of petri net discovery algorithms. In: Jensen, K., van der Aalst, W.M.P. (eds.) Transactions on Petri Nets and Other Models of Concurrency II. LNCS, vol. 5460, pp. 225–242. Springer, Heidelberg (2009). https://doi.org/10.1007/978-3-642-00899-3_13
6. Fuller, A., Fan, Z., Day, C., Barlow, C.: Digital twin: enabling technologies, challenges and open research. IEEE Access 8, 108952–108971 (2020)
7. Giua, A., Silva, M.: Petri nets and automatic control: a historical perspective. Ann. Rev. Control 45, 223–239 (2018). https://doi.org/10.1016/j.arcontrol.2018.04.006
8. Gusikhin, O., Lewis, D., Miteff, J.: Integration of plant floor information for scheduling and control. SAE Tech. Paper Ser. (1996). https://doi.org/10.4271/961648
9. Huang, C., Wang, S.: A hierarchical Bayesian generation framework for vacant parking space detection. IEEE Trans. Circ. Syst. Video Technol. 20(12), 1770–1785 (2010). https://doi.org/10.1109/TCSVT.2010.2087510
10. Kotb, A.O., Shen, Y., Huang, Y.: Smart parking guidance, monitoring and reservations: a review. IEEE Intell. Transp. Syst. Mag. 9(2), 6–16 (2017)
11. Lin, T., Rivano, H., Le Mouël, F.: A survey of smart parking solutions. IEEE Trans. Intell. Transp. Syst. 18(12), 3229–3253 (2017). https://doi.org/10.1109/TITS.2017.2685143
12. Lourenco, J., Gomes, L.: Animated graphical user interface generator framework for input-output place-transition petri net models. In: van Hee, K.M., Valk, R. (eds.) Applications and Theory of Petri Nets, pp. 409–418. Springer, Berlin Heidelberg, Berlin, Heidelberg (2008)

13. Ma, Z., Li, Z., Giua, A.: Marking estimation in a class of time labelled petri nets. IEEE Trans. Autom. Cont. **65**(2), 493–506 (2020)
14. Makke, O., Gusikhin, O.: Petri net-based smart parking information system. In: Berns, K., Helfert, M., Gusikhin, O. (eds.) Proceedings of the 6th International Conference on Vehicle Technology and Intelligent Transport Systems (VEHITS 2020), Prague, Czech Republic, May 2–4, 2020, pp. 385–393. SCITEPRESS (2020). https://doi.org/10.5220/0009583403850393
15. Màrmol, E., Sevillano, X.: Quickspot: a video analytics solution for on-street vacant parking spot detection. Multimedia Tools Appl. **75**(24), 17711–17743 (2016) https://doi.org/10.1007/s11042-016-3773-8
16. NRCan: 2019 fuel consumption guide (2015). https://www.nrcan.gc.ca/energy/efficiency/communities-infrastructure/transportation/idling/4459 Accessed 15 Dec 2019
17. NRCan: 2019 fuel consumption guide (2019). https://www.nrcan.gc.ca/sites/www.nrcan.gc.ca/files/oee/pdf/transportation/tools/fuelratings/2019FuelConsumptionGuide.pdf Accessed 15 Dec 2019
18. Rozenberg, G., Engelfriet, J.: Elementary net systems. In: Reisig, W., Rozenberg, G. (eds.) ACPN 1996. LNCS, vol. 1491, pp. 12–121. Springer, Heidelberg (1998). https://doi.org/10.1007/3-540-65306-6_14
19. Ru, Y., Hadjicostis, C.N.: Sensor selection for structural observability in discrete event systems modeled by petri nets. IEEE Trans. Autom. Cont. **55**(8), 1751–1764 (2010). https://doi.org/10.1109/TAC.2010.2042348
20. Seymer, P., Wijesekera, D., Kan, C.D.: Smart parking zones using dual mode routed bluetooth fogged meshes. In: VEHITS, pp. 211–222, January 2019). https://doi.org/10.5220/0007734802110222
21. Sun, W., Stoop, E., Washburn, S.S.: Evaluation of commercial truck parking detection for rest areas. Transp. Res. Rec. **2672**(9), 141–151 (2018) . https://doi.org/10.1177/0361198118788185
22. Yang, R., Li, B., Cheng, C.: A petri net-based approach to service composition and monitoring in the IoT. In: 2014 Asia-Pacific Services Computing Conference, pp. 16–22, December 2014. https://doi.org/10.1109/APSCC.2014.11
23. Zhang, Y., Wang, W., Du, W., Qian, C., Yang, H.: Coloured petri net-based active sensing system of real-time and multi-source manufacturing information for smart factory. Int. J. Adv. Manuf. Technol. **94**(9), 3427–3439 (2018). https://doi.org/10.1007/s00170-017-0800-5

Adaptive Heterogeneous V2X Communication for Cooperative Vehicular Maneuvering

Daniel Bischoff[1,3]($\boxtimes$), Florian A. Schiegg[2]($\boxtimes$), Tobias Meuser[3]($\boxtimes$), Dieter Schuller[1]($\boxtimes$), and Ralf Steinmetz[3]($\boxtimes$)

[1] Opel Automobile GmbH, 65423 Ruesselsheim, Germany
{daniel.bischoff,dieter.schuller}@stellantis.com
[2] Corporate Research, Robert Bosch GmbH, 31139 Hildesheim, Germany
florian.schiegg@de.bosch.com
[3] Multimedia Communications Lab, TU Darmstadt, 64283 Darmstadt, Germany
{daniel.bischoff,tobias.meuser,ralf.steinmetz}@kom.tu-darmstadt.de

Abstract. Cooperative Vehicular Maneuvering (CVM) can increase traffic efficiency and safety by enabling vehicles to organize and perform concerted driving maneuvers cooperatively. However, since Vehicle-to-Everything (V2X) communication, which constitutes a key enabler for CVM, decreases with increasing distances between cooperating vehicles, only poor CVM performance and therewith only poor traffic efficiency and safety improvements can be achieved at vast distances and under heavy traffic load. In the work at hand, we extend our CVM approach and propose a novel adaptive heterogeneous V2X communication approach exploiting benefits from cellular and ad-hoc communication in large-scale scenarios. We show that our proposed CVM approach is able to avoid traffic jams under high traffic load. With our proposed communication approach, we significantly improve the Quality of Communication (QoC) in terms of Age of Information (AoI) by 15% and the CVM performance in terms of average velocity by 3.2% compared to the ad-hoc approach.

Keywords: V2X communication · Cooperative vehicular maneuvering · MCM · Quality of communication · Cooperation cost · LTE

1 Introduction

In past years, the number of vehicles has grown tremendously and might even continue to grow in the near future, whereas the infrastructure remains the same. As a consequence, traffic jams will become more severe, especially on motorways

The German Federal Ministry for Economic Affairs and Energy (BMWi) supports this research within the project IMAGinE - Intelligente Manöver Automatisierung - kooperative Gefahrenvermeidung in Echtzeit (Intelligent maneuver automation - cooperative hazard avoidance in real time).

© Springer Nature Switzerland AG 2021
C. Klein et al. (Eds.): SMARTGREENS 2020/VEHITS 2020, CCIS 1475, pp. 228–254, 2021.
https://doi.org/10.1007/978-3-030-89170-1_12

and in urban areas. While past research activities primarily focused on traffic safety regarding Advanced Driver Assistance System (ADAS), vehicle efficiency, in addition to safety, is considered increasingly important [6].

In this context, V2X communication constitutes a promising research area to address traffic efficiency and safety for both human drivers and autonomous vehicles. Because it enables sharing the information perceived by own sensing capabilities and received from other vehicles, V2X leads to increased perception of the relevant environment beyond the vehicles' local sensor perception [24]. By allowing the exchange of driving intentions for traffic coordination, V2X enables CVM [19] to increase traffic efficiency.

Radio propagation introduces attenuation of signal strength due to (i) path loss, (ii) shadowing, and (iii) fading as well as message latency and collision due to the limited channel bandwidth. In the work at hand, we use the term QoC to indicate the quality of message propagation in terms of reliability and latency. Considering realistic radio propagation effects is indispensable when relying on wireless information such as CVM applications.

CVM leverages high distances between communicating vehicles to coordinate early. Communication technologies such as cellular communication can be employed for realizing V2X communication at large distances. The larger the distance between the communicating parties, the higher susceptible the communication is to faults for the reasons mentioned above (path loss, shadowing, fading). At small distances between the communicating parties, reliable communication at low latency is required during cooperation to inform about changes in time. Here, ad-hoc communication technologies such as Intelligent Transportation System-G5 (ITS-G5) appear to be more appropriate for realizing V2X communication.

Hence, one single communication technology might not be able to satisfy the requirements in all situations [34], i.e., to start coordination early and enable communication reliably and at low latency during cooperation. Thus, applying a heterogeneous communication for CVM seems appropriate to account for realistic environments.

While heterogeneous V2X dissemination strategies that aim at providing fairness of channel usage have already been examined by related work (cp. Sect. 6), CVM requires peak QoC for the cooperation vehicles immediately before and while executing the cooperating maneuver. In contrast, lower QoC levels are sufficient for initiating CVM at larger distances. Furthermore, decentralized maneuver coordination in small-scale scenarios with a limited number of cooperation vehicles, utilizing simplified communication channels, has also been considered in related work. In the work at hand, we focus on a real-world large-scale intersection scenario accounting for a more realistic communication channel. Thus, we consider high communication requirements for CVM.

In summary, we pose and address the following research question in this paper:

"What is the impact of communication on CVM, and can we improve CVM by applying a heterogeneous communication approach?"

Correspondingly, we contribute and propose to

- extend our large-scale CVM planning and execution approach [2],
- analyze the impact of communication on CVM performance,
- present our adaptive heterogeneous communication approach for CVM and provide a corresponding evaluation.

The rest of the paper is structured as follows: In Sect. 2, we define our system model, including the scenario, decentralized CVM, the applied V2X communication, and the problem formulation. Section 3 extends and optimizes CVM for large-scale scenarios. In Sect. 4, we describe our adaptive heterogeneous communication approach for CVM. Section 5 focuses on the experimental setup and provides detailed evaluation results. In Sect. 6, we discuss related work along with its limitations and emphasis on the enhancements provided by the work at hand. Finally, Sect. 7 summarizes and concludes the paper.

2   System Model

In the following, we describe our system model, which we implement and evaluate in a simulation environment. We consider a concrete urban intersection in Aschaffenburg, Germany, from the Kooperative Perzeption (cooperative perception) (Ko-PER) project [29] with high vehicular traffic load as our scenario. The specific scenario and involved traffic flows will be explained in Subsect. 2.1.

With a high vehicular traffic load, we expect a traffic jam to occur within the intersection due to the drivers' or fully-automated vehicles' limited coordination capability without communication. To counteract a traffic jam occurrence, we propose to use decentralized CVM, which leverages V2X communication. Therefore, we briefly explain the considered V2X coordination mechanism in Subsect. 2.2.

Decentralized CVM relies on V2X communication to exchange driving intentions and coordinate the maneuver. Wireless communication encounters propagation effects in real-world environments such as path loss, fading, and latency. These effects degrade the QoC and cause Maneuver Coordination Messages (MCMs) to arrive late or get lost. The propagation effects can have various effects on different communication technologies. We consider a combination of ad-hoc and cellular communication for our adaptive heterogeneous communication approach, where we explain both communication technologies in Subsect. 2.3.

2.1   Scenario

The considered scenario is an urban intersection in Aschaffenburg, Germany, as depicted in Fig. 1, where buildings surround the intersection and obstruct the Line-of-Sight (LoS) to the other arms. Traffic lights control the vehicle flows from all four arms.

The traffic flow in this intersection was analyzed in detail with video cameras in [29], where valid scenarios were extracted in [13]. Like [2], where the QoC for

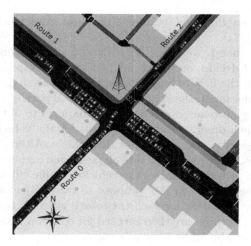

Fig. 1. Ko-PER intersection in Aschaffenburg, Germany. Figure adapted from [16].

CVM was examined in detail, we consider the scenario where vehicles approaching from the north-west and south-east wait at a red traffic light. Vehicles from the north-east (Route 2) drive straight at a green light, and vehicles from the south-west can either drive straight (Route 0) or turn left (Route 1) both at a green light. Vehicles with the intention to turn left have to wait for an open gap in the oncoming traffic flow from the north-east. Further, vehicles approaching from the south-west with the intention to drive straight must wait for vehicles to find a gap and drive left. Traffic jams for vehicles from the south-west increase with an increased density of the traffic flow from the north-east. To avoid the formation of a traffic jam, vehicles with a left-turn intention require cooperation from vehicles driving straight from the north-east.

All vehicles are fully automated, equipped with V2X communication, and have CVM enabled. In particular, we consider the European Telecommunication Standard Institute (ETSI) ITS-G5 for ad-hoc and Long Term Evolution (LTE) for cellular communication, where every vehicle has access to both communication technologies. In this work, all vehicles solely rely on the environment perception provided by V2X communication, i.e., vehicles are not equipped with any other environmental sensors such as cameras or radars.

2.2 Decentralized Cooperative Vehicular Maneuvering

CVM is a promising mechanism to improve traffic efficiency in highly congested scenarios [19]. In general, the coordination can be arranged in a centralized or decentralized way. In centralized approaches, a central authority observes the traffic in certain areas and decides for the best maneuvers to improve the traffic efficiency, i.e., they leverage an increased extended environmental perception avoiding egoistic maneuvers by single vehicles. On the downside, centralized approaches lack scalability and require additional infrastructure close to the coordination points [21].

In the paper at hand, we focus on a decentralized approach, where each vehicle requests and decides on CVM independently. [18] proposes a decentralized approach: With the help of trajectories, the authors suggest to describe the future path of vehicles for the longitudinal and lateral path as a function of time. In contrast to highly automated driving, CVM requires to obtain a set of different trajectories, which describe different options for the vehicle considering the current position, velocity, and heading of the vehicle. After generating a set of different trajectories, [18] proposes to rate all generated and received trajectories, where the trajectory, which optimizes the vehicle's traffic efficiency is rated with the lowest cost. The authors in [19] propose to rate trajectories distributively and send the respective rating for each trajectory via V2X communication.

All generated trajectories are then checked for collision with trajectories from other vehicles received by V2X communication.

As suggested in [18], the vehicle commits to the cheapest planned trajectory, which has to be collision-free, or we need to have right-of-way for the colliding trajectory. The principle of CVM is depicted in Fig. 2, where we annotate exemplary costs for the different types of trajectories. In order to optimize our traffic efficiency, we can optionally request a desired trajectory (orange). The desired trajectory must have a collision with another received planned trajectory (black), where we do not have the right-of-way and must be cheaper than our current planned trajectory. A vehicle receiving a desired trajectory with a collision with its planned trajectory can offer cooperation by considering a more expensive but collision-free alternative trajectory (green) as its planned trajectory. Intuitively, we offer cooperation if the cooperating vehicle's invested cost is adequate, i.e., below a threshold c_t. As shown in Fig. 2, the Cooperation Vehicle (CV) from top has cost of $c_{cv,plan} = 0.0$, and $c_{cv,coop} = 0.3$ for the planned and cooperative trajectories, respectively. Therefore, we can obtain the induced cost by offering cooperation as $c_{cv,diff} = c_{cv,coop} - c_{cv,plan} = 0.3$. The Requesting Vehicle (RV) from bottom issues cost of $c_{rv,plan} = 0.4$, $c_{rv,des} = 0.0$, $c_{rv,alt} = 1.0$ for the planned, desired, and alternative trajectories, respectively. Hence, the gain in traffic efficiency in terms of cooperation cost can also be obtained by the difference in cost as $c_{rv,diff} = c_{rv,plan} - c_{rv,des} = 0.4$. If the cooperation vehicle from top cooperates, its cost increases by 0.3, whereas the cost for the requesting vehicle from the south decreases to 0.4. If $c_{cv,diff} + c_t < c_{rv,diff}$ holds, cooperation would be offered in this scenario.

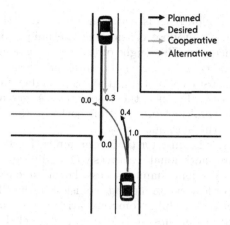

Fig. 2. Intersection scenario illustrating CVM showing different types of trajectories with their respective costs. (Color figure online)

2.3   V2X Communication

CVM relies on the exchange of MCMs over V2X communication. For the paper at hand, we assume that the vehicle's information is current, and the processing of incoming and outgoing messages is instantaneous. That way, no additional latency is introduced to the exchange of V2X messages.

To keep track of the QoC of each message, we timestamp each MCM, which is already common for ETSI ITS-G5 messages such as the Cooperative Awareness Message (CAM) [10].

We adopt and extend the dissemination strategies mentioned in [20]. For ad-hoc communication, we use Single Hop Broadcast (SHB), where messages are disseminated to vehicles in the direct communication range of our vehicle. [20] obtained a communication distance of approximately less than 300 m. For cellular communication, we use Geocast, where vehicles send their messages to a base station mentioning a destination area, which is bit-wise encoded as a Geohash. The base station forwards the messages via Unicast to all vehicles within the respective Geohash.

Radio propagation effects such as path loss and fading impact the QoC causing unreliable V2X communication. To describe these effects for both considered communication technologies, we use the scalable and realistic V2X channel model proposed in [1]. We describe the path loss for LoS with the Two-Ray Ground reflection model, reflecting the attenuation caused by the reflection on the ground surface. In the case of a blocked LoS, we use a knife-edge model, which has been previously used for V2X channels in [4] to describe the respective attenuation caused by shadowing and the path loss using the Friis model [8]. Further, we describe the destructive and constructive interference caused by multipath propagation with the Jakes model [12], considering the transmitter's and receiver's relative velocity in a deterministic way. Therefore, the amount of dominant radio propagation path is static, and we obtain the delay spread in a stochastic way. In [1], we propose considering the unique properties of ad-hoc and cellular communication: The height of the antennas is considered to determine the los condition. By considering the antenna's height, the probability of one or even multiple obstacles blocking the los is higher for ad-hoc compared to cellular communication. Further, the base station's increased antenna height reduces the number of multiple propagation paths at the receiver, due to less reflecting objects near the antenna.

The channel capacity is finite for both communication technologies. Cellular communication requires additional resources to coordinate the channel, whereas ETSI ITSG5 relies on random channel access. For ad-hoc communication, messages can get delayed or lost due to message collisions if the Channel Busy Ration (CBR) is high. In contrast, cellular communication can efficiently use the channel resources but requires an up- and downlink channel. Further, the Unicast transmission is inefficient, as the same information is transmitted multiple times to different receivers, and the information has to be processed in the back-end.

The induced channel load also depends on the number of sent messages per vehicle. For the paper at hand, we set the message generation frequency static to analyze the impact of imperfect communication better. However, message generation rules for CVM are an essential aspect to decrease the induced channel load, which is an open topic for future work.

3   Maneuver Coordination

The following section describes our proposed extensions to the large-scale CVM coordination algorithm proposed in [2]. Therefore, we divide the maneuver coordination process into maneuver planning in Subsect. 3.1 and introduce maneuver execution in Subsect. 3.2.

3.1   Maneuver Planning

Following the structure proposed in [2], we divide the maneuver planning application in Trajectory Generation, Processing, and Cooperation.

Trajectory Generation. The trajectory generation's goal is to obtain a set of trajectories, which describes possible options of the vehicle's future moving behavior within a limited amount of time referred to as time horizon w. r. t. its current position and velocity.

As vehicles drive on roads, the movement direction is restricted according to the lane's specifics, reducing the complexity of trajectories to describe future moving behavior. To extract the movement behaviour from the trajectory at the receiver side, vehicles also require to have the same understanding of the road topology. Similar to [2], we describe a trajectory using a set of trajectory sections, where each trajectory section consists of a set of longitudinal and lateral polynomials. The longitudinal polynomial describes the progress on a lane as a function of time. The lateral polynomial is the lateral offset within the respective lane as a function of the longitudinal progress. Hence, we need a new trajectory section to change the lane or transition to the next lane following our vehicle route. We can reference each trajectory section's start with its latitude and longitude absolute position, i.e., the start reference point of the respective lane. Further, we might require multiple lateral and longitudinal polynomials for one trajectory section to describe the vehicle movement changes. For now, we use polynomials of the second degree, i.e., a constant acceleration model. Thus, to allow vehicles to accelerate, keep the current velocity, decelerate, and wait in standstill within one lane, we might require a maximum of four longitudinal polynomials for one trajectory section.

All generated trajectories share the same time horizon such that they are comparable for further processing, i.e., cost annotation. To reach the envisaged time horizon, we might obtain multiple trajectory sections for the next lanes considering the current velocity, acceleration, and position of the vehicle w. r. t. respective lane's properties. Unlike described in [2], where we vary the vehicle's velocity for different endpoints, we propose to vary the acceleration to obtain multiple trajectories ranging from negative to positive values. For positive values, we accelerate to the respective lane's velocity limit and remain the velocity for the rest of this lane. We also ensure to reach the next lane's velocity limit at the end of the current lane with a constant deceleration, which is the same for all generated trajectories and can be specified. We decelerate to standstill and stay at the respective position for the rest of the time horizon for negative values.

Let us assume a straight lane with a maximum allowed velocity $v_{\text{lane,max}} = 13\,\text{m/s}$, and a vehicle starting to drive on this lane with a velocity $v_{\text{start}} = 8\,\text{m/s}$.

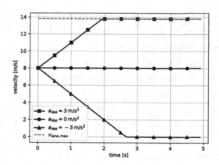

Fig. 3. Acceleration approach to obtain different trajectories for a vehicle enabling CVM.

Figure 3 depicts the velocity of the vehicle v over the time horizon t_{th} for three different accelerations a_{des}. The trajectory starts with the current velocity of the vehicle v_{start} at $t_{\text{th}} = 0\,\text{s}$. For $a_{\text{des}} = 3\,\text{m/s}^2$, we accelerate to $v_{\text{lane,max}}$, and hold the velocity for the rest of the lane. For $a_{\text{des}} = 0\,\text{m/s}^2$, we remain the velocity v_{start} for this lane. We slow down from v_{start} for negative accelerations, where, in our example, we decelerate to a standstill for $a_{\text{des}} = -3\,\text{m/s}^2$.

Compared to our approach in [2], this approach significantly decreases the number of generated trajectories, as we control the generation of trajectories with the acceleration step size of a_{des}. For different a_{des}, we can obtain trajectories of different length, ranging from the maximum to the minimum reachable trajectory length within the envisaged time horizon. For small acceleration step sizes, we obtain more trajectories, which allows for more possible driving maneuvers but increases the computation time for the trajectory processing described in the following.

Trajectory Processing. We perform a collision check using our generated and the received trajectories. In case another vehicle indicates to cooperate with our vehicles (cooperation offer or request), i.e., mentioning our station id in the MCM, we attach the station id, trajectory class (planned or desired), and trajectory type to each of our trajectories. In case of a received desired trajectory, we also denote the difference in cost compared to the other stations planned trajectory for further processing.

To guarantee traffic safety, we define a safety area at the front of vehicle, i.e., vehicles avoid colliding with this safety area, yielding

$$d_{\text{s,front}} = v * t_{\text{s}} + d_{\text{m}}, \tag{1}$$

where t_{s} and d_{m} are the safety area time and distance margin. $d_{\text{s,front}}$ increases with increasing velocity v, where d_{m} ensures a safety distance to the vehicle in front for $v \to 0$. We also add a static safety area at the back of the vehicle $d_{\text{s,back}} = d_{\text{m}}$ to avoid vehicles turn sharply after a vehicle passes the intersection. For the paper at hand, we consider $d_{\text{m}} = l_{\text{w,veh}} = 1.8\,\text{m}$ and $t_{\text{s}} = 1\,\text{s}$, where $l_{\text{w,veh}}$ is the width of the vehicle.

We differentiate the collision type as safety margin and vehicle collision, i.e., the collision circles introduced in [2] have one of the mentioned collision types. Trajectories with vehicle collisions should be avoided at all costs and we allow for safety margin collision for the vehicle acting on a cooperative maneuver. Here, the safety margin collision is only allowed with the vehicle offering cooperation to avoid aborting the cooperation immediately in case of a collision. Even though the cooperating vehicle aims to avoid a collision while cooperating, it cannot always be guaranteed due to the nature of an event-discrete simulator and imperfect communication.

We propose a mechanism to improve the efficiency of the trajectory collision check from [2]. Therefore, we obtain the length of both trajectories l_{traj} and the distance between both vehicles $d_{\text{t,r}}$. If

$$d_{\text{t,r}} > \max(l_{\text{traj,1}} + d_{\text{s,front,1}} + d_{\text{s,back,1}} + 0.5 \cdot d_{\text{l,veh,1}},$$
$$l_{\text{traj,2}} + d_{\text{s,front,2}} + d_{\text{s,back,2}} + 0.5 \cdot d_{\text{l,veh,2}})$$

holds, we expect no collision, where $d_{\text{l,veh}}$ is the length of the respective vehicle. Further, for each time step, we obtain the distance between both vehicles within the time step. If

$$d_{\text{t,r}} > \max(d_{\text{s,front,1}} + d_{\text{s,back,1}} + d_{\text{l,veh,1}}, d_{\text{s,front,2}} + d_{\text{s,back,2}} + d_{\text{l,veh,1}})$$

holds, we also expect no collision.

For each trajectory conflict, we obtain the right-of-way for our trajectories using the cooperative function trigger.

Cooperative Function Trigger. A key module in our proposed CVM architecture is the cooperative function trigger. Among other supportive functionalities, which we briefly describe in the following, the cooperative function trigger is responsible for determining potential cooperative functions for each generated trajectory.

While obtaining a set of possible trajectories, the trajectory generation module calls the cooperative functions trigger to get the respective trajectory's cooperative function within the envisaged time horizon, where each lane is composed as a trajectory section. We detect the cooperative functions using map information of the respective lane. In most common traffic simulators, such as [16], two roads are connected via a junction. Roads and junctions contain lanes, where the lanes of the roads and junctions are connected. We can also obtain the connection of each lane, which contains the maneuver type of each lane. We implement turning at junctions, merging on motorways, cooperative lane change and obviously no cooperative function for the paper at hand. As an example, lanes belonging to a junction and turning left or right without having right-of-way are denoted as turning at junctions. Driving straight or having the right-of-way while turning left or right within a junction is not denoted as a cooperative function, as we are not expecting the need for cooperation. There is also no cooperative function on straight roads, except if the planning module decides to change the lane within the road. After obtaining the distance to the next cooperative maneuver, we take the planned trajectory assigned by the cooperation logic and iterate through the list of cooperative functions. Here, each cooperative function is assigned to a unique lane. In case we found a cooperative function, we can obtain the distance to the lane from the map module using our current position.

Besides the aforementioned functionality, the cooperative function trigger also analysis trajectory conflicts and identifies the right-of-way for trajectory processing. Furthermore, the cooperative function trigger also handles the cooperation state changes supporting the cooperation logic.

Cooperation Logic. Now, we apply the cooperation logic on our obtained trajectories required for decentralized CVM as described in Subsect. 2.2 from the trajectory processing, where all trajectories contain information about potential trajectory conflicts, the respective right-of-way, and potential cooperation negotiations.

From our obtained trajectories, we select the cheapest planned trajectory, which is collision-free or has the right-of-way over other planned trajectories. If another station requests cooperation, we also search for the cheapest alternative trajectory, which requires to be collision-free with the requesting station. For collisions with other planned trajectories, we need to have the right-of-way.

Further, we only consider offering cooperation if $c_{\text{cv,diff}}+c_\text{t} < c_{\text{rv,diff}}$, as explained in Subsect. 2.2.

We select the cheapest trajectory with collision and without right-of-way as our desired trajectory, where this trajectory also requires to be cheaper as our planned trajectory.

Next, we propose our Cooperation State Machine handling the respective cooperation states of our vehicle.

Cooperation State Machine. Depending on the selected trajectory or combination of trajectories, we switch to the appropriate cooperation state. Therefore, we propose five states: *Default, Request, Acting Request, Acting Offer, and Emergency.* The states and transitions are depicted in Fig. 4.

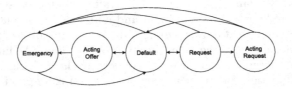

Fig. 4. Cooperation state machine with all five cooperation states and the allowed transitions.

All vehicles start in the *Default* cooperation state. From this state, we can switch to all other states and switch back to this state as well.

We switch to the *Request* state if we request a cooperative maneuver and wait for cooperation, i.e., send a desired in addition to the planned trajectory. As long as we request cooperation, we stay in the *Request* state and switch back to the *Default* state if we no longer require cooperation, e.g., we are suddenly too close to the cooperation point, or the vehicular traffic changed.

In case we recognize that another vehicle offers us cooperation, we switch to the *Acting Request* state. We stay in the *Acting Request* state until we reach the cooperation point and ensure not to reach the cooperation point earlier than promised with our desired trajectory at the start of the cooperation. We cancel the cooperation if we cannot reach the cooperation point in time to avoid unnecessary costs for our cooperation partner and define a cooperation timeout to avoid toggling.

In case we decide to offer cooperation with a valid alternative trajectory, we transition from the *Default* to the *Acting Offer* state. We ensure not to arrive at the cooperation point earlier than promised with our cooperative planned trajectory in this state. We transition back to the *Default* state after arriving at the cooperation point. Like the *Acting Request* state, we define a cooperation timeout to avoid toggling.

In the rare case that we cannot obtain a valid planned trajectory from our cooperative trajectories, i.e., collision-free or no right-of-way, we obtain a planned trajectory from the emergency trajectories to avoid any collision with other vehicles and switch to the *Emergency* state, i.e., we obtain cooperative trajectories in the range $a_{\text{dec,coop}} = [-3 \ldots 3]\,\text{m/s}^2$ and emergency trajectories in the range $a_{\text{dec,emer}} = [-3 \cdots -10]\,\text{m/s}^2$. We stay in the *Emergency* state as long as we require an emergency trajectory. From this state, we can only transition to the *Default* state if we no longer require an emergency trajectory. Additionally, we define a cooperation timeout after being in the *Emergency* state.

3.2 Maneuver Execution

The created planned trajectory describes the future movement behavior of our vehicle we promise to our environment. As long as we are not cooperating, i.e., being in the *Default* or *Request* state, our planned trajectory should reasonably match a human driver's or fully-automated vehicle's driving behavior. In other words, the planned trajectory aims to emulate the traffic simulator's driving behavior. When cooperating with other vehicles, i.e., being in the *Acting Request* or *Acting Offer* state, our planned trajectory deviates from the driving behaviour of the traffic simulator. Further, CVM also increases the environmental awareness of vehicles. Even without an explicit cooperation partner, we can passively cooperate and increase our traffic efficiency, i.e., we can find a potential gap identified from the trajectories of other vehicles. Therefore, we propose to control all cooperating vehicles from the traffic simulator and handle their longitudinal and lateral control.

For all cooperating vehicles, we obtain the latest planned trajectory from the maneuver planning module. As our simulator is event-discrete, we need to obtain the longitudinal and lateral acceleration for the next time step from the first longitudinal and lateral polynomial of the planned trajectory and send it as a request to our vehicle.

4 Adaptive Heterogeneous Communication

CVM leverages high communication distance and requires a high QoC while performing a cooperative maneuver, i.e., outdated information caused by high latency or unreliable communication decreases the efficiency of CVM, which has already been shown analytically in [3]. Therefore, we propose a heterogeneous dissemination strategy explicitly designed to improve the QoC targeting CVM. The main requirements of our approach are to (i) inform the local environment about our future driving behavior, (ii) increase the communication range to coordinate and start to cooperate early, and (iii) minimize the AoI to cooperation partners while cooperating.

We expect that one communication technology is insufficient to fulfill the requirements above. The authors in [14,17,22] show that ad-hoc communication is limited in range. Further, the reliability suffers shadowing, which likely occurs in scenarios such as an intersection. Likewise, cellular communication with Unicast transmission exceeds the channel load, where the latency can be unbounded.

We investigate existing heterogeneous approaches in Sect. 6 and find that none of the approaches focus on the needs of CVM, where a bilateral communication is required to coordinate the cooperative maneuver. In previous V2X applications such as the cooperative awareness or collective perception [24], the primary focus is to inform the environment, which requires an unidirectional communication, i.e., these applications are not expecting a response to their message.

The structure of our proposed adaptive heterogeneous approach is depicted in Fig. 5 and can be briefly summarized as follows: First, to inform our local environment, we broadcast our MCMs via ITS-G5. If we are in cooperation, we monitor the QoC of our cooperation partner for the ad-hoc communication interface. In case the QoC is insufficient to coordinate the maneuver, we additionally use cellular communication to increase the QoC for our cooperation partner.

If we are not cooperating, we determine the need for cooperation w.r.t. the scenario our planned trajectory is currently covering. To increase our local awareness and detect potential cooperation partners as early as possible, we aim at extending our communication range using cellular in addition to ad-hoc communication. We elaborate more on the approaches above in the following.

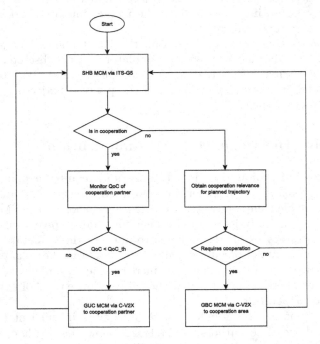

Fig. 5. Flow diagram showing the adaptive communication approach for CVM.

4.1   Quality of Communication

To improve ad-hoc communication, ETSI proposes to measure, estimate, and share the QoC in terms of CBR [11]. Unfortunately, the CBR targets the lower-layer communication stack and might be unsuited to improve the application performance of CVM, which also applies to the Packet Delivery Ratio (PDR) and latency as their impact on the application performance is challenging to obtain.

We propose using the AoI τ introduced in [15] and already applied on CVM in [3]. According to [9], we save the latest information of objects extracted from received V2X messages such as the MCM. Using the timestamp of these objects, we can obtain the AoI according to Eq. 2 as

$$\tau_t = t_{\mathrm{msg,cur}} - t_{\mathrm{msg,last}}, \tag{2}$$

where $t_{\mathrm{msg,cur}}$ and $t_{\mathrm{msg,last}}$ denote the time when the current and last message were created at the transmitter, respectively.

Further, to smoothen the measurement, we suggest to obtain a series of measurements of τ for each object separately and apply an exponential smoothing function such that we give more relevance to recent measurements using Eq. 3, yielding

$$\tau_t^\star = \alpha \cdot \tau_t + (1 - \alpha) \cdot \tau_{t-1}^\star, \tag{3}$$

where α and $1 - \alpha$ denote the weighting of the present and past measurement, respectively. As we propose using heterogeneous communication, we need to differentiate the received messages by the used communication interface to keep track of the AoI for each communication technology separately. However, only the latest received MCM for each object will be processed by the maneuver planning application.

As a downside of our definition in Eq. 3, we obtain $\tau_t^\star$ as the difference in timestamp for the previously and currently received message. Unless we are not receiving a subsequent message, we are not updating Eq. 2, which falsifies the actual AoI in case of a high PDR, i.e., the AoI remains low although the information ages over time.

Therefore, we propose to use the current absolute time t_{cur} to obtain an observation of $\tau_t^\star$ denoted as $\tau_{t,\mathrm{obs}}^\star$. That way, we are not updating $\tau_t^\star$ with t_{cur}. One could also easily obtain the AoI as the time difference between the last received message and the current time. However, our observation $\tau_{t,\mathrm{obs}}^\star$ can be shortly after receiving an MCM, which would lower $\tau_t^\star$ leading to a too optimistic value for the AoI. Hence, according to Eq. 4, we only consider t_{cur} if $t_{\mathrm{cur}} > \tau_t^\star$ holds, yielding

$$\tau_{t,\mathrm{obs}}^\star = \begin{cases} \alpha \cdot t_{\mathrm{cur}} + (1 - \alpha) \cdot \tau_t^\star & \text{, if } t_{\mathrm{cur}} > \tau_t^\star \\ \tau_t^\star & \text{, otherwise.} \end{cases} \tag{4}$$

Further, the Local Dynamic Map (LDM) continuously updates and deletes outdated entries according to their specified lifetime t_{lt}. Once we receive a new object, the LDM does not have past observations for $\tau_{t-1}^\star$. We propose to set

$\tau_{t-1}^{\star} = t_{\text{lt}}$ for this case, as we have not received any messages of the respective object for at least t_{lt}.

4.2 Radio Access Technology (RAT) Selection

We propose a three-step dissemination approach to fulfill the requirements above, following the flow diagram in Fig. 5.

First, to inform the local environment about our current planned maneuver, we always disseminate our MCM via ad-hoc communication using SHB. Compared to the cooperative awareness, which disseminates the current position and velocity via Broadcast to the local environment, the MCM further increases the local awareness as we communicate our future planned maneuver to allow for a proactive traffic adaptation.

In addition to the local environmental awareness, we continuously evaluate our need for cooperation within our current planning horizon. In case our planned trajectory covers a cooperative function scenario, e.g., turning at junctions or merging on motorways, we disseminate our current MCM via cellular Geocast targeting the area of relevance surrounding the potential cooperation point. Geocast, as already used in [20], is a grid-based dissemination approach, where V2X messages are disseminated to the respective grid, which is encoded as a Geohash. Therefore, we obtain all Geohashes required to cover a circle area with the radius r_{circle} and attach them to the MCM. The parameter r_{circle} depends on the maximum allowed velocity for the respective scenario and the time horizon of our trajectory such that we cover all potential vehicles. We forward the message to the cellular base station, which, in turn, disseminates the message to all vehicles within the respective Geohashes. The proposed mechanism is illustrated in Fig. 6.

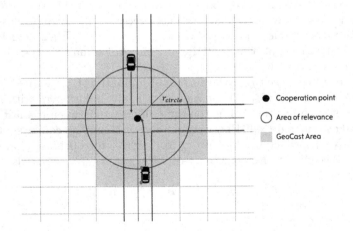

Fig. 6. Intersection scenario, where the vehicle from the bottom determines the cooperation point yielding an area of relevance covering the GeoCast Area in yellow. (Color figure online)

Vehicles, potentially requiring cooperation, will keep sending the MCM via both interfaces until passing the cooperative function scenario. Other vehicles, which are also approaching the scenario but do not require cooperation, e.g., driving straight, will continue solely using the ad-hoc communication interface while being in the *Default* cooperation state. In case these vehicles recognize a cooperation conflict via one of the given interfaces and switch to the *Acting Offer* state, we aim at improving the QoC while keeping the channel utilization at a minimum. Therefore, vehicles being in the *Acting Offer* state monitor the AoI of their cooperation partners for the ad-hoc communication technology, as described in Subsect. 4.1. Assuming channel reciprocity, we expect our cooperation partners to receive messages from us with a similar AoI as we receive messages from them. In case $\tilde{\tau} > \tau_{\mathrm{th}}$ holds, where we denote τ_{th} as our threshold AoI, we use cellular Geo-Unicast solely to reach our cooperation partners and improve the QoC for them. Geo-Unicast keeps the amount of redundant information and cellular channel utilization at a minimum. Furthermore, it can also significantly increase the QoC to relevant vehicles, which are involved in the cooperation. We set τ_{th} according to the 1.5 of the inverse of the used message frequency yielding $\tau_{\mathrm{th}} = 1.5/f_{\mathrm{msg}}$. That way, we keep the QoC high in case of packet loss experienced on the ad-hoc communication interface.

For the paper at hand, we assume a constant message generation rate for all states over both communication technologies and, in line with [26], we propose to deactivate Decentralized Congestion Control (DCC) for ad-hoc communication. Reducing the message generation rate will increase the AoI, which might be unnecessary in most situations. As the channel capacity is a limited resource, we highly recommend advanced and adaptive generation rates on the application layer, which are left for future work.

5 Evaluation

In the following section, we analyze the performance of our proposed CVM and adaptive heterogeneous V2X communication approach within a simulation environment using a realistic scenario described in Sect. 2.

Therefore, we describe our simulation environment, briefly introducing the simulation setup. Subsequently, we explain the reference approaches used throughout this evaluation, and, finally, present the results w. r. t. the V2X communication and CVM performance.

5.1 Simulation Environment

Following the simulation structure in [2], we use Simulation of Urban Mobility (SUMO) 1.0 [16] to represent the vehicular traffic flow and the road network. The architecture is depicted in Fig. 7. We extract the Ko-PER intersection from Open Street Map (OSM) using Netconvert, which is part of the SUMO package. Further, we use OMNeT++ 5.4.1 [31] to simulate the communication network, where we connect the traffic simulator SUMO with the network simulator OMNeT++ using Veins 5.0 [28].

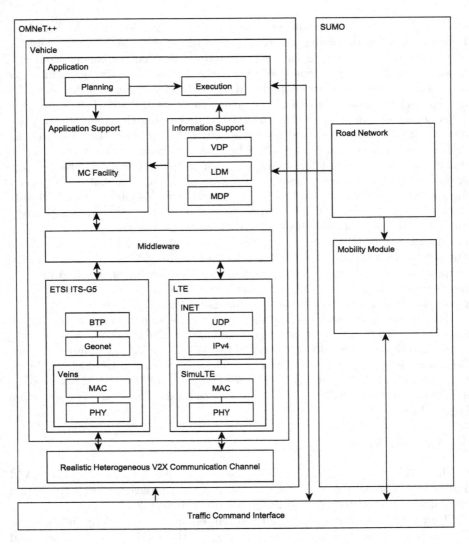

Fig. 7. Simulation architecture showing the components of the network simulator OMNeT++ [31] and the connection of the traffic simulator SUMO [16].

Veins uses the Traffic Command Interface (TraCI) to obtain traffic relevant data from each vehicle, such as the position, velocity, and acceleration, where we extend Veins to enable CVM. Veins also implements the network interface card, i.e., Medium Access (MAC) and Physical (PHY) layer.

We use SimuLTE [32] to implement the cellular LTE network. SimuLTE extends the INET framework of OMNeT++ implementing the MAC and PHY layer in the back-end and for the user interfaces below the Unified Data Protocol (UDP) and IPv4 layers from INET.

We extend the ETSI ITS-G5 interface by a GeoNetworking Protocol (GNP) and a Basic Transport Protocol (BTP) in [2] and incorporate our heterogeneous V2X channel model proposed in [1].

As suggested in [2], we implement a middleware to connect the communication interfaces to the application support modules, containing the maneuver coordination facility. The information support contains modules for data providers such as the Vehicle Data Provider (VDP), LDM, and Map Data Provider (MDP) module required by the application support and applications to create trajectories and MCMs. In this work, we implement the maneuver execution module on the application layer, which access the mobility control of the respective vehicle of the traffic simulator SUMO via TraCI. To obtain trajectories, we require information from the road network provided by the MDP module. The MDP module parses the road network from SUMO via XML.

5.2   Reference Approaches

In order to evaluate and compare our approach, we explain our considered reference approaches. Our baseline is the driver implemented by SUMO without any CVM enabled refered to as *No CVM*. To obtain the upper limit of CVM, we use a perfect communication model, which does not introduce any packet loss and latency, called *Ideal* in the following. We compare the performance and show the degradation to the perfect communication model introducing our realistic V2X channel model using the ETSI ITS-G5 communication interface, which we refer to as *Ad-hoc*. Finally, we apply our adaptive heterogeneous communication approach to increase the communication range and overall QoC while performing a CVM, which we refer to as *Adaptive*.

5.3   Results

In the following, we present our results evaluating our proposed approach. For this purpose, we adopt the simulation parameters for the ad-hoc and cellular LTE communication interface from [2] and [1], respectively.

As depicted in Fig. 1, we place the cell tower for LTE and a Road Side Unit (RSU) in the center of the intersection. The RSU is responsible for measuring the CBR and will not induce any more traffic load on the ad-hoc channel. We also adopt the traffic density from [2] and perform each simulation run for 500 s.

First, we evaluate the impact of the message generation rate and time horizon of trajectories on the CBR for ad-hoc communication. Next, we observe the QoC in terms of the AoI while performing a cooperative maneuver and the distance to the cooperation point when starting CVM. Finally, we evaluate the quality of CVM in terms of the average velocity of vehicles for the different approaches mentioned above.

Quality Of Communication. Let us first take a look on the induced channel load of MCMs for *Ad-hoc* communication considering our proposed realistic

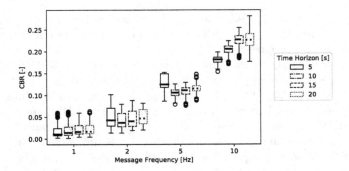

Fig. 8. Distribution of the CBR for ad-hoc communication where the respective message frequency and time horizon apply to all vehicles within the simulation run.

channel model in Fig. 8. We investigate the CBR for message generation rates ranging between $f_{msg} = [1, 2, 5, 10]$ Hz and a time horizon $t_{th} = [5, 10, 15, 20]$ s. For the rest of this evaluation, we set the cost threshold to $c_t = 0.2$. For $c_t \to 0$ the cooperating vehicle is more willing to offer cooperation, whereas for $c_t \to 1$ the cooperating vehicle will tend to decline cooperation requests. A more detailed analysis of cost threshold and how it impacts the overall traffic efficiency is left for future work.

As shown in Fig. 7, we only broadcast MCMs on the channel and DCC remains deactivated. Also, we have not added any security header to the MCMs, which would obviously increase the CBR further.

Note that MCMs from vehicles which stopped at a red light are rather small in size, i.e., they do not send a desired trajectory and the planned trajectory only represents the current position as the vehicle will not move in the near future. However, also small packet sizes contribute to the CBR due to the random access of the channel considering ETSI ITS-G5.

In Fig. 8, we can see an increase in the CBR for higher message frequencies, where $f_{msg} = 10$ Hz induces a CBR of more than 20%.

For $f_{msg} = 10$ Hz, we also observe a significant increase in the CBR by up to 5% from $t_{th} = 5$ s to $t_{th} = 10$ s. This effect reduces with decreasing message frequency and even inverses for $f_{msg} = 5$ Hz. Here, we observe a higher CBR for $t_{th} = 5$ s compared to $t_{th} = 10$ s. We argue that this effect occurs as the probability of coordination is significantly reduced when decreasing t_{th} such that the cooperation vehicle keeps sending desired trajectories in addition to the planned trajectory. Further, due to less successful cooperations, the traffic congestion also increases within the intersection, which also increases the CBR. We observe that a traffic jam is present for all routes for $f_{msg} < 5$ Hz and $t_{th} < 10$ s.

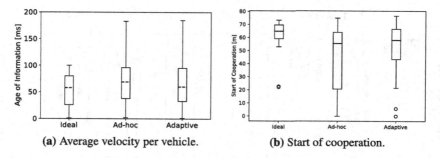

(a) Average velocity per vehicle.   (b) Start of cooperation.

Fig. 9. Distribution of the experienced AoI and start of cooperation for $t_{th} = 10\,$s while performing a cooperative maneuver.

Next, let us take a look on the QoC experienced by vehicles while cooperating, which is depicted in Fig. 9. From Fig. 9a, we can observe that we experience a similar AoI for the *Ad-hoc* and the *Adaptive* approach, where a significant number of measurements are below 100 ms.

Note that this measurement reflects the current AoI to the respective cooperation partner while executing a cooperative maneuver. The experienced AoI can be between 0...100 ms for a message frequency $f_{msg} = 10\,$Hz considering a perfect channel (refer to the *Ideal* approach in Fig. 9a, i.e., we can process the received information shortly after or just before receiving an updated message.

For *Ad-hoc* communication, the median AoI is at 69 ms while cooperating, where our *Adaptive* approach is able to keep the AoI below a median of 60 ms. From the measurements, we can also obtain an average AoI of 54 ms, 171 ms, and 153 ms for the *Ideal*, *Ad-hoc*, and *Adaptive* approach, respectively, where our *Adaptive* approach targets an AoI following Sect. 4 of 150 ms.

With our adaptive approach, we are able to decrease the median AoI experienced by vehicles while cooperating by 15.0%.

Let us also analyze the start of cooperation, where we focus on the distance to the cooperation point. We clearly see that the ideal approach outperforms the *Ad-hoc* and *Ideal* approach with a median of 65 m and an average of 62 m. Compared to that, *Ad-hoc* is able to start the cooperation at a median distance of 55 m and an average of 42.7 m. Our adaptive approach leverages an early coordination at large distances enabling to start the cooperation at a median of 58 m and an average of 53 m. Hence, our *Adaptive* approach allows to start the cooperation earlier compared to the *Ad-hoc* approach by 7.3%.

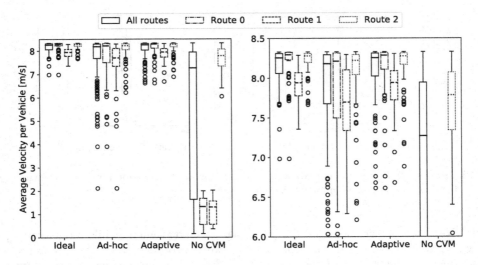

Fig. 10. Distribution of the average driven velocity per vehicle w. r. t. to the respective routes for different approaches for $t_{\mathrm{th}} = 10\,\mathrm{s}$.

Quality of CVM. Let us now focus on the quality of CVM w. r. t. the average velocity driven on different routes in Fig. 10.

Therefore, let us first take a look on the approach without using CVM, denoted as *No CVM*, i.e., controlled by a simple SUMO driver. We clearly see that a traffic jam occurs as Route 0 and 1 almost drop to a velocity of $1\,\mathrm{m/s}$. In contrast to that, vehicles driving straight on Route 2 approaching from northeast almost reach the maximum velocity of $8.33\,\mathrm{m/s}$ leveraging their right-of-way in the intersection. Noticeably, the median average velocity for all routes is comparable high even though a traffic jam occurs for Route 0 and 1. That is because we show the distribution of the average velocity per vehicle, where we have a high traffic flow for Route 2 and a low traffic flow caused by the traffic jam for Route 0 and 1. As the traffic density from Route 2 is very high, we have more measurements for this route.

Let us now take a look on the approaches leveraging CVM and start with the *Ideal* approach. Considering a perfect V2X communication channel, we clearly see that CVM is able to significantly increase the traffic efficiency for all routes compared to the previous approach with *No CVM*. Surprisingly on the first sight, our approach also seems to outperform *No CVM* for Route 2 even though we offer cooperation. That is because SUMO slows down for lanes without the right-of-way, which occurs in the given scenario as depicted in Fig. 1. As our approach only relies on V2X communication as the environmental sensor, we are not decelerating unless we detect a conflict with another planned trajectory.

Now, let us take a look on the *Ad-hoc* approach. From Fig. 10, we can observe that we are able to significantly improve the velocity for all routes compared to *No CVM*, almost reaching the performance of the *Ideal* approach. If we take a closer look at the average velocity per vehicle on the right of Fig. 10, we can observe a degradation in the median average velocity per vehicle over all routes by approximately 0.6%. A noticable difference in the average velocity can be observed for Route 1, which is the route requesting cooperation. The median of the average velocities per vehicle decreases by 3.2% for the *Ad-hoc* approach. We experience a higher overall AoI as seen in Fig. 9a so that we cannot react to a changed planned trajectory immediately, which increases the costs for all routes.

Compared to that, our *Adaptive* approach is able to reach the performance of the *Ideal* approach. With the *Adaptive* approach, we leverage an early coordination by sending MCMs via the LTE interface while being in the *Request* state. Further, we also increase the QoC in terms of AoI while being in a cooperation.

6 Related Work

In the following, we focus on related work, targeting CVM and heterogeneous V2X communication.

6.1 Cooperative Vehicular Maneuvering

Coordinating CVMs using V2X communication can be organized in a centralized or decentralized manner, where decentralized approaches partition the computational complexity and do not require additional infrastructure support. On the contrary, centralized approaches can reach a global optimum to increase traffic efficiency. Let us first analyze existing decentralized CVM approaches.

One of the first approaches leveraging V2X communication to coordinate CVM has been proposed in [7]. To coordinate CVM, the authors introduce seven different messages and aim to coordinate the maneuver explicitly. Subsequently, they subdivide a cooperative maneuver in *Sense*, *Model*, *Plan*, and *Act* phases, thereby providing a modular and flexible architecture.

The authors in [6] propose a trajectory-based CVM approach, which aims to be more flexible than the work in [7] and can be applied to different use-cases. The path planning creates trajectories using target points from the road map, where the authors select the best trajectory combination considering the own created and received trajectories. The authors conclude that the creation and comparison of trajectories are computationally costly.

The work in [18] extends the previous generic trajectory-based approach and introduces a planned and desired trajectory enabling implicit coordination. Hence, as required in [7], any confirmation messages for coordination are obsolete, thereby saving coordination time and message overhead.

The authors in [33] extend the approach proposed in [7] and implement CVM into a microscopic simulation framework, considering a lightweight communication channel model. The authors introduce explicit coordination to minimize the impact of imperfect communication and propose message generation rules for MCMs.

In decentralized approaches, vehicles solve the cooperation conflict themselves, whereas in centralized approaches a central entity obtains coordination to optimize the overall traffic flow. The authors in [5] propose a hybrid approach and extend the work in [18], introducing the support of road infrastructure to further increase the traffic efficiency leveraging centralized and decentralized coordination. They also evaluate different types of message generation rules for CVM, where dynamic rules can reduce the overall message overhead by granting more resources to relevant vehicles.

Focusing on an on-ramp merging scenario, the work in [21] proposes a centralized CVM approach, where the cooperation process is solved using fuzzy logic. In this approach, the computational complexity to detect a conflict is lowered as the authors only focus on the arrival time of vehicles, i.e., the vehicles' longitudinal path close to the on-ramp. A central entity aims to increase the traffic efficiency by coordinating the vehicles' arrival time to the merging point.

In conclusion, the recent literature already proposes mechanisms for CVM, where the approaches range from centralized to decentralized covering explicit and implicit approaches. In our work, we adopt the idea of a decentralized trajectory-based explicit approach. However, the related work currently evaluates CVM only in small-scale scenarios and simplifies or neglects radio propagation effects.

To overcome these limitations, we propose a trajectory generation and processing, lowering the computational complexity of maneuver planning to enable large-scale evaluations in microscopic simulations. Here, we perform the cooperative maneuver by taking over the vehicles' control from the traffic simulator. That way, we can control all vehicles within the simulation or only vehicles performing a cooperative maneuver. We apply a realistic V2X channel model, which covers propagation effects such as shadowing, small-scale fading, and path loss. We evaluate the impact of imperfect communication on the performance of CVM. Subsequently, we propose an adaptive heterogeneous V2X communication approach explicitly designed for CVM.

6.2   Heterogeneous V2X Communication

Exploiting heterogeneous networks to improve the QoC for V2X communication has already been thoroughly studied in the recent literature [34, 35]. Cluster-based approaches can be organized in a decentralized or centralized topology. They aim to reduce the local channel load and extend the communication range to other groups of vehicles.

[30] proposes a decentralized cluster approach using multi-hop communication, where the cluster head requires to have both communication interfaces, i.e., 802.11p and LTE. Further, the cluster head is selected using the average velocity to its cluster members to avoid unnecessary cluster formations. Information is shared within a cluster, and the cluster head extends the range to other vehicles beyond the communication range via LTE. [30] also allows multi-hop communication so that cluster members can reach their cluster heads. The proposed

approach aims to reduce the latency while improving the reliability and minimizing the cellular network load. A centralized cluster approach is proposed in [23], where a central entity is responsible for the cluster formation which aims to improve the cluster formation and stability. To reduce the impact of a cluster break-up, [20] proposes a game-theoretic approach to subscribe to relevant data via cellular communication and offload it via ad-hoc communication.

A context-aware heterogeneous V2X communication approach is proposed in [27] and subsequently extended in [25]. Following the approach, vehicles measure their current environment and autonomously select the best-suited communication technology for the target V2X application. The authors show that their proposed approach improves the QoC in throughput per vehicle and overall CBR.

In summary, the related work proposes centralized and decentralized cluster-based offloading approaches, which are unsuited to be used for CVM applications as the offloading process causes additional latency. A heterogeneous context-aware dissemination approach leveraging decentralized and autonomous coordination is promising to improve the QoC for CVM. However, we think that obtaining the best communication technology solely from the respective application requirements based on communication metrics does not exhibit the full potentials of a heterogeneous V2X approach for CVM.

To overcome this limitation, we propose an adaptive heterogeneous approach based on ad-hoc communication extending the local environmental perception of relevant vehicles. Further, we add cellular Geo-Unicast communication if the current context causes a low QoC, although a high QoC is required. Finally, we take advantage of cellular Geo-Broadcast to extend our environmental perception beyond the direct communication range of ad-hoc communication.

7   Conclusion

This paper extends our large-scale maneuver coordination approach proposed in [2] in terms of scalability for the trajectory generation and trajectory collision check. In particular, we improve the generation of trajectories using different unique accelerations for each trajectory obtained from an acceleration profile. Also, we propose a cooperation state machine to ensure the promised cooperative trajectory execution and explain our approach executing the planned maneuver microscopic traffic simulator. Furthermore, we propose an adaptive dissemination strategy using the advantages of both ad-hoc and cellular communication. We use ad-hoc communication to inform the local environment exhibiting minimum latency. To coordinate a maneuver earlier, we need an extended communication range, where we propose using cellular Geo-Broadcast if our current planned trajectory covers a cooperative function. We also use cellular Geo-Unicast to improve the QoC while cooperating with other vehicles. In our evaluation, we show that CVM significantly impacts the communication channel, where we observe a CBR of 25% for a message frequency of 10 Hz within our scenario.

252 D. Bischoff et al.

We also show that our proposed adaptive approach outperforms ad-hoc communication in terms of QoC and quality of CVM, which we measure in terms of the average velocity per vehicle. In particular, our proposed CVM approach is able to avoid any traffic jams considering an ideal communication channel. We also show that the limited range of ad-hoc communication significantly impacts the quality of CVM. Therefore, our adaptive heterogeneous communication approach is able to improve the mean AoI by 15% and the average velocity within our scenario for all routes by up to 3.2%. We obtain the QoC from past measurements at the transmitter side, assuming a reciprocity channel to adjust our dissemination strategy to improve the QoC and the receiver side of cooperating vehicles. A reciprocity channel is a strong assumption especially in vehicular networks, which are prone to high fluctuation of the wireless channel. We aim at improving this approach using collaboration: Vehicles in front of us already experience the QoC we will experience within the next seconds. Therefore, these vehicles can share their connectivity map with us, which can, in turn, adjust their dissemination strategy proactively.

Despite an adaptive dissemination using heterogeneous communication technologies, the message generation rate is crucial to improve the efficiency of CVM. In our future work, we aim at proposing an adaptive generation rate using the cooperation relevance of vehicles assigning more resources to a vehicle requiring or acting cooperation.

References

1. Bischoff, D., et al.: Safety-relevant V2X beaconing in realistic and scalable heterogeneous radio propagation fading channels. In: Proceedings of the International Conference on VEHITS, vol. 5. SCITEPRESS, May 2019
2. Bischoff, D., Schiegg, F.A., Meuser, T., Schuller, D., Dycke, N., Steinmetz, R.: What cooperation costs: quality of communication and cooperation costs for cooperative vehicular maneuvering in large-scale scenarios. In: VEHITS, pp. 394–405 (2020)
3. Bischoff, D., Schiegg, F.A., Meuser, T., Steinmetz, R.: Impact of imperfect communication on cooperative vehicular maneuvering at intersections. In: IEEE 91th VTC Spring, pp. 1–5 (2020)
4. Boban, M., Vinhoza, T.T.V., Ferreira, M., Barros, J., Tonguz, O.K.: Impact of vehicles as obstacles in vehicular ad hoc networks. IEEE J. Sel. Areas Commun. **29**(1), 15–28 (2011). https://doi.org/10.1109/JSAC.2011.110103
5. Correa, A., et al.: Infrastructure support for cooperative maneuvers in connected and automated driving. In: IEEE Intelligent Vehicles Symposium, pp. 20–25 (2019)
6. Düring, M., Franke, K., Balaghiasefi, R., Gonter, M., Belkner, M., Lemmer, K.: Adaptive cooperative maneuver planning algorithm for conflict resolution in diverse traffic situations. In: ICCVE, pp. 242–249 (2014)
7. Franke, K., Gonter, M., Düring, M., Lemmer, K., Balaghiasefi, R., Kücükay, F.: A reference architecture for CISS/CDAS within the field of cooperative driving. In: ICCVE, pp. 357–363 (2014)
8. Friis, H.T.: A note on a simple transmission formula. Proc. IRE **34**(5), 254–256 (1946)

9. Intelligent Transport Systems: Local Dynamic Map. Standard, ETSI (2014)
10. Intelligent Transport Systems: Specification of cooperative awareness basic service. European standard, ETSI (2014)
11. Intelligent Transport Systems: ITS-G5 access layer specification for its operating in the 5 GHz frequency band. European standard, ETSI (2019)
12. Jakes, W.C.: Microwave Mobile Communications. Wiley, New York (1974)
13. Jesenski, S., Stellet, J.E., Schiegg, F.A., Zöllner, J.M.: Generation of scenes in intersections for the validation of highly automated driving functions. In: IEEE Intelligent Vehicles Symposium, pp. 502–509 (2019)
14. Karoui, M., Freitas, A., Chalhoub, G.: Performance comparison between LTE-V2X and ITS-G5 under realistic urban scenarios. In: IEEE VTC-Spring 2020 (2020)
15. Kaul, S., Gruteser, M., Rai, V., Kenney, J.: Minimizing age of information in vehicular networks. In: 2011 8th Annual IEEE Communications Society Conference on Sensor, Mesh and Ad Hoc Communications and Networks, pp. 350–358 (2011)
16. Krajzewicz, D., Hertkorn, G., Rössel, C., Wagner, P.: SUMO (Simulation of Urban MObility); an open-source traffic simulation. In: Proceedings of the 4th middle East Symposium on Simulation and Modelling (MESM 2002) (2002)
17. Kuehlmorgen, S., Schmager, P., Festag, A., Fettweis, G.: Simulation-based evaluation of ETSI ITS-G5 and cellular-VCS in a real-world road traffic scenario. In: 2018 IEEE 88th Vehicular Technology Conference (VTC-Fall), pp. 1–6, August 2018. https://doi.org/10.1109/VTCFall.2018.8691011
18. Lehmann, B., Günther, H., Wolf, L.: A generic approach towards maneuver coordination for automated vehicles. In: 21st ITSC, pp. 3333–3339 (2018)
19. Llatser, I., Michalke, T., Dolgov, M., Wildschütte, F., Fuchs, H.: Cooperative automated driving use cases for 5G V2X communication. In: IEEE 2nd 5G World Forum, pp. 120–125 (2019)
20. Meuser, T., Bischoff, D., Richerzhagen, B., Steinmetz, R.: Cooperative offloading in context-aware networks: a game-theoretic approach. In: Proceedings of the 13th ACM International Conference on Distributed and Event-Based Systems, DEBS 2019, pp. 55–66. Association for Computing Machinery, New York (2019). https://doi.org/10.1145/3328905.3338535
21. Milanes, V., Godoy, J., Villagra, J., Perez, J.: Automated on-ramp merging system for congested traffic situations. IEEE Trans. Intell. Transp. Syst. **12**(2), 500–508 (2011)
22. Mir, Z.H., Filali, F.: LTE and IEEE 802.11 p for vehicular networking: a performance evaluation. EURASIP J. Wirel. Commun. Netw. **2014**(1), 89 (2014)
23. Remy, G., Senouci, S., Jan, F., Gourhant, Y.: LTE4V2X: LTE for a centralized VANET organization. In: 2011 IEEE Global Telecommunications Conference - GLOBECOM 2011, pp. 1–6 (2011)
24. Schiegg, F.A., Brahmi, N., Llatser, I.: Analytical performance evaluation of the collective perception service in C-V2X Mode 4 networks. In: IEEE ITSC, pp. 181–188 (2019)
25. Sepulcre, M., Gozalvez, J.: Heterogeneous V2V communications in multi-link and multi-rat vehicular networks. IEEE Trans. Mobile Comput. 1 (2019). https://doi.org/10.1109/TMC.2019.2939803
26. Sepulcre, M., Mira, J., Thandavarayan, G., Gozalvez, J.: Is packet dropping a suitable congestion control mechanism for vehicular networks? In: 2020 IEEE 91st Vehicular Technology Conference (VTC2020-Spring), pp. 1–5 (2020)
27. Sepulcre, M., Gozalvez, J.: Context-aware heterogeneous V2X communications for connected vehicles. Comput. Netw. **136**, 13–21 (2018)

28. Sommer, C., German, R., Dressler, F.: Bidirectionally coupled network and road traffic simulation for improved IVC analysis. IEEE Trans. Mob. Comput. **10**(1), 3–15 (2011)

29. Strigel, E., Meissner, D., Seeliger, F., Wilking, B., Dietmayer, K.: The Ko-PER intersection laserscanner and video dataset. In: 17th ITSC, pp. 1900–1901 (2014)

30. Ucar, S., Ergen, S.C., Ozkasap, O.: Multihop-cluster-based IEEE 802.11P and LTE hybrid architecture for VANET safety message dissemination. IEEE Trans. Veh. Technol. **65**(4), 2621–2636 (2016)

31. Varga, A., Hornig, R.: An Overview of the OMNeT++ simulation environment. In: Proceedings of the 1st International Conference on Simulation Tools and Techniques for Communications, Networks and Systems & Workshops, pp. 60:1–60:10 (2008)

32. Virdis, A., Stea, G., Nardini, G.: Simulating LTE/LTE-advanced networks with SimuLTE. In: Simulation and Modeling Methodologies, Technologies and Applications, pp. 83–105 (2015)

33. Xu, W., Willecke, A., Wegner, M., Wolf, L., Kapitza, R.: Autonomous maneuver coordination via vehicular communication. In: 49th Annual IEEE/IFIP International Conference on Dependable Systems and Networks Workshops (DSN-W), pp. 70–77 (2019)

34. Zekri, A., Jia, W.: Heterogeneous vehicular communications: a comprehensive study. Ad Hoc Netw. **75–76**, 52–79 (2018). https://doi.org/10.1016/j.adhoc.2018.03.010

35. Zheng, K., Zheng, Q., Chatzimisios, P., Xiang, W., Zhou, Y.: Heterogeneous vehicular networking: a survey on architecture, challenges, and solutions. IEEE Commun. Surv. Tutor. **17**(4), 2377–2396 (2015)

The Fadhloun-Rakha Car-Following Model: A Novel Formulation Capturing Driver, Vehicle, Roadway, and Weather Variables

Karim Fadhloun[1], Hesham Rakha[1]([✉]) [iD], Amara Loulizi[2] [iD], and Jinghui Wang[1]

[1] Virginia Tech Transportation Institute, Virginia Tech, 3500 Transportation Research Plaza, Blacksburg, VA, USA
`{karim198,hrakha,jwang}@vt.edu`
[2] LR11ES16 Laboratoire de Matériaux, d'Optimisation Et d'Environnement Pour La Durabilité, Ecole Nationale d'Ingénieur de Tunis, Tunis, Tunisia
`amlouliz@vt.edu`

Abstract. The research presented in this paper validates and compares the performance of the Fadhloun-Rakha (FR) car-following model to other state-of-the-art car-following models, including: the Wiedemann, the Frietzsche, the Gipps, the Rakha-Pasuparthy-Adjerid (RPA) and the Intelligent Driver Model (IDM) models. The FR model converges to a steady-state formulation (in our case the Van Aerde model), separates the human from the machine-in-the-loop, models vehicle dynamics, and ensures asymptotic stability of the traffic stream. The uniqueness of the FR model include: (1) explicitly modeling the driver throttle and brake pedal input in a single continuous equation; (2) explicitly capturing driver perception and control inaccuracies and errors; (3) modeling vehicle dynamics using a point-mass model; (4) allowing for shorter than steady-state following distances when following faster leading vehicles; and (5) ensuring collision-free driving. The validation effort, which is conducted using naturalistic driving data, demonstrates that the FR model generates trajectories that are more consistent with empirically observed driver following behavior when compared to the five aforementioned models. Furthermore, the FR model is the only formulation that allows for an explicit and simple independent tuning of driver, roadway, and/or vehicle characteristics allowing it to capture the impact of driver, vehicle, road surface, tire, road topology, and weather conditions on the modeling of car-following behavior. To demonstrate this fact, a sensitivity analysis is conducted demonstrating the robustness of the FR model in capturing several aspects of the road/vehicle/driver system in a concise and precise manner.

Keywords: Rakha-Pasumarthy-Adjerid car-following model · Car-following behavior · Vehicle dynamics · Vehicle longitudinal motion

1 Introduction

Due to the continuous technological advancement and proliferation of computational tools both at the level of hardware and software, traffic engineering is becoming more

© Springer Nature Switzerland AG 2021
C. Klein et al. (Eds.): SMARTGREENS 2020/VEHITS 2020, CCIS 1475, pp. 255–278, 2021.
https://doi.org/10.1007/978-3-030-89170-1_13

and more simulation-oriented. Relying on computerized traffic simulations for planning, urbanization and environmental purposes can be cast as a two-edged activity. On the one hand, microscopic simulation software allow the user to evaluate and estimate the outcomes of different potential scenarios in a fast and cost effective manner and, most importantly, without inducing any bottlenecks or disrupting the flow of vehicles in the real world. On the other hand, it is imperative to not forget that the results returned by traffic simulators are directly correlated to the accuracy and precision of the different models and logics incorporated in them. Subsequently, it is necessary to ensure that whatever implemented in this type of software, would constitute good descriptors of real traffic conditions and empirical behavior.

A main component of microscopic simulation software is the car-following model. Car-following models [1–8] predict the temporal and spatial behavior of a following vehicle when the time-space profile of the leading vehicle is known. The outputs of car-following models directly impact several other factors and measures of effectiveness (MOE), such as vehicle energy/fuel consumption and emissions.

This paper describes a research effort that aims to validate a new innovative acceleration-based car-following model, which is the Fadhloun-Rakha (FR) model. The methodology and the procedure that led to the functional form of the model was described extensively in a previous work by Fadhloun and Rakha [9]. The validation of the proposed model is conducted by comparing its performance against the performance of other car-following models. The Gipps [10], Frietzsche [3], Wiedemann [11, 12], the IDM [8] and the RPA models [13, 14] were selected as controls of the proposed model because of their wide use and their implementation in some of the most famous traffic simulators (AIMSUN [15], PARAMICS [16], VISSIM [17] and INTEGRATION [18, 19]). The dataset used in the validation procedure is extracted from the naturalistic data of the 100-Car study that was conducted by the Virginia Tech Transportation Institute [20, 21].

Concerning the layout, this paper is organized as follows. First, an overview of the Fadhloun-Rakha (FR) model is provided along with the other state-of-the-practice car-following models mentioned above. Subsequently, the dataset used in this study is briefly described and the analysis related to the calibration procedure as well as the validation process of the FR model is presented. The validation of the model is conducted in two stages. First, a quantitative and qualitative comparative study is conducted for the purpose of evaluating the model performance. Second, the main advantage of the FR model, which relates to its ease of tuning and flexibility in terms of capturing different dynamic characteristics (engine power, weather, road grade, human behavior, vehicle type), is highlighted using a sensitivity analysis. Finally, the conclusions of the paper are drawn and insights into future work are provided.

2 Background

In this section, a brief description of the logic behind each of the studied models is provided in a chronological order.

2.1 Wiedemann Model

The Wiedemann model [11] is a psycho-physical car-following model that is widely known in the traffic engineering community due to its integration in the microscopic multi-modal traffic simulation software VISSIM [17]. The initial formulation of the model [11], proposed in 1974, was calibrated mostly based on conceptual ideas rather than real traffic data. As a result, a much-needed recalibration of the model [12] was performed in the early-1990s using an instrumented vehicle.

The Wiedemann model framework, as implemented in VISSIM, uses five bounding functions in the $\Delta v - \Delta x$ domain—AX, ABX, SDX, SDV and $OPDV$—to define the thresholds between four traffic regimes—free driving, closing-in, following and emergency. Depending on the traffic regime in which the following vehicle is located, the acceleration is set equal to a predefined specific rate. The mathematical expressions of the five regime thresholds are given in Eqs. (1–5).

$$AX = L_{n-1} + [AX_{add} + AX_{mult} \times RND1] \tag{1}$$

$$ABX = AX + [BX_{add} + BX_{mult} \times RND1]\sqrt{\min(u_{n-1}, u_n)} \tag{2}$$

$$SDX = AX + [EX_{add} + EX_{mult} \times (NRND - RND2)] \times [BX_{add} + BX_{mult} \times RND1]\sqrt{\min(u_{n-1}, u_n)} \tag{3}$$

$$SDV = \left(\frac{\Delta x - L_{n-1} - AX}{CX}\right)^2 \tag{4}$$

$$OPDV = SDV \times [-OPDV_{add} - OPDV_{mult} \times NRND] \tag{5}$$

Where $RND1$, $RND2$ and $NRND$ are normally distributed parameters that aim to model the randomness associated with different driving patterns and behaviors, L_{n-1} is the length of the leading vehicle in meters, u_{n-1} is the lead vehicle speed in (m/s), Δx is the spacing between the lead and the following vehicles, and CX is a model parameter that is assumed to be equal to 40. Finally, the remaining variables, named using the standard format P_{add} or P_{mult}, are the model parameters requiring calibration.

It is noteworthy to mention that the formulations of Eqs. (1–5) could be further simplified by removing the random driver-dependent parameters for the specific case of this study. In fact, the randomness inducing parameters are of no use when calibrating the model against empirical data of a single driver. With that being said, Eqs. (1–5) are modified by applying the generic transformation of Eq. 6 resulting in a significant reduction of the number of calibration parameters. The resultant set of equations, defined in Eqs. (7–11), requires the calibration of a total of four parameters.

$$P_{cal} = P_{add} + P_{mult} \times P_{rand} \tag{6}$$

$$AX = L_{n-1} + AX_{cal} \tag{7}$$

$$ABX = AX + BX_{cal}\sqrt{\min(u_{n-1}, u_n)} \tag{8}$$

$$SDX = AX + EX_{cal} \times BX_{cal}\sqrt{\min(u_{n-1}, u_n)} \tag{9}$$

$$SDV = \left(\frac{\Delta x - L_{n-1} - AX}{40}\right)^2 \tag{10}$$

$$OPDV = -SDV \times OPDV_{cal} \tag{11}$$

2.2 Gipps Model

Gipps model [10], developed in the late-1970s and implemented in the traffic simulation software AIMSUN [22], is formulated as a system of differential difference equations. Using a time step Δt that aims to model the reaction time of drivers, the model computes the following vehicle speed u_n at time $t + \Delta t$ as a function of its speed and the leading vehicle speed u_{n-1} at the preceding time step t.

As shown in Eq. 12, the speed of the following vehicle is estimated by determining the minimum of two arguments. The first term governs the cases characterized by uncongested traffic and relatively large headways. Under such conditions, the following vehicle speed increases until the free-flow speed of the facility u_f is reached. The model formulation is also inclusive of a condition that ensures that u_f is never exceeded once achieved. The second argument of the model is attained when congestion prevails and speeds are constrained by the behavior of the vehicles ahead of them. Due to the collision avoidance mechanism it implements, the congested regime branch is the one responsible for making the Gipps model collision-free.

$$u_n(t + \Delta t) = min\left(\begin{array}{c} u_n(t) + 2.5.A_{max}^{des}.\Delta t\left(1 - \frac{u_n(t)}{u_f}\right)\sqrt{0.025 + \frac{u_n(t)}{u_f}} \\ D_{max}^{des}.\Delta t + \sqrt{\left(D_{max}^{des}.\Delta t\right)^2 - D_{max}^{des}\left[2(\Delta x - L_{n-1}) - \Delta t.u_n(t) - \frac{u_{n-1}^2(t)}{\widehat{D}_{n-1}}\right]} \end{array}\right) \tag{12}$$

Where A_{max}^{des} and D_{max}^{des} are the respective desired maximum acceleration and deceleration of the following vehicle in m/s^2, and $\widehat{D}_{n-1}$ denote the maximum deceleration rate of the leading vehicle in m/s^2. Those three parameters are the ones requiring calibration for Gipps model.

2.3 Frietzsche Model

Frietzsche model [3] is a car-following model that shares the same structure as Wiedemann model. In this model, six threshold parameters are used to define five driving regimes. The thresholds are defined for four gap (Δx) values and two differences in speed (Δv) values between the leading and the following vehicles. The four gap threshold parameters, AR, AS, AD, and AB are presented in Eqs. (13–16); while the two differences in speed thresholds, PTP and PTN, are given in Eqs. (17–18). We note that the expression of the acceleration rate a_n associated with the "closing in" regime is given in Eq. (19–20).

$$AR = s_{n-1} + T_r \times u_{n-1} \tag{13}$$

$$AS = s_{n-1} + T_s \times u_n \tag{14}$$

$$AD = s_{n-1} + T_d \times u_n \tag{15}$$

$$AB = AR + \frac{\Delta u^2}{\Delta b_m} \tag{16}$$

$$PTP = K_{PTP}(\Delta x - s_{n-1})^2 + f_x \tag{17}$$

$$PTN = -K_{PTN}(\Delta x - s_{n-1})^2 - f_x \tag{18}$$

$$a_n = \frac{u_{n-1}^2 - u_n^2}{2d_c} \tag{19}$$

$$d_c = \Delta x - AR + u_{n-1}.\Delta t \tag{20}$$

Where T_r, T_s, T_D and Δb_m are calibration parameters expressed in seconds. For the remainder of this study d_{max}, f_x, K_{ptp} and K_{ptn} are set equal to -6 m/s^2, 0.5, 0.002 and 0.001.

2.4 The Intelligent Driver Model

The IDM model [8] is a kinematics-based car-following model that is widely used for the simulation of freeway traffic. It was developed in 2000 by Treiber et al. [8] with the main objective of modeling the longitudinal motion of vehicles as realistically as possible under all traffic situations. The fame of this model is mainly due to its mathematical stability, which results in stable vehicle trajectories and smooth acceleration profiles. The acceleration function of the intelligent driver model (IDM) car-following model is presented in Eqs. (21–22).

$$a_n(u_n, s_n, \Delta u_n) = a\left(1 - \left(\frac{u_n}{u_f}\right)^\delta - \left(\frac{s^*(u_n, \Delta u_n)}{s_n}\right)^2\right) \tag{21}$$

$$s^*(u_n, \Delta u_n) = s_j + u_n T + \frac{u_n \Delta u_n}{2\sqrt{a.b}} \tag{22}$$

Where s^* denotes the steady state spacing, a is the maximum acceleration level, b is the maximum deceleration level, δ is a calibration parameter and T is the desired time headway.

260 K. Fadhloun et al.

2.5 Rakha-Pasumarthy-Adjerid Model

The RPA model [13, 14] is a car-following model that controls the longitudinal motion of the vehicles in the INTEGRATION traffic simulation software [18, 19]. The model is composed of three main components: the steady-state, the collision avoidance and the vehicle dynamics models. Using the three components, the RPA model computes the speed of the following vehicle as shown in Eq. 23.

$$u_n = min\left(u_n^{VA}, u_n^{CA}, u_n^{DYN}\right)$$ (23)

Here u_n^{VA}, u_n^{CA} and u_n^{DYN} are the speeds calculated using the three modules described previously and which expressions are given in what follows.

First-Order Steady-State Car-Following Model. The RPA model utilizes the Van Aerde nonlinear functional form to control the steady-state behavior of traffic. The latter model was proposed by Van Aerde and Rakha [23–25] and is formulated as presented in Eq. 24.

$$s_n^{VA} = c_1 + \frac{c_2}{u_f - u_n} + c_3 u_n$$ (24)

Here s_n^{VA} is the steady state spacing (in meters) between the lead and the following vehicles, u_n is the speed of the follower, in (m/s), u_f is the free-flow speed expressed in m/s, and c_1 (m), c_2 (m^2/s) and c_3 (s) are constants used for the Van Aerde steady-state model that have been shown to be directly related to the macroscopic parameters defining the fundamental diagram of the roadway.

Finally, it should be noted that from the perspective of car-following modeling, the main objective is to determine how the following vehicle responds to changes in the behavior of the leading vehicle. Subsequently, a speed formulation is adopted for the Van Aerde model, as demonstrated in Eq. 25, which is easily derived from Eq. 24 using basic mathematics.

$$u_n^{VA} = \frac{-c_1 + c_3 u_f + s_n - \sqrt{\left(c_1 - c_3 u_f - s_n\right)^2 - 4c_3\left(s_n u_f - c_1 u_f - c_2\right)}}{2c_3}$$ (25)

Collision Avoidance Model. The expression of the collision avoidance term is shown in Eq. 26 and is directly related to a simple derivation of the maximum distance that a vehicle can travel to decelerate from its initial speed to the speed of the vehicle ahead of it while ensuring that, in the case of a complete stop, the jam density spacing between the two vehicles is respected.

$$u_n^{CA} = \sqrt{(u_n)^2 + 2b(s_n - s_j)}$$ (26)

Here b is the maximum deceleration at which the vehicles are allowed to decelerate and s_j is the spacing at jam density.

Vehicle Dynamics Model. The final component of the RPA model is the vehicle dynamics model [26, 27] that ensures that the vehicle's mechanical capabilities do not limit it from attaining the speeds that are dictated by the steady-state component. this model computes the typical acceleration of the following vehicle as the ratio of the resultant force to the vehicle mass M (Eq. 27). The resultant force is computed as the difference between the tractive force acting on the following vehicle F_{n+1} (Eq. 28) and the sum of the resistive forces acting on the vehicle which include the aerodynamics, rolling and grade resistances.

$$a_n^{DYN} = \frac{F_n - \left(0.5\rho C_d C_h A_f u_n^2 + MgC_{r0}(C_{r1}u_n + C_{r2})/1000 + MgG\right)}{M} \tag{27}$$

$$F_{n+1} = \min\left(3600\eta\frac{\gamma P}{u_n}, M_{ta}g\mu\right) \tag{28}$$

Here η is the driveline efficiency (unitless); P is the vehicle power (kW); M_{ta} is the mass of the vehicle on the tractive axle (kg), which is equal to the proportion of mass on the tractive axle p_{ta} multiplied by the total mass M; γ is the vehicle throttle level (taken as the percentage of the maximum observed throttle level that a certain driver uses); g is the gravitational acceleration (9.8067 m/s^2); μ is the coefficient of road adhesion or the coefficient of friction (unitless); ρ is the air density at sea level and a temperature of 15 °C (1.2256 kg/m^3); C_d is the vehicle drag coefficient (unitless), typically 0.30; C_h is the altitude correction factor equal to $1-0.000085h$, where h is the altitude in meters (unitless); A_f is the vehicle frontal area (m^2), typically 0.85 multiplied by the height and width of the vehicle; C_{r0} is a rolling resistance constant that varies as a function of the pavement type and condition (unitless); C_{r1} is the second rolling resistance constant (h/km); C_{r2} is the third rolling resistance constant (unitless); m is the total vehicle mass (kg); and G is the roadway grade (unitless).

The acceleration computed using the dynamics model is then used to calculate the maximum feasible speed u_n^{DYN} using a first Euler approximation.

2.6 Fadhloun-Rakha Model

The Fadhloun-Rakha (FR) model [9] is an acceleration-based car-following model that uses the same steady-state formulation and respects the same vehicle dynamics as the RPA model. Additionally, the model uses very similar collision-avoidance strategies to ensure a safe following distance between vehicles.

The mathematical expression of the FR model, presented in Eq. 29, estimates the acceleration of the following vehicle as the sum of two terms. The first term models the vehicle behavior in the acceleration regime, while the second governs the deceleration regime.

$$a_n = F \times a_n^{DYN} + CA(u_n, s_n, \Delta u_n) \tag{29}$$

In the acceleration regime, the vehicle behavior is governed by the vehicle dynamics, as demonstrated in Eq. 27 to ensure that vehicle accelerations are realistic. A reducing multiplier F (Eq. 30), which ranges between 0.0 and 1.0, is then applied to the vehicle dynamics acceleration. The F factor is a function that is sensitive to X_n (Eq. 31) which represents the ratio of u_n/s_n divided by the ratio of the steady state speed to the steady state spacing u_n^{VA}/s_n^{VA}. It aims to guarantee that two objectives are met. First, it ensures the convergence of the vehicles' behavior towards the Van Aerde steady state model. Second, it attempts to model human behavior and the different patterns of driving by acting as a reduction factor to the vehicle dynamics model.

$$F(X_n) = e^{-aX_n}\left(1 - X_n^b e^{b(1-X_n)}\right)^d \tag{30}$$

$$X_n = \frac{s_n^{VA}}{s_n} \bullet \frac{u_n}{u_n^{VA}} \tag{31}$$

Where a, b, and d are model parameters that are calibrated to a specific driver and model the driver input to the gas pedal.

The second term in the expression of the FR model considers vehicle deceleration to avoid a collision with a slower traveling lead vehicle as shown in Eqs. (32–33). As shown, collision avoidance is ensured by the function CA, which computes the needed deceleration to apply as the ratio of the square of the kinematics deceleration needed to decelerate from the current speed to the leading vehicle speed at a desired deceleration level that is set by the user.

$$d_{kinematics} = \frac{\left[u_n^2 - u_{n-1}^2 + \sqrt{\left(u_n^2 - u_{n-1}^2\right)^2}\right]}{4\left(s_n - s_j\right)} \tag{32}$$

$$CA(u_n, s_n, \Delta u_n) = \frac{d_{kinematics}^2}{(d_{desired} - gG)} \tag{33}$$

Where d_{des} is the desired deceleration level.

Finally, to model the effect of the driver error in estimating the leading vehicle speed and the distance gap between the two vehicles, two wiener processes are incorporated in the model formulation at the level of u_{n-1} and s_n. Additionally, a white noise signal is added to the model's expression to capture the driver's imperfection while applying the gas pedal. The compounding effect of those three signals makes the model output more representative of human driving behavior.

At a first glance, the mathematical expression of the FR model might seem complex due to the high number of variables involved. However, most of these parameters have fixed values that are either constant or dependent on specific characteristics of the road and the vehicle. Despite the latter, the research team recognizes that the model in its current form is oriented towards a potential user that is interested in modelling specific scenarios with a high level of detail. For the average user who is just looking to use the model for testing purposes in a standard setting, the formulation of the FR model could be further simplified.

With that in mind and for the purpose of highlighting the practicality and ease of implementation of the model, we proceeded to create a family of sub-models that are specific to different vehicle categories. The different models, shown in Table 1, present a simplified formulation of the vehicle dynamics model for different vehicle groups (sedans, SUVs, buses, heavy trucks) in a standard road setting (dry and flat asphalt road in a good condition).

Table 1. Summary of the dynamics model for different vehicle categories.

Vehicle category	Vehicle dynamics model
LDV sedan	$a_{max} = \min\left(\frac{400000}{M.u}, 6.86p_{ta}\right) - 0.029\frac{u^2}{M} - (0.0004u + 0.056)$
Midsize SUV	$a_{max} = \min\left(\frac{572000}{M.u}, 6.86p_{ta}\right) - 0.048\frac{u^2}{M} - (0.0004u + 0.056)$
Pick-up truck	$a_{max} = \min\left(\frac{862000}{M.u}, 6.86p_{ta}\right) - 0.072\frac{u^2}{M} - (0.0004u + 0.056)$
Bus	$a_{max} = \min\left(\frac{918000}{M.u}, 6.86p_{ta}\right) - 0.232\frac{u^2}{M} - (0.0004u + 0.056)$
Heavy-duty truck	$a_{max} = \min\left(\frac{1530000}{M.u}, 6.86p_{ta}\right) - 0.516\frac{u^2}{M} - (0.0004u + 0.056)$

On a side note, it is noteworthy to mention the reason for which the weight of the vehicle was kept as a variable rather than a constant for the different vehicle categories shown in Table 1. The reason relates to the fact that even small changes in the vehicle weight might have a significant impact on the resulting maximum acceleration profile. That is especially true for the case of heavy trucks for which the load factor of the trailer defines a big range for the total truck weight.

3   Naturalistic Dataset

The data used herein represents a small subset that was extracted from the naturalistic driving database generated by the 100-Car study [20] that was conducted by the Virginia Tech Transportation Institute (VTTI) in 2002. In fact, VTTI initiated a study where 100 cars were instrumented and driven by a total of 108 drivers around the District of Columbia (DC) area. The resulting database from the 100-Car study [20] contained detailed logs of more than 207,000 completed trips with a total duration of around 20 million minutes of data.

The naturalistic dataset that was used to validate the proposed model contains information relating to 1,659 car-following events that spans over a duration of around 13 h which is significant for the task of validation of car-following models. The car-following data composing the dataset comes from six different drivers and was collected on a relatively short segment of the Dulles Airport access road (approximately an 8-mile long section) in order to maintain facility homogeneity.

Finally, it is noteworthy to state that both the characteristics of the different vehicles are known due to the naturalistic nature of the dataset. This makes the determination of the different FR and RPA model variables straightforward and exclusive of bias.

4 Parameter Calibration of the Various Models

For each of the studied models, a certain number of inputs is needed. These inputs can be categorized into two groups. The first category comprises the inputs that are the same for the different models, namely the time-space and the time-speed profiles of the leading vehicle, the starting location and speed of the following vehicle as well as the free-flow speed (u_f) which was estimated specifically for each car-following event along with any other variables related to the roadway. The use of the free-flow speed distribution shown in Fig. 1, instead of a constant value across all of the events, is justified by the significant heterogeneity of the driver behavior during the free driving phase. In fact, drivers do not necessarily drive at the speed limit of the facility when there is no vehicle ahead of them.

Besides that, the desired speed of a certain naturalistic event was set equally across all of the studied models in order to maintain the homogeneity of driver behavior and road facility for that specific event.

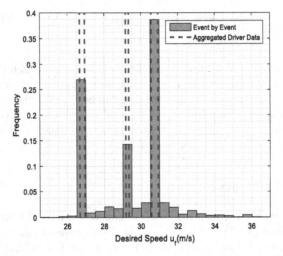

Fig. 1. Distribution of the free-flow speed for the naturalistic events [28].

As a side remark, we note that the jam density k_j, the capacity q_c and the speed-at-capacity u_c, which are needed to generate a simulated trajectory in the case of the formulations of the RPA model and the FR model, were estimated using the calibration procedure proposed by Rakha and Arafeh [29]. However, unlike the free-flow speed, those parameters were calibrated using the bulk data of each driver given their minor influence on the resulting model outputs. The estimated values for the latter driver-specific parameters are presented in Table 2 along with the needed vehicle-specific parameter values in Table 3.

The remaining input variables consist of model-specific parameters that require calibration depending on the researcher's objectives. Since this study aims to validate a new car-following model by comparing its performance to that of other state-of-the-art models, the different parameters need to be calibrated such that the resulting simulated

Table 2. Values of k_j, q_c and u_c for each driver [28].

Driver	k_j (veh/m)	q_c (veh/s)	u_c (m/s)
Driver_124	0.091	0.865	22.22
Driver_304	0.150	0.833	19.00
Driver_316	0.075	0.464	21.36
Driver_350	0.080	0.529	21.28
Driver_358	0.087	0.447	19.53
Driver_363	0.131	0.906	23.69

Table 3. Characteristics of the different vehicles [28].

Driver	Vehicle characteristics			
	P (kW)	M (kg)	C_d	A_f (m^2)
Driver_124	90	1190	0.36	2.06
Driver_304	90	1090	0.40	2.00
Driver_316	90	1090	0.40	2.00
Driver_350	90	1090	0.40	2.00
Driver_358	145	1375	0.40	2.18
Driver_363	145	1375	0.40	2.18

behavior of the following vehicle matches its observed behavior as closely as possible. The calibration procedure of the different parameters of each model was conducted heuristically taking the speed RMSE as the error objective function. The choice to optimize each model with regards to the speed RMSE is judged reasonable given that the optimization operation was done on an event-by-event basis. In fact, we opted to calibrate each model separately for each car-following event rather than for the dataset as a whole. Even though that exponentially increased the computation time, a more fair comparison between the results is made possible as each model was allowed to propose its best possible fit for each of the 1659 naturalistic events. Hence, the different model outputs are incorporative of the effect of the strength points of each model.

Finally, given the presence of noise in the proposed model, the calibration was conducted using a bi-level procedure. First, the model parameters were calibrated deterministically without the consideration of the noise signals. Next, to model the effect of the noise, the optimized parameters of the first step were used to run a total of 1000 simulations in order to have valid model outputs and to determine the 95% confidence interval of the results.

5   Results and Model Validation

Having access to the calibrated parameters, the speed profiles were obtained for each car-following event of the naturalistic dataset. The corresponding speed outputs ensure a minimal RMSE between a model's predictions and the measured data over its whole timespan. To illustrate the results, the probability distribution of the speed RMSE of the different models is plotted in Fig. 2. The figure demonstrates that the FR model performs better overall in terms of fitting the observed data than the other models. That is demonstrated by the fact that its RMSE distribution is higher than those of the other models towards the lower end of the speed errors (between 0 and 0.5). Then, as the RMSE keeps getting bigger and bigger, the tendency is reversed and the RMSE distribution of the FR model becomes the smallest.

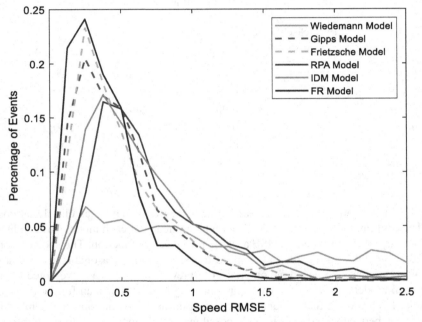

Fig. 2. Probability distribution of the speed RMSE for the different models [28].

Further Characteristics of the calibration errors are presented in Table 4. The table demonstrates that the lowest values for the mean, the median and the standard deviation are observed in the case of the FR model. These results are consistent with Fig. 2 and further support the robustness and the flexibility of the FR model in comparison to the other models.

To better quantify statistically the difference in performance between the proposed model and the other five models, the rank of the new model was determined for each event based on the calculated RMSE value (the resulting mean of the 1000 trials). The ranking was sorted in an increasing direction of the RMSE value with the best model

Table 4. Characteristics of the calibration errors for the different models.

	FR	RPA	Gipps	Wiedemann	Frietzsche	IDM
Mean	0.685	1.182	0.844	3.848	0.913	1.223
Median	0.553	1.029	0.724	2.801	0.712	0.983
Std Dev	0.639	0.642	0.593	3.464	0.725	0.944

being the one offering the lowest error. Table 5 shows the results of this analysis where the rank distribution of the proposed model is presented. From the table, one can see that the FR model outperformed the other ones. In fact, this model offered the best fit to the empirical data for about half of the considered events (735 out of 1659 events). Furthermore, the number of events for which the fit of the proposed model was in either the first or the second position, represents about two thirds of the total cases (1126 out of 1659 events).

The quantitative analysis was taken a step further as the proposed model was compared face-to-face with each of the studied models. That would allow for a better understanding of the new model's performance. Figure 3a and Fig. 3b present the results of this comparison in terms of the optimized speed RMSE and the one computed from the resulting acceleration profiles, respectively. In terms of speed error, the FR model is demonstrated to significantly outperform the other models. In fact, its speed RMSE was smaller than that found using the RPA, Gipps, Wiedemann, Frietzsche, and the IDM models in between 65% to around 90% of the events.

The previous stated values do not confer enough information about the new model performance by themselves as they do not quantify the percentages by which the error function was reduced. Consequently, the bar chart of Fig. 3 is complemented by Table 6 which presents key measures (mean, median and standard deviation) about the distribution of the relative percentage decrease in the speed RMSE. For instance, it is found that for the 90% of the total events for which the proposed model formulation outperformed the Wiedemann model, the error reduction percentage had a median equal to 85%. In the case of the RPA model, the FR model resulted in an average decrease of the RMSE that is around 56% for the 88% of the events for which it was the best.

When considering face-to-face comparisons in terms of the resulting acceleration data from the optimized speed profiles, only the Wiedemann and the IDM model outperformed the FR model as it can be observed in Table 5 and Table 6. While the IDM model is known for its excellent fit to acceleration data due to its smooth expression, the results of the Wiedemann model seem intriguing at first. In fact, it is found that the results are justified by the structure of the Wiedemann model itself as it will be described later.

In order to examine the performance of the different models qualitatively, the resulting simulated speeds are presented for some sample events. In fact, Fig. 4 plots the variation of the observed and simulated speed profiles for four different events over time. For each subplot (Fig. 4a through Fig. 4d), the results from the studied models are drawn in order to compare their predictions with the observed naturalistic behavior. For example, for the event presented in Fig. 4a, the driver accelerated from about 85 km/h to around 94 km/h, maintained his/her speed around that value, then re-accelerated to

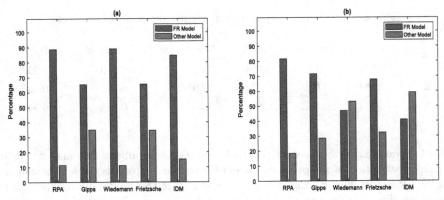

Fig. 3. Comparison of the proposed FR model performance to the performance of the other models: a. Based on the speed RMSE; b. Based on the acceleration RMSE [28].

Table 5. Rank of the FR model in terms of goodness of fit as a percentage of the total number of events using the speed RMSE [28].

Rank	Rank distribution (%)
1	44.30
2	23.57
3	16.88
4	11.63
5	3.32
6	0.30

Table 6. Distribution characteristics of the decrease percentage in the speed RMSE for head-to-head comparisons [28].

	Best model	Mean	Median	Standard deviation
RPA model	FR model	56.33	58.68	23.76
Gipps model		45.43	46.97	22.45
Wiedemann model		77.02	85.72	20.96
Frietzsche model		45.65	46.91	22.78
IDM model		50.51	53.46	21.50
RPA model	RPA model	26.62	22.76	18.76
Gipps model	Gipps model	43.25	45.66	23.33
Wiedemann model	Wiedemann model	43.94	45.49	24.41
Frietzsche model	Frietzsche model	35.97	35.87	22.10
IDM model	IDM model	30.36	27.54	20.87

about 97 km/h and tried to maintain that speed until the end of the event. This behavior was well captured by most of the studied models, except that at the end of the event all models predicted a decrease in speed. This is mainly due to the fact that all the studied models take into account a minimum safe distance in order to avoid collision with the leading vehicle. Given that the collision avoidance logics of the models judged that the spacing maintained by the driver is unsafe for such high speeds, a decrease in speed was predicted to keep a safe distance and to ensure that the collision avoidance conditions are met. That opposes the actual driver behavior who maintained his/her driving speed despite being unsafely close to the leading vehicle. Looking roughly into this event, it is the FR model that traces better the actual driver behavior, followed by the IDM model, then Gipps, the RPA and Frietzsche models, and lastly Wiedemann model.

It is worth clarifying at this level the reasons behind the steep decrease in speed observed in the output of the Wiedemann model. The observed speed drop, which occurs 30 s after the start of the event, is due to the nomenclature of Wiedemann model itself. In fact, similar data cliffs were found to be present in a noticeable number of other events for this model. Such behaviors result from the abrupt change in the acceleration value when transitioning from one traffic regime to another. Besides the latter aspect, the crossing of one of the boundaries delimiting the different regions of the Wiedemann model was found to result in another disparity in the model output when compared to most of the other models (FR, RPA, Gipps, IDM). The concerned disparity is observed when the following vehicle remains in the same traffic region for the entire duration of the car-following event, hence arising the possibility of having a constant acceleration over the entire duration of the car-following maneuver. The previous two drawbacks are also manifested in the Frietzsche model due to its similar structure, however their presence is not as prevalent. For instance, one such case in which the following vehicle remained within the same traffic regime for Frietzsche model is shown in Fig. 4c. The figure illustrates a scenario in which the driver was trying to maintain his/her desired speed of 100 km/h with minor fluctuations. Since the vehicle started and finished its trip within the "Free Driving" regime, the Frietzsche model resulted in a constant speed profile for the entire event. However, the latter aspects of Frietzsche and Wiedemann models do not necessarily connote an inability to propose a fitted speed that matches empirical data. As a matter of fact, while all the models captured the empirical behavior of the event presented in Fig. 4b, the Frietzsche model was the best in terms of tracing the actual speed profile. All other models slightly over-predicted the maximum reached speed.

Finally, concerning the event described by Fig. 4d, the speed profile suggests that the highway is heavily congested. The driver decelerated from about 32 km/h to come to an almost complete stop for a few seconds. This was followed by an oscillatory behavior due to a succession of accelerations and decelerations. Despite the repeating oscillations, the FR model traced almost perfectly the driver behavior for the entire timespan. The RPA model gave reasonable predictions for this event as well. Overall, as a qualitative measure, the different events presented in the figure are consistent with the goodness of fit results presented earlier. The Gipps model along with the FR and RPA model appear to capture the naturalistic data considerably well.

Next, the acceleration profiles derived from the calibrated speed data were examined. For illustration purposes, a sample event was chosen to visualize and compare the simulated acceleration profiles to empirical data.

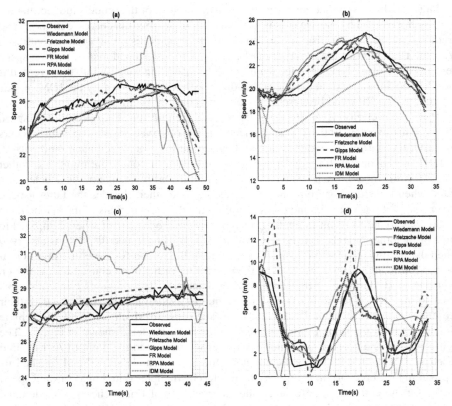

Fig. 4. Variation of the simulated speeds over time of four sample events [28].

The different profiles are presented in Fig. 5. For clarity of the figure as the overlap between the outputs of the studied models is significant, the results are presented in each sub-figure (Fig. 5a through Fig. 5f) along with the observed acceleration of the driver. During this 2-min car-following event, the driver had acceleration and deceleration maneuvers with maximum values of 1.6 m/s² and 2.1 m/s², respectively. As shown by Fig. 5a, the Wiedemann model results in a zero constant acceleration mainly because the modeled vehicle behavior remained within the boundaries of one of the traffic regimes for the total event duration.

More importantly, the illustrated constant acceleration behavior of the Wiedemann model, which was confirmed across several other car-following events, gives a plausible explanation of the extremely low values found when the RMSEs related to the acceleration data were computed. By avoiding the oscillatory behavior of the other models and, more importantly, staying within the maximum acceleration and deceleration values without overshooting, a constant acceleration profile would result in a better fit to the empirical behavior in terms of the RMSE value. Setting aside the car-following events with a constant simulated acceleration, the Wiedemann model resulted in a stepped acceleration profile similar to the acceleration-time diagram of the Frietzsche model plotted in Fig. 5b. As for Gipps model, the FR model and the RPA model (Fig. 5c, Fig. 5d, and Fig. 5e, respectively), they resulted in acceleration values that closely followed the field data even though the maximum predicted deceleration was relatively overestimated. More precisely, the IDM model traced the actual acceleration profile the best for this specific event followed by the FR model formulation. Generally speaking, the new model was found to be the best in terms of mimicking the real driver behavior as it successfully avoided the acceleration fluctuations produced by the other models that are far in excess of those observed at the level of the empirical data. Even more, the significance and contribution of the latter finding is further amplified given the fact that the FR model formulation is inclusive of three noise signals. Those noises attempt to account for the driver's errors related to estimating the model input variables—the distance gap to the leading vehicle along with its speed—as well as his/her imperfection while applying the gas pedal. Notwithstanding the fact that the other models are exclusive of such errors giving them a statistical edge, their predicted acceleration profiles were still outperformed by the acceleration predictions of the FR model except for the IDM model which provides comparable results.

From a traffic researcher standpoint, acceleration data can be cast as the most important output of a car-following model. In fact, acceleration information is the starting point for the computation of other measures of effectiveness (MOEs). Two specific MOEs that are very sensitive to the accuracy of predicted accelerations and quite important from an environmental perspective, are fuel consumption and emissions estimations. With that in mind, it seemed necessary to examine the behavior of the maximum acceleration distribution of the bulk dataset given its major impact on any fuel consumption or emissions calculation.

Subsequently, the observed and predicted maximum acceleration of each model were extracted for each event and plotted as shown by Fig. 6. We note here that the maximum acceleration data is sorted from the highest value to the lowest for each model independently of the others. This means that the event numbered as one, for example, in the figure is not the same physical event for all the studied models or that calculated from the measured speed data. It is just the physical event that resulted in the highest maximum observed or modeled acceleration. In other words, the figure does not allow making event-by-event comparisons between the different models. The main purpose of the plot is to compare the empirical maximum acceleration distribution of the whole dataset to the ones resulting from the calibration of the different studied models.

As a side note, since 1000 simulations were run using the logic of the FR model to estimate the mean and the dispersion of the results, the simulated maximum acceleration using the new model formulation is plotted using the mean and the 95% confidence interval of the data which is shown by the light bounded area in Fig. 6. Qualitatively speaking, the figure demonstrate the superiority of the FR model in terms of its ability of replicating the maximum acceleration behavior of the naturalistic dataset. In fact, the

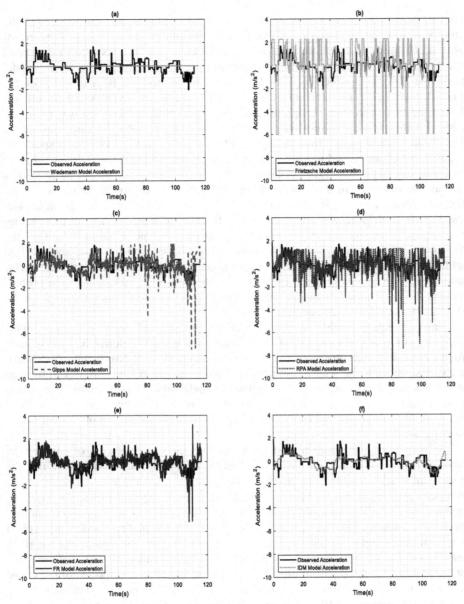

Fig. 5. Variation of the simulated acceleration over time of a sample car-following event: a. Wiedemann model; b. Frietzsche model; c. Gipps model; d. RPA model; e. FR model; f. IDM Model [28].

observed data appears to be successfully covered by the breadth of the 95% confidence interval of the model output.

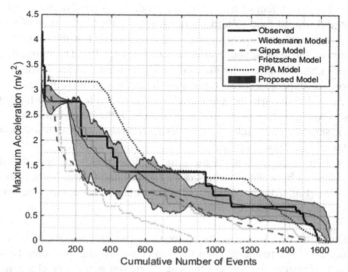

Fig. 6. Comparison of the maximum acceleration behaviour of the naturalistic dataset to the outputs of the different models [28].

From the above analysis, one can confirm that the FR model succeeds the most in terms of fitting the empirical following behaviour of the vehicles. As discussed, it was demonstrated to result in the smallest errors and to recreate most of the accelerations patterns of the observed trajectories. However, the above analysis does not highlight the main contribution of the FR model over the other ones. Specifically, the main advantage offered by the FR model lies in its ease of tuning to capture different specific characteristics of both the vehicle, the driver and the road conditions such as engine power, weather conditions, and road grade on the vehicle. The model robustness is further complemented by its inclusion of parameters that are reflective of the human-in-the-loop element separately from the vehicle dynamics variables. That allows for modeling the driver/vehicle system as two separate entities rather than one as is the case for most car-following models. In other words, the model is able to emulate the variability resulting from human behavior randomness even when the same vehicle is operated in a similar road setting.

6 Model Robustness to Driver/Vehicle/Roadway/Weather Parameters

To illustrate some of the aforementioned points, the research team proceeded to perform a simple sensitivity analysis in which a one kilometer trip is simulated for different case scenarios. In each of the scenarios, all the model parameters were set to a fixed value except for one. That would allow visualizing its impact on the generated trajectories. Initially, the following case scenarios are considered:

- *Scenario 1*: the coefficient of friction of the road, μ is varied between 0.1 and 0.8 in order to model several road conditions ranging from icy to dry as shown in Fig. 7a.
- *Scenario 2*: different vehicle categories are considered. For the vehicle categories, we opted to use those presented earlier in Table 1 (Fig. 7b). The figure demonstrates that the sedan, the SUV and the pickup truck performances are close to each other. Furthermore, as expected, those three vehicle categories were trailed by the heavy vehicles. As a side remark, the semi-truck was assumed to be fully loaded resulting in the observed significant delay in comparison with the other vehicles.
- *Scenario 3*: several road grades were investigated ranging from a 4% downhill to a 4% uphill at 2% increments (Fig. 7c).
- *Scenario 4*: two configurations of the same vehicle model are considered to evaluate the differences between all-wheel drive (AWD) and forward-wheel drive (FWD) configurations (Fig. 7d). As anticipated, the simulated trajectories demonstrate the superiority of the all-wheel drive version.

Looking into the first scenario, the trajectories presented in Fig. 7a are consistent with the expected effect resulting from the considered road conditions. However, it is only tentative to consider that the coefficient of friction is the sole characterizing factor of such conditions. In fact, it was demonstrated by Rakha et al. [30] that inclement weather has a significant impact on the fundamental diagram of the facility. Depending on the precipitation and the visibility levels, reduction factors are applied to the characterizing parameters of the steady state behavior. In that context, Fig. 7a could be cast as a representation of the specific case in which the weather is clear (no precipitation and high visibility) regardless of the road condition. To illustrate the effect of the road condition in conjunction with the weather conditions, Fig. 8a is presented. The figure highlights the impact of the precipitation and the visibility levels on the produced trajectories when the road is snowy. Specifically, the figure plots two cases against each other: the first one is characterized by a snowy road and a clear weather, while the second case involves a snowy road, heavy snow precipitation and low visibility. The findings further demonstrate the robustness of the FR model as it could be easily tuned to account for the impact of inclement weather if desired. In fact, the integration of the methodology proposed by Rakha et al. [30] into the FR model is a simple and straightforward task.

Next, in order to complement Fig. 7c which illustrates the effect of the road grade for a light-duty vehicle, we propose to investigate the case of heavy vehicles. In that regard, Fig. 8b replicates scenario 3 when a fully loaded semi-truck is considered. The results illustrate the ability of the FR model to capture the amplified impact that the road grade has on heavy vehicles in comparison to passenger cars. The importance of the results presented in Fig. 7 and Fig. 8 resides in the fact that they prove that the acceleration profiles generated by the FR model are reflective of the vehicle type and its environment. This makes the estimations of other measures of effectiveness that are based on the acceleration data (fuel consumption, emissions, etc.) more accurate and precise when compared to the other car-following models.

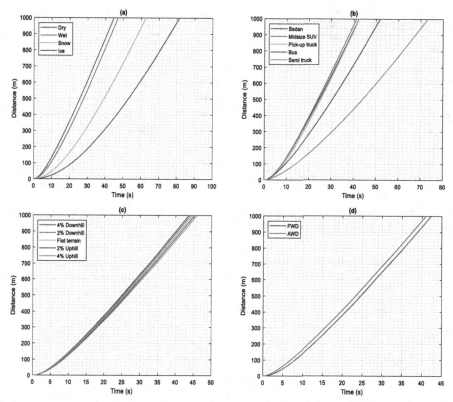

Fig. 7. Effect of different model parameters on the simulated trajectories: a) Coefficient of road friction; b) Vehicle category; c) Road Grade; d) All wheel drive vs. forward wheel drive.

Here, it might be argued that some of the above criteria could be captured by some of the other car-following models with only minor changes. For instance, the maximum acceleration parameter in the IDM model could be modified to capture the effect of the road grade through deducting the deceleration level resulting from the grade resistance. While that is technically correct, the FR model remains more robust and simple to use as no modifications are needed to capture the effect of most of the parameters characterizing vehicle dynamics and road conditions.

Finally, the FR model robustness in relation to capturing human behavior variability is investigated. As a reminder, the FR model applies to the vehicle dynamics acceleration model a driver input parameter F (Eq. 30) to model different patterns of driving. That is achieved through varying a set of three parameters (a, b, and d) in an attempt to simulate different driver inputs to the accelerator (gas pedal). For illustration purposes, a two kilometer trip is simulated for different value sets (a, b and d) using the same vehicle and road environment. The resulting trip trajectories are plotted in Fig. 9. The significant breadth of coverage of the trajectories demonstrates the success of the FR model in relation to modeling human behavior variability.

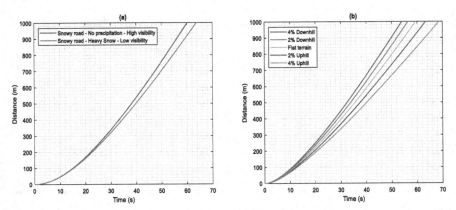

Fig. 8. Effect of different model parameters on the simulated trajectories: a) Inclement weather; b) Road grade for a fully loaded semi-truck.

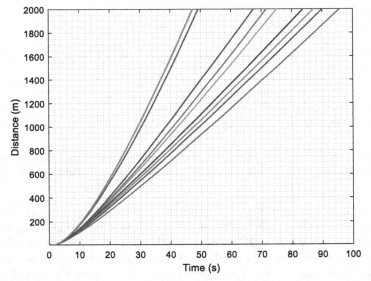

Fig. 9. Effect of different (a, b, and d) parameter values on the simulated trajectories.

7 Conclusions and Future Work

The research presented in this paper validates and compares the performance of the Fadhloun-Rakha (FR) car-following model to other state-of-the-art car-following models. The uniqueness of the FR model include: (1) explicitly modeling the driver throttle and brake pedal input in a single continuous equation; (2) explicitly capturing driver perception and control inaccuracies and errors; (3) modeling vehicle dynamics using a point-mass model; (4) allowing for shorter than steady-state following distances when following faster leading vehicles; and (5) ensuring collision-free driving.

Using naturalistic data from six drivers the FR model was demonstrated to outperform the five state-of-the-art car-following models. While the RMSE, used herein, is a good indicator of the ability of a car-following model to replicate empirical behavior from a statistical perspective, it is not sufficient to confirm that it would be the best with regards to every aspect of traffic engineering. This study demonstrated that the FR model is the only formulation that allows for an explicit and simple independent tuning of driver, roadway, and/or vehicle characteristics allowing it to capture the impact of driver, vehicle, road surface, tire, road topology, and weather conditions on the modeling of car-following behavior. To demonstrate this fact, a sensitivity analysis demonstrated the robustness of the FR model in capturing several aspects of the road/vehicle/driver system in a concise and precise manner.

Acknowledgments. The authors acknowledge the financial support provided by the University Mobility and Equity Center (UMEC) and the Department of Energy through the Office of Energy Efficiency and Renewable Energy (EERE), Vehicle Technologies Office, Energy Efficient Mobility Systems Program under award number DE-EE0008209.

References

1. Chandler, R.E., Herman, R., Montroll, E.W.: Traffic dynamics: studies in car following. Oper. Res. **6**(2), 165–184 (1958)
2. Drew, D.R.: Traffic flow theory and control (1968)
3. Fritzsche, H.-T.: A model for traffic simulation. Traffic Eng. + Control **35**(5), 317–321 (1994)
4. Gazis, D.C., Herman, R., Rothery, R.W.: Nonlinear follow-the-leader models of traffic flow. Oper. Res. **9**(4), 545–567 (1961)
5. Jiang, R., Wu, Q., Zhu, Z.: Full velocity difference model for a car-following theory. Phys. Rev. E **64**(1), 017101 (2001)
6. Newell, G.F.: A simplified car-following theory: a lower order model. Transp. Res. Part B: Methodol. **36**(3), 195–205 (2002)
7. Olstam, J.J., Tapani, A.: Comparison of Car-following models (2004)
8. Treiber, M., Hennecke, A., Helbing, D.: Congested traffic states in empirical observations and microscopic simulations. Phys. Rev. E **62**(2), 1805 (2000)
9. Fadhloun, K., Rakha, H.: A novel vehicle dynamics and human behavior car-following model: model development and preliminary testing. Int. J. Transp. Sci. Technol. **9**, 14–28 (2020)
10. Gipps, P.G.: A behavioural car-following model for computer simulation. Transp. Res. Part B: Methodol. **15**(2), 105–111 (1981)
11. Wiedemann, R.: Simulation des Strassenverkehrsflusses. Schriftenreihe des Instituts für Verkehrswesen der Universität Karlsruhe, Karlsruhe, Germany (1974)
12. Wiedemann, R., Reiter, U.: Microscopic traffic simulation: The simulation system MISSION, background and actual state, in CEC Project ICARUS (V1052), Final Report, Brussels. pp. 1–53 in Appendix A (1992)
13. Rakha, H., Pasumarthy, P., Adjerid, S.: A simplified behavioral vehicle longitudinal motion model. Transp. Lett.: Int. J. Transp. Res. **1**(2), 95–110 (2009)
14. Sangster, J., Rakha, H.: Enhancing and calibrating the rakha-pasumarthy-adjerid car-following model using naturalistic driving data. Int. J. Transp. Sci. Technol. **3**(3), 229–248 (2014)

15. Barceló, J.: GETRAM/AIMSUN: a software environment for microscopic traffic analysis. In: Proceedings of the Workshop on Next Generation Models for Traffic Analysis, Monitoring and Management (2001)
16. Smith, M., Duncan, G., Druitt, S.: PARAMICS: microscopic traffic simulation for congestion management (1995)
17. PTV-AG, VISSIM 5.40–01 User Manual. Karlsruhe, Germany (2012)
18. Van Aerde, M., Rakha, H.: INTEGRATION © Release 2.30 for Windows: User's Guide – Volume I: Fundamental Model Features, M. Van Aerde & Assoc., Ltd., Blacksburg (2007)
19. Van Aerde, M., Rakha, H.: INTEGRATION © Release 2.30 for Windows: User's Guide - Volume II: Advanced Model Features, M. Van Aerde & Assoc., Ltd., Blacksburg (2007)
20. Dingus, T.A., et al.: The 100-car naturalistic driving study, Phase II-results of the 100-car field experiment (2006)
21. Sangster, J., Rakha, H., Du, J.: Application of naturalistic driving data to modeling of driver car-following behavior. Transp. Res. Rec.: J. Transp. Res. Board **2390**, 20–33 (2013)
22. Soria, I., Elefteriadou, L., Kondyli, A.: Assessment of car-following models by driver type and under different traffic, weather conditions using data from an instrumented vehicle. Simul. Model. Pract. Theory **40**, 208–220 (2014)
23. Van Aerde, M., Rakha, H.: Multivariate calibration of single regime speed-flow-density relationships [road traffic management]. In: Vehicle Navigation and Information Systems Conference, 1995, Proceedings, in Conjunction with the Pacific Rim TransTech Conference, 6th International VNIS. 'A Ride into the Future' (1995)
24. Rakha, H.: Validation of van aerde's simplified steady-state car-following and traffic stream model. Transp. Lett.: Int. J. Transp. Res. **1**(3), 227–244 (2009)
25. Wu, N., Rakha, H.: Derivation of van aerde traffic stream model from tandem-queuing theory. Transp. Res. Rec.: J. Transp. Res. Board **2124**(1), 18–27 (2009)
26. Rakha, H., et al.: Vehicle dynamics model for predicting maximum truck acceleration levels. J. Transp. Eng. **127**(5), 418–425 (2001)
27. Rakha, H., Snare, M., Dion, F.: Vehicle dynamics model for estimating maximum light-duty vehicle acceleration levels. Transp. Res. Rec.: J. Transp. Res. Board. **1883**(1), 40–49 (2004)
28. Fadhloun, K., et al.: A validation study of the fadhloun-rakha car-following model. In: Proceedings of the 6th International Conference on Vehicle Technology and Intelligent Transport Systems - Volume 1: VEHITS (2020)
29. Rakha, H., Arafeh, M.: Calibrating steady-state traffic stream and car-following models using loop detector data. Transp. Sci. **44**(2), 151–168 (2010)
30. Rakha, H., Farzaneh, M., Arafeh, M, Sterzin, E.: Inclement weather impacts on freeway traffic stream behavior. Transp. Res. Rec. **2071**(1), 8–18 (2008)

Container Handling Operation Modeling and Estimation

Sergej Jakovlev[1,2(✉)], Tomas Eglynas[1], Mindaugas Jusis[1], Miroslav Voznak[1,2], Pavol Partila[1], and Jaromir Tovarek[1]

[1] Klaipeda University, Universiteto al. 17, 92294 Klaipeda, Lithuania
[2] VSB-Technical University of Ostrava, 17. Listopadu 15, 70833 Ostrava, Czech Republic

Abstract. This paper presents the initial research findings from the Klaipeda port quay crane monitoring activities related to the Blue economy development initiative in the Baltic Sea and demonstrates the effectiveness of the modelling of the spreader movement patterns. The use case study demonstrates the possibility to monitor the cargo handling processes using ICT sensory equipment and to address the problem of information system deployment in harsh industrial environments. Custom made monitoring and data transmission sensory units were developed and placed on the quay crane spreader and AGV to detect the movement speed and the accelerations in 3D space. Theoretical and use-case scenarios are presented and discussed briefly. Initial results suggested that crane operators' involvement in the control of the cargo movement produced incorrect control patterns (joystick movements) that delayed port operations. Each control movement of the joystick needs to have direct real-time feedback from the spreader (actual movement of the cargo). Feed-back control functionality will allow adjusting the spreader movement ac-cording to the operator and will decrease the cargo transportation time during constant breaks.

Keywords: Data acquisition · Communication technology · Engineering · Systems design

1 Introduction

Klaipeda Sea Port has distinguished itself in the Baltic Region due to its rapid increase in cargo flows and adoption of Blue Economy regulations and strategies, that require a decrease of CO2 and other harmful gasses in the industry surrounding the Sea Port and related to Port activities (including shipbuilding, bulk cargo transit, fossil fuel transship, fishing and production). Many practitioners and action method-ology developers in the transport chain did research in this area. Ranging from communication and control systems application with deep insights and relevant reviews, economical calculations, and practical use cases [1–4]. Overall, the possibility to adopt new technologies in such closed environments is a rare opportunity. In practice, the realization of complex control solutions limited by cost efficiency in comparison to standardized and commonly used solutions [5, 6].

C. Klein et al. (Eds.): SMARTGREENS 2020/VEHITS 2020, CCIS 1475, pp. 279–289, 2021.
https://doi.org/10.1007/978-3-030-89170-1_14

The adoption of new ideas is difficult even to "modern minds" [7]. In practice, it is difficult to come close to working equipment and to acquire agreement for their monitoring on-site. The initial visual analysis suggested developing new ideas on how to lower fluctuations of the containers' gripper. Its movements are random in nature, due to external impacts, such as wind or physical contact with other objects. It is difficult to predict such random deviations in practice [2]. In comparison, European ports such as Rotterdam or Hanover apply new systems for vibration decrease in the cables during lowering procedures. Dampening control systems decrease unnecessary strains arising during the accelerated movement of containers by synchronizing operators' actions with the total lowering process engines and control units. Artificial Intelligence (AI) systems with stochastic algorithms for efficient learning and fast adoption to unlikely events are used in scenarios with high risks [1].

Control and coordination of opera-tor movement is a task for unconventional systems, mainly used to solve competence shortage problems in engineering, medicine, and explorations environments [8, 9]. Today, most Baltic Sea Region Ports handled automated systems, but only on the surface. Context procedures and IT operations automated in most "brutal" fashion. Equipment is bought, but not relied upon to solve critical tasks. That is why the inclusion of the quay crane even in modern ports is still innovation-theoretical. In reality, the crane opera-tor has to wait for the Automated Guided Vehicle (AGV) or the AGV has to wait for the operator to finish his unloading routine, even when the most modern control systems are used.

Klaipeda city Containers terminal (LKAB "Smeltė") located in the Klaipeda Port is among the fastest-growing Sea Ports in the entire region. Container traffic volume has increased in Klaipeda Port in 2020 drastically, yet the operational efficiency has halted due to new EU and inner company regulations and globalization standards. The most effective means to enhance the container handling operations is to im-prove the existing systems by synchronizing the operations on a technological level, taking into account the technological deviations and the nature of the problems addressed by the personnel on-site. Essentially, it would in general improve the level of services provided, which can be realized by fully utilizing invested resources such as berths, cranes, yards, and handling equipment. Depending on the actual position of the AGV or the crane, decisions are made systematically to slow down the speed of movement so that the target point is reached at the same time by all involved bodies. This saves both energy resources and technical resources, and increases crane and consequently, the entire port efficiency.

In this article, we try to analyze the use case from the LKAB "Smelte" terminal, by estimating the operational efficiency of the loading procedures using the containers handling equipment (namely the quay crane and AGV).

2   Description of the Monitoring Equipment

In the experimental research DL1 - MK2 data logger/analyzer was used to acquire and transfer statistical data. It uses a three-axis accelerometer. Dynamical characteristics are examined, including acceleration, speed, and position. GPS antenna is used to increase accuracy. Movement speed detection accuracy set to 0.16 km/h due to technical reasons and data logging accuracy set to 1% due to irregularities in the electronics.

Figure 1 demonstrates the used equipment. Also, horizontal and vertical acceleration sensors have a standard industry set accuracy level of 0.05 m/s^2 with maximum detection acceleration set to 20 m/s^2. Higher speeds and accelerations are statistically unlikely due to technological and structural reasons.

Fig. 1. Demonstration of the secured case with DL-1 MK2 Datalogger [11, 12].

The mounting point was set on the spreader, shown in Fig. 2. This position was chosen as a more reliable and safer due to constant movements and obstructions, unnecessary hits in all areas. Battery life was not an essential part of the equipment. Its full capacity lifetime was enough to function regularly for the entire period of experimentation (8 000 mAh).

DL1 – MK2 data logger chosen because it allows all the data to be referenced to not just time, but also a position during the 3D movement. This allows the data to be interpreted in a strict understandable way, referenced clearly to the actual position and time stamp. Braking points and gripper usage was analyzed with the built-in 3-axis accelerometer enhanced for high downforce applications.

It is capable of detecting minute changes with a 100 Hz update rate on all attached sensors and accelerometer channels. It also provides 8 analog channels (with 0–20 V battery voltage) for sensor inputs ready for additional measurements and 2 CAN channel with up to 1 M baud rate with 14 CAN filter per channel (CAN 2.0 compatible). The logger itself has IP50 environmental protection (Fig. 2).

Fig. 2. Demonstration of the Data Acquisition sensory hardware placement on the crane spreader [11].

The spreader placement position was secured with handles, but due to the harsh working environment, it was decided to add additional protection via the secured hard plastic mounting case. The maximum power consumption is set to 1.6 W.

3 Theoretical Model of the Movement

To ensure a deeper understanding of the problem addressed in this work, we have analyzed the movement patterns for the quay cranes during the containers handling operations and made simulations with the lab tested equipment (Fig. 3). Here, on the right side of the figure under number - 1, we demonstrate the lab test-bed designed to simulate the movement pattern in a small-scale model, and under number - 2, we demonstrate the spreader with the movement control electronics attached.

We analyzed the theoretical part of the mechanics of the movement and the influence occurring during the actual procedures that affect the operator's actions (Fig. 4). These Figures provide casual movement patterns for loading and unloading procedures. Figure 4 also demonstrates the theoretical positional movement of the container unloading procedure which corresponds to the real-life case studies presented in Fig. 10.

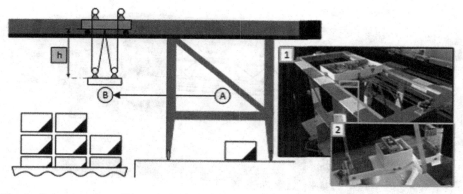

Fig. 3. Demonstration of the quay crane movement points (A and B) along the x-axis and the height h for y-axis movements [12].

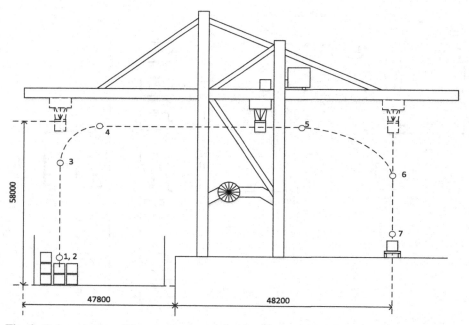

Fig. 4. Demonstration of the quay crane model with critical points of the movement of the spreader (1 to 7), showing the actual position of the container during these operations with the real.

The provided theoretical simulation model (Fig. 5) is yet to finish during the course of the project, but already, we can see the pattern of the movement, which in theory, could provide details and visual confirmation of the accuracy of the lab test-bed.

During the modeling phase, we have analyzed several velocity profiling models, and the best results were achieved using the S-shape velocity profiles, programmed suing MATLAB Simulink (Fig. 6).

284   S. Jakovlev et al.

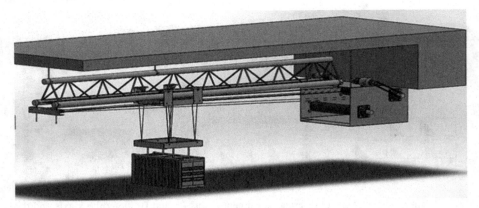

Fig. 5. Demonstration of the quay crane simulation model for the test-bed.

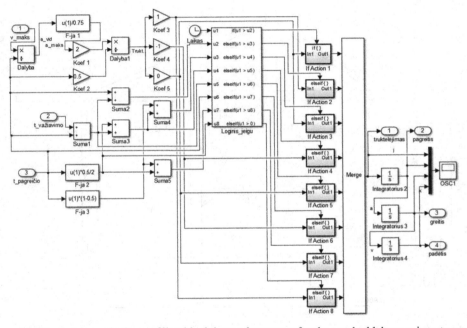

Fig. 6. S-shape velocity profiling block internal structure for the test-bed lab experiments.

The Simulink model has been tested with an S-shaped entry profile when the crane trolley control system is an open type (without feedback) and the crane spreader is with the load with a rope length of 1.9 m and the traveling speed is 0.2 m/s. The following Fig. 7 demonstrates the developed Simulation software used with the S-shape profile to simulate the velocity decrease during movements on the test-bed.

Also, during the simulation and test-bed experimentations, due to the absence of a controller, the spreader was delayed in responding to the control task, while using the

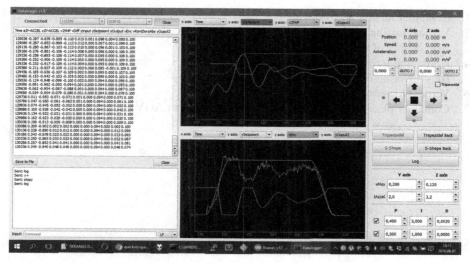

Fig. 7. Developed software for the simulations.

PID controllers, dynamic error reached a mere 1.3% that does not significantly affect system operations. The velocity of the load oscillations reaches almost 0.15 m/s and it dampens with the 7.7% percentage decrease for each amplitude of the oscillation with the 0.374 Hz frequency. We acknowledge, that in current systems, AI enriched control models may prove effective, but to the mechanical nature of the problem, the S-shape profile proved to be far more effective in real-time scenarios on the test-bed [12]. So, the conclusion is drawn, that future research will address the AI enrichment of the control units while making comparative analysis with the S-shape profiling method.

4   Experimental Measurement Results

The number of container loading and unloading measurements set to 278, due to port operations strict rules and cooperation agreements for the measurement period. Crane operators were warned that measurements took place during their working hours to avoid legal problems. During the meeting with the working crane operators and truck drivers (who are also AGV operators), discussions were made to address the importance of these measurements and to see the vector of improvement. Some of the crane operators even expressed appreciation for the research. Each measurement had its deviation and irregularity, considering the operator "best choice" scenario set by the operational manual. The following Figs. 8, 9 and 10 demonstrate the actual position of the ICT sensory unit during the case study in Klaipeda sea Port and the accelerations of the shipping container during movements.

The following figure shows the same pattern movement described by the theoretical model and the simulation using the velocity S-shape profiles. Each container varied in mass, therefore, the average mass of 20 metric tons considered for the mean calculations. At this exact measurement, the mass of the container was measured at 19.220 kg. Figures demonstrate 7 stages of operational consideration:

1. Container raising with hooking;
2. Vertical raising of the container;
3. Bias raising of the container;
4. Horizontal transportation of container;
5. Bias lowering of the container;
6. Vertical lowering of the container;
7. Container placement on the transport means (truck or AGV).

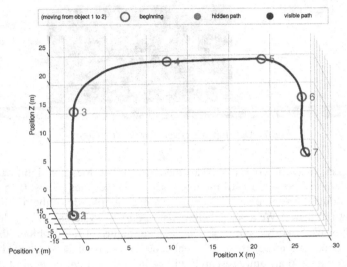

Fig. 8. Spreader position detection and movement points during the container unloading operation from the ship [13].

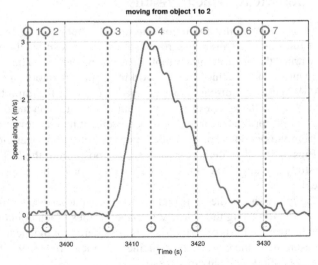

Fig. 9. Demonstration of spreader speed actual values during the 7 stages of operation [13].

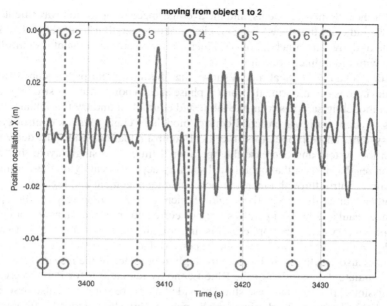

Fig. 10. Demonstration of spreader and container sway oscillation during the 7 stages of operation [13].

The following figures demonstrate the actual speed values during these 7 stages for the process, described in earlier that correlate with the theoretical research findings [11, 12]. These figures demonstrate the spreader and container sway oscillation values. These values are of high importance, because higher values correlate with the actual speed of the operation during the 7th stage, by lowering the speed of container positioning on the transport means or AGV. The overall transportation process is then prolonged to compensate the sway and keep up with the work standard for the safety of cargo and security of operation.

These operations are mostly synchronized with the on-site AGV operators and working standards to keep up with the ship unloading procedure. Yet, due to technological reasons, delays occur daily.

5 Conclusions

Initial results suggest that during the operator did not maintain the same speed during the horizontal transfer of the container. The operator made sudden joystick control movements to stop the transportation process for a short period. Figure 10 demonstrates the ladder shape of the speed values, which correlates with the initial suggestion. This is due to operator mistake, lack of experience, and unsynchronized actions between AGV or truck and the crane. Each ladder produces additional oscillation, which is kept up to the final 7th stage. The operational standard regulates the maximum speed of the spreader movement. Due to these factors, each container was transported with an average of 8.1

s delay for the 278 measurements, and the average speed of operation was calculated as 40.4 s. This indicates that the working efficiency of the operation is only 80%. Each crane is capable of delivering much more container if the operator movement is controlled by a system with pre-defined control models.

The developed theoretical model shows that the movement patterns are strict, and serious deviations occur during the control phase at each point. Authors strongly suggest using the modeling samples from the lab tested equipment and try to evaluate the possibilities to adapt using AI enriched control models in crane joystick control systems. Such a system can help operators in critical control situations and thus, decrease the stress on the system and decrease the operational time for a single cycle. Initial data collection results suggest that operational stability depends heavily on the optimization of operation control through inner transport chain management and regulations.

In other words, the productivity and efficiency of the crane rely on the operator experience. Faults done by operators are not corrected in a due manner, though new regulations and systems are applied. This, in turn, allows constant mistakes to happen and will provide other operators with false context data.

Authors also would like to indicate the high importance of the research done by the EU, to stimulate the adoption of the Blue Economy regulations for Ports to crease the CO_2 emissions [10]. The use case study provided in this research was also described in brief in [13] and can help to eliminate the human-machine boundaries for future control systems for heavy industry. These are the primary results gained after the initial testing of the equipment in the terminal. In the future work will include the examination of the AGV control models, as well as new methods to collect data, ranging from 5G to LoRaWAN networks. Additional AI models will be developed and taught during the experimental phase with the AGV and spreader to detect movement patterns remotely with a less than dynamic 1% error.

Acknowledgements. This research has received funding from European Regional Development Fund (project No 01.2.2-LMT-K-718–03-0001) under grant agreement with the Research Council of Lithuania (LMTLT).

References

1. Tuan, L.A., Cuong, H.M., Van Trieu, P., Nho, L.C., Thuan, V.D., Anh, L.V.: Adaptive neural network sliding mode control of shipboard container cranes considering actuator backlash. Mech. Syst. Signal Process. **112**, 233–250 (2018)
2. Golovin, I., Palis, S.: Robust control for active damping of elastic gantry crane vibrations. Mech. Syst. Signal Process. **121**, 264–278 (2019)
3. Henikl, J., Kemmetmüller, W., Kugi, A.: Modeling and simulation of large-scale manipulators with hydraulic actuation. IFAC Proc. **45**(2), 780–785 (2012)
4. Sha, M., et al.: Scheduling optimization of yard cranes with minimal energy consumption at container terminals. Comput. Ind. Eng. **113**, 704–713 (2017)
5. Jakovlev, S., et al.: Cargo container monitoring data reliability evaluation in WSN nodes. Elektron. ir Elektrotechnika **119**(3), 91–94 (2012). https://doi.org/10.5755/j01.eee.119.3. 1371

6. Andziulis, A., et al.: Priority based tag authentication and routing algorithm for intermodal containers RFID sensor network. Transport **27**(4), 373–382 (2012). https://doi.org/10.3846/16484142.2012.750622
7. Eglynas, T., Jakovlev, S., Bogdevičius, M., Didžiokas, R., Andziulis, A., Lenkauskas, T.: Concept of cargo security assurance in an intermodal transportation. In: Marine Navigation and Safety of Sea Transportation: Maritime Transport and Shipping (2013). https://doi.org/10.1201/b14960-39
8. Jakovlev, S., Bulbenkiene, V., Andziulis, A., Adomaitis, D.: E-services providing complex containers cargo conditions monitoring information system. In: International Conference on Management of Emergent Digital EcoSystems, MEDES'11, pp. 293–296 (2011). https://doi.org/10.1145/2077489.2077543
9. Jakovlev, S., Voznak, M., Andziulis, A., Kurmis, M.: Communication technologies for the improvement of marine transportation operations. IFAC Proc. (IFAC-PapersOnline) **46**(15), 469–474 (2013)
10. Kavakeb, S., Nguyen, T.T., McGinley, K., Yang, Z., Jenkinson, I., Murray, R.: Green vehicle technology to enhance the performance of a European port: a simulation model with a cost-benefit approach. Transp. Res. Part C Emerg. Technol. **60**, 169–188 (2015)
11. Jakovlev, S., Eglynas, T., Jusis, M., Gudas, S., Pocevicius E., Jankunas, V.: Analysis of the efficiency of quay crane control. In: 7th IEEE Workshop on Advances in Information, Electronic and Electrical Engineering (AIEEE), Liepaja, Latvia, pp. 1–3 (2019). https://doi.org/10.1109/AIEEE48629.2019.8977009
12. Eglynas, T., Jusis, M., Jakovlev, S., Senulis, A., Partila P., Gudas, S.: Research of quay crane control algorithm with embedded sway control sub-routine. In: 27th Telecommunications Forum (TELFOR), Belgrade, Serbia, pp. 1–4 (2019). https://doi.org/10.1109/TELFOR48224.2019.8971115
13. Jakovlev, S., Eglynas, T., Jusis, M., Gudas, S., Jankunas, V., Voznak, M.: Use case of quay crane container handling operations monitoring using ICT to detect abnormalities in operator actions. In: Proceedings of the 6th International Conference on Vehicle Technology and Intelligent Transport Systems - Volume 1: VEHITS, pp. 63–67 (2020). https://doi.org/10.5220/0008880700630067

Simulated Pedestrian Modelling for Reliable Testing of Autonomous Vehicle in Pedestrian Zones

Qazi Hamza Jan, Jan Markus Arnold Kleen[✉], and Karsten Berns[✉]

Technische Universität Kaiserslautern, Kaiserslautern, Germany
{hamza,j_kleen15,berns}@cs.uni-kl.de
http://www.agrosy.uni-kl.de

Abstract. Pedestrian zones are increasing in lengths and the relevant authorities are aiming at introducing autonomous vehicles to such zones for different purposes like transportation vehicles, delivery vehicles and cleaning vehicles. As the name suggests, pedestrian zones are crowded by pedestrian having highest priority. Vehicles in such zones should take special care regarding the safety of the people. Unlimited situations can occur from the pedestrians. Hence, it becomes crucial to test such vehicles before deploying in real-world to ensure safety of the people and the environment. Therefore, there is a need to have a realistic behaviors of pedestrians in simulation for critical testing of autonomous vehicles. The major novelty in this paper is the generation of virtual pedestrians which avoid obstacles realistically and to provide a platform for accurate and easy testing of autonomous vehicles in pedestrian zones. These virtual pedestrians avoid all kinds of obstacles based on self-awareness while progressing towards the goal. Main feature of these pedestrians are based on direction and speed heuristics. The goal is to have minimum number of parameters to generate test scenarios with realistic behaving pedestrians for autonomous systems. A thorough experimentation is done to validate the system. In the final experiment, a real-world scene is recreated from the simulation and the results are compared. It is seen visually that both the trajectories from the simulation and real-world highly resemble to each other. By slightly tweaking the parameters, one can generate different test scenario.

Keywords: Pedestrian simulation · Autonomous vehicles · Pedestrian zone · Virtual pedestrians

1 Introduction

With the increase usefulness of autonomous vehicles, the demand for these systems is increasing in different sectors such as agriculture, forestry, urban transport, construction and so on. In the past few years, demand for autonomous shuttles in pedestrian zones is also growing. Pedestrian zones are public areas reserved for pedestrians and prohibited for most of the auto-mobile traffic. These areas include city centres, tourist attractions, airports, university campuses and so on. Two main reasons for having autonomous shuttles in such zones is:

© Springer Nature Switzerland AG 2021
C. Klein et al. (Eds.): SMARTGREENS 2020/VEHITS 2020, CCIS 1475, pp. 290–307, 2021.
https://doi.org/10.1007/978-3-030-89170-1_15

- the difficulty in reaching from one point to another in pedestrian zones.
- lack of conventional transport system in such zones.

As the population is growing normal streets are converted to pedestrian zones in order to sustain the open environment. This will allow more accessibility and easy flow of huge crowds. To accomodate the elderly and disabled people to traverse such huge zones, it is relevant to have a particular transport system which can safely carry passengers through these crowded environments. Therefore, it becomes important to have a system which is safe and reliable and can carry people in a smooth manner. There are already few companies, for example, EasyMile [1] and Navya [2] which have autonomous vehicles in testing phase. These vehicles are driving in a restricted environment to verify its credibility. [3] shows lack of interaction could result in collision and how important it is to have interaction with the pedestrians.

Reliability and safety are crucial aspects when developing a system for autonomous shuttles in pedestrian zones. Pedestrians can include children, juveniles and senior. Different factors effect the behavior of such road user [17–19] Hence, these systems should ensure safety of pedestrians at all cost. For this reason, it becomes important to test the system thoroughly before launching in the real-world scenario. Since, the testing cannot be performed around real people due to high risk of system failure, therefore, we provide simulated pedestrians which exhibits a realistic behavior similar to pedestrians walking in pedestrian path for testing autonomous vehicles. These behaviors include avoiding vehicles in a uniform manner, going parallel to vehicle in a small area etc. Throughout the length of this paper, the simulated pedestrians will be called virtual pedestrians to differentiate between real-world pedestrians and simulated pedestrians. The simulated system should be capable of fast testing scenarios which include:

- fast generation of virtual pedestrians.
- randomness in their behavior.
- capability of avoiding static and dynamic obstacle.
- behavior avoidance for vehicles.
- moving of virtual pedestrians towards a specific goal.
- additional behaviors for virtual pedestrians like texting, talking on the phone and so on.

This work is the extension of already published paper [4]. This work addresses the problem of validating autonomous systems in the vicinity of pedestrians. This paper highlights a detailed description of generating virtual pedestrians for easy and quick testing of autonomous vehicles in a pedestrian zone. The generated virtual pedestrians have knowledge of their surroundings and can move on the given way-points. These virtual pedestrians can differentiate between other pedestrians and the vehicle to get a reasonable trajectory. Our simulation offers a variety of parameters to construct scenarios. The goal of this system is to have virtual pedestrians which mimic real-world pedestrians.

In the next section, related work specifically to pedestrian simulation in the domain of autonomous vehicles is presented. Following, a detailed description of methodology is discussed. Section 5 compares the results of our method with already existing methods. In the final section, we deduce the results for our virtual pedestrians.

2   Related Work

As already mentioned, autonomous vehicles are functioning more and more in pedestrian paths. Researchers are actively working on different navigation strategies. These navigation strategies include avoiding any kind of confusion with the pedestrian along with the continuous flow of the vehicle. The authors in [5] have focused on interaction modules to grab pedestrian's attention. This strategy is useful for crowded environment to avoid freezing robot problem. Their focus is also on pedestrian zone and they have performed experiments in simulated environment.

Carla [7], another open-source tool to support autonomous driving in simulation has recently been introduced. It provides different cities and town models along with variety of sensors. It also aims at facilitating autonomous driving system in urban environment. For realistic scenes in urban environment, Carla offers pedestrian on side-walks. The pedestrian modelled in Carla navigate by location based cost. Carla requires information of the town for example map for the navigation of virtual pedestrians. These virtual pedestrians are designed to walk on footpath and occasionally cross the road. They do not provide specific avoiding behavior of pedestrians to vehicle.

Some researchers are working on crowd evacuation models. Authors in [13] have used social force model in high density environment. They have modified social force model for bi-directional pedestrian streams. In [14], the authors have used residual network based scene-independent crowd simulation (ResNet-SICS) framework to simulate crowd simulation. It is a data driven approach in which data-driven crowd properties quantization (DCPQ) method is proposed. Authors in [15] have used virtual reality (VR) head-mounted display for pedestrian simulation. This enables simulation of pedestrians in virtual environment. Users can act as pedestrians, drive a car or just visualize a scene. They have a client-server architecture where the user can interact with each other. For crowd formation, it would require large number of people for testing. Hence, for dense crowd vehicle testing is not feasible.

A similar case for testing conflict of pedestrian and vehicle is presented in [16]. They have used Surrogate Safety Measures (SSMs) to validate Pedestrian Protection System (PPS). They have considered three SSMs; Pedestrian Classification Time to Collision (PCT), Total Braking Time to Collision (TBT) and Total Minimum Time to Collision (TMT). They have used PreScan for building the simulation. There some pedestrian simulation softwares like [20] used for planning, managing and optimizing pedestrian flow in urban environment in buildings. This simulation would be useful for vehicles inside buildings. But they do not offer high quality rendering. Another open-source framework for pedestrian simulation is [21]. It offers pedestrian dynamics at microscopic level. The models include gradient navigation model, social force model, and optimal steps model. For variety of situations, another pedestrian simulation tool [22] can be used. This simulation offers to study the flow of pedestrians. This software does not specializes in vehicle pedestrian interaction since we expect different reaction of pedestrians to a vehicle.

However, our system offers virtual pedestrians which can freely walk around a pedestrian path towards their goal point. They have high rendering and perform different animations like texting, talking on a phone etc.

3   System Architecture

Due to increase in pedestrian zone lengths and growth in automated systems, driver-less vehicles are surfacing in pedestrian zones as well. These vehicles can be delivery vehicles, transport vehicles or waste collection vehicles. Each vehicle has its own purpose and drives accordingly. For example, a delivery vehicle has to make way door to door to deliver packages. On contrary, transport vehicles need to carry passengers from one point to another. For all such vehicles it is observed that pedestrians show a common behavior. Pedestrians would always try to avoid colliding with all such vehicles only if they are aware of the approaching vehicle. For unaware pedestrians, it becomes important to either give signals from the vehicle or cross them safely from a side, if space available. Due to high dynamicity in pedestrian zones, all such vehicles are obligated to be tested thoroughly before inaugurating it for its main purpose. For testing, a similar virtual dynamic environment must be created.

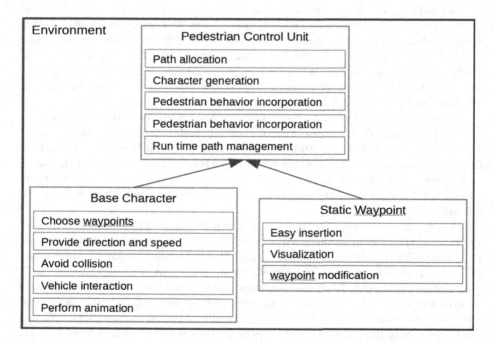

Fig. 1. A block diagram of the system is shown. It consists of three main modules. All the functionalities are enlisted in their respective module briefly [4].

This paper proposes to implement pedestrians in simulation for such driverless vehicles which are designed to navigate in pedestrian path. The main objective in designing such system is to provide virtual pedestrians with identical characteristics to that of real-world pedestrians. The fundamental behavior of the virtual pedestrians to account for is walking towards their goal and avoiding any kind of obstacle. For testing purposes, the system should provide flexibility to incorporate other behaviors as well. According to Federal Highway Administration University Course on Bicycle and Pedestrian Transportation [6], there exist pedestrians with different age groups. Based on their age group pedestrians have different actions and responses towards vehicles. The age groups are summarized in the following:

- Infants and toddler (age 0 to 4)
- Young children (age 5 to 12)
- Pre-teens (age 13 to 14)
- High school aged (age 15 to 18)
- Adults (age 19 to 40)
- Middles aged adults (ages 41 to 65)
- Senior Adults (ages 65+)

Based on the experience and peripheral vision, every age group reacts to a particular situation. Infant and toddlers are impulsive and unpredictable and are developing peripheral vision. Young children lack experience and short for drivers to see. Pre-teens also lack experience but ride more frequently under risky condition. They have a sense of invulnerability. High school aged are very active and are capable of travelling at higher speed. Adults are fully aware of traffic environment and interested in improving conditions. Whereas, middle aged adults may slowing of reflexes. The senior adults have difficulty hearing vehicles approaching from behind.

Therefore, it is essential to have different age groups of pedestrians in testing environment. This system develops virtual pedestrians that can be easily spawned in the environment and have randomness in their behaviors. It enables different crossing behaviors for the same trajectory of the vehicle and the same goal points of the virtual pedestrian. In addition, this behavior can be changed by changing the position of goal points which are discussed in detail in the later section.

Outline of our system architecture is given in Fig. 1. The figure shows main modules of the system in the environment. Each of the module is dependent on each other. The Pedestrian Control Unit (PCU) handles major of processing, i.e., from path allocation to run time path management. Base Character (BC) passes waypoints given from user interface in PCU to every virtual pedestrians. It also does the collision avoidance for each virtual pedestrian. Static Waypoint (SW) are separate unit which are automatically attached to the PCU. SW are the trajectory points on which virtual pedestrians are intended to navigate. Each module in the Fig. 1 has been explained in the following subsections.

For the sake of high quality perception, we have used Unreal Engine [8]. Unreal Engine is a state of the art gaming engine. It has a photo-realistic rendering, dynamic physics and effects and lifelike animations. It offers built-in class for character animation. Unreal engine uses Artificial Intelligence to perform certain actions. The decision making is done using behavior trees. It also uses artificial intelligence perception system to retrieve information from the environment. The collision avoidance in Unreal Engine is done using Reciprocal Collision Avoidance (RVO) [12]. This method is based on avoiding collision using velocity of the agents. Every agent should have information about the velocity of other agent. This is done by observing the velocity of other agent. No central coordination among the agents is required to solve the collision problem in RVO. Consequently, the agent can only observe the velocity of other agents. If all the agents select velocity other then the reciprocal velocity then it guarantees that the agent will not collide. Comparison of RVO method with our system is given in the experimentation.

3.1 Pedestrian Control Unit

PCU has been designed for managing all the virtual pedestrians in the environment. PCU acts as the main unit in all the modules given in Fig. 1. The idea to have a main unit is to make an interface where user can easily define parameters for test scenarios. This interface is made simple to accomodate all possible parameters. All the information given by the user is further carried out to other modules.

Suitable parameters are specified for a user to shape a scenario. Some fundamental parameters for scene creation are as following:

- number of pedestrians existing in the environment
- pedestrians existing as single or in group
- walking speed of virtual pedestrians
- type of animation required along with walking
- number of people in a group
- visible way points for debugging
- removal of virtual pedestrians after path completion

3.2 Base Character

Base Characters are the physical entity in the environment. To show the physical entity in the simulation, geometrical shapes exist in simulation. These pieces are known as mesh. Every model designed in Unreal Engine is a static mesh. These meshes can be made complex to clearly replicate a human. Advantage of the meshes in Unreal Engine is that it is rendered using graphic card, hence, enabling high quality replicas. For autonomous vehicle testing it becomes important to use these complex meshes to offer the system a realistic stream of virtual pedestrians. Later, these are used for object detection algorithms [9] and specifically for face detection [10].

3.3 Static Waypoint

When creating a test scenario, it is already defined where the virtual pedestrians can manuever. It is done by assigning them goal points. These goal points are known as Static Waypoint (SW). SWs are placed in the environment where the pedestrians are required to walk. Normally, they are placed on the pedestrian path where the vehicle is required to drive. For example, when placed exactly at the centre of the pedestrian path, the virtual pedestrians and vehicle always comes face to face. In this case either pedestrian or the vehicle has to give the way.

A threshold is defined to detect when the virtual pedestrian has reached the SW. This radius around the SW is known as epsilon. Every virtual pedestrian enters the radius of the SW at least once when following the path assigned. If the radius is large, the virtual pedestrians upon entering the radius of the SW directly turns towards the next SW. It would create problems at the corner SWs because the virtual pedestrian might walk outside of the pedestrian path to follow its trajectory if there is curvy path. If the radius is very less and there is an obstacle on the SW, then either the virtual pedestrians will wait for the SW to be cleared or go to the next SW after waiting too long. For testing purposes,

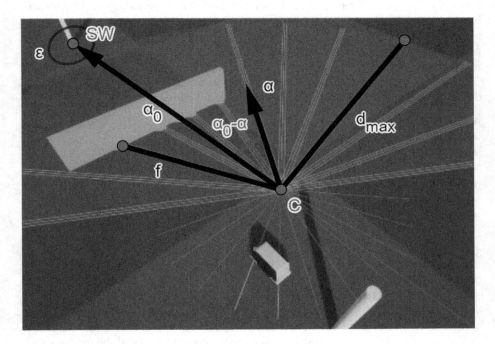

Fig. 2. Simulation view of virtual pedestrian c in the vicinit of vehicle and an obstacle. Two static waypoints as start and goal are show by cylinder shape. The maximum view of the virtual pedestrian c is d_{max}. α are the directions defined and α_0 is the direction towards the goal point. f is the distance to the obstacle [4].

it should be decided how big epsilon should be. For different values of epsilon, virtual pedestrians behaves differently.

Behavior of virtual pedestrians also depends on the placement of the SWs. The further the SWs are placed, easily the pedestrians give way to the vehicle. Nearer the SWs, more precisely the virtual pedestrians follows the path.

4   Proposed Approach

To provide a realistic testing platform for autonomous vehicle testing in a pedestrian path, we propose to generate virtual pedestrians that move along a predefined path and avoid obstacles on its way. This reaction is also observed in humans. Generally, a person tends to avoid collision with other people or any object in their path. This behavior can be achieved if the person is aware of its surrounding. For the same reason, the virtual pedestrians in the proposed approach are aware of its surrounding. It can sense the obstacles in their path.

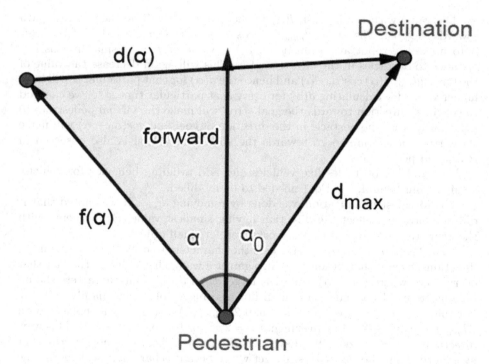

Fig. 3. To find the direction we use law of cosine. $d(\alpha)$ is the weighted distance towards the goal form the direction of α [4].

4.1 Walking Direction of Virtual Pedestrians

The direction of each virtual character is defined by using direction heuristics. At every time step, the virtual character has to re-evaluate its direction. It would calculate directions over its surrounding based on its awareness. As can be seen in Fig. 2, point c is the center of the virtual character from where it finds the direction. The green lines show the view of the virtual pedestrian. d_{max} is maximum distance the virtual pedestrian can sense. Discrete viewing angles have been defined by α, and α_0 is the direction to the goal point. We have used the minimization problem from [11].

$$d(\alpha) = d_{max}^2 + f(\alpha)^2 - 2d_{max}f(\alpha)\cos(\alpha_0 - \alpha) \qquad (1)$$

$f(\alpha)$ is the distance to collision in direction of α. As the angle from the goal point α increases, the $cos(\alpha_0 - \alpha)$ decreases making the whole term $2d_{max}f(\alpha)\cos(\alpha_0 - \alpha)$ in Eq. 1 to decrease. Hence, the weighted distance in direction $d(\alpha)$ for that particular angle will increase. This can be clearly seen in Fig. 3

The value with the highest $d(\alpha)$ is selected which will be the shortest path towards the goal. The term $2d_{max}f(\alpha)\cos(\alpha_0 - \alpha)$ is also effected by $f(\alpha)$. This is to make the robot avoid obstacles. If the value of $f(\alpha)$ is small means less distance to obstacles in the direction of α. This will again decrease the value of the term $2d_{max}f(\alpha)\cos(\alpha_0 - \alpha)$ and hence the $d(\alpha)$ for that particular α will have higher value. By calculating $d(\alpha)$ for every α at particular time step, we can find the optimal direction towards the goal. $f(\alpha)$ will make the virtual pedestrian to move away from the obstacle in the direction of goal and $cos(\alpha_0 - \alpha)$ will make the virtual pedestrian to go towards the goal. This action is also observed in real-world pedestrians.

To avoid big obstacles like vehicles and add avoiding behavior for vehicles coming from behind, the Eq. 1 needed to be modified.

The foremost modification was done by removing d_{max}^2. It was noted that it did not have any effect the direction having smallest value. Experiments with the heuristics determined that it works well for small objects.

Next, $2d_{max}f(\alpha)\cos(\alpha_0 - \alpha)$ causes the characters to only choose very direct directions, even if that means walking against a wall. This is due to the fact that every $d(\alpha)$, where $(\alpha_0 - \alpha) > 90°$, is larger than $d(\alpha_0)$. But characters should be able to avoid not only very small but also bigger obstacles mainly vehicles. For this reason, $\alpha_0 - \alpha$ is valued less and $2d_{max}f(\alpha)\cos(\alpha_0 - \alpha)$ is replaced with $2d_{max}f(\alpha)\cos(\frac{\alpha_0 - \alpha}{x})$. In experiments $x = 2$ seems to work quite well. This way, directions with $(\alpha_0 - \alpha) > 90°$ have a chance to be picked. It is noteworthy that avoidance of small objects does not get worse because characters still choose the most direct direction. Hence, the Eq. 1 is modified to Eq. 2.

$$d(\alpha) = f(\alpha)^2 - 2d_{max}f(\alpha)\cos(\frac{\alpha_0 - \alpha}{x}) \qquad (2)$$

As already mentioned, the reaction of real-world pedestrians to static and dynamic obstacles is always different. For the static obstacle, they feel easy passing nearby but when subjected to a vehicle, these pedestrians have mixed reactions. Normally, they already set out a way for the vehicle to pass. On this account, $f(\alpha)^2$ is added to Eq. 2. This ensures that the virtual pedestrian will not collide with the vehicle. If there is no other way to avoid the vehicle then the virtual pedestrian will choose a different walking speed. A sample of implementation is shown in Fig. 4.

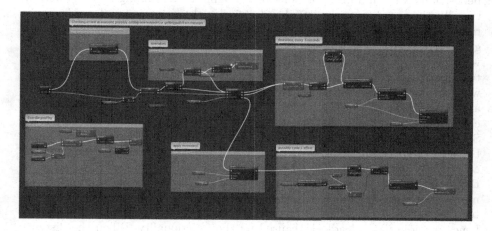

Fig. 4. Direction heuristics implementation in Unreal Engine using blueprints.

4.2 Walking Speed of Virtual Pedestrians

Since it is impossible to assign walking speed to countless virtual pedestrians, a range of walking speed is given. The upper and lower limit of the walking speed range for every virtual pedestrian is defined by the user. A preferred walking speed v_{pref} is defined and used as the upper limit for every virtual pedestrian. Velocity for every virtual pedestrian is then calculated as:

$$v = \min(v_{pref}; \frac{f(\alpha)}{t_{coll}}) \tag{3}$$

A constant minimum time to collision t_{coll} is always positive, so the character can never walk against any obstacle. The virtual pedestrian waits if the vehicle crosses the chosen direction of the pedestrian, similar to a pedestrian crossing a road in real life. For near moving vehicle v is set to zero.

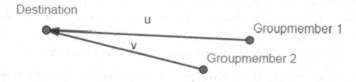

Fig. 5. The distance to group for group member 2 is $\|u - v\|$ [4].

Grouping of Virtual Pedestrians. When driving a vehicle in a pedestrian zone, different interactions can occur with pedestrians. One aspect of these interactions depends on the number of pedestrians in the environment. Pedestrians are walking in singles or a group. Single pedestrians have their independent path whereas pedestrians in a group need to remain together. Virtual pedestrians in a group walk on their own and there is no central decision-maker. Making virtual pedestrians walk in a group is done by changing their walking speeds. Conventionally, the speed for each virtual pedestrian in the group is equal, so the group remains together. It can happen that virtual pedestrian can walk away from the group. For such a scenario, the character who is away from the group needs to wait for the whole group. But being in the group every virtual pedestrian needs to respect each other personal space similar to real-world pedestrians. To know when a character needs to wait, two constants are defined; a preferred distance and a maximum distance to the group. Figure 5 shows how these distances are calculated. Considering that every member of the group should have the same SW. Here the distance of every virtual pedestrian to the group is the difference between the personal distance to current SW and the maximum distance to the current SW in the group. The reason to measure distance in this way is to allow the group to split or walk around the obstacle. This behavior is important for narrow paths where vehicle crosses from the center. This check always guarantees that at least one member of the group is not waiting for the whole group, hence, avoiding any deadlocks caused by the functionality. When the distance between the character and group increases, the character waits for the group by looking towards the group. As the group reaches the near the distant character and maximum distance becomes equal to the preferred distance, the character starts walking at its regular speed.

In PCU, the grouping behavior can be selected. There is an option to enable or disable grouping behavior. When enabled, also designate the number of groups and how many characters in a group.

5 Experiments

Pedestrian zones mainly involve pedestrians. Each of these pedestrians acts differently. There is very little probability that a pedestrian going towards the same goal at different times will react to a certain situation in exactly the same way. Due to this reason, there is an indefinite number of reactions from a single situation happening repeatedly. These reactions depend on the size of the crowd, the maturity of people, their motives, and awareness level.

In order to validate the virtual pedestrian's behavior, we have conducted several experiments that include experiments from individual characters to a group of characters and from tackling static obstacles to dynamic obstacles.

5.1 Two Individual Characters and a Vehicle Crossing

A test scenario is created which involves two individual virtual pedestrians crossing a vehicle from the front. This test is done to comprehend the behavior of

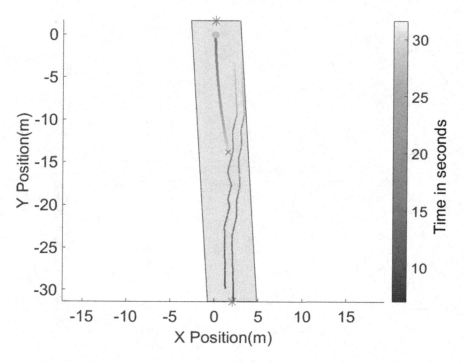

Fig. 6. Time-plot of two individual characters crossing a vehicle from the front [4].

single virtual pedestrians in a pedestrian zone. A time-plot of the test is shown in Fig. 6.

The gray color presents the pedestrian zone where the virtual pedestrians cannot strictly walk out of the area. The lower and upper red stars are the start and goal static waypoint respectively. The green dot and red cross is the start and goal point of the vehicle respectively. It can be noticed that as the characters walk towards the goal SW, it can realize the approaching vehicle from the front. The characters do not wait for the vehicle to get near rather they in advance start making way for the vehicle to pass. In this test, the vehicle was intentionally steered towards virtual pedestrians to analyze their behavior. The more vehicle is steered towards the characters, the more characters go away from the path. Both virtual pedestrians adopt almost the same pattern.

5.2   Group of Virtual Pedestrians

As defined earlier, group of virtual pedestrians are number of pedestrians which remain together. In order to analyse the grouping behavior of characters, two different situations are considered.

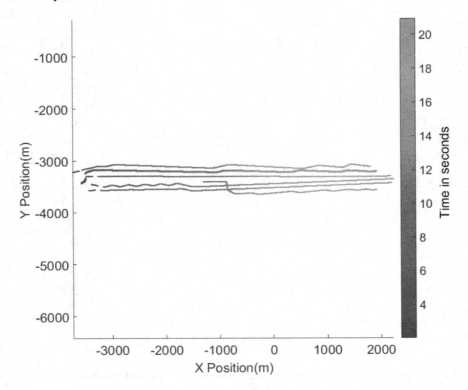

Fig. 7. Group of characters walking towards the goal without obstacle.

Group of Characters Without Obstacle. Firstly, group of six virtual pedestrians are spawned in an open environment as can be seen in Fig. 7. These virtual pedestrians simply walk from start to goal SW. It can be observed that one virtual pedestrian at 12 s waits for the whole group. As the group approaches, the character starts walking along. There is also randomness in their path. This is also realistic since people sometimes change position during their walk.

Group of Characters with Obstacle. Secondly, group of five virtual pedestrians are spawn in open environment. However, there is a static obstacle in red shown in Fig. 8. As the virtual pedestrians are spawned, they directly walk towards the corner of the obstacle. Despite having an obstacle in their path, the virtual pedestrians remain in a tight group and in between they change their position. This kind of stochasticity of individual pedestrian in the group is routinely observed in real world situation.

5.3   Comparison with Real World Pedestrians

To validate our system, we compare it with the real world pedestrians. Our campus is modeled in the simulation as can be seen in Fig. 9. The same area in

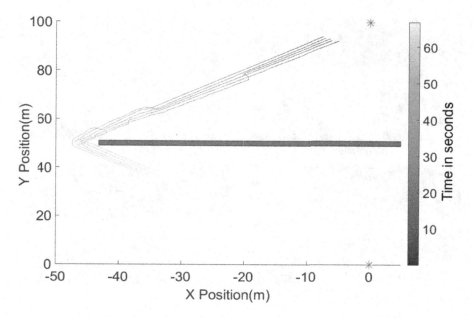

Fig. 8. Group of characters walking towards the goal with obstacle [4].

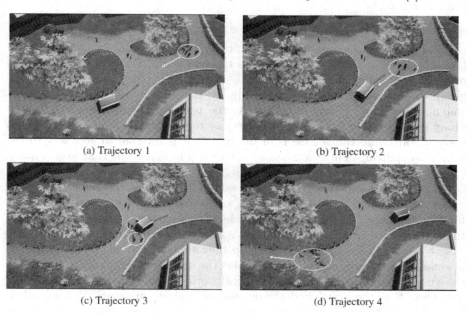

(a) Trajectory 1

(b) Trajectory 2

(c) Trajectory 3

(d) Trajectory 4

Fig. 9. Group of six characters walking towards an approaching vehicle in a narrow pedestrian zone [4].

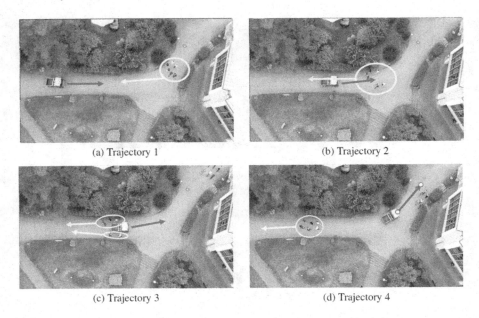

(a) Trajectory 1   (b) Trajectory 2

(c) Trajectory 3   (d) Trajectory 4

Fig. 10. Group of six pedestrians walking towards an approaching vehicle in a narrow pedestrian zone.

the real world can be seen in Fig. 10. Initially, testing is done in simulation and later the same scenario is re-created in the real-world. Figure 9 shows a group of six characters walking towards a goal. A vehicle is made to pass through this group to see a splitting behavior. In Fig. 9a, the yellow circle shows characters walking in a group in one direction. As the vehicle approaches in Fig. 9b, the group starts to split in advance to give way to the vehicle. Since the path has a small width and the vehicle is in the center, it is rational to give way to the vehicle by splitting. This phenomenon is seen in Fig. 9c. As the vehicle goes away, the group joins together.

In real-world experimentation, the same location and the same number of pedestrians are told to walk towards the same goal point as in simulation. It can be seen from the Fig. 10 that as the vehicle approaches, the pedestrians show the same behavior done in simulation. Although they do not cross the vehicle exactly at the same location neither do they split exactly in the same way as in simulation but overall behavior remains the same. It is impossible to recreate the same situation from simulation to real-world and vice versa. From Fig. 10a, it is clear that the group pedestrians and vehicle are approaching each other. The vehicle in this experiment is driven by a driver. In Fig. 10b, the pedestrians become aware of the vehicle and start splitting. Figure 10c shows almost similar trajectories as Fig. 9c in simulation. And finally, all the pedestrians get together in the last image.

5.4   Comparison with RVO

This paper also compares our virtual pedestrians with characters using RVO offered by Unreal Engine. The comparison can be seen in the plot shown in Fig. 11. Two virtual pedestrians of our system and two characters using RVO are made to cross each other. The above trajectories crossing each other is from our virtual pedestrians and the lower two trajectories from the RVO method. Our system equally shares the same responsibility to avoid each other, whereas, in RVO method one of the virtual pedestrian changes its trajectories. The other one does not even slightly change.

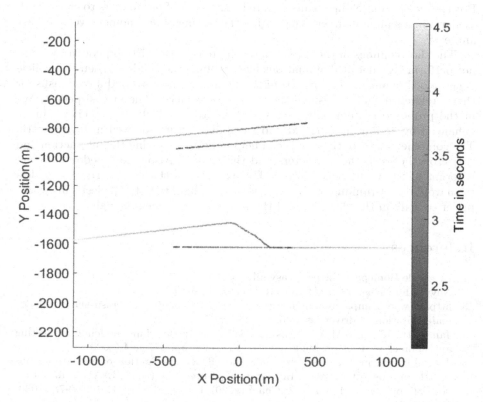

Fig. 11. Group of six pedestrians walking towards an approaching vehicle in a narrow pedestrian zone.

6   Conclusion

This paper proposes and implements virtual pedestrians in simulation, which is easily configurable for continuous testing. The generated virtual pedestrians possess realistic characteristics in terms of interacting with the vehicle and other pedestrians. These interactions include avoiding vehicles, crossing vehicles from a safe distance, going nearby vehicles when there is no space. From the experiments, it can be inspected that characters for different instances show reasonable behaviors, which is also expected in the real-world. The plots in Fig. 6 demonstrates that the characters distinguish between static and dynamic obstacle by giving way beforehand. The virtual pedestrians in plot 8 show the grouping behavior and how important it is to remain together to form the group. Also, the group passes around the obstacle to follow the shortest distance towards the goal. These behaviors are normally expected in humans when they want to cross a vehicle or wall in their path. Finally, a comparison with the real-world situation is done in Fig. 9 where the same scenario was recreated from Fig. 10. Both show very matching results. There is a number of parameters to create each scenario in a simple manner. This makes the testing of autonomous vehicles fast and easy.

The shortcomings in the given approach are that the virtual pedestrians cannot perform very detailed animations like grabbing the children when the vehicle is nearby. Humans use other gestures for communication to find a consensus for their preference while crossing other people or vehicles. The virtual pedestrians in the proposed system only uses visual aid to avoid obstacles. They can be enhanced by adding hearing aid and signaling gestures as well in future work. The combined effect of these aids can help in better realizing the interaction and trajectory between the characters and the vehicle. Also, these pedestrians are ignorant of the weather conditions. For example, if the rain starts, the pedestrian would start running or if there is strong sunlight then the pedestrians would prefer to walk in the shade even if the route becomes long enough.

References

1. EasyMile Homepage. https://easymile.com/
2. Navya Homepage. https://navya.tech/en/usecases/city/
3. https://www.tampabay.com/news/perspective/a-google-cars-crash-shows-the-real-limitation-of-driverless-vehicles/2267980/
4. Jan, Q.H., Kleen, J.M.A., Berns, K.: Self-aware pedestrians modeling for testing autonomous vehicles in simulation. In: VEHITS, pp. 577–584 (2020)
5. Jan, Q.H., Klein, S., Berns, K.: Safe and efficient navigation of an autonomous shuttle in a pedestrian zone. In: Berns, K., Görges, D. (eds.) RAAD 2019. AISC, vol. 980, pp. 267–274. Springer, Cham (2020). https://doi.org/10.1007/978-3-030-19648-6_31
6. Turner, S., Sandt, L., Toole, J., Benz, R., Patten, R.: Federal Highway Administration University Course on Bicycle and Pedestrian Transportation. Publication No. FHWA-HRT-05-133. US Department of Transportation (2006)
7. Dosovitskiy, A., Ros, G., Codevilla, F., Lopez, A., Koltun, V.: CARLA: an open urban driving simulator. arXiv preprint arXiv:1711.03938 (2017)
8. EasyMile Homepage. https://www.unrealengine.com/en-US/
9. Molchanov, V.V., Vishnyakov, B.V., Vizilter, Y.V., Vishnyakova, O.V., Knyaz, V.A.: Pedestrian detection in video surveillance using fully convolutional YOLO neural network. In: Automated Visual Inspection and Machine Vision II, vol. 10334, p. 103340Q. International Society for Optics and Photonics (2017)

10. Sun, X., Wu, P., Hoi, S.C.H.: Face detection using deep learning: an improved faster RCNN approach. Neurocomputing **299**, 42–50 (2018)
11. Moussaïd, M., Helbing, D., Theraulaz, G.: How simple rules determine pedestrian behavior and crowd disasters. Proc. Nat. Acad. Sci. **108**(17), 6884–6888 (2011)
12. Lake, A.T.: Reciprocal collision avoidance and navigation for video games (2012)
13. Taherifar, N., Hamedmoghadam, H., Sree, S., Saberi, M.: A macroscopic approach for calibration and validation of a modified social force model for bidirectional pedestrian streams. Transportmetrica A Transp. Sci. **15**(2), 1637–1661 (2019)
14. Yao, Z., Zhang, G., Dianjie, L., Liu, H.: Learning crowd behavior from real data: a residual network method for crowd simulation. Neurocomputing **404**, 173–185 (2020)
15. Perez, D., Hasan, M., Shen, Y., Yang, H.: AR-PED: Augmented Reality Enabled Pedestrian-in-the-Loop Simulation. No. 19–06083 (2019)
16. Alghodhaifi, H., Lakshmanan, S.: Simulation-based model for surrogate safety measures analysis in automated vehicle-pedestrian conflict on an urban environment (Conference Presentation). In: Autonomous Systems: Sensors, Processing, and Security for Vehicles and Infrastructure 2020, vol. 11415, p. 1141504. International Society for Optics and Photonics (2020)
17. Ishaque, M.M., Noland, R.B.: Behavioural issues in pedestrian speed choice and street crossing behaviour: a review. Transp. Rev. **28**(1), 61–85 (2008)
18. Willis, A., Gjersoe, N., Havard, C., Kerridge, J., Kukla, R.: Human movement behaviour in urban spaces: implications for the design and modelling of effective pedestrian environments. Environ. Plan. B Plan. Des. **31**(6), 805–828 (2004)
19. Harrell, W.A.: Factors influencing pedestrian cautiousness in crossing streets. J. Soc. Psychol. **131**(3), 367–372 (1991)
20. https://www.anylogic.com/airports-stations-shopping-malls/
21. http://www.vadere.org/
22. https://www.oasys-software.com/products/pedestrian-simulation/

The Impact of COVID-19 Experience on Smart City and Future Mobility

Oleg Gusikhin[(✉)](ORCID)

Global Data Insight and Analytics, Ford Motor Company,
22001 Michigan Avenue, Dearborn, MI, USA
ogusikhi@ford.com

Abstract. This paper discusses the challenges and opportunities of the existing technologies and practices in the context of Smart City and Future Mobility to cope with pandemics. The overview shows a need to accelerate the deployment of Smart City and Smart Mobility technologies and revisit strategic supply chain planning models. It shows that advancements in IoT, communication, AI and Analytics play a crucial role in enabling rapid innovation in order to address immediate needs raised by COVID-19. The overview and discussion focus on five areas: Smart City Technologies, Robust Supply Chain of critical items, Smart Mobility, Connected and Intelligent Vehicles, and Ambient Intelligence.

Keywords: COVID-19 · Smart city · Robust supply chain · Smart mobility · Connected vehicles · Ambient intelligence

1 Introduction

In just a short period of time, COVID-19 has changed the lives of people around the globe. In the absence of a vaccine, society has focused on mitigation actions, such as contact tracing, surveillance, social distancing, hygiene, quarantine, and masks. Each of these response actions created significant opportunities and expectations for applications of advanced technology, including the Internet of Things (IoT), Analytics, Artificial Intelligence (AI), Robotics, and Smart Mobility.

On one hand, technology and business innovations of the last decade help to endure the challenges of the pandemic. For example, the abundance of online delivery services provided a critical lifeline for the replenishment of food, medication and household items while complying with a shelter-in place order. Established businesses like Amazon, FedEx, UPS as well as the relatively new entrants Door Dash, Postmates, and Grab, all experienced surge in demand and growth. Video conferencing and cloud computing allowed to keep workers productive operating from home offices. Social media keeps friends and family connected. Wearables and contactless health monitoring, Medical Chatbots, telemedicine addresses many personal healthcare needs without the risk of virus exposure during medical office visit. Additive manufacturing helped alleviate the shortages of critical supply, such as face shields and masks.

C. Klein et al. (Eds.): SMARTGREENS 2020/VEHITS 2020, CCIS 1475, pp. 308–321, 2021.
https://doi.org/10.1007/978-3-030-89170-1_16

Analytics and AI are being brought to the forefront to address a variety of challenges posed by the pandemic. They guide governments and businesses in assessing risks, coordinating mitigation actions and planning the recovery. Scientists around the world are actively trying to harness AI to accurately forecast the virus spread, develop a vaccine, or create new testing methods.

On the other hand, the outbreak highlighted significant gaps in societal readiness to address pandemic challenges. It raised a new set of priorities for future research and development to efficiently address a potential second wave and to better prepare for any future outbreaks. In the meantime, there are many ongoing attempts for a rapid innovation to leverage already existing tech in new ways, identify and expand best practices, reprioritize and pull ahead promising development close to production-ready stage, and revisit failed processes and strategies.

This paper focuses on the effect of COVID-19 on Smart City and Future Mobility technology and practices. Section 2 overviews challenges and opportunities of leveraging Smart City Technology in an attempt to better predict and contain the virus spread. Section 3 discusses the need for municipalities to insure the robustness of the supply chain of critical items, leveraging the capabilities of the local manufacturing base to fulfill the shortages in the time of global crisis. Section 4 discusses the effect of the pandemic on different smart mobility options. Section 5 overviews connected and intelligent vehicle features and services that can be useful in times of pandemic and social distancing. Section 6 discusses how elevated hygiene risk awareness may change user experience requirements to Human Machine Interface (HMI) and Ambient Intelligence, specifically in application to ride-hailing services and shared autonomous vehicles. Finally, the conclusion summarizes key points of the discussion.

2   Smart City Technology

As COVID-19 is spreading around the world, many cities and governments are trying to leverage their digitization investments and are turning to existing Smart City Technologies [16] to help better prepare and limit the spread of the virus. Smart City Technologies, combining Internet of Things, Communications, Cloud Computing and Data Analytics, enable comprehensive modeling, forecasting and decision analysis. They also appear to have a promise to tackle contact tracing, enforcement of social distancing and quarantine orders and public risk screening, although, many of those attempts draw strong criticism from privacy advocates raising legitimate concerns about protection and safety of personal information.

The ubiquity of smart phones and their capabilities to track location and proximity interactions with other phones make them a viable tool to identify potential virus exposures and communicate alerts for a need of testing or self-quarantine. The aggregated geolocation data, collected from individual phones, has been widely used for years for real-time traffic or to determine busy times of businesses and public places. For COVID-19, using this aggregated data Google and Apple released downloadable Community Mobility Reports that highlight movement-trend differences at country, state, county or regional levels. This aggregated data can be very valuable for epidemiology models to better track disease spread and localize the outbreaks [13]. To take more radical measures, a number of countries implemented more pervasive individual geolocation tracking with different degrees of privacy protection.

The efficiency of the phone-based tracking method depends on the penetration of the apps among the community. That in turn depends on the social responsibilities of the citizens and the trust in the service providers for protection of private data. The team of MIT researchers [15] suggests that the efficient contact tracing tools should be citizen-centric, privacy-first solutions that are open source, secure, and decentralized. Despite the promise of the technology, the efficacy app-based contact tracing has not been proven in many countries. As an alternative, many businesses deployed contact tracing and social distancing warnings using proprietary wearable devices to insure the safe return to work practices.

Camera-based surveillance and video analytics is another technology that cities are trying to explore. For example, camera-based system and face recognition have been used to enforce self-quarantine orders and identify the violators. Thermal imaging technology is also gaining a momentum enabling the efficient screening for potential fervor from a distance. Recently, potential for wastewater surveillance emerged as a complimentary tool to measure the presence of infectious diseases in cities or municipalities [23]. Another promising approach is analytics of wearables data. [14] reports that the analysis of aggregated Fitbit resting heart rate trends can possibly improve real-time and geographically refined influenza surveillance.

Although these technologies have limitations, according to reports, each of them had some degree of success at different stages of virus spread. It is very likely that they provided a sizable contribution to the overall flattening of the curve. The advantage of the combined implementation of these technologies is the ability to collect a more accurate and comprehensive data set for analytics modeling and reporting. However, the public privacy concern is one of the biggest challenges that needs to be addressed for the wide deployment of electronic surveillance.

3   Resilient Supply Chain of Critical Items

One of the biggest issues raised by the pandemic is the resilience of the supply chain of critical items. In the face of the pandemic, one of the key themes across the globe was the shortage of critical medical supplies such as face masks, hand sanitizers, COVID-19 test kits, and ventilators.

To address severe medical shortages, the US Center for Disease Control (CDC) updated the Personal protective equipment (PPE) usage guidelines to incorporate contingency and crisis strategies that can help to stretch critical supplies. These strategies include PPE reuse guidance and the use of PPE procured from sources not regulated by Food and Drug Administration (FDA), including public donations and the local manufacturing base. To ramp up the local production of critical medical supply, the FDA has temporarily loosened restrictions on who can make medical devices and PPE and provisioned emergency use authorization.

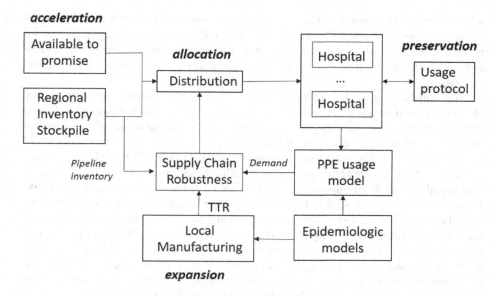

Fig. 1. Model of robust supply chain of critical items.

Many private businesses repurposed their production capacity to fulfill the urgent need of frontline workers. Fashion and apparel companies make face masks and medical gowns, perfume makers and distilleries produce hand sanitizer, and automotive companies manufacture face shields, respirators and mechanical ventilators. Hundreds of companies with additive manufacturing equipment mobilized to join the effort to fulfill the needs for PPE. At the end of March 2020, the Federal Emergency Management Agency (FEMA) established a Supply Chain Stabilization Task Force to close the gap between what private sector can provide and the needs of healthcare end-users by applying the four-prong approach of Preservation, Acceleration, Expansion and Allocation [4].

[20] overviews a comprehensive set of supply chain vulnerability analysis and mitigation methods. Specifically, an advance warning and forecast along with alternative sourcing arrangements are critical tools during an unprecedented surge of demand and global supply chain disruption. [12] presents the framework of a viable supply chain that adapts three structural designs–agility-oriented, resilience-oriented, and survival-oriented–based on the operating environment. The COVID-19 global supply chain disruption is an example of a survival-oriented environment. That is when the regular sources of the supply chain are unavailable, and the system may seek alternative, potentially non-traditional supply sources (such as automotive companies producing PPE and ventilators), employ strict rationing of the product between customers, and utilize strategies to reduce the demand (such as PPE reuse and flattening the curve). COVID-19 has demonstrated how the supply chain of critical items switched into a survival-oriented mode of operation. This transition, however, has been happening in an

ad-hoc basis. For several weeks, the front-line workers dealing with COVID-19 patients experienced significant shortages of PPEs. Consequently, it is crucial to establish the framework that will guide the authorities to control the switch between different modes of Supply Chain operation in a timely and coordinated manner.

[19] emphasized the need for governments to establish a stress tests for supply chain of critical goods and services similar to the stress tests for banks instituted after the 2008 financial crisis. The authors also outlined one of the efficient frameworks to analyze the robustness of supply chain that is based on the concepts of time-to-survive (TTS) and time-to-recovery (TTR) [18]. TTS is the maximum amount of time the system can function without performance loss if a supply of a particular item is disrupted. In the case of emergency planning, TTS should be calculated as the available pipeline inventory divided by expected daily consumption that can be determined from epidemiological models. TTR represents the time which takes the supplier to recover to full functionality, or in the case of a consumption surge, the time to ramp up the production to fulfill new demand level. In the case of global supply chain disruption, TTR may mean the time to establish alternative or supplemental sources of production and procurement. It may include the time to establish the production of critical items by the local manufacturing base from the abundance of raw materials and components. The robust supply chain is defined as the case when $TTR < TTS$.

For example, Ford ramped up the production of face masks to 225,000 per day in less than two weeks from the kick-off the project [5]. Using this as TTR, public health administrations can determine when healthcare providers should switch to contingency or crisis item usage strategies or how to distribute the existing pipeline inventory (Fig. 1).

Large companies, such as Ford or General Motors, can rapidly develop the production of necessary supplies by utilizing their extensive resources: engineering talent, manufacturing capabilities, purchasing, and logistics networks. Additionally, there is an extensive network of small manufacturers, including facilities with 3D printing equipment. In contrast to large companies, many small manufacturers could not address the problem alone but may set up production as a coalition. In order to efficiently leverage the network of small businesses, local administrations need to integrate and coordinate diverse production capabilities, design and engineering services, and logistics.

In order to efficiently incorporate local manufacturing capabilities into city emergency planning, city administration should create and maintain maps of local manufacturing capabilities into the needs of healthcare providers. This map should include an estimate of the TTR for each product. Assessing the existing medical supply chain for different scenarios of inventory usage will provide the TTS values. Comparing those TTR and TTS parameters for each of the critical items can help cities to estimate gaps in the current supply and local production capabilities and to take appropriate long-term, medium-term, and short-term mitigation actions, respectively: incentivizing private businesses in the development of needed capabilities, setting appropriate inventory levels of critical items, and determining the times switch to PPE conservation protocols and the times to initiate local production (Fig. 1).

4   Smart Mobility

Public transit is a major source of concern during the pandemic. Public transport presents a significant risk for virus spread. On the other hand, it is needed for essential employees to commute to work. Consequently, it is critical to maintain steady and safe operation of public transit with proper disinfection and driver protection protocols. To reduce the potential of virus exposure it is necessary to control the flow of passengers to provision maintenance of social distancing. Different cities implemented different approaches: from complete shutdown in Wuhan to increasing transportation frequency in Copenhagen.

Social distancing and quarantine orders are changing the transit demand pattern: while many businesses and entertainment venues are closing, destinations serving essential businesses may experience an increase in passengers. The transportation agencies need to dynamically adapt to the changes by altering schedules and routes. This requires the system that can optimize new schedules subject to new capacity constrains as well as the means to efficiently communicate those changes to commuters.

The cities that implemented integrated multi-modal transportation systems may leverage its capabilities by controlling the flow of passengers, providing tracking of potential coronavirus exposures and efficiently communicating dynamic changes in routes and schedules. For example, Mobility Broker [2], implemented in city of Aachen, Germany provides a single app to access city buses, trams, rail, shared bikes and shared cars. Most of municipal employees, faculty and students of Aachen University as well as many citizens are subscribers for the Mobility Broker. In the case of a pandemic, the city can leverage the Mobility Broker to control the access to public transportation and limit the number of passengers for each ride. The system will also help to insure the cleaning between the rides on a shared vehicle or bike. Non-essential personnel may be granted a limited number of rides at certain times for specific routes for trips to grocery stores, pharmacies or to care for elders. The Mobility Broker can be also efficiently used to track potential exposures to COVID-19. When one of the passengers tests positive for coronavirus, his/her routes can be matched with the routes of other passengers and notifications alerts can be sent through the app.

Taxi and Ride-hailing services are the most affected sectors of smart mobility. At the same time, as the demand on ride hailing services plummeted, the demand for home deliveries is soared. For example, Uber reported that in the second quarter of 2020, its mobility gross booking fell 75% compared to 2019, while its delivery services grew 106% [21]. The mobility companies that diversified their business are shifting their capacity to delivery services. Uber in addition to Uber Eats, launched two new services: Uber Connect that delivers non-food items from selected retailers and Uber Direct that allows people to post the packages to relatives and friends.

The pandemic highlighted opportunities and challenges for autonomous vehicles. There are many reports from China describing the use of autonomous vehicles to deliver food, medication, and tests to the areas significantly affected by the virus. Mayo Clinic in Florida uses the NAVYA autonomous shuttles to transport samples between test sites and laboratory to limit potential coronavirus exposure. However, most of the major developers of autonomous vehicles suspended their testing as it requires a safety driver on board of each vehicle and significant back office personnel.

One of the approaches that can accelerate the deployment of driverless vehicles on public roads is teleoperation. There is already a number of companies that provide teleoperation services to the autonomous vehicle industry. In the long run, the idea is to create centralized teleoperation centers where one person has the potential to help several vehicles and thus reduce the number of safety drivers required [3]. During pandemic time, the benefits of individual transportation may easily justify the expense of even one-to-one pairing of a teleoperator with each vehicle.

5   Connected and Intelligent Vehicles

The pandemic experience showed that it may be too early to dismiss the value of personal vehicle as a thing of the past in favor of new shared mobility models. Personal vehicles present a safer alternative to shared mobility to travel to grocery, pharmacy or to work location to perform an essential job. Connected Vehicles technology and telematics services may play a considerable role in maintaining vehicle operational reliability, reducing insurance expenses due to reduction of driving activity, minimizing the need for physical contact in drive-through services or serve as a conduit for integrated digital health applications.

"Shelter in place" orders resulted in significant drop in the driving of majority of the population. One way to translate this decreased mileage into reduced premium on vehicle insurance is through usage-based coverage offered by many insurance companies. Typically, this type of insurance requires installation of the telematics dongle provided by the insurance company that can remotely monitor mileage and behaviors. The embedded telematics may substantially simplify switching to usage based insurance. For example, Ford launched collaboration with the Nationwide SmartRide program starting with 2020 Ford and Lincoln vehicles that leverage vehicle embedded modem. Signing up for this type of insurance can be done merely using owner FordPass or LincolWay app.

In the case of prolonged vehicle parking, it is recommended to start the vehicle at least once a week to maintain its condition. Connected vehicle remote start on demand or scheduled start, where it is permitted, can help address this issue. The ability to remotely control windows and heating, ventilation, and air conditioning (HVAC) helps to refresh cabin air. Although there is no evidence that COVID-19 can contaminate HVAC systems, a CDC representative recommended to run ventilation system "blow out" with recirculation off and heater at max temperature with doors or windows open before entering a car [11]. Furthermore, Ford announced the development of original variation of the precondition feature for heated sanitizing of vehicle interior surfaces, which is ready to be deployed in existing police interceptors [22]. This connected feature warms the engine up to an elevated level and turns the heat and fan settings to high to get the temperature inside to 133 °F (56 °C) for 15 min. According to the Ohio State University department of microbiology, these temperature and time parameters would reduce viral concentrations by more than 99% on surfaces and in the air.

During the pandemic, it is even more important than ever that the vehicle is properly maintained and will not fail during the trip. Connected vehicle apps can provide the diagnostics and prognostics information regarding the health of the vehicle and alert any immediate need for maintenance. Providing a direct connection to the service shop, the service appointment can be scheduled in such a way that the wait time is minimized. The service shop can automatically check the availability of required service and the replacement parts.

To reduce physical interactions, many service shops offer vehicle pickup and delivery services. It may be critical if the owner is in self-isolation or he/she just wants to avoid additional trips due to exposure concerns. Phone as a key technology may be very useful for such type a service to provide access to the vehicle electronically without any need for in person interactions. The access key with a location of the vehicle can be send to the service shop, where the technician can pick it up and drop it off at the agreed location. Using remote control functionality the technician can initiate a system "blow out" before entering the car.

The pandemic resulted in a surge of drive-through services, as it appears to be a safer alternative to in-store shopping. In addition to traditional drive-through services, such as fast food, banking and pharmacy, there is a surge of emerging ad-hoc services from virus testing to drive-through grocery pick up. The weak link in many of these services, however, is the need to physically interact with the attendant including payment handling. Even with the established drive-through services, the driver might not have the app on their phone. The connected vehicle infrastructure can offer the possibility to dynamically provide ordering and payment options through the vehicle infotainment interface. For example [10] presents the concept of Dynamic SmartDeviceLink Apps that can be activated within specific context, such as proximity of a drive-through business. The appropriate backend infrastructure may enable the rapid deployment of such new services by established as well as new businesses.

Advanced vehicle technology provides an effective platform for a deployment of digital health and wellness applications. There is a rapid growth of screening apps, wearables analytics for advanced diagnostics and medical chat bots. For example, Apple in collaboration with CDC developed a screening app that is used to dispatch patients. Stanford Medicine scientists launched new research to detect early signs of viral infection, including COVID-19, through data from wearables [1]. University of Cambridge is developing an app that can recognize COVID-19 cough, while Carnegie Mellon is developing an app to recognize disease from the voice and cough. There is a rise of chat bots that provide personalized information regarding the virus, that help recognize the symptoms and offer personalized advice on the course of action. Driver status monitoring has been one of the important areas of Automotive Research and Development for many years. The earlier applications focused on drowsiness and impairment [6], emotional state [8], and most recent applications included measurement of driver's vitals using build-in sensors or wearables to support comfort and ambient intelligence [9]. Vehicle voice interface has also been a major focus of automotive HMI design advancing from a simple list of keyword controls to seamless integration with Personal Voice Assistants [17]. As a result, the vehicle presents an ultimate environment to provide personal health monitoring incorporating vitals measurement, cough recognition and medical chat bots.

6   Ambient Intelligence

COVID-19 raised public sense of awareness about surroundings, especially in shared spaces. People now are much more cognizant about cleanness of surfaces and air quality. It creates a need for accelerated development of Ambient Intelligence and Smart Environment technologies that can leverage advancements in IoT, Machine learning and Analytics.

According to CDC, although the main way to contract coronavirus is through person to person transmission, it may be possible to get infected by touching a surface that has the virus on it and then touching their own face. This possibility brought an elevated hygiene risk awareness resulting in both more meticulous hand washing and avoidance of high-touch surfaces in public places.

Touchscreens have been a mainstream HMI approach of the past decade. The interactive digital kiosks market is one of the fastest growing, catering to airports, shopping centers, restaurants and many other customer facing businesses. The pandemic is most likely to change HMI user experience requirements by pivoting from touchscreen to touchless technologies and ambient intelligence. Many modern buildings already have such technology, utilizing automatic doors, faucets, and light switches operated by proximity and infrared sensors, restricted access doors and turnstiles operated by RFID cards or face recognition camera, and NFC payment readers. According to reports, many buildings in China have adopted voice-controlled systems and there is even an elevator featuring holographic display. The switch from touch interfaces to touchless smart environment is fully aligned with patterns of technical systems evolution, such as increased use of field (e.g. substituting mechanical means with sensory) and decreased human involvement [26]. COVID-19 simply accelerates this evolution.

These user requirement changes will also affect HMI design in ride-hailing services, and specifically in shared autonomous vehicles. Most likely, it will accelerate the advancement and adaptation of voice, gesture and holographic HMI technologies. Use of the rider's own phone to control vehicle functionality is another efficient and effective approach. The Smart Phone is already a main gateway to reserve the ride and it is logical to use it to control vehicle ambient environment. Figure 2 shows the example of controlling vehicle infotainment functions using rider's phone app.

Fig. 2. Passenger phone control of vehicle functions.

Cleaning and disinfection of the autonomous vehicle between the rides is another important aspect of customer care. Amid the coronavirus, many taxi and ride-hailing providers established a protocol to clean the vehicle between each ride. How can it be done in the case o autonomous vehicles without the need to bring it to the depot for each ride? The heated sanitizing feature discussed in the previous section is one of the options that can be used. UV light is another practical approach that has been widely adapted for disinfection amid COVID-19. [7] describes the application of a mini-drone that can be deployed inside the autonomous vehicle between rides to inspect the cleanliness of the inside, especially in hard to reach places (Fig. 3). Integrating a UV lamp with such a drone may offer an efficient disinfection mechanism.

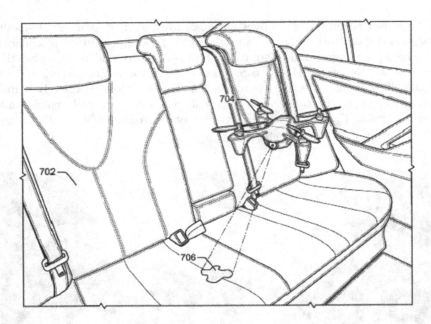

Fig. 3. Inspection drone for autonomous vehicle.

COVID-19 also raised concerns regarding air quality. First, there are concerns directly related to the possibility to catch the virus if the prior rider was infected. More generally, several recent studies [24] show that there is a direct link between pollution exposure and coronavirus death rate. These findings reinforce OEMs priority in efforts to reduce vehicle emissions and specifically electrification. In a short term, they drew special attention to in-vehicle air quality management technologies. That includes the advanced filtration system, such as high-efficiency particulate air filters (HEPA) featured in Tesla Model X and Model S Bioweapon Defense Mode. There is also a large market of brought-in air quality sensors and car cup holder air purifiers, ionizers and fresheners. In addition to advanced air filters and 3rd party IoT devices and sensors, it is critical that the vehicle climate control and brought-in gadgets are properly managed and coordinated. To this end, vehicle connectivity architecture needs to provision seamless integration of external IoT devices and cloud services [25]. [9] describes an intelligent management of climate control leveraging vehicle SmartDeviceLink integration with smartphone app connected to brought-in PM2.5 sensor and cloud analytics. The system informs vehicle occupants about the internal and external air quality levels, prevents dirty air from entering the cabin by closing the recirculation gate when poor external air is detected, and refreshes air in cabin rapidly when excessive pollutant is detected inside the cabin.

7   Conclusions

The paper discusses the challenges and opportunities of the existing technologies and practices in the context of Smart City and Future Mobility to cope with the pandemic. The overview shows that there is a need to accelerate the deployment of Smart City and Smart Mobility technologies, and to revisit strategic supply chain planning models. Furthermore, it shows that advancements in IoT, communication, AI and Analytics play a crucial role in enabling rapid innovation in an attempt to address immediate needs raised by COVID-19. The overview and discussion focuses on five areas: Smart City Technologies, Robust Supply Chain of critical items, Smart Mobility, Connected and Intelligent Vehicles, and Ambient Intelligence.

Many cities around the world are actively trying to leverage their existing digitalization efforts. Phone tracking and video analytics are the most common technologies that have been applied to modeling and mitigations activities. This aggregated data and analytics allow to enhance the earlier warning, forecast, and decision analysis. Another common application area is social distancing and quarantine order enforcement, contact tracing, and public risk screening. The novel areas in wearable data analytics and wastewater surveillance show the promise to further enhance problem identification and forecast capabilities. Thermoimaging is emerging as an effective public risk screening technique. Privacy is the key issue that needs to be addressed for a wide deployment of these technologies.

The disruption of the global supply chain that resulted in shortages of critical items clearly demonstrated the need for robust supply chain design and planning. The experience showed that the local administrations need to rely on their own manufacturing base to fulfill the shortages in times of crisis. Emergency inventory management should use the models for robust supply chain planning, incorporating the times for manufacturers to ramp up the production.

Smart Mobility technologies may play a crucial role during the pandemic. This overview highlighted the following observations: Integrated Mobility as Service Platforms enable effective dynamic management of the transportation network and control of passenger flow to match capacity with the changing travel demand pattern and social distancing requirements. Mobility providers can strengthen their business proposition by diversifying between ride-hailing and delivery services. Autonomous vehicles can play a significant role during the pandemic. Teleoperation can accelerate the deployment of autonomous vehicles.

Personal vehicles provide the best protection outside the home when one needs to travel for food, medication or to place of essential work. Connected vehicle technologies can help to maintain reliable vehicle conditions and to leverage usage-based insurance. Connected interactive ad-hoc services may help to reduce the need for physical interactions in drive-through businesses. Advanced vehicle technologies can be used for personal health monitoring.

The pandemic substantially affected user experience requirements on ambiance and interfaces with public space environments. It elevated hygiene risk awareness regarding touch surfaces and air quality. There is a need for accelerated development of Ambient Intelligence and Smart Environment with a focus on health and wellness, specifically in autonomous vehicles in application to shared mobility.

References

1. Armitage, H.: Stanford medicine scientists hope to use data from wearable devices to predict illness, including COVID-19 (2020). https://med.stanford.edu/news/all-news/2020/04/wearable-devices-for-predicting-illness-.html
2. Beutel, M.C., et al.: Mobility service platforms - cross-company cooperation for transportation service interoperability. In: Proceedings of the 20th International Conference on Enterprise Information Systems ICEIS, vol. 1, pp. 151–161. INSTICC, SciTePress (2018). https://doi.org/10.5220/0006705501510161
3. Daw, A., Hampshire, R.C., Pender, J.: Beyond safety drivers: staffing a teleoperations system for autonomous vehicles, pp. 1–55. ArXiv abs/1907.12650, https://arxiv.org/abs/1907.12650 (2020)
4. FEMA: Coronavirus (COVID-19) pandemic: supply chain stabilization task force (2020). https://www.fema.gov/fema-supply-chain-stabilization-task-force
5. Ford-Online: How ford's manufacturing machine pivoted to building one million face shields per week (2020). https://www.at.ford.com/content/dam/atford/fna/images/articles/2020/04/face_shields/Face_Shield_Timeline.pdf
6. Gusikhin, O., Filev, D., Rychtyckyj, N.: Intelligent vehicle systems: applications and new trends. In: Cetto, J.A., Ferrier, J.L., Costa dias Pereira, J., Filipe, J. (eds.) Informatics in Control Automation and Robotics, vol. 15, pp. 3–14. Springer, Heidelberg (2008). https://doi.org/10.1007/978-3-540-79142-3_1
7. Gusikhin, O., Jales Costa, B., Goh, M.: Vehicle inspection systems and methods (2020). https://patentscope.wipo.int/search/en/detail.jsf?docId=US2978102777
8. Gusikhin, O., Klampfl, E., Filev, D., Chen, Y.: Emotive driver advisor system (EDAS). In: Cetto, J.A., Ferrier, J.L., Filipe, J. (eds.) Informatics in Control, Automation and Robotics. Lecture Notes in Electrical Engineering, vol. 89, pp. 21–36. Springer, Heidelberg (2011). https://doi.org/10.1007/978-3-642-19539-6_2
9. Gusikhin, O., Makke, O., Yeung, J.C., MacNeille, P.: Smartdevicelink application to intelligent climate control. In: Proceedings of the 13th International Conference on Informatics in Control, Automation and Robotics (ICINCO 2016). vol. 1, pp. 234–240 (2016). https://doi.org/10.5220/0005997002340240
10. Gusikhin, O., Shah, A., Makke, O., Smirnov, A., Shilov, N.: Dynamic cloud-based vehicle apps - information logistics in disaster response. In: Proceedings of the 4th International Conference on Vehicle Technology and Intelligent Transport Systems RESIST, vol. 1, pp. 626–635. INSTICC, SciTePress (2018). https://doi.org/10.5220/0006815606260635
11. Huetter, J.: CDC offers perspective on handling autos, vehicle HVAC amid COVID-19 threat (2020). https://www.repairerdrivennews.com/2020/05/04/cdc-offers-perspective-on-handling-autos-vehicle-hvac-amid-covid-19-threat/
12. Ivanov, D.: Viable supply chain model: integrating agility, resilience and sustainability perspectives-lessons from and thinking beyond the COVID-19 pandemic. Ann. Oper. Res. 1–21 (2020). https://doi.org/10.1007/s10479-020-03640-6
13. Panigutti, C., Tizzoni, M., Bajardi, P., Smoreda, Z., Colizza, V.: Assessing the use of mobile phone data to describe recurrent mobility patterns in spatial epidemic models. Roy. Soc. Open Sci. 4(5), 1–13 (2017). https://doi.org/10.1098/rsos.160950

14. Radin, J.M., Wineinger, N.E., Topol, E.J., Steinhubl, S.R.: Harnessing wearable device data to improve state-level real-time surveillance of influenza-like illness in the USA: a population-based study. Lancet Digital Health **2**(2), 85–93 (2020). http://www.sciencedirect.com/science/article/pii/S2589750019302225
15. Raskar, R., et al.: Apps gone rogue: maintaining personal privacy in an epidemic. CoRR ArXiv abs/2003.08567 https://arxiv.org/abs/2003.08567 (2020)
16. Sanchez-Corcuera, R., et al.: Smart cities survey: technologies, application domains and challenges for the cities of the future. Int. J. Distrib. Sens. Netw. **15**, 1–36 (2019). https://doi.org/10.1177/1550147719853984
17. Shah, A., Gusikhin, A.: Integration of voice assistant and smartdevicelink to control vehicle ambient environment. In: Proceedings of the 6th International Conference on Vehicle Technology and Intelligent Transport Systems, pp. 522–527. INSTICC, SciTePress (2020). https://www.scitepress.org/Link.aspx?doi=10.5220/0009465305220527
18. Simchi-levi, D., et al.: Identifying risks and mitigating disruptions in the automotive supply chain. Interfaces **45**, 375–390 (2015). https://doi.org/10.1287/inte.2015.0804
19. Simchi-Levi, D., Simchi-Levi, E.: We need a stress test for critical supply chains. Harvard Bus. Rev. (2020). https://hbr.org/2020/04/we-need-a-stress-test-for-critical-supply-chains
20. Stecke, K.E., Kumar, S.: Sources of supply chain disruptions, factors that breed vulnerability, and mitigating strategies. J. Mark. Channels **16**(3), 193–226 (2009). https://doi.org/10.1080/10466690902932551
21. Uber: Uber announces results for second quarter (2020). https://investor.uber.com/news-events/news/press-release-details/2020/Uber-Announces-Results-for-Second-Quarter-2020/default.aspx
22. Wilson, M.: Ford kills COVID-19 with ingenious car heater hack (2020). https://www.fastcompany.com/90510004/ford-kills-COVID-19-with-ingenious-car-heater-hack
23. Wu, F., et al.: SARS-COV-2 titers in wastewater are higher than expected from clinically confirmed cases. medRxiv (2020). https://www.medrxiv.org/content/early/2020/04/07/2020.04.05.20051540.full.pdf
24. Wu, X., Nethery, R.C., Sabath, B.M., Braun, D., Dominici, F.: Exposure to air pollution and COVID-19 mortality in the united states. medRxiv (2020). https://www.medrxiv.org/content/early/2020/04/07/2020.04.05.20054502
25. Yeung, J., Makke, O., MacNeille, P., Gusikhin, O.: Smartdevicelink as an open innovation platform for connected car features and mobility applications. SAE Int. J. Passeng. Cars Electron. Electr. Syst. **10**, 231–239 (2017). https://doi.org/10.4271/2017-01-1649
26. Zlotin, B., Zusman, A.: Patterns of Technological Evolution, pp. 1438–1446. Springer, New York (2013). https://doi.org/10.1007/978-1-4614-3858-8_40

Author Index

Printed in the United States
by Baker & Taylor Publisher Services